STUDIES IN ANCIENT HISTORY

I

ASSYRIAN COLONIES IN CAPPADOCIA

by

LOUIS LAWRENCE ORLIN
THE UNIVERSITY OF MICHIGAN

1970
MOUTON
THE HAGUE · PARIS

LIBRARY OF CONGRESS CATALOG CARD NUMBER 68-54391

Printed in The Netherlands by Mouton & Co., Printers, The Hague

To my wife, Carol

PREFACE

Our knowledge of the Assyrian Colonies of Cappadocia is chiefly derived from the so-called "Cappadocian" tablets, cuneiform documents written in an old dialect of Assyrian, and originating from three sites in Anatolia — Kültepe, Alişar Hüyük and Boğazköy. The documents are private records, being the business notes, memoranda and letters of Assyrian traders who lived in these and other places in Asia Minor on a more or less permanent basis during the more than one hundred-fifty years separating the reigns (inclusively) of Erišum I and Šamši-Adad I, kings of Assyria (ca. 1940-1781 B.C.). There are no historical documents either from Mesopotamia or from Anatolia to illuminate the origins of these merchant communities, but much information about the day-to-day activities of their inhabitants has been extracted from the document sources. An occasional text also allows some special insight into political conditions of the time, but most of what we know about these conditions, and of political institutions generally, must be painstakingly culled out from every type of context.

The main outlines of the political situation seem clear enough when we would consider the relationships of the colonies to each other, to *Kârum Kaniš*, chief executive of them all, and subsequently, of the whole number to Assur, capital of Assyria during our period and nearly 500 miles from *Kaniš*. All the evidence shows that the Assyrian government controlled a network of some twenty-one communities of its traders abroad, administering them by executive fiat from Assur, and sending its envoys to *Kârum Kaniš*. For their part, the Assyrian traders fully acknowledged the sovereignty of Assyrian law, and continued to employ Assyrian customs and traditions in a region populated primarily by non-Semites. We may speak with assurance of an Assyrian "colonial system". But serious differences of opinion arise to the question of the nature and the extent of Assyrian power over the areas in which the trader communities were located.

Our sources, as shall be seen, attest the existence of numerous indigenous governments, headed by princes, whose palaces often were situated in the same towns where the Assyrian communities are found. These princes are thought by many scholars to have been vassals of an Assyria which had conquered Anatolia in this early period; but the opinion has also been set forth that they were fully autonomous rulers who had sanctioned the establishment of the Assyrian communities through some sort of treaty relationships, which guaranteed protection of Assyrian trading interests as well as insured economic advantages to themselves. On the surface, the presence in Anatolia of a highly integrated network of Assyrian settlements with legal responsibilities to Assur appears to demand a conclusion that force played a part in its establishment, but a survey of the political information contained in the Cappadocian tablets shows that the local princes reserved to themselves important rights and privileges of action not consistent with their being considered vassals.

Because of the differences of interpretation on the very important political question the writer was led to begin a study of the Old Assyrian settlements in the mid-1950's. The controversy over what political characteristics these settlements represented in their own time, which claimed the continued attention of such eminent scholars as the late Prof. Julius Lewy, of Professors Landsberger, Goetze and Gelb, to mention but a few who wrote about them during the past decades, stood as a challenge to a student of Assyriology who also had a deep interest in the political theory and practice of the ancient world. Accordingly, I offered *Assyrian Colonies in Cappadocia* as a doctoral thesis to the then Department of Near Eastern Studies and the Graduate Faculty of the University of Michigan in 1960. My special purpose was to bring into focus all the textual information that had a bearing on the Old Assyrian settlements so as to come to some resolution of the problem, and to try to distinguish some fundamental questions that ought to be asked from the point of view of political theory. To my knowledge the dissertation presented the first attempted and provisional synthesis of the subject in recent years, and was published by University Microfilms, Inc., Ann Arbor, under its dissertation project.

Mouton and Co. accepted my study for publication just a few months before the work of Paul Garelli, *Les Assyriens en Cappadoce* appeared in Europe as a monograph of the Bibliothèque Archéologique et Historique de l'Institute Français d'Archéologie d'Istanbul [v. XIX, 1963]. Garelli's study represents a thoroughgoing treatment of a number of areas that I could but touch upon in passing, especially in matters of economics and commerce. Through a true coincidence each of us proceeded independently of the other, and it is pleasant and gratifying to find that his conclusions about the character of Assyrian commercial imperialism are similar to my own. I have in no way attempted to review his book in preparing my own for the press, though where I differ from him in matters of text-reading or interpretation [primarily in Chapter Four] I have indicated in the notes.

Since 1960 several major volumes of Old Assyrian texts have appeared as well as a number of articles containing publications of texts with commentaries. In addition, work has gone forward steadily at Kültepe, where new tablets continue to be unearthed, and at Boğazköy. In a real sense one writes on the subject of the Old Assyrian settlements only to be seriously overwhelmed by new materials with each passing year.

In first preparing this work for publication I altered sections of the original manuscript to accomodate the then most important new references, and also expanded my treatment of the indigenous political situation in Anatolia to consider the stages through which the threshold of the Old Hittite Kingdom was reached, as well as to offer a glimpse of contemporaneous events in Mesopotamia [Appendix C]. It was impossible to convert my original study into a work on the early second millennium in Anatolia and Mesopotamia. This remains a desideratum for the future.

But many problems connected with the composition of this study in the press since 1965 have delayed its appearance, a regrettable but unalterable circumstance of book production involving extremely complicated and technical subject matter. Since the submission of this work to the publisher a new collection of relevant bibliographical items has appeared. Although these items have contributed to the rising store of knowledge about the Old Assyrian Period and about specific issues of colonial life and trade, it was impossible to incorporate the newest information into this work, which had by then reached proof-stage. The most noteworthy additions are P. Garelli's, "Tablettes cappadociennes diverses (lettres)", RA 59 (1965), 149-176, and RA 60 (1966), 93-152, Karl Hecker's, *Die Keilschrifttexte der Universitätsbibliothek Giessen* (= *Berichte und Arbeiten aus der Universitätsbibliothek Giessen 9*, Giessen, Universitätsbibliothek, 1966), and M. T. Larsen, *Old Assyrian Caravan Procedures* (Istanbul, 1968). One should also note the recent article by Franz Fischer, "Boğhazköy und die Chronologie der altassyrischen Handelsniederlassungen in Kappadokien", *Istanbuler Mitteilungen* (1965), 1-16. Other articles have been appended to the bibliographical sections of Appendix A, but have not been included in the final bibliography at the end of this study. Furthermore, some new archaeological references have been included together in an Addendum to Appendix B.

It remains to express sincere gratitude to a number of scholars from whose life-long studies of Old Assyrian questions and occasional personal remarks I learned tremendously about the subject. The work of the late Prof. Julius Lewy represented an indispensable source of teaching to me, and if I came to differ with his major conclusions, my debt to his pioneering investigations of linguistic and textual matters, as to his personal kindness (and that of Mrs. Lewy) to me, is nonetheless great. To Prof. I. J. Gelb of the Oriental Institute, University of Chicago, who always found time for a kind word of encouragement, and to him and Prof. A. L. Oppenheim, also of the Oriental Institute, for permission to consult the files of the Assyrian Dictionary, I express deep appreciation.

At the University of Michigan a number of scholars gave generously of their time and insights, and it is a pleasant duty to thank Prof. George E. Mendenhall of the Department of Near Eastern Languages and Literatures, Prof. James H. Meisel, Department of Political Science, and Profs. Paul J. Alexander and Gerald S. Brown of the Department of History, for their help. Most of all, I owe an inestimable debt of gratitude to Prof. George G. Cameron, Chairman of the Department of Near Eastern Languages and Literatures, whose standards of scholarly excellence are ever to be emulated, and without whose friendship, encouragement and guidance, always freely and generously given, this study could not have been accomplished.

The publication of this work is assisted by a grant from funds derived from income on the endowment of the Horace H. Rackham School of Graduate Studies of the University of Michigan, for which I thank the Board of Governors.

Finally, to my wife, who shared with me the long task which this study entailed, and who assisted me in uncounted ways, I offer affectionate thanks.

TABLE OF CONTENTS

Preface 7

List of figures and maps 13

List of abbreviations and symbols 15

PART 1: THE OLD ASSYRIAN SETTLEMENTS AND THE BACKGROUND OF CAPPADOCIAN TRADE

I. Introduction and geographical milieu 23

II. Cappadocian trade and the structure of the old Assyrian political system 45

PART 2: POLITICAL RELATIONSHIPS BETWEEN THE ASSYRIAN SETTLEMENTS AND THE ANATOLIAN PRINCIPALITIES

III. The Anatolian rulers and their principalities 73

IV. Indications of diplomatic relationship between Assyrians and Anatolians 114

V. Survey of Assyrian-Anatolian political encounters during the Main period of Assyrian activity in Anatolia 139

PART 3: CONCLUSIONS

VI. The Assyrian "community" and the Anatolian communities: toward a definition of Assyrian "colonization" 161

Appendix A. The old Assyrian documents 184

Appendix B. Chronological and stratigraphical notes on the old Assyrian settlements 199

Appendix C. The old Assyrian colonies in the setting of Anatolian cultural history 224

Bibliography 248

Index 265

LIST OF FIGURES AND MAPS

MAPS

1. The Kingdoms of Anatolia during the period of the old Assyrian settlements 111

FIGURES

1. Chart showing political references associated with Anatolian towns 76
2. Scheme of the stratification on the Terrace-Mound at Kültepe 201
3. Scheme of the correlations in stratigraphy between the Terrace-Mound and the City-Mound at Kültepe 215
4. Scheme of the correlations in stratigraphy between Kültepe, Alishar Hüyük, and Boğazköy 219
5. Proposed relative chronology of the old Assyrian period . . . 222

ABBREVIATIONS AND SYMBOLS

BOOKS AND PERIODICALS

AAA	*Annals of Archaeology and Anthropology.*
AASF	*Annales Academiae Scientiarum Fennicae.*
ACIO	*Actes du congrès internationale des orientalistes.*
ADOG	*Abhandlungen der Deutschen Orient-gesellschaft.*
AfO	*Archiv für Orientforschung.*
AHDO	*Archives d'histoire du droit orientale.*
AHK	B. Landsberger, "Assyrische Handelskolonien in Kleinasien aus dem dritten Jahrtausend", *AO*, 24 (1925), 1-36.
AIBL	*Académie des inscriptions et belles-lettres. Comptes-rendus*, Paris.
AJA	*American Journal of Archaeology.*
AJSL	*American Journal of Semitic Languages and Literatures.*
An Or	*Analecta Orientalia.*
6	G. R. Driver, *Cappadocian Texts at Oxford* (1933) 69-70, Pls. I-VIII.
27	W. von Soden, *Das akkadische Syllabar* (1948).
33	W. von Soden, *Grundriss der akkadischen Grammatik* (1952).
An St	*Anatolian Studies.*
AO	*Der alte Orient.*
AOB	*Altorientalische Bibliothek.*
APAW	*Abhandlungen der Preussischen Akademie der Wissenschaften.*
ARM	*Archives royales de Mari.*
Ar Or	*Archiv Orientální.*
ATHE	B. Kienast, *Die altassyrischen Texte des orientalischen Seminars der Universität Heidelberg und der Sammlung Erlenmeyer-Basel* (Berlin, 1960).
Bab.	*Babyloniaca.*
BANE	*The Bible and the Near East* (Albright Festschrift), ed. G. E. Wright (New York, 1961).
BASOR	*Bulletin of the American Schools of Oriental Research.*
Bez., Glossar	C. Bezold, *Babylonisch-assyrisches Glossar.*
BIN	*Babylonian Inscriptions in the Collection of J. B. Nies.*
IV	A. T. Clay, *Letters and Transactions from Cappadocia* (1927).
VI	F. J. Stephens, *Old Assyrian Letters and Business Documents* (1944).
BKS	*Boghazköi-Studien.*
BO	*Bibliotheca Orientalis.*
BoTU	*Boghazköi-Texte in Umschrift.*
CAD	*The Assyrian Dictionary of the Oriental Institute of the University of Chicago.*
CAH	*Cambridge Ancient History.*

CCT	S. Smith, *Cuneiform Texts from Cappadocian Tablets in the British Museum*, Part I (1921).
II-IV	S. Smith, *Cuneiform Texts from Cappadocian Tablets in the British Museum*, Parts II-IV (1924-1927).
V	S. Smith and D. J. Wiseman, *Cuneiform Texts from Cappadocian Tablets in the British Museum*, Part V (1956).
Chantre	Kültepe texts in E. Chantre, *Mission en cappadoce* (1898) 93-109, Pls. XXI-XXII and IV, 7, V, 8f.
CSQ	*The Culver-Stockton Quarterly.*
CT	*Cuneiform Texts from Babylonian Tablets in the British Museum.*
De Clercq	Cappadocian tablet in *Collection De Clercq*, II (1900) 174f.
Deimel, SL	A. Deimel, *Sumerisches Lexikon.*
Delitzsch, HWB	Fr. Delitzsch, *Assyrisches Handwörterbuch.*
DOG	*Deutsche Orientgesellschaft.*
DTCFD	*Ankara Üniversitesi. Dil ve Tarih-Coğrafya Fakultesi Dergisi.*
DTCFY	*Ankara Üniversitesi. Dil ve Tarih-Coğrafya Fakultesi Yayinlari.*
Edinburgh	A. H. Sayce, "Cappadocian Cuneiform Tablets from Kara Eyuk", in *Bab.*, 2 (1911) 65-80.
EHA	S. Smith, *Early History of Assyria* (1928).
EL I and II	G. Eisser and J. Lewy, *Die altassyrischen Rechtsurkunden vom Kültepe* (= *MVaG*, 33, 1930, and 35,3, 1935).
ERV	*Ebert's Reallexikon der Vorgeschichte.*
Florilegium	*Recueil de travaux dédies a M. le marquis Melchior de Vogue* (1909).
Gol.	V. S. Golenischev, *Vingt-quatre tablettes de la collection W. Golenischeff* (1891).
HEM	*Halil Edhem Memorial.*
HGN	J. Garstang, *Interim Page Index of Hittite Geographical Names of Asia Minor* (unpublished).
HO	*Handbuch der Orientalistik.*
HSS	*Harvard Semitic Series.*
HT	L. W. King, *Hittite Texts in the Cuneiform Character from Tablets in the British Museum* (1920).
HUCA	*Hebrew Union College Annual.*
IAIMK	*Izvestiia Rossiiskoi Akademii Istorii Material'noi Kul'tury.*
IAK	E. Ebeling, B. Meissner, and E. F. Weidner, *Die Inschriften der altassyrischen Könige* (1926) (= *AOB*, 1).
ICK I	B. Hrozný, *Inscriptions cunéiformes du Kültepe*, I (1952).
II	L. Matouš, *Inscriptions cunéiformes du Kültepe*, II (1962).
IEJ	*Israel Exploration Journal.*
IHN	L. A. Mayer and J. Garstang, *Index of Hittite Names* (= *British School of Archaeology in Jerusalem*, Supplementary Papers, I, 1923).
ILN	*Illustrated London News.*
JAOS	*Journal of the American Oriental Society.*
JCS	*Journal of Cuneiform Studies.*
14	P. Garelli and D. A. Kennedy, "Seize tablettes cappadociennes de l'Ashmolean Museum d'Oxford", (1960), 1-22.
Jena	cf. *TuM.*
JEOL	*Vooraziatisch-Egyptisch Gezelschap "Ex Orient Lux". Jaarbericht.*
JHS	*Journal of Hellenic Studies.*
JJP	*Journal of Juristic Papyrology.*
JKAF	*Jahrbuch für Kleinasiatischen Forschung.*
JNES	*Journal of Near Eastern Studies.*

JRAS	*Journal of the Royal Asiatic Society of Great Britain and Ireland, London.*
JSOR	*Journal of the Society of Oriental Research.*
JSS	*Journal of Semitic Studies.*
KAH	*Keilschrifttexte aus Assur historischen Inhalts* (= *WVDOG*, 16 and 37).
KB	*Keilinschriftliche Bibliothek.*
KBo	*Keilschrifttexte aus Boghazköi.*
IX	H. Otten, *Keilschrifttexte aus Boghazköi*, IX (Berlin, 1957).
KKL	*Khorsabad King List.*
Kleinasien (1933)	A. Goetze, *Kulturgeschichte des alten Orients* (= *Handbuch der Altertumswissenschaft*, 3 Abt., 1 Teil, 3 Bd., 3 Abs., 1 Unterabs (1933).
(1957)	*Idem.*, 2nd. Ed.
KTBl	J. Lewy, *Die Kültepetexte der Sammlung Rudolph Blanckertz, Berlin* (1929).
KTHahn	J. Lewy, *Die Kültepetexte aus der Sammlung Frida Hahn*, (Berlin, 1930).
KTP	F. J. Stephens, "The Cappadocian Tablets in the University of Pennsylvania Museum", *JSOR*, 11 (1927) 101-36.
KTS	J. Lewy, *Die altassyrischen Texte vom Kültepe bei Kaisarije* (1926).
KUB	*Keilschrifturkunden aus Boghazköi.*
LC	Fr. Thureau-Dangin, *Lettres et contrats de l'époque de la première dynastie babylonienne* (*TCL*, I).
Leiden	F. M. Th. Bohl, "Mededeelingen uit de Leidsche Verzameling van Spijkerschrift-Inscripties II. Oorkonden uit de Periode van 2000-1200 v. Chr.", *Mededeelingen der Koninklijke Akademie van Wetenschappen. Afdeeling Letterkunde*, Deel 78, Serie B, No. 2 (1934), 36-43.
Liv.	T. G. Pinches, "The Cappadocian Tablets Belonging to the Liverpool Institute of Archaeology", *AAA*, I (1908), 49-80, and Pls. XVII-XXX.
LSS	*Leipziger Semitistische Studien.*
MAOG	*Altorientalische Gesellschaft, Berlin. Mitteilungen.*
MDOG	*Deutsche Orient-Gesellschaft, Berlin. Mitteilungen.*
74	H. G. Guterbock, "Texte" (1936), 64f.
77	K. Bittel and R. Naumann, "Kappadokische Tontafeln" (1939), 23.
MKAWB	*Koninklijke Academie voor Wetenschappen, Letteren en Schone Kunsten van België*, Klasse der Letteren, 22/23 (1960), 3-48. Mededelingen. (= G. Goossens, *Het Ontstaan van het Assyrisch Rijk*).
MVaG	*Vorderasiatisch-aegyptische Gesellschaft, Berlin. Mitteilungen.*
OBM	W. F. Leemans, *The Old Babylonian Merchant, his Business and his Social Position* (1950).
OIC	*Chicago. University. The Oriental Institute. Oriental Institute Communications.*
OIP	*Chicago. University. The Oriental Institute. Oriental Institute Publications.*
27	I. J. Gelb, *Inscriptions from Alishar and Vicinity* (1935).
OLZ	*Orientalische Literaturzeitung.*
Or Chr	*Oriens Christianus.*
7	P. E. van der Meer, "Fünf kappadokische Geschaftsbriefe", (1932), 126f.
Or ns	*Orientalia, nova series.*
Or Suec	*Orientalia Suecana.*
PAPS	*Proceedings of the American Philosophical Society.*
PICO	*Proceedings of the International Congress of Orientalists.*
PNC	F. J. Stephens, *Personal Names from Cuneiform Inscriptions of Cappadocia* (YOS, XIII, 1, 1928).
PSBA	*Proceedings of the Society of Biblical Archaeology, London.*

4	T. G. Pinches, "Communication" (cf. the 'Cappadocian' tablet in the British Museum) (1882) 11-18, and 28-32.
6	A. H. Sayce, "The Cuneiform Tablets of Kappadokia", (1883-84) 17-25.
19	A. H. Sayce, "Assyriological Notes", (1897) 286-91.
RA	*Revue d'assyriologie et d'archéologie orientale.*
8	Fr. Thureau-Dangin, "La date des tablettes cappadociennes", (1911) 142-151.
21	S. Smith, "Miscellanea", (1924) 89f.
RAI 2	*Compte rendu de la seconde rencontre assyriologique internationale organisée à Paris de 2 au 6 Juillet 1951 par le Groupe François Thureau-Dangin (1951).*
RB	*Revue Biblique.*
RHA	*Revue Hittite et Asianique.*
66	P. Garelli and D. A. Kennedy, "Un nouveau prince anatolien?", (1960), 37-44.
RHR	*Revue de l'Histoire des Religions.*
RLA	*Reallexikon der Assyriologie.*
RT	*Recueil de Travaux.*
18	J. V. Scheil, "Tablette cappadocienne", (1896), 74f.
31	*Idem.*, "Texte cappadocienne ninivite", (1919), 55f.
SATK	J. Lewy, *Studien zu den alt-assyrischen Texten aus Kappadokien* (Berlin, 1922).
SeD 2	B. Hrozný, "Über eine unveröffentlichte Urkunde vom Kültepe (ca. 2000 v. Chr.)", *Symbolae Paulo Koschaker dedicatae* (Leiden, 1939) 108-111 (= *Studia et documenta ad iura Orientis antiqui pertinentia* II).
Šil.	V. K. Shileiko, "Documenty iz Giul-tepe", *IAIMK*, 356-364.
SUP	A. H. Sayce, "The Cappadocian Cuneiform Tablets of the University of Pennsylvania", *Bab.*, 6 (1912), 182-192.
Syria	*Revue d'art oriental et d'archéologie — Paris.*
TC	Georges Contenau, *Tablettes cappadociennes* I (= *TCL*, IV).
II	Fr. Thureau-Dangin, *Tablettes cappadociennes,* II (= *TCL*, XIV).
III	J. Lewy, *Tablettes cappadociennes,* III (= *TCL*, XIX-XXI).
TTAED	*Türk Tarih Arkeologya ve Etnografya Dergisi.*
4	B. Landsberger, "Vier Urkunden vom Kültepe", (1940), 7-31.
TTC	Georges Contenau, *Trente tablettes cappadociennes* (Paris, 1919).
TTKY	*Türk Tarih Kurumu Yayinlari.*
TuM	J. Lewy, *Die Keilschrifttexte aus Kleinasien* (= *Texte und Materialien der Frau Professor Hilprecht Collection of Babylonian Antiquities im Eigentum der Universität Jena, I*).
VAB	*Vorderasiatische Bibliothek.*
VAS	*Vorderasiatische Schriftdenkmaler.*
VAT	*Tablets of the Vorderasiatischen Abteilung (der Staatlichen Museen in Berlin) with inventory number.*
YOS	*Yale Oriental Series.*
WZKM	*Weiner Zeitschrift für die Kunde des Morgenlandes.*
ZA N.F.	*Zeitschrift für Assyriologie und verwandte Gebiete. Neue Folge.*
ZDMG	*Deutsche morgenlandische Gesellschaft. Zeitschrift.*
ZVSGI-ES	*Zeitschrift für vergleichende Sprachforschung auf dem Gebiete der indogermanischen Sprachen.*
ZSS	*Savigny-Stiftung für Rechtsgeschichte. Zeitschrift.*

MISCELLANEOUS

The following symbols are used:

[ ]	Wholly lost.
{ }	Partially lost.
⟨ ⟩	Omitted by scribe.
《 》	Pleonastically written by scribe.
( )	Supplied by the author.
!	Sign abnormal in form, but must be read as transliterated.
...	Lost or unreadable signs, number uncertain or unessential.
^	Long vowel.
d	Deity.
GN	Geographical name.
PN(NN)	Personal name.

PART ONE

THE OLD ASSYRIAN SETTLEMENTS AND THE BACKGROUND OF CAPPADOCIAN TRADE

I

INTRODUCTION AND GEOGRAPHICAL MILIEU

Near the eastern limits of the great central Plateau of Anatolia, astride heavily traveled trade routes which, in ancient times, converged upon it from all directions, rises the mound of Kültepe, site of the imposing ancient city of Kaniš. On its northeastern side, nearly contiguous to it, stands a flat terrace far less prominent in appearance. Here, during the nineteenth and eighteenth centuries before Christ, successive generations of enterprising Assyrian traders built up a flourishing community which has become known to us as *Kârum Kaniš*.[1] For a period variously estimated as a century or a century and a half, this community represented the most important of a number of Assyrian trading communities which, like itself, were situated in major cities of Anatolia.[2]

The history of *Kârum Kaniš* reaches back to the mid-twentieth century, most likely to the reign of Erišum I of Assyria (ca. 1940-1900 B.C.) but no extant documents confirm this. On the terrace mound of Kültepe the third inhabitation stratum above virgin soil, Level II, contains the first evidence of Assyrian occupation — thousands of clay tablets in an old dialect of Assyrian, found in the houses and offices of its trader residents.[3] Of the previous inhabitants on the terrace we know very little. The first occupants, those of Level IV, were users of a so-called "Cappadocian" pottery, a gaily-painted and geometrically-decorated ware which gave way after a short period of life at the dawn of the second millennium to a pottery whose style and technique remained relatively homogeneous and essentially different from it for many centuries thereafter.[4] Already in Level III on the terrace the Cappadocian

[1] The chronology used in this study is that of Sidney Smith (Hammurabi = 1792-1750 B.C.).

[2] For a discussion of the chronology of the Assyrian period in Anatolia see Appendix B.

[3] For the stratigraphy at Kültepe and other Old Assyrian sites, *ibid.* The documentary source material is surveyed in Appendix A.

[4] See T. Özgüç, TTKY V Seri — No. 10 (1950) 210f. Also pertinent are A. Goetze,

ware had practically petered out, but whether the occupants of this stratum belonged to a different population group we cannot tell. By the time of Level II, the Assyrians are fully established as occupants of the terrace mound.

If the history of *Kârum Kaniš* fades away into the darkness of the early second millennium, it is but slightly different with the record of Kaniš, the city, itself. The large mound which covers over the remains of this city is currently being excavated, but the lowest strata have only recently been reached. We may surmise that as early as the reign of Narâm-Sîn of Akkad (ca. 2350 B.C.) the city of Kaniš entered history, for its king at that time, Zipani, is alleged to have participated in a revolt against the Akkadian conqueror, but we know nothing of the events which followed in the city's career until the time of the Assyrians, some five hundred years later.[5] With the exception of this text and one other which may embody reliable tradition about the earliest history of Anatolia, but which is a late redaction and therefore untrustworthy, there is no historical record of events which antedate Assyrian occupation of the settlements that are the subject of this study.[6]

It is impossible, then, to know by what stages or under what circumstances the merchants arrived in Anatolia, at the present time. But however much we lack information about these important details, it is perfectly apparent that they fashioned a highly organized commercial enterprise, an international import-export business in the fullest sense.

Kleinasien (1957), 43-44, and *idem*, "The Cultures of Anatolia", in *Proceedings of the American Philosophical Society*, 97 (1953), 220.

[5] The relevant text is CT XIII, 44 ii 4f., to be read with an early variant Hittite version from Boğazköy, 2, BoTU, 3 (= KBo, III, 13). The former is a neo-Assyrian account, the latter Old Hittite. Since several of the names of the kings who are alleged to have banded together against Narâm-Sîn are Amoritic, it is reasonable to suppose that the author of the oldest version was working from an even older historical source, although the character of the extant account is half-legendary. The Old Hittite version has been studied by B. Hrozný, "Narâm-Sîn et ses ennemis d'après un texte hittite", *ArOr*, 1 (1929), 65-76, with pertinent bibliography. Generally, see H. G. Güterbock, "Die Historische Tradition ...", *ZA*, N.F. 8 (v. 42) (1934) 2f., and *ZA*, N.F. 10 (v. 44) (1938), 45f.

[6] In addition to the text cited in the previous footnote, the so-called *šar tamḫari*, "King of Battle" text (*VAS*, XII, 190, 193) represents less a historical than a literary account of an expedition alleged to have been made by Sargon of Akkad to Anatolia for the protection of Akkadian merchants installed at *Burušḫattum* or its vicinity. The version cited here was found at El Amarna in Egypt. Variants in the Hittite language coming from Boğazköy are 2, *BoTU*, 1 and 2 (= *KBo*, III, 9 and 10). Translations and discussions may be found in E. F. Weidner, "Der Zug Sargons von Akkad nach Kleinasien", *BKS*, 6 (1922); W. F. Albright, "The Epic of the King of Battle, Sargon of Akkad in Cappadocia", *JSOR*, 7 (1923) 1-20; P. Dhorme, "Les nouvelles tablettes d'el Amarna. IV. La tablette de Sargon l'Ancien", *RB*, 33 (1924), 19-32.

From Assur, the eastern terminus and financial center of the trade, the merchants imported a metal, *annâkum*, textiles and wool, in return for which they filled orders for copper, Anatolian garments and a variety of small manufactures.[7] Caravans carrying these goods were regularly dispatched to towns on both sides of the Taurus Ranges, and traveled along routes that were safe and secure. To regulate their financial affairs the merchants employed an intricate system of bookkeeping, under which their outstanding accounts were registered in public registry offices, whether these were located in Assur or in one of the Anatolian settlements.

These settlements were essentially of two types, and were designated either as *kârum* or *wabârtum* (var: *ubârtum*). These terms may be understood to mean different things according to the contexts in which they appear. Each, first of all, refers to a settlement as a physical entity. But beyond this, each may also connote the community of persons in such a settlement, as well, finally, as the particular administrative or executive body which oversees the affairs of such a community.[8] A glimpse into the etymological history of *kârum* will serve to illustrate the origins of its various meanings.

The term is a loan-word in Semitic from the Sumerian *kar*, meaning "quay" or "dam embankment". Originally it signified the earthen banks built up along the waterfronts of Mesopotamian river and canal towns, which served as unloading depots for the cargo carriers plying the waterways of the lower Tigris-Euphrates Valley river systems. The markets which naturally tended to grow up along these quay areas gradually came to bear the same designation as the quay itself, as finally did the specialized community of traders who functioned in, and most likely lived near, these markets. Through extensions of usage, the term also came to be employed to designate the administrative and judicial boards which supervised the business activities with which the traders were concerned. Thus, in sum, three levels of meaning for *kârum* may be discerned: it is a term which is applied to define a trading area; the trading community of that area; and the administration, in the narrow sense, of that community.[9]

[7] See Chapter II, below, for a survey of Cappadocian trade.

[8] For the meaning of *kar/kârum* in Early Mesopotamia see A. Walther, "Das altbabylonische Gerichtwesen", *LSS*, 6 (1917), 79-80.

[9] I. J. Gelb provides useful analogies: "The same development of meanings as in *kârum*, originally 'commercial settlement', later 'judicial power', can be observed in the words 'pharaoh (great house)' or 'Porte', originally a place where justice was executed, later 'justice' or the ruler himself. Cf. also the English term 'court', originally only the place where justice was dealt out", *OIP*, 27 (1935), 12, n. 141.

In Mesopotamia, the *kârum* of a Sumerian or Semitic city was a specialized trading and market quarter, and its trader population, composed as it was of the citizenry of the town, shared with other groups within the urban organization a common heritage of ancestry, language and religion.[10] But in Cappadocia, the Old Assyrian *kârum* displays different characteristics.

It was still, to be sure, primarily a trading community. But its meaning can no longer be sought with reference to its functioning role *within* a fully Semitized urban environment. In Cappadocia it signifies more the entire Semitic community residing in a foreign city.[11] By virtue of its establishment and position within a distinctly non-Semitic population area, it has become not only an outpost of Mesopotamian culture abroad, but also a community empowered to represent the Assyrian government in negotiations with indigenous Anatolian rulers and their administrations. Thus while the designation, *kârum*, was the same for the Mesopotamian and for the Anatolian community of Semitic traders, it describes institutions which were in fact quite different, and made so because of the different circumstances under which they existed. The *kârum* of Anatolia belongs to a different class of political organization from its namesake in Mesopotamia, a class which shall but loosely be designated for the moment as a "colony".

According to the Cappadocian texts published to date there were eleven colonies of the *kârum*-type, and ten *wabârâtum* (pl.).[12] These

[10] For the Mesopotamian *kârum* as a specialized quarter, cf. W. F. Leemans, *The Old Babylonian Merchant: His Business and His Social Position* (Leiden, 1950), 63, and A. L. Oppenheim, "A Bird's-Eye View of Mesopotamian Economic History" (Chapter III), in K. Polanyi, C. M. Arensberg and H. W. Pearson (eds.), *Trade and Market in the Early Empires* (Glencoe, Ill., 1957), 30-31. For administrative and judicial functions of the *kârum* in this area, cf. A Walther, *Das altbabylonische Gerichtswesen*, *op. cit.*, 70-80, and W. F. Leemans, *The Old Babylonian Merchant... op. cit.*, 71, and 104f.

[11] This opinion anticipates one of our conclusions. In the history of Cappadocian research various opinions on this point have been expressed, the chief being those of Benno Landsberger, who argued that *kârum* designated the entire community so characterized, and Julius Lewy, who means by it the principal quarter and governing body of an Anatolian town, i.e., an arm of the Assyrian government which Lewy alleges exercised imperial authority in Anatolia. We agree with Prof. Lewy that the *kârum* represented a specific quarter of an Anatolian town populated primarily by Assyrians (see fn. 18, below), but depart from his interpretation of its political character.

[12] The list of *kârum* and *wabârtum* (sg.) settlements is given below. The term *wabârtum* has been the object of various interpretations. Most recently Prof. Lewy has seen in it a collective derived from *ubâru*, "resident alien", "emigrant", "neighbor", hence a community of such ("On Some Institutions of Old Assyrian Empire", *HUCA*, 27 [1956], 59, n. 250 and 60, n. 252). Earlier Lewy saw in the term the idea of "Station" or "Militärposten" (*KTHahn* [1930] 6), a view to which Gelb, *OIP*, 27 (1935), 36, in

were well-distributed in an area extending from Assyria to the Plain of Konya in the southwestern reaches of the Anatolian Plateau, a rough distance of about six hundred miles east to west. The evidence of personal and place names in our sources shows fairly clearly that Anatolia in the early second millennium was populated to a large extent by Hattians — speakers of Hattic.[13] These represent the autocthonous population. From the existence of a considerable number of Indo-European names it seems clear that the Assyrian colonies existed during a period which finds Indo-Europeans already forming an important part of the Anatolian population.[14] In addition to the Hattic and Indo-European names found in our texts, a relatively insignificant number of Hurrian names has been noticed, but it is reasonable to suppose that the people who bore these names represent only isolated individuals who found employment with the Assyrian caravans, at a time when perhaps the main body of the Hurrians was still distributed in the fringe mountainous areas of Eastern Anatolia and Mesopotamia.[15]

Within their own group, the Assyrians, themselves, reflect a dual ethnic origin. Many of their names are Assyro-Babylonian in construction, but many are West-Semitic.[16] However it would be incorrect to

part subscribed. Another translation, offered by M. David, *OLZ*, 36 (1933), col. 214f., was "Fremdenniederlassung". While it is perfectly clear that the *wabâratum* of Anatolia have legal and commercial jurisdiction over the Assyrian traders, and that they form a class of settlement subordinate in importance to the *kârum*, and especially to *Kârum Kaniš*, the superior of all the Assyrian settlements, the specific character of these communities is unknown. The view of von Soden, *AnOr*, 33 (1952), 58, that *wabârtum* is a noun meaning "Handelsamt" is derived from *post hoc* considerations.

13 For Hattic see A. Goetze, *Kleinasien* (1957), 45-47, with literature there cited.

14 For the arrival of the Indo-Europeans in Anatolia and the complex linguistic problems related thereto, *ibid.*, Further useful but frequently divergent discussions may be found in E. Bilgiç, "Die Ortsnamen der 'kappadokischen' Urkunden im Rahmen der alten Sprachen Anatoliens", AfO 15 (1954-51) 1-37; A. Goetze, "Some Groups of Ancient Anatolian Proper Names", *Language* 30 (1954) 349-359; *idem*, "The Linguistic Continuity of Anatolia as Shown by its Proper Names", *JCS*, 8 (1954), 74-81; *idem*, "The Theophorous Elements of the Anatolian Proper Names from Cappadocia", *Language*, 29 (1953), 263-277; I. J. Gelb, "A Contribution to the Proto-Indo-European Question", *JKAF*, 2 (1951), 23-36; B. Landsberger, "Assyrische Königsliste und 'Dunkles Zeitalter'", *JCS*, 8 (1954), Exkurs 1 und 2, 120-133.

15 See H. G. Güterbock, "The Hurrian Element in the Hittite Empire", *JWH*, 2 (1954) 383 and A. Goetze, *Kleinasien* (1957), 61-63 for Hurrian generally, with the literature there cited.

16 See F. J. Stephens, *PNC* (1928), 4-5, and 74-95. Also relevant are J. Lewy, "Zur Amoriterfrage", *ZA*, N.F. 4 (v. 38) (1929) 243-272; *idem*, "Les textes paléo-assyriens et l'Ancien Testament", *RHR*, 110 (1934), 29-65; *idem*, "*TC*, 100; *LC*, 242 und das Eherecht des altassyrischen Rechtsbuches, *KAV*, Nr. 1", *ZA*, N.F. 2 (v. 36) (1925), 139-161; B. Landsberger, "Über die Völker Vorderasiens im dritten Jahrtausend", *ZA*, N.F. 1 (v. 35) (1924); 213-238.

assume that the Assyrian traders came to Anatolia as the result of a migration of West Semites, perhaps *before* the main body of Assyrians entered their northern Mesopotamian homeland, as has been thought in the past, for chronological indications make it certain that the trader colonies were founded during the tenure of the Old Assyrian Dynasty at Assur.[17]

Although we have but two clear archaeological indications of it — gained from the excavations at Kültepe and at Alişar Hüyük — it appears that the Assyrians typically lived in their own quarter or section of an Anatolian city, and there they carefully maintained their own Semitic customs in religious and secular matters.[18] As a homogeneous group they wrote their own language, worshipped their own gods, and for the most part followed the dictates of Assyrian law. They used their own calendar for dating their financial documents, and also employed traditional Mesopotanian weights and measures and monetary value ratios.[19] However, they relied upon Anatolian craftsmen for the domestic utility items, such as pottery, which they required.

Despite their being a close, Semitic-oriented group, which even treated their non-Semitic neighbors as cultural inferiors according to indications in the sources,[20] they nevertheless mixed with their neighbors to an extent that some scholars in the past have been unwilling to admit. The traders might marry indigenous women and maintain them as "secondary" wives, all the time being responsible for the support of Assyrian wives and families in Assyria.[21] As settled residents they naturally engaged in

[17] The earlier opinion of A. T. Clay postulating an empire of Amurru in the upper Euphrates Valley which antedated the civilization of Babylonia and Assyria, was used as the basis for the belief in a Semitic migration to Cappadocia in early times by Ferris Stephens, "Studies of the Cuneiform Tablets from Cappadocia", *Culver-Stockton Quarterly*, 2, No. 2 (1925), 17f. The reader is referred to Appendix B of this study for the most recent chronological indications.

[18] That the Assyrians considered the *kârum* a specific quarter is evident from *CCT*, III, 4:40f., discussed briefly by J. Lewy, "On Some Institutions of the Old Assyrian Empire", *HUCA*, 27 (1956), 36, n. 128. Although clear evidence of Assyrian merchant inhabitation appears at Boğazköy, the topographical situation is still confused (see Appendix B). The appearance of only five tablet fragments of "Cappadocian" style at Yorgan Tepe (*Nuzi*) does not permit meaningful conclusions about the presence of an Old Assyrian community there. As for the maintenance of their own customs by the Assyrians, some allusion to this is made in almost every article on the Cappadocian Period. The reader is referred to the list of titles in the bibliography, and to specific notices in the footnotes of this study.

[19] See, for example, B. Landsberger, *AHK* (1925), 1-36, and G. Eisser and J. Lewy, *EL*, I and II, *passim*.

[20] See J. Lewy, "On Some Institutions ..." *op. cit.*, 15, n. 65 [16].

[21] *Ibid.*, 3-10. Further, see J. Lewy, "*TC*, 100; *LC*, 242 und das Eherecht des altassyrischen Rechtsbuches KAV Nr. 1", *op. cit.*, and B. Hrozný, "Über eine unver-

business with the indigenous inhabitants, and because of their financial resources they frequently lent money to non-Assyrians, thereby enormously stimulating local commercial activities as well, incidentally, as garnering substantial profit from interest payments on debts owed to them.[22] But beyond this, it should be noted that while the Assyrian *kârum* or *wabârtum* was a full-fledged residence area (as will be shown below), its members led an itinerant existence. They were caravaners, constantly on the move. They depended, therefore, on the Anatolian farmer and craftsman for food and domestic services to a large measure.[23]

The opportunity for the type of social and business interrelationships that have been mentioned was largely occasioned by the physical nearness of the *kârum* to its host city, as well as by a favorable climate of opinion under which symbiotic relationships were maintained. Discussion of this climate must be reserved for later, but some description of the Anatolian city complex may be undertaken. For this purpose the city of Kaniš with its *kârum* may well serve as a model.[24]

The city-mound rises to a height of twenty-three meters above the surrounding plain and appears as a raised circular terrace with steep sides on all but its northern and northeastern perimeter. Excavation has uncovered here the remains of large, monumental-type buildings, one of which was certainly the palace of the city's administration. No doubt future soundings will reveal many more impressive remains of structures belonging to the indigenous residents.

About two hundred meters away from the large city-mound, facing the easily approachable northern and eastern slopes, stands the *kârum*-terrace whose surface rises about two and one-half meters above ground level. Annual excavations in this terrace since 1948 have revealed many

öffentlichte Urkunde vom Kültepe (ca. 2,000 v. Chr.)", *SeD*, 2 (1939), 108-111.

22 See EL I and II *passim*. Debts owed by Anatolians were usually payable at harvest time (*ana harpî*) or at the festival of a god, which probably also was connected with harvesting activities. Usually the original loan was made against the pledge of servitude for one or more members of the debtor's family should he default.

23 J. Lewy maintains that the Assyrian population of Alişar Hüyük practised farming ("On Some Institutions ...", *op. cit.*, 61-64). Prof. Lewy may rightly suggest that because one Assyrian asks another to send him certain agricultural products and sheep and rams, the products in question are available for purchase from an agricultural population. But this does not necessarily mean that the addressee of the pertinent letters — Nabi-Enlil, in *OIP*, 27, 5 and 6, lived among farmers who were *Assyrian*. That Nabi-Enlil appears to have purchased lambs from a man bearing an Assyrian name (cf. *OIP* 27, 34:4-6) is immaterial without further context, as is the reference to payments made to Kukkulanum and Adad-naṣir (*OIP*, 27, 31: Rev. 11-15), cited in Lewy, *ibid.*, 64, n. 267.

24 See Appendix B for a detailed survey of the excavations.

buildings which testify to the character of the *kârum* as a residence quarter as well as a commercial station. Large, two-storied houses were found here, some with open courtyards. In these houses the Assyrian merchants set aside rooms for use as offices, and in these rooms great numbers of business documents were found, some in large vase-containers which acted as filing cabinets.[25]

In addition to the houses the *kârum* contained buildings which served as administrative meeting places, temples and shrines, and warehouses and stables. The chief "public" building of the *kârum* was the *Bît Kârim*, or "*Kârum*-House", whose functions will be described in a later chapter. In addition the *kârum* probably had pasturage lands for the use of its caravan animals, and a market area certainly was set aside within its precinct.[26] Indeed, excavation shows that during the most flourishing period of Assyrian inhabitation at *Kârum Kaniš*, the period designated as Level II, the *kârum* area was so crowded that the houses practically touched each other.[27] We cannot think of *Kârum Kaniš* as anything but a substantially appointed residence quarter designed for continued use; certainly it was not a small and insignificant trading post as has been thought by some in the past.

That the Assyrian residence area at Kültepe-*Kaniš* (and at Alişar Hüyük) was situated below the city-mound, and somewhat away from it, has led scholars to think that the Assyrians were excluded from the main city area, and that they must have enjoyed some kind of extra-

[25] Many of the Cappadocian tablets were originally found by Hrozný in groups of from ten to two hundred-fifty, regularly dispersed in the earth, but almost always beside them were fragments of large vases in which they had originally been deposited. Hrozný also found several still inside a large intact vase. See B. Hrozný, "Rapport préliminaire sur les fouilles tchéchoslovaques du Kültépé (1925)", *Syria*, 8 (1927), 5f. For the more recent finds of the *Türk Tarih Kurumu*, see the relevant bibliography in Appendix B.

[26] For remarks on the possible site of the *Bît Kârim* at Kültepe cf. T. Özgüç, *TTKY*, V, Seri — No. 10 (1950), 151 and *idem*, *TTKY*, V Seri No. 12 (1953), 121. The *Bît Kârim* probably housed the *Kârum*-treasury, cf. Chapter Two, n. 88 and 127, below, and the "Treasury of the Caravaners", for which cf. Chapter Two, n. 88. That the *kârum* had its shrines and chapels is learned *inter alia* from *Bab*. 6, 186, which mentions a Temple of Aššur in *Kârum Uršu*, and the frequent references to oath-taking in "the gate of the god" (*bâb ilim:* cf. e.g., *KTHahn*, 31:5, and the comments in *EL* I, p. 119, n. (c), etc. The existence of market areas is deduced from the appearance of the title *rabi mahîrim*, 'chief of the market', (cf. *TC*, III, 253:1 and *BIN*, VI, 226:5f) as well as *TC*, III, 262A:3f, where a slave (*ṣubrum*) is mentioned as being purchased in the market, etc.

[27] Cf. T. Özgüç, *TTKY*, V, Seri — No. 10 (1950), 121f., and *idem*, *TTKY*, V Seri — No. 12 (1953), 114f.

territorial status.[28] But it is entirely normal that a commercial area designed to accommodate a busy caravan trade be situated in accessible places on the edges of cities, and not necessarily atop high citadel mounds.[29] In passing it should be said that no inferences of a political nature drawn from topographical observations are valid in this instance. For we have already noted that were it not for the presence of certain specifically Assyrian objects in the *kârum* area — the cuneiform documents and seals and seal impressions in the Mesopotamian style — the *kârum* could have been mistaken for any typically Anatolian settlement.[30]

If the Assyrian *kârum* in Anatolia as typified by *Kârum Kaniš* was substantially constructed and capable of handling a large volume of overland trade, the location of each in an important city shows how well and advantageously distributed was the entire number of colonies. We may conveniently survey the geography of these colonies so as to understand the extent of Assyrian trading operations in Anatolia.[31]

The region bearing this name consists essentially of an extensive and irregular plateau ringed on all sides by high mountain ranges. In the North, East and South, the mountain ring is well defined, being two to four thousand feet higher than the plateau it surrounds; but on the West, towards the Aegean coastlands, the hills are fewer and less imposing. Here the approaches to the plateau run out as fingers of ridges which separate deep inlets. Between these ridges the rivers descending from the highlands have fashioned broad and fertile valley plains.

The central plateau thus forms a homogeneous region to which access is not especially easy except from the Aegean side. On the North, for the most part, the Pontic Mountains reach nine thousand feet, and descend right to the seacoast. This precludes the existence of more than a few harbors. The ranges, themselves, follow the coast, and consist of parallel ridges between which rivers have formed deep-lying valleys. Natural routes through these mountains are few.

On the South the Taurus Mountains form an imposing barrier. The

28 For the latest expression of this idea, cf., J. Klima and L. Matouš, "Les tablettes 'cappadociennes'", *RAI*, 2 (1951), 59, and Goetze, *Kleinasien* (1957), 72.

29 Even today in the Near East caravan markets still cling to the outskirts of cities.

30 Cf. H. Çambel, *Or*, ns 20 (1951), 246-247.

31 The following survey is freely taken from W. B. Fisher, *The Middle East*, 2nd. Ed. (London and New York, 1952) 293-338. Also see L. Dudley Stamp, *Asia*, 8th. Ed. (London and New York, 1950), 69-105, and H. H. von der Osten, "Anatolische Wege", in *Eranos* (*Acta Philologica Suecana A Vilelmo Lundström Condita*), 49 (1951), 65-84. The reader is further referred to the following maps: Faik Sabri Duran, Türkiye,

Taurus chain, properly speaking, comprises a series of fold ranges dominated by the Taurus Dağ, which is one of four separate massifs cut by river action. This chain runs parallel to the Anti-Taurus in a north-east, southwest direction. Together, the Taurus and the Anti-Taurus form the huge mountain border between Anatolia and Syria. To the west of the main Taurus Range extend the ridges of the Western Taurus, which can be traced from the district of Fethiye north-eastwards toward Afyonkarahisar, and then south-eastward toward Silifke.

As in the North, no coastal plain is present except for that between Ağva and Alanya (the Plain of Antalya), and the Cilician Plain, which lies in the north-east corner of the Mediterranean. The scarcity of coastal plain in the South is due to the sheer drop of the Western Taurus to the edge of the sea over most of its domain. On the whole, stream outlets to the Mediterranean are not characteristic of this region, but rather there are numerous mountain lakes, most of which are saline.

The main Taurus Range on the south and south-east rim of the Anatolian Plateau is distinctly narrower than the Western Taurus, and much higher. In the Aladağlar region the range reaches twelve thousand feet. A number of narrow and precipitous river valleys have been cut right through the mountain barrier and one such defile, forms the well-known Cilician Gates, a relatively easy but rather indirect route between Central Anatolia and the Mediterranean Coast.

As the Taurus Chain sweeps away toward the north-east from the Mediterranean, it becomes reinforced by the parallel chain of the Anti-Taurus. Gradually the combined ranges approach the Northern Pontic Ranges, and finally merge with them to form the region of the Eastern Highlands. There is little physical unity here since the extensive and continuous mountain ranges of the North fall away on the South first into broken plateau country, and finally into an undulating plain which continues through Northern Mesopotamia. Further disunity arises from the presence of several large river basins — those of the Aras (Araxes), Euphrates and Tigris. Passes through the Taurus and the Anti-Taurus are few, a condition which severely limits the ease of communication between Anatolia and Mesopotamia.

The central Anatolian Plateau, itself, consists of a rolling upland containing numerous sunken basins that are occupied by marshes and mud-flats, and also many massifs that consist either of volcanic cones or horst-blocks. The general level of the plateau surface lies between three

1:2,000,000 (Kanaat Yayinlari, Istanbul); and *Karte der türkischen Republik*, 1:2,500,000, *Petermann's Geographischer Mitteilungen* (v. 81) (1935), Tafel 22.

and five thousand feet, while the upland masses reach six to eight thousand feet above sea level. The general character of the plateau is steppe-land whose aspect is extremely dreary. It is snow-covered and wind-swept in winter, dry and brown in summer.

The streams on the northern flank of the plateau have cut back through the mountain ring and now drain wide areas of the plateau itself. The basins of the Sakarya, the Kizil Irmak (Halys), and the Yesil Irmak cover more than half the plateau. The rivers, themselves, are often deeply entrenched below the level of the plateau surface, and their vallyes are irregular and discontinuous. The whole surface of the northern plateau is deeply eroded, and precipitous valley walls and sheer, rugged hillsides are to be seen in many districts.

The enclosed basins of the South-west are disposed in a rough crescent between Afyonkarahisar on the West, Konya on the South, and Kayseri on the East. In the absence of drainage there are no deep valleys, and the whole region is open and undulating.

Because of its enclosed nature much of the central Plateau of Anatolia is arid and supports little plant or animal life. Its climate is similar to that of the steppe-lands of Russia. Winter temperatures on the surface do not rise much above the freezing point. In the valleys snow lies continuously for two to four months. Summers are very hot and dry, and feature violent dust storms. The total rainfall over considerable areas does not exceed ten inches. East of the Plateau, in the mountains of Armenia, conditions are even more severe, for witner temperatures here fall consistently below fifteen degrees Fahrenheit. Nearly all the valleys and plains in the mountain masses of Armenia are blocked with snow for four or five months of the year.

The vegetation of the plateau-steppe is scanty. Over vast areas there are no trees except for lines of willows along the water-courses. Herbage consists mainly of grass and small shrubs. On the whole cultivation is restricted to the neighborhood of rivers, or to the few areas (such as the region of Kayseri) where rainfall is unusually abundant. For the greater part, the central Plateau is bare and monotonous country given over to grazing.

However forbidding are its land features and climate, the Anatolian Plateau and its mountain fringes still possess great treasure in forests and minerals. Both the eastern and the western reaches of the Pontic Chain in the North are extensively wooded, but the Taurus and the Anti-Taurus in the South are less so. The riches of the latter, however, are to be found in substantial deposits of copper, silver and lead, and in smaller deposits of gold — the metals for which the Mesopotamian king and trader alike searched most frequently in Asia Minor.[32]

Despite the obstacles presented by the difficult terrain through which they had to pass, and the long distances they had to overcome, the Assyrian caravans traveled to and from the different colonies, and between Anatolia and Assyria, with a minimum of inconvenience. Consisting of heavily-laden donkeys, the caravans passed by easy stages between towns along the trade routes, employing local guides, and using the services of guards who kept the roads free of bandits most of the time.[33] Easily traversed, direct routes were generally used, but sometimes the caravaners chose alternate roads which were more sheltered and secret.[34]

A survey of these routes and the locations of the Assyrian colonies on them shows how vast an area was regularly traversed by the caravans we have been discussing. To be sure, many of the locations which will be proposed below are tentative, and some have been the subject of long debate, yet generally they appear to the writer to be sound. Before passing on to a discussion of these, however, it is convenient to present a list of the names of the colonies with the references to them from the sources:

THE "KÂRUM"-SETTLEMENTS

Burušḫattum:	*CCT*, I, 19b:9; III, 4:41-43; V, 12b:17; *EL*, 330a:16; 331:1; 332:48; 334:1; 335:26; 337:20; 338:24; 339:1; 340:y + 2; *ICK*, I, 26a:1; *KTHahn*, 14:33; *TC*, III, 273:16-17.
	Bît Kârim:
	CCT, I, 19b:3-5; 22a:3-5; II, 8-10; V, 38a:5, 15, 17, 23, 30, 32; *ICK*, I, 190:14 (*Bît Qar !-ri-im*); *TC*, 37:9-11; III, 165:35, 38, 42; *TuM*, I, 27b:7f.
Durḫumit:	*AnOr*, VI, 12:5; *ATHE*, 22A:15; 22B:6-7; *CCT*, V, 10b:22-23; *EL*, 278B:1; *ICK*, I, 86:33; *ICK*, II, 141:33; *TC*, 35:3-4(?).
Ḫaḫḫum:	*CCT*, II, 49a:16; *EL*, 243:19; 275:1; 314:13; 315:17.
Ḫattuš:	I. J. Gelb in R. S. Hardy, *AJSL*, 58 (1941), 179, n. 6.

[32] A most comprehensive work on the location of ancient mines, the qualities of ancient metals, and techniques of metal working is R. J. Forbes, *Metallurgy in Antiquity* (Leiden, 1950).

[33] See Chapter VI, below.

[34] See E. Bilgiç, *Die einheimischen Appellativa der kappadokischen Texte und ihre Bedeutung für die anatolischen Sprachen* (= *DTCFY*, No. 96, 1954, 43-44.)

Hurama:	*BIN*, VI 32:4; *EL*, 252:24; *ICK*, I 61:3, 21.
Kaniš:	*EL*, 225:14; 238:16; 239:21; 245:41; 247:27; 248:28; 249:x+2; 250:27; 253:x+2; *et passim*.
	Bît Kârim: *passim*.
Niḫria:	*EL*, 210A:3, 9; 210B:7, 11.
Tawinia (*Tamnia*):	*HUCA*, 27 (1956), 45, n. 170.
Uršu:	*EL*, 255:23; 256:16; *SUP*, 7:3.
Waḫšušana:	*BIN*, VI, 183:20; *CCT*, V, 12a:22-23; 15c:16-17; *EL*, 238:30; 251:18; 258:9; 262:25; 263:22; 265:30; 268:32; 277:1; 316:11; 330:16; 336:x+9; *ICK*, I, 159:3-7; *ICK*, II, 139:32; *Jena*, 440:1; *TC*, 32:3; 60:2; 111:13; III, 275:1.
	Bît Kârim: *BIN*, IV, 218:21-22.
Zalpa:[35]	*Chantre* 11:3f., Rs. x+6.
	Bît Kârim: *BIN*, VI, 167:8f.

THE "WABARTUM"-SETTLEMENTS

Badna:	*KTHahn*, 3:4, 23f.
Ḫanaknak:	*EL*, 260:17.
Karaḫna:	*HUCA*, 27 (1956), 59, n. 251.
Mama:	E. Bilgic, *AfO*, 15 (1945-51), 30 and 34; *idem*, *Belleten*, 17, No. 65, fig. 36, 1.4.
Šalatuwar:	*KTHahn* 16:22; See *KTP*, 10:3f. and 20.
Šamuḫa:	*VAT*, 6209:3f. (cf. *HUCA*, 27 [1956] 70, n. 301); *VAT*, 9295 (*OLZ*, 29 [1926] 756 and *EL* I, p. 182); Kt b/k 21:23-27 in *TTKY*, *VII Seri — No*. 28, 66, n. 10a.
Tuḫpia:	*EL*, 271:12f.
Ulama:	*EL*, 282A:1; 282B:1f.
Wašhania:	*HUCA*, 27 (1956), 60, n. 251; Kennedy and Garelli, *JCS*, 14:5:30.
Zalpa:	*EL*, 267A:13.

In discussing the locations of the Old Assyrian settlements listed abovc it is desirable to begin with *Kârum Kaniš*, the most important of all. We recall that its remains have been excavated at Kültepe.

Kültepe is situated slightly west of a north-sourth line running between Samsun on the Black Sea, and Tarsus in the Cilician Plain. It lies some eleven kilometers south of the Kizil Irmak (Halys) where that river cuts

[35] Two different Zalpas may come into question — Zalpa/Zalpuwa and Zalpaḫ. See A. Goetze, *Kleinasien* (1957), 74, n. 12.

a great circle through the Anatolian Plateau toward the northeast. Nineteen kilometers further to the south-west lies Kayseri (Gr.: Caesarea Mazaca). The situation of Kültepe allows it to dominate the approaches to the Taurus and the Anti-Taurus on the East and South-East, and the Cilician Gates on the South. Furthermore, it lies at the intersection of many lines of communication which converge upon it from all directions.

The ancient city of *Kaniš*, then, was at the hub of a system of routes which radiated from it to all points of the compass. To the south lay *Kârum Waḫšušana*, which should probably be located in the area around modern Niğde.[36] Far to the south-west lay *Kârum Burušḫattum*. The location of this important site must be sought in the rough square of land area defined by the modern towns of Obruk, Konya, Kadinhani and Cihanbeyli, directly south-west of Tuz Gölü, or "Salt Lake".[37]

The route to both of these *kârû* from Kültepe-*Kaniš* was the same as far as *Wašḫania*, the seat of a *wabârtum*. *Wašḫania* was approximately one day's journey south-west of *Kaniš*, and hence must be looked for in the general area of İncesu.[38] At *Wašhania* the main route to the South bifurcates, a branch going on to *Waḫšušana* by way of the town of *Mal-*

[36] Although the writer has spent considerable time studying the Cappadocian itineraries and other geographical source material, he cannot reproduce here all or even a major portion of his results. The footnotes which follow, therefore, contain but a part of the pertinent references, and the reader is accordingly directed to the most readily available published commentaries. On the situation of *Waḫšušana* see J. Lewy, "Naram-Sin's Campaign to Anatolia in the Light of the Geographical Data of the Kültepe Texts", *HEM*, I (1947), 14-15, and E. Bilgiç, "Die Ortsnamen ...", *op. cit.*, 21. Both agree to localizing it near modern Niğde, though for different reasons.

[37] This on consideration of the Cappadocian itinerary *TC* III 165 and relevant information from later Hittite sources. *Burušḫattum* of the Old Assyrian Period appears in Hittite as *Burušḫanda*, *Burušḫandumnan* (*IHN*, 11), *Baršuḫanda* and *Paršḫunta* (*HGN*, 16). According to the Hittite text *KUB*, VI, 45-46, *Paršḫunta* is in the Lower Country, a part of the Hittite land in the southern Anatolian Plateau bordering on the land Arzawa (Goetze, *Kizzuwatna*, 23). The Cappadocian text *TC*, III, 165 offers the following sequence of towns between *Kaniš* (modern Kültepe) and *Burušḫattum:* (1) *Kaniš* (2) *Wašḫania* (3) *Nenašša* (4) *Ulama* (5) *Burušhattum*. That the route must have been south-westerly, terminating south of the Tuz Gölü, is supported by additional information from Hittite sources, which aid in the localization of the individual stations. See subsequent footnotes.

[38] Cappadocian *Wašḫania*, the first station after *Kaniš* according to *TC*, III, 165, appears as *Wašḫaniya* in the Hittite text *KUB*, XXVI, 43 and 58, where it is placed in the district of *Ḫarziuwa* (25f.), a place also cited in the Cappadocian text *KTS*, 35a:7. *Ḫarziuwa*, according to *KUB*, XXI, 6a (and as judged by Garstang, *HGN*, 6), was on one side of the territory raided by Hittite enemies from *Walma* (= *Cappadocian* "*Ulama*", station No. 3 of *TC*, III, 165); it appears to have been situated in the south-west region of the Halys River (Kizil Irmak) Basin. Bilgiç, "Die Ortsnamen ...", *op. cit.*, 21, places *Wašḫania* in the vicinity of modern İncesu; Lewy, "Naram-Sin's Campaign ...", *op. cit.*, 15, situates it at modern Nevşehir, about 45 km. west of İncesu.

lita, which lay somewhere in the area of the modern town, Yeşilhisar.[39] The other branch, going in a south-westerly direction, reached *Nenašša*, which various scholars have placed at Aksaray.[40] From *Nenašša* it proceeded to ancient *Ulama* (var: *Walama*), the seat of an Assyrian *wabârtum*. This town should be located somewhat south of Tuz Gölü (Salt Lake), and on the north-eastern perimeter of the Plain of Konya.[41] Leaving *Ulama*, the south-westerly route arrived directly at *Burušḫattum*. We know little about the roads which must have connected *Kârum Burušḫattum* and *Kârum Waḫšušana*, the two most southerly *kârû* of Anatolia proper. Either between these places, or somewhere south of *Waḫšušana* lay the ancient town of *Šalatuwar*, wherein an Assyrian *wabârtum* was located.[42]

In the area north and north-west of Kültepe-*Kaniš*, within the Kizil Irmak (Halys) Basin, were situated several *kârû* and *wabârâtum*. The sites of two of these may positively be identified. At Boğazköy, which later was to become the seat of the Hittite capital, *Ḫattušaš*, were found the remains of *Kârum Ḫattuš*. Small numbers of Cappadocian tablets have been found, or excavated, here for many years. Similarly, at Alişar Hüyük, inhabitation strata containing Cappadocian tablets have been uncovered, but it is not positively known whether the settlement here may have been a *kârum* or a *wabârtum*. Unfortunately, it is also unclear what name the site bore during the Cappadocian Period.[43]

[39] See Bilgiç, "Die Ortsnamen ...", *op. cit.*, 21-22. Lewy favors a slightly more westerly location, on the modern Nevşehir-Niğde road, "Naram-Sin's Campaign ...", *op. cit.*, 14-15.

[40] *Nenašša*, the next station after *Wašḫania* on the *Kaniš-Burušḫattum* road (*TC*, III, 165), is also known in Hittite sources (*IHN*, 35; *HGN*, 15), and is generally linked with the *Nanassos* of Ptolemy. See E. Bilgiç, "Die Ortsnamen ...", *op. cit.*, 20, n. 148.

[41] *Ulama*, station No. 3 on the *Kaniš-Burušhattum* road (*TC*, III, 165), was called *Walma* in Hittite times (*HGN*, 24-25), a variant spelling also known in the Cappadocian tablets (*BIN*, IV 31:17; *TC*, III, 271:22). In the Annals of Muršiliš (A. Goetze, *MVAG*, 38 [1933]), 1. 51, it is situated by the Astarpa River, near the Arzawan frontier. As a land, it borders on the Hulaya River, which is associated with *Paršḫunta/Burušḫattum* (among others) in the Lower Land, according to *KUB*, VI, 46-46, no. 37. Garstang equates the Hulaya River Land with the Plain of Konya (*HGN*, 7). Bilgiç, "Die Ortsnamen ...", *op. cit.*, 20, places *Ulama* somewhat south of the Tuz Gölü.

[42] Lewy notes that caravans sent from *Waḫšušana* to *Burušḫattum* used a road passing by *Šalatuwar*, and on the basis of other evidence as well, postulates that *Šalatuwar*, was situated on one side of a triangular road system — *Wašḫania-Waḫšušana*, *Wašḫania-Burušḫattum* and *Burušḫattum-Wahšušana* — between the latter two cities; he identifies it with *Salaberina*, a station on the Tabula Peutingeriana, which he proposes lay somewhere south of modern Helvadin, at the foot of the Hasan Dağ. ("Naram-Sin's Campaign ...", *op. cit.*, 14-15, w.n. 15 and 18. Bilgiç prefers a localization further to the south-east) "Die Ortsnamen ...", *op. cit.*, 22, w.n. 156.

[43] Lewy argues that the ancient name of Alişar Hüyük was *Amkuwa*, and that it was

Since we have no memoranda of any intineraries followed in this area which would allow us to gauge distances between the Assyrian colonies located therein, the identification of such colonies is even less precise than usual. Somewhere in the near vicinity of Boğazköy, but either to the north or south, lay *Kârum Tawinia* (var: *Tamnia*).[44] Also the town of *Zalpa* must be sought in the same general area.[45] There is a question of whether our sources refer to two towns of this name (the other possibility being *Zalpaḫ*, in Syria), or not.[46] Accordingly, it is also unclear whether the *wabârtum* attested at *Zalpa*, and *Kârum Zalpa*, belong to the same town. Historical texts from the later Hittite period associate *Zalpa* both with *Ḫattuš* and *Kaniš*, and it probably was situated not too far from Alişar Hüyük.[47]

In the eastern part of the Kizil Irmak Basin the town of *Durḫumit* was located. This is the same town known to the Hittites as *Dur/Turmitta*, and was the seat of a *kârum* in the Cappadocian Period. Most likely, it was located between Alişar Hüyük and Sivas, an important modern town on the road leading north from Kayseri.[48] In the same general area, but probably to the east or south-east of *Durḫumit* lay *Tuḫpia*, where a *wabârtum* was located.[49]

The towns which we have been discussing all lay generally to the north or south of *Kârum Kaniš*, and at the present time there is no evidence which points to a conclusion that settlements of Assyrian traders were located further to the west in Anatolia than the region around the Plain

a *wabârtum*, "On Some Institutions ...", *HUCA*, 27 (1956), 60-64, w. n. 257-259f. Gelb also thought it probable that Alişar Hüyük = 'Amkuwa', *OIP*, 27 (1935), 9.

44 The observations of Goetze, *RHA*, 1 (1930), 27, and Garstang, "Hittite Military Roads in Asia Minor", *AJA*, 47 (1943), 47. Goetze suggests Alaca Hüyük, slightly to the north-east of Boğazköy, while Garstang equates *Tawinia* with *Tavium*, at Nefesköy, about 20 km. south of Boğazköy.

45 At the present time it seems clear only that *Zalpa* was located in the Halys River (Kizil Irmak) Basin. Bilgiç has collected many references which seem to show that *Zalpa* was not too far from *Hattuš*, *Kaniš* and Alişar Hüyük, among others ("Die Ortsnamen ...", *op. cit.*, 30-31.

46 Cf. footnote 35, above.

47 Cf. Lewy, "On Some Institutions ...", *op. cit.*, 60, n. 253 for references to the discussion of the eminent place which Zalpa held in Hittite tradition.

48 Cf. Bilgiç, "Die Ortsnamen ...", *op. cit.*, 28-30 [29]. Garstang, "Hittite Military Roads ...", *op. cit.*, 55f., places it at modern Yeni Han, slightly north-west of modern Sivas. Goetze, *Kleinasien* (1957), *op. cit.*, 72, includes it with the northern group of cities — *Hattuš*, *Tuḫpia*, *Zalpa* and *Tawinia*, all for him lying between Boğazköy and Merzifon.

49 The close geographical association of *Tuḫpia* with *Durḫumit/Durmitta* is evident from Hittite sources, and is fully discussed in the references given in footnote 48, above.

of Konya. We may therefore turn to the east, and to a discussion of the Assyrian settlements in the mountainous areas of the Taurus and the Anti-Taurus, as well as a few in North Syria. Here some detailed account of the trade routes is possible both because our sources provide sufficient data, and because the number of roads through the mountains between Anatolia and Syria is necessarily limited to the number of traversable passes.

Our sources seem to attest two routes through the Taurus, a northern and a southern.[50] The northern passed through the town of *Timilkia*, which was neither a *kârum* nor a *wabârtum*, but nevertheless an important caravan city in our period. Its ultimate destination was *Ḫaḫḫum*, the seat of an Assyrian *kârum*, whence it ran on into the Plain of North Syria.[51] The more southerly route went by way of *Mama*, a *wabârtum*, and *Uršu*, a *kârum*, before it, too, entered North Syria and joined with the northern branch to form a common road to Mesopotamia.[52] Several *kârum*-settlements and *wabârâtum*, as we shall see, were located in the mountainous terrain between *Uršu*, on the southern route, and *Ḫaḫḫum*, on the northern.

The locations of both these ancient towns have long been a highly controversial matter. We are persuaded that *Ḫaḫḫum* is to be sought for in the vicinity of the modern town of Harput, which is situated about one hundred kilometers northeast of Malatya.[53] We also accept the

[50] The reader is referred to A. Goetze, "An Old Babylonian Itinerary", *JCS*, 7 (1953), 51-72, and Bilgiç, "Die Ortsnamen ...", *op. cit.*, 22-30 [24f.], for the relevant discussions. We are persuaded that the general reconstructions made by these two scholars are more probable than that of J. Lewy in "Studies in the Historic Geography of the Ancient Near East", Or ns. 21 (1952), 265-292 (= II. *Old Assyrian Caravan Roads in the valleys of the Ḫabur and the Euphrates and in North Syria*"), and *ibid.*, 393-425 ("Old Assyrian Caravan Roads ...", concluded). Our reasons for departing from Lewy include, among others, his insistence that *Ḫaḫḫum*, a key station on the *Kaniš-Assur* road, is to be localized in Northern Syria or Eastern Cilicia (273, against which we argue in footnote 53), and his identification of Cappadocian *Ta/Dar(a)kum* with *Terqa* of the Mari Period (274f.), which we feel is unconvincing. Both these attributions result in Lewy's taking the Old Assyrian route along the Euphrates against the evidence cited by Bilgiç and Goetze, above.

[51] That *Timilkia* was an important station between *Kaniš* and *Ḫaḫḫum* is attested, among others, in *CCT*, IV, 18a, while *BIN*, IV, 114:18f. gives the parallel connection *Timilkia-Ḫaḫḫum*. Cf. Bilgiç, "Die Ortsnamen ...", *op. cit.*, and Goetze, "An Old Babylonian Itinerary", *op. cit.*, 69.

[52] Cf. Bilgiç, "Die Ortsnamen ...", *op. cit.*, 24-27, and Goetze, "An Old Babylonian Itinerary", *op. cit.*, 72 (sketch-map).

[53] The localization of *Ḫaḫḫum* has long been a controversial matter. The town is attested as early as the period between the end of the Old Akkadian Dynasty and the beginning of *Ur*, III, and is evidently the same *Ḫaḫḫum* which appears in the Gudea Inscription with reference to the gold coming from its mountains. (For the references

conclusions of Sidney Smith that *Uršu* must be placed somewhere in the area extending from the Amanus Ranges of Lebanon to the Euphrates

---

see Gelb, "Studies in the Topography of Western Asia", *AJSL*, 55 [1938], 75). The identification of *Ḫaḫḫum* with *Ḫaḫḫas* of the Hittite Imperial Period (cf. A. Goetze, "Hattušiliš; den Bericht über sein Thronbesteigung nebst den Paralleltexten", *MVaG*, 29 [1925], 34f., 1. 17), was made by Lewy ("'Kappadokische' Tontafeln und Frühgeschichte Assyriens und Kleinasiens", *OLZ*, 29 [1926], 966, w. n. 4, and "Zur Amoriterfrage", *ZA*, nf 4 [38] [1929] 262f., n. 5), and Garstang ("Hittite Military Roads ...", *op. cit.*, 50, n. 46), and was accepted by Gelb ("Studies ...", *op. cit.*, 76).

Bilgiç ("Die Ortsnamen ...", *op. cit.*, 27-28), in reviewing the relevant studies of Garstang ("*Šamuḫa* and Malatya", *JNES*, 1 [1942] 452) about *Ḫaḫḫas*, agrees with that scholar about its association with ancient Pattiarik and *Šamuḫa* in the area of Malatya and its northern hinterland. Bilgiç places *Šamuḫa* in the immediate area of Malatya, Pattiarik in the area of modern Pertek, about 125 km. north-east of Malatya, for since the Hittite king Hattušiliš encountered and defeated in *Ḫaḫḫas* the Gasga people, who had based themselves in *Pattiariga*, *Ḫaḫḫas* must be sought in the close vicinity.

The Cappadocian tablets offer loosely corroborative information. The text *TC* 18, consisting of instructions to a certain Assur-nada, and most likely sent from *Assur* to him while he was en route to *Kaniš*/Kültepe, tells him that if he is afraid to go to *Ḫaḫḫum* he should split up his caravan into three parts, each to proceed to *Kaniš* separately. One part is to leave from *Mama*, a station between *Uršu* and *Kaniš*, probably closer to *Uršu*. Upon word of its safe arrival, the second part is to set out from *Uršu*, as is the third (lines 32-46).

We must infer that the text (*TC*, 18) reached Assur-nada in some place along the relatively direct route from *Assur* to the approaches of the Anti-Taurus, at a point before the road bifurcated — one branch going via *Ḫaḫḫum*, the other via *Uršu*. Since we are persuaded that *Uršu* is to be located west of the Euphrates and close to it, between modern Birecik and Cerablus (ancient *Carchemish*, for which see footnote 54, below), it appears to follow that *Ḫaḫḫum* must lie in the area east and north of *Uršu*, since Assur-nada, the caravaner of *TC* 18 presumably could have reached it first.

When all of the preceding information is considered with the fact that Gudea of *Lagaš* took gold from the mountains of *Ḫaḫḫum*, and with the discussion by R. J. Forbes, *Metallurgy in Antiquity* (Leiden: 1950), 151, relative to the location of gold deposits in Asia Minor, it becomes extremely probable that *Ḫaḫḫum* is to be localized in the vicinity of modern Harput, about 100 km. north-east of Malatya, for with the exception of rich mines south of the Caucasus, in Armenia, and deposits south of Lake Van and in surrounding mountains, the only deposits of gold in Eastern Asia Minor that are anywhere in the vicinity of the Old Assyrian route are the deposits of gold in the Taurus near Harput. Other deposits known to Herodotus and to Strabo occur in the extreme western part of Asia Minor.

Finally, the area of Harput is feasible as the location-area of *Ḫaḫḫum* because it satisfies the conditions of the above-mentioned Hattušiliš text, it being located about 20 km. south and slightly west of Pertek, where Bilgiç (*loc. cit.*), places Pattiarik; and it lies directly on the route through the Anti-Taurus beginning at modern Diyarbekir and proceeding via Ergani, Maden, Elazig to the Euphrates crossings at Keban, or near Malatya, whence the route proceeds to Kayseri and Kültepe via the Tohma Su, Darende, Gürün and Sariz. Because Garstang's localizing of *Ḫaḫḫum-Ḫaḫḫas* at Kangal (*loc. cit.*) is too far from a source of gold, and is also quite a bit north of the usual route between the Malatya area and Kayseri, and because of Bilgiç's arguments that *Ḫaḫḫum* and *Pattiarik* must be close to the Euphrates, *Ḫaḫḫum*-Kangal must be rejected.

River north of modern Cereblus (ancient *Carchemiš*), most probably very close to the western bank of that river.[54] So situated, it commands the approaches to the area of modern Maraş, the southern terminus of three important passes cutting through the Taurus.

By beginning at Kültepe-*Kaniš*, we may trace the routes leading through these passes into North Syria, and more conveniently discuss the locations of the *kârû* and *wabâratum* on the mountain fringes of Eastern Anatolia than otherwise. We recall that the southern route mentioned above led to Maraş. It could arrive there either by passing through the modern town of Göksun, or through Elbistan.

Considering the Göksun passage first, the route from Kültepe-*Kaniš* reached Göksun after passing through the Göz Bel Pass, a fairly easy passage capable of taking light wagon traffic; another road to Göksun goes by way of the Gök Bel, which is a less important and more difficult pass.[55]

From Göksun it is possible to reach Maraş by two routes. One cuts through the Ahir Bel Pass, and crosses the Gök Su and the Ceyhan (*Pyramos*) River. The other, which is far more difficult, goes through the Keban Pass, and then continues around the Dolaman Dağ before it finally crosses the Ceyhan River and arrives at Maraş. Writing in 1893, and though they themselves had never traversed it, the Englishmen

[54] Attempts by various scholars to localize *Uršu* have produced much disagreement. The reader is referred to Sidney Smith, "*Uršu* and *Haššum*", *AnSt*, 6 (1956), 35-43 for the latest review and appraisal. Here Smith adduces reasons for rejecting Urfa as a probable site of *Uršu*, in part because of evidence from the Mari texts (especially, *ARM*, XV, 184) which strongly suggests that *Uršu* must have been situated on the west side of the Euphrates and close enough to the river for a beacon-light signal from the opposite bank to have been seen by its inhabitants. Beyond this, we believe that Smith is persuasive on the point that *Ibla* and *Uršu* at some times must have overlapped in territory. He points out that the land *Uršu* could also be called *Ibla*, *KI*. (*Loc. cit.*, 39), and that: "Ibla was the old geographical name, Uršu was the city which became the capital of an enlarged city state." (*Loc. cit.*, 40). His conclusion is that the land *Uršu* extended from the Amanus to the Euphrates north of *Carchemish* (Cerablus), and thus covered the approaches to Syria, but that the extension of the land to the west bank of the Euphrates does not fix the site of the city, except generally. (*Loc. cit.*, 42).

[55] The material which follows in the texts and the notes has been condensed from material contained in scholarly studies and travel diaries. The chief sources used are D. G. Hogarth and J. A. R. Munro, "Modern and Ancient Roads in Eastern Asia Minor", *Royal Geographical Society*, Supplementary Papers, 3 (1890-93), Part 5 (London, 1893), 643-739; W. M. Ramsay, *The Historical Geography of Asia Minor* (London, 1890) (= *Royal Geographical Society*. Supplementary Papers, 4); J. G. C. Anderson, "The Road System of Eastern Asia Minor", *JHS*, 17 (1897), 22-44. A general description of the routes and passes through the Taurus and the Anti-Taurus systems, west to east, is given in Hogarth and Munro, *loc. cit.*, 657-670, to be read with Ramsay, *loc. cit.*, 55f., with further references there given.

Hogarth and Munro had it on local opinion that the Göksun-Maraş passage was by far the easiest of all through the Eastern Taurus.[56]

Returning to our starting point at Kültepe-*Kaniš*, we may discuss the route which goes to Maraş by way of Elbistan. From the Kültepe region a more easterly route than that which goes to Göksun leads through the Kuru Çay Pass, an easy passage also capable of carrying light wagon traffic, to Elbistan. From Elbistan to Maraş one alternative route leads south through Firnis. The first part, leading to Firnis, crosses the Hurma Su, and passes round the western shoulder of the Berut Dağ. From Firnis it eventually crosses the Ceyhan River and traverses the very steep Ahir Dağ before it reaches Maraş.[57]

The second way of getting to Maraş from Elbistan is more direct than that which passes through Firnis, but it is also far more difficult. This alternative route crosses the İcme Su after leaving Elbistan, passes through Ambararasi and Hacinoğlu, and cuts through the extremely precipitous Kusuk Pass. The going is very difficult, and becomes easier only as the route approaches Maraş.[58]

From a consideration of these roads through the Taurus, it is highly probable that such a town as *Uršu*, whose importance in the Mari period as well as in the Cappadocian is evident, was located just at the entrance to the Maraş system of passes. The situation of ancient *Mama*, which lay between *Uršu* and *Kaniš*, must assuredly be either on the Maraş-Göksun, or the Maraş-Elbistan, route.

Having discussed the southern route between Anatolia and Syria, it remains for us to describe the northern. From Kültepe-*Kaniš* it must roughly have followed an easterly course through the Upper Sariz Valley to Gürün and Darende before it reached the area of Malatya. From this region it would have gone to ancient *Ḫaḫḫum* in the Harput area before reaching North Syria through the Ergani Pass, north of Diyarbekir. Such a route would have cut through the Kuru Çay Pass into the Sariz Valley, and then have followed the course of the Tohma Su until that stream joined the Euphrates slightly north-east of Malatya.[59]

[56] Cf. Hogarth and Munro, *loc. cit.*, 660, but especially Anderson, *loc. cit.*, 28.

[57] Cf. Hogarth and Munro, *loc. cit.*, 661-665.

[58] *Ibid.*, 665-667. In light of the extreme difficulties of the Kusuk passage as reported by Hogarth and Munro, we question whether Goetze is entirely justified in pushing the extreme western portion of his Old Assyrian route, Euphrates-*Kaniš*, through it ("An Old Babylonian Itinerary", *op. cit.*, 69). This minor criticism in no way decreases our respect for his general conclusions.

[59] Cf. Bilgiç, "Die Ortsnamen ...", *op. cit.*, 28; Garstang, "Hittite Military Roads ...", *op. cit.*, 47f.; Ramsay, *loc. cit.*, 270-280 and the maps of routes in Eastern Cappadocia and Armenia Minor.

It seems also probable that the Assyrian merchant caravans used a third route between Anatolia and North Syria. This is a route which branches off the Gürün-Darende-Harput road and cuts south from the area of Malatya through Polat and Besni, following which it can connect either to routes going west to Maraş, or east to Samsat.[60] In the area south of Malatya, and considerably south of Harput, where we situated ancient *Ḫaḫḫum*, the towns of *Ḫurama*, seat of a *kârum*, and of *Šamuḫa*, which claimed a *wabârtum*, must have been located.[61]

The routes through the mountains discussed above all joined a direct route to Mesopotamia which passed through North Syria. This skirted the headwaters of the Baliḫ and the Ḫabur, tributaries of the Euphrates. Branches of this route led into the valleys of these rivers. As it passed eastward, the main route hugged the Sinjar Hills and made its way down the Tigris to *Assur* (Qal'at Sherqat), the eastern terminus of the caravans.[62]

Two *wabârâtum* — at *Ḫanaknak* and at *Batna* — are to be sought in North Syria, though it is not clear where they are located.[63] The last of the *kârum*-settlements under consideration, *Kârum Niḫria*, must lie in the triangle of land formed by imaginary lines between Mardin, Siverek

[60] Cf. Hogarth and Munro, *loc. cit.*, 657, and Ramsay, *loc. cit.*, 276 and 279.

[61] Goetze's discussion of Hittite passages mentioning *Lawazantia* (= *Cappadocian Luḫusaddia*) and *Ḫurama* (*Kizzuwatna and Hittite Geography*, New Haven, 1940 [= *YOR*, 22], 72-73 w. n. 289), favors a localization of the latter in Eastern Anatolia toward the Euphrates. Two bits of information derived from Cappadocian texts support the positioning of *Ḫurama* in the general area of the approaches to the Anti-Taurus west of the Euphrates and somewhat east and north of *Uršu* (n. 54, above): *EL*, 243 mentions *Ḫurama* in connection with *Ḫaḫḫum*, while *TC*, II 27 suggests its relative closeness to *Timilkia* (n. 51, above). It appears to follow that *Ḫurama* must lie in the mountainous area between Cerablus (ancient *Carchemiš*) and Malatya.

As for *Šamuḫa*, Goetze, *Kleinasien* (1957), 72, places it in the area between the Upper Halys (Kizil Irmak) and the Upper Euphrates, while Bilgiç generally agrees by placing it in the vicinity of *Ḫaḫḫum*, "Die Ortsnamen ...", *op. cit.*, 26-27.

[62] Cf. Goetze, "An Old Babylonian Itinerary", *op. cit.*, 72, (sketch-map).

[63] Goetze, *ibid.*, 68, equates *Batna*(*e*) with Sürüc, between Urfa and Birecik; Bilgiç notes that *Batna* must have been situated in the vicinity of *Timilkia*, for which see n. 51 and 61, above ("Die Ortsnamen ...", *op. cit.*, 28, n. 200).

As for *Ḫanaknak*, its possible location in North Syria is suggested by the element *Ḫana* in its name, though I am unable to propose a localization.

A *wabârtum* not discussed in the text — that at *Karaḫna* — also resists localization. It appears to be associated with Hittite *Taggašta* and *Marišta* (Garstang, *HGN*, unpublished). Garstang localizes these towns in the general area of the Lower Halys ("Hittite Military Roads ...", *op. cit.*, 54f.). That *Karaḫna* may have been further to the south is suggested by the appearance of its name in the Egyptian text of the treaty between Hattušiliš III and Ramses II, hence perhaps in North Syria, as Garstang notes in *IHN* (1923), 26.

and Diyarbekir.[64] So situated, it commands the easternmost approaches to Anatolia from North Syria — the Ergani Pass.

The total view offered by the sources, then, shows a large network of Assyrian trading centers, each connected to the others by direct and well-traveled routes, and the entire system linked to *Assur*, the capital of Assyria during our period. We may turn our attention now to the commerce which passed through these settlements, and provide a sketch of the backgrounds of Cappadocian trade.

[64] *Niḫria* is also known from the Mari Letters (*ARM*, I 19:4, and *ibid.*, 103:8), where it appears to be associated with the land of *Kudmuḫ*. The Cappadocian tablets suggest that *Nihria* was relatively near *Ḫaḫḫum* (*CCT*, II, 22). Both Bilgiç ("Die Ortsnamen ...", *op. cit.* 23), and G. Dossin ("Un cas d'ordalie par le dieu fleuve d'après une lettre de Mari", *SeD*, 2 [1939], 116-117), agree in placing *Niḫria* west of *Kudmuḫ*, which they locate in the area north of modern Cizre and Nusaybin, hence approximately in the triangle formed by connecting lines between Mardin, Siverek and Diyarbekir. So located, *Niḫria* lies astride the approaches to the Anti-Taurus before the Ergani Pass. Prof. Mendenhall informs me that in light of an almost total absence of mounds in the approach areas to the Ergani Pass System on a direct line from Midyat to Diyarbekir, the route from *Assur* to the area of Malatya probably made the approach to the north somewhere near, or west of, Siverek.

II

CAPPADOCIAN TRADE AND THE STRUCTURE OF THE OLD ASSYRIAN POLITICAL SYSTEM

The Old Assyrian Dynasty came to power in the midst of the twentieth century before Christ. Its first ruler was Puzur-Aššur I, but we know nothing of the events which brought him to the throne of Assur. Previous to his accession, Assyria had been vassal to various dynasties of Southern Mesopotamia. As early as the twenty-fourth century, Sargon of Akkad had campaigned there, as had his successors, especially Narâm-Sîn, who conquered Assyria and built temples in Nineveh.[1] Later, under the Third Dynasty of Ur, governors of Assur served Sumerian kings.[2]

The opportunity for Assur to emerge from her vassalage and become an independently-ruled land arose, without doubt, during the period when Ur III was progressvely weakened by the attacks of hostile city rivals. In the realignment of power following the fall of Ur, Assur became but one of several contenders for primacy, others being the cities of Eshnunna, Isin, Larsa and Mari. Under Ilu-šuma, the grandson of Puzur-Aššur I, Assyria was strong enough to interfere in the affairs of southern cities; in one text he asserts that he established the "freedom" of such places as Akkad, Ur, Nippur, Awal, Kismar and Der.[3]

[1] Cf. S. A. Pallis, *The Antiquity of Iraq* (Copenhagen, 1956), 578.

[2] Cf. the Inscription of Zâriqum, city-governor of Assur during the reign of Bur-Sin, third ruler of the powerful Third Dynasty of Ur: Assur 21982, published in *KAH*, II, 2, and in W. Andrae, *Die archaischen Ischtar-Tempel*, 106f. and pl. 64c given in *IAK*, II, 1.

[3] Cf. Assur 20488, unpublished (Photo Assur 6209f.), transliterated and translated as *IAK*, IV, 2. The pertinent lines are *Rev* (2), 13-30. Another text of Ilušuma, Assur, 19977 published in *KAH*, II, 4, and by Andrae, *Die archaischen Ischtar Tempel, op. cit.*, 115f. with pl. 65, and appearing as *IAK* IV, 1, mentions in *Rev.* (*2*): 1-3 that Ilušuma established the "freedom" of the Akkadians.

The meaning of the phrase "to establish the freedom (of something)" (*andurârum/ adurârum šakanum*) is explained by the authors of *IAK* as follows: the idiom can be used with reference to men or to things. If used of men, it means freedom from bondage and compulsory service, protection against unjust treatment, as well as political freedom from foreign rule; if used of things, it indicates exemption from commercial duties (free trade) or only moderate taxes on commerce (*IAK*, 8, n. 6).

J. Lewy takes issue with the above by translating *andurârum* as "free movement",

The course of Assyrian political development which reaches its culmination in Ilušuma's activities (though very little is know of it), witnesses a permanent change from a semi-nomadic to an urban style of life. The Khorsabad King List records that the earliest Assyrian rulers lived in tents; these kings may have begun to reign in the days when Akkadian conquerors campaigned in the North.[4] There is no doubt that Assyria came gradually, but quite thoroughly, under first Akkadian, then Sumerian, cultural influences. By the time of Ur III cities are prominent in Assyria, although they seemed to have served mainly as fortresses to insure the peace of the land. When Assur was finally able to rule itself, it could draw upon models of Southern Mesopotamian urban organization for its own development, though certain of its customs and institutions are indigenous, and were never established in the South.

A glimpse of the ancient Mesopotamian city and its institutions may well serve to introduce the institutions of Assur and set the stage for a discussion of Cappadocian trade during the Old Assyrian period. Until the present time, the available data has seemed to indicate that the cities were primarily "temple communities". It is thought that each was held by the ancient Mesopotamian to have been ruled by a god,[5] who owned both the land and the population living on it. The temple was called "the god's house", and in the opinion of Frankfort, it functioned "actually as the manor-house on an estate, with the community laboring in its

---

"unrestricted traffic", without accepting the notion of "exemption from taxes". Cf. "Some aspects of Commercial Life in Assyria and Asia Minor in the Nineteenth Pre-Christian Century", *JAOS*, 78 (1958), 99, w.n. 68, where Lewy alludes to the text Assur 16850 (= *KAH*, II, 11, also published as *IAK*, V, 7), an inscription of the Old Assyrian King Irišum, son of Ilušuma, who established the *andurârum* of silver, gold, copper, lead, wheat, wool and a few cheap commodities, during his reign.

[4] The historicity of the earliest Assyrian kings is doubtful. Kings No. 17 through 26 of the Khorsabad King List (= *KKL*) are "ancestors" of Šamši-Adad I (*KKL*, 39), and are not, or hardly, from Assyria proper. As for kings *KKL*, 1-16, many of the names seem artificial: there are six "rhyming pairs" (e.g., Zuabu: Nuabu; Didânu: Ḫanu; Imṣu: ḪAR-ṣu; etc.). All except three are of unlikely historicity for the later Sargonic and entire Ur III period. So W. Hallo, "Zâriqum", *JNES*, 15 (1956), 221, n. 9. It is entirely possible that none of the Assyrian King List rulers began rule before the latter part of Ur III.

[5] Cf. H. Frankfort, *The Birth of Civilization in the Near East* (New York, 1956), 63. Not all scholars are in agreement with the recapitulation which follows in the text. Prof. I. J. Gelb, on the basis of a study of Old Akkadian tablets, especially those in the collection of the Chicago Natural History Museum, came to the tentative conclusion that early Mesopotamian society was a feudal society based on private property. Cf. *Old Akkadian Inscriptions in Chicago Natural History Museum* (= *Fieldiana: Anthropology* v. 44, no. 2, 1955), 181-182).

service".[6] The central political theory of these communities, according to the same author, was a kind of "state socialism":

> The belief that man fulfilled the purpose of his being by serving the gods had very remarkable consequences for the structure of early Sumerian society. Since the citizens projected the sovereignty of their community into their god, they were all equal in his service. In practice this service took the form of a cooperative effort which was minutely organized. The result was a planned society, and the remains of the Protoliterate period show that it existed then, although it is better known from Early Dynastic times.[7]

The idea of a planned society in the earliest historic periods does not, however, imply a corresponding political despotism. On the contrary, the temple communities seem to have practised what has been called (perhaps unfortunately), "primitive democracy".[8] To judge from the earliest myths, in which the political organization of the gods may be held to reflect a situation prevailing on earth at the time of their composition, ultimate authority rested in a general assembly of citizens, whose deliberations were directed by a leader.[9] Verdicts of the assembly became law after proper debate and voting. In such debate, the opinions of the elders carried the greatest weight.[10]

The leader in the earliest assemblies was chosen by the assembly itself, usually to meet a specific crisis. The crisis past, the leader *pro tem* would return his commission and authority to the assembly.[11] Jacobsen has compared the leader chosen in this *ad hoc* manner to the Old Testament "Judge", who was a powerful individual to whom people in trouble turned for help in getting their rights.[12]

The assembly as a sovereign body was gradually forced into the background in the face of political necessity. The leader became a permanent feature of government.[13] Popular will ultimately gave way to personal rule (though the assembly was still recognized), for the leader's position and influence were now guaranteed by direct ties of allegiance between himself and members of his household and soldiery, and so perpetuated.

6 *Ibid.*, 54.
7 *Ibid.*, 64.
8 The term was coined by Th. Jacobsen, "Primitive Democracy in Ancient Mesopotamia", *JNES*, 2 (1943), 159. Were it not for the possibility of confusing Early Mesopotamian ideas of freedom with those of Greek and later society — ideas which are significantly different — the designation would be excellent.
9 Cf. Th. Jacobsen, "Primitive Democracy ...", *op. cit.*, 167-171, and *idem*, "Early Political Development in Mesopotamia", *ZA*, nf 18 (v. 52) (1957), 101-104.
10 *Ibid.*, "Early Political Development ...", 102, w. n. 14.
11 *Ibid.*, 104.
12 *Ibid.*, 110-111.
13 *Ibid.*, 113ff.

This is the situation observable for the period of our first historical texts. Dynasties become the order of the day, while the authority of the ruler is glorified, even sanctified. In the person of the sovereign, the political and the religious tendencies of ancient Mesopotamian culture meet. At once he is the mundane protector of city and land, as well as the divinely-favored superman; in his office he combines the chief symbols of power and fortune.

The drift of early Sumerian history is toward the consolidation of large land areas under a single king, until under the Old Akkadian Dynasty (and subsequently under the Third Dynasty of Ur), the pattern of large standing armies, strategically located garrisons, and widespread systems of provincial administrations is firmly established as a fact of Mesopotamian political life.

The rise of a strong executive system, under which the palace replaces the temple as the most prominent institution of the city or national organization, appears to have produced an alteration in the traditional balance of power between these two institutions.[14] The temple seems originally to have had exclusive control of the means of production — the seed for planting, the draft animals, the implements of cultivation.[15] There is much evidence to suggest that it allotted these to the citizens, who seem each to have been enrolled on its lists.[16] And subsequently, after the harvest, the temple appears to have apportioned out a share of grain and other products to its members in accordance with their rank and the amount and type of service they had contributed.[17] Under this system the temple was the chief landlord, employer and storekeeper in the ancient Mesopotamian city.

As such, it naturally required a large staff of officials to administer its services and reckon its accounts. Because of the apparent magnitude of its interests and operations, it became bureaucratic to a high degree.[18] Special associations, or guilds, of functionaries and workmen begin to appear amongst the citizenry.[19] Each of these associations was directed by a foreman in its work, and one of them, the association of the DAM.-KAR, or "professional trader", is of special interest to us.

[14] For the usurpation of power by dynastic lines, *ibid.*, 122f.

[15] Cf. Frankfort, *Birth of Civilization, op. cit.*, 65f. and S. A. Pallis, *The Antiquity of Iraq, op. cit.*, 490-491.

[16] Cf. Frankfort, *Birth of Civilization, op. cit.*, 66-69.

[17] *Ibid.*

[18] *Ibid.*, 72-73.

[19] *Ibid.*, 69. Cf. also I. Mendelsohn, "Gilds in Babylonia and Assyria", *JAOS*, 60 (1940), 68-72, which deals, however, with guilds in Old Babylonian times and later. Cf. note 31, below.

The importance of the DAM.KAR in the economic life of ancient Mesopotamia may readily be seen if we consider how ill-suited the region is for anything but agriculture. It is an alluvial country, nourished by deposits of sediment brought down by the Tigris and the Euphrates Rivers. It contains no deposits of stone or metals, nor is there good timber available for building. From the earliest times in its history the inhabitants of the Mesopotamian river valleys had to import vital materials from neighboring countries, for which they paid by exchanging products of the soil.[20] In the development of inter-regional commerce, the professional merchant was all-important.[21]

Frankfort has held that the DAM.KAR in Sumerian society was exclusively concerned with export and import, and did not trade locally with the members of his own community, but this view has been reasonably challenged.[22] On the whole, however, the DAM.KAR was the prime mover in inter-city and international trade. That he received an allotment of land for his services to the community indicates the degree of his importance in the life of the ancient city.[23]

Though he was primarily an employee of the temple in early periods, the DAM.KAR was able to build up a store of capital for his private commercial use.[24] No doubt this was possible because he was able, much like other land-holding members of the community, to accrue surpluses over and above the produce he owed the temple at harvest time, and to use these surpluses to make loans at interest to less prosperous citizens. Further, he could finance private trading enterprises, and reap profit from his participation as creditor, as well as claim special commissions for particular services to other businessmen.[25]

From the time of the Old Akkadian Dynasty to the brilliant Third Dynasty of Ur, the hold of the temple upon the economic life of the Mesopotamian city appears to have loosened to the extent that more and

[20] A most important work devoted entirely to the DAM. KAR (= Semitic *tamkârum*) is W. F. Leemans, *The Old Babylonian Merchant: His Business and His Social Position* (Leiden, 1950).

[21] Cf. Leemans, *The Old Babylonian Merchant* ..., *op. cit.*, 1-4.

[22] Cf. Frankfort, *The Birth of Civilization* ..., *op. cit.*, 74, contradicted by Leemans, *The Old Babylonian Merchant* ..., *op. cit.*, 41, where it is stated that (during the period of Lugalanda and Urukagina at Lagaš): "It was mainly the commerce with other towns and countries that was carried on by the *damkara*, but they also figured in local trade, especially in the sale of fish".

[23] Cf. Leemans, *The Old Babylonian Merchant* ..., *op. cit.*, 43. Also, the Sumerian *damkara* could own property of their own (*ibid.*, 45f.).

[24] *Ibid.*, 45-47.

[25] *Ibid.*, 46.

more contracts between private individuals appear.[26] This is also the period in which political power is more concentratedly centralized in the secular, rather than the religious institution. The effect of this shift of emphasis is seen in the emergence of the palace as an important entrepreneur, as important, perhaps, as the temple. The DAM.KAR now is seen to serve both institutions, and accounts are kept for him in both.[27] But he continues to serve his own interests as well, and he functions, then, both as government trader and as private entrepreneur.

The Hammurabi Law Code of Old Babylonian times (ca. late eighteenth century), shows us the DAM.KAR (Semitic: *tamkârum*), not only as an itinerant trader,[28] but also as one who employs agents in his business.[29] He also appears as a capitalist *par excellence*, and as a moneylender.[30] He has fully emerged as a "public trustee", whose services are offered both to government officials and to private citizens, and whose activities are regulated by law. As a "public trustee", he functions both as a citizen of his city, and as a member of the professional group, the association of *tamkârû*.[31]

To attempt to trace the development of private trading enterprise further would be irrelevant to our purpose, but it suffices to say that during the Old Assyrian Period, in Assur, a great number of trading companies existed.[32] These were organized most often as family enterprises, and were headed by patriarchs.[33] It is not entirely clear from our

[26] *Ibid.*, 42.
[27] *Ibid.*, 43f.
[28] *Ibid.*, 6-10.
[29] *Ibid.*, 22-35.
[30] *Ibid.*, 11-21.
[31] Leemans, *The Old Babylonian Merchant ...*, *op. cit.*, points out that there appear to be no convincing traces of an organization of *damkara* in Ur III times, although if the title *gal-damkara* may be taken as indicating the existence of such an organization, there was one in the preceding period (47, and 41). In Larsa during the reigns of Rim-Sin and Warad-Sin, the *tamkârû* appear to have formed a special group, "who perhaps lived in one quarter of the town" (63). For the Old Babylonian Period, Leemans says: "Actually not a single trace of guild organisations is extant in the Old Babylonian sources, not even a word to denote such a corporation. But while we reject the existence of guilds as we conceive them, in Babylonia, it cannot be denied that those who pursued a certain profession did form a certain group in the community." (68). For the full argument and a rejection of Mendelsohn, cited in note 19, above, cf. pp. 67-68.
[32] These are referred to in the Cappadocian tablets as *ellatum* (sg.), whose meaning can be rendered either as "trading caravan" or "trading company", according to context. Cf. A. Salonen, "Hippologica Accadica", *AASF*, Helsinki, 1956, 201-202.
[33] It is well-known that the Cappadocian tablets frequently show three active generations of the same families in Anatolia: cf. the family of Pušukin at Kaniš, studied in J. and H. Lewy, "The Origin of the Week and the Oldest West Asiatic Calendar", *HUCA*, 17 (1942-43), 82, n. 337; the families of Buṣuttaa, Ṭâb-aḫum and Luzina at

sources that these companies were composed of *tamkârû* exclusively, or seen, for that matter, primarily; for the role of the *tamkârum* in Old Assyrian trade is obscure. He is, to be sure, a necessary functionary, but the most important entrepreneurs are rarely reported to be *tamkârû*. Rather, it is the entrepreneur who makes use of the *tamkârum* in his operations.[34]

Whereas in earlier periods of Mesopotamian history the amount of private enterprise is restricted and rather marginal, in the Old Assyrian period, by contrast, it is significantly enlarged. The entrepreneur's activities still fall under public supervision, and he continues to serve the interests of palace and temple, but now most of his trade is what might be called "company trade".[35] Yet, as shall be seen below, there appears to have been a great deal of cooperative enterprise between companies.

The origins of Cappadocian trade, as we have already pointed out, are hidden from view. It is rather too facile an explanation that in the ancient Near East "trade follows the flag",[36] and that the system of Assyrian *kârû* and *wabâratum* in Anatolia represents the rewards of an Old Assyrian conquest of the regions across the Taurus.[37] This view will be examined later in detail, but at this point we would merely mention our own solution to this problem: trade between Assyria and Cappadocia was sanctioned by commercial treaties drawn between high

Kaniš, cited by K. Balkan from newly excavated and unpublished tablets, *TTKY*, VII, Seri — No. 28, 46; the family of Kiki, *PNC* (1928), 51, etc. These families were related to the great merchants of Assur.

34 This is to be seen in many Cappadocian tablets. The *tamkârum* is usually referred to as such, without being named. Cf. B. Landsberger, *AHK* (1925), 12-20, and *idem*, "Kommt *Ḫattum* 'Hettiterland' und *Ḫatti'um* 'Hettiter' in den Kültepetafeln vor?", *ArOr*, 18, 1/2 (1950), 332, n. 15; and K. Polanyi, "Marketless Trading in Hammurabi's time" (Chapter II), in K. Polanyi, C. M. Arensberg and H. W. Pearson (eds.), *Trade and Market ...*, *op. cit.*, 24-25.

35 Whereas in earlier periods considerable amounts of goods owned by palaces and temples were carried as part of the *tamkârum's* stocks, in the Old Assyrian texts these appear to play a minor role. We mean by this that although the government of Assur — manifested through the palace and assembly of that city — had the power to tax and regulate the movement of trade goods (see below), the latter were mostly obtained privately, although certain precious commodities like *amûtum* (see later) could only be gotten through government agencies. Our texts report the occasional movement of "temple-goods" (*ikribu*. Cf. B. Landsberger, *AHK* (1925), 15, and J. Lewy, "Les textes paléo-assyriens et l'Ancien Testament", *RHR*, 110 (1934), 42, n. 25). Additionally, royal personages of Assur are seen occasionally to make use of the trading facilities. Cf., e.g., the text *OIP*, 27, 58:24, and J. Lewy, "On Some Aspects of Commercial Life ...", *op. cit.*, 100, w.n. 75.

36 J. Lewy, "'Kappadokische' Tontafeln und Frühgeschichte Assyriens und Kleinasiens", *OLZ*, 29 (1926), 756.

37 Cf. Chapters Three and Six for full discussion.

representatives of the Assyrian government and the individual rulers of Anatolian towns where the Assyrians sought to establish commercial conclaves. Nothing was of greater concern to Assyria than opening up the rich treasure-bearing regions of Anatolia as a market for her own exports, and as a permanent area of commercial exploitation. We strongly believe that the Old Assyrians accomplished what no other Mesopotamian power had succeeded in doing previously — systematically knitting together a vast trading "empire" in a foreign area without recourse to war. The instrument by which she originated this commercial domination was the good-will of the traders who made the first contacts; her success in creating and sustaining a large network of settlements across the Taurus was guaranteed by the formal and orderly relations which developed between herself and the indigenous principalities of the new area, all of which were sustained by oaths of mutual assistance and regard which were theoretically guarded by the deities of each side.

Admittedly, this is an inference from the political and economic information given in the Cappadocian sources only, but in the absence of relevant documents for the early political history of Assyria it is still viable. Nothing in the sources supports the idea that the Assyrians maintained troops in Anatolia, nor has excavation produced any evidence of military occupation. By and large we are dealing with Assyrian private citizens, commercial entrepreneurs, who were efficiently organized for the purpose of carrying on a large-scale international commerce, as the existence of the *kârû* and *wabârâtum* testifies.

The success and continuity of Cappadocian trade depended upon a complex organization and a specialized division of labor. The lifeblood of the trade was the wealthy, private entrepreneur, the *ummeânum*, who supplied the necessary capital and goods.[38] Usually (though not exclusively) resident at Assur, the *ummeânum* commissioned the *tamkârû* to do business for him. However, he might also finance small, itinerant traders (*šamalla'û*) directly.[39] Depending upon the *ummeânum's* resources, he could be powerful enough to direct a large trading firm (*ellatu*), or by contrast, he could simply and occasionally employ *tamkârû*

[38] For this term cf. B. Landsberger, "Solidarhaftung von Schuldnern in den babylonisch-assyrischen Urkunden", *ZA*, N.F. 1 (v. 35) (1924), 22, and *idem*, "Zu Driver's Übersetzungen: kappadokischer' Briefe", *ZA*, N.F. 4 (v. 38) (1929), 278; KTHahn, 14; *OIP*, 27, p. 35, n. to line 33, w.n. 8.

[39] On *šamalla'um* cf. *EL*, II, 101a; 103a (107f.); 164g; 167d. The word means "pouch-carrier", "sack-carrier"; cf. Leemans, *The Old Babylonian Merchant* ..., *op. cit.*, 31, n. 99. For the relationships between the *šamalla'um* and the *tamkârum* in the Hammurabi Period, Leemans, *op. cit.*, 22-35.

or *šamalla'û* on a smaller scale. Sometimes he pooled his resources with other entrepreneurs to create partnerships, and accordingly he was able to share the profits forthcoming from shareholding in a large enterprise.[40]

The *ummeânum* could function also as a money-lender, or banker.[41] As such, he was interested in collecting interest (*ṣibtum*) on his loan, or sharing in the profit (*nêmelum*) won through its use. He would invest a certain amount of money, usually silver or gold, with a traveling merchant. The capital thus given was called *naruqqum*, the name which designated the bag or sack in which the trader carried his weight-stones.[42] At the end of a stated period of time the contractee-trader had to return a multiple of the capital originally received by him, the amount of which was determined by the amount of time for which the original investment was made.[43] This period of time could be reckoned in years, months, or units of five days (*ḫamuštum*).[44] Should the trader have been successful enough to acquire money over and above the amount of return originally agreed upon, he would divide the surplus with his *ummeânum*.[45] Under the so-called *nêmelum*-contract, a type different from the *naruqqum*-contract just mentioned, the itinerant trader was entitled to one-third (*šalšâtum*) of the proceeds for himself.[46]

In addition to his being a money-lender and investor, the *ummeânum* was an exporter *par excellence*. Ever concerned with finding markets for his surplus domestic goods, he supplied his itinerant employees with merchandise destined either for direct sale to native Anatolian consumers, or for delivery to his agents or regional representatives abroad. These men served as his distributors, and were active in gauging the market conditions prevalent at any given time. As more or less permanent residents of the *kârû* and *wabârâtum* in Anatolia, they were members of the trading companies directed by the *ummeânû* from their home offices in Assur.[47] Often, the Assyrian regional representatives were blood-

[40] Cf. *TTAED*, 4:1.

[41] Cf. Landsberger, "Solidarhaftung von Schuldner ...", *op. cit.*, 278.

[42] Cf. H. Lewy, "Marginal Notes on a Recent Volume of Babylonian Mathematical Texts", *JAOS*, 67 (1947), 308, and Leemans, *The Old Babylonian Merchant* ..., *op. cit.*, 31, n. 99.

[43] Cf. H. Lewy, "Marginal Notes ...", *op. cit.*, 308-309, w.n. 15-26.

[44] Cf. e.g., the range of debt-tablets published in *EL*, I, pp. 14-86, etc.

[45] Cf. H. Lewy, "Marginal Notes ...", *op. cit.*, 308, w.n. 15.

[46] For a full discussion and interpretation of the economic ramifications of this type of contract, with many citations of texts, cf. *EL*, II, 103, n. (a).

[47] A special study devoted to classifying the membership of the major firms remains to be made. At present fairly reliable indications of such membership may be inferred from studying the letters sent and received by certain of the well-known residents of

relations to them, and served, therefore, to protect the interests of family investments.[48]

The functions of these representatives were to disburse goods which they had ordered from Assur in the name of various purchasers, and to supervise the acquisition and subsequent shipment of Anatolian goods to Assur. As a clearing agent for orders to Assur, an important merchant in one of the *kârû* or *wabârâtum* would receive money in advance from a purchaser, who was usually a colleague. He would acknowledge receipt of this money by drawing up a document, properly witnessed, and handing it to the purchaser.[49] As the latter, himself, may have been an itinerant trader, he would often commission a *tamkârum* to represent his interest, and the *tamkârum* would then hold the receipt, and be generally responsible for claiming the shipment of ordered goods when it arrived from Assur.[50] He might then have to transship the newly-arrived merchandise to his principal in another town.

In a transaction originating in Anatolia, and involving the purchase of goods from Assur, several distinct phases can be observed. The merchant broker in one of the colonies would transfer the money he had received from a colleague-client to a trusted functionary, or carrier.[51] This carrier would then proceed with the earliest available caravan, and deliver both order and purchase money in Assur, often to a specific exporter.[52] If the desired goods were available for the taking, the original carrier, or one of his own trusted employees, might return to Anatolia with them by the next outgoing caravan.[53] But sometimes it happened that the exporter could not supply the needed items at the moment, and he therefore issued a promissory note acknowledging his obligation to deliver them at a

Kaniš or Assur. Frequently the letters mention that someone is the representative of the sender, e.g., "he who is like me" (*ša kîma iati*), etc.

[48] One must be careful, however, not to assume, wherever the term "father" (*abu*) is used by one man to address another, that there is always a filial relationship involved, for *abu* is frequently used as a term of respect, meaning "superior". Cf. J. Lewy, "Apropos of a Recent Study in Old Assyrian Chronology", *Or ns*, 26 (1957), 28, w.n. 4.

[49] One of the frequently encountered types of disputes between traders involves the validity of debt, or obligation, tablets, especially when the holder claims he has not been satisfied.

[50] Examples in Landsberger, *AHK* (1925), 19-20.

[51] Typically, silver or gold from Anatolia is shipped to Assur, in return for which goods (usually called *luqûtum*) are sent out. Carriers such as Kukkulanum, who appears, e.g., in *EL*, 108, *EL*, 139, *EL*, 312 and *KTHahn*, 24; Aššur-Malik, son of Luzina, in *EL*, 149; and others, passed back and forth between Kaniš and Assur, as well as Kaniš and other Assyrian trading settlements, carrying goods and metals.

[52] Cf. e.g., *EL*, 140, and *KTHahn*, 24.

[53] Cf. e.g., *BIN*, IV, 12; *EL*, 295; *EL*, 313 among many possible examples of the movement of goods.

specified future date. In such circumstances the exporter frequently was obliged to pay interest on the purchase money he had received, this to be added to the value of the goods forthcoming. Since market conditions fluctuated, it frequently happened that the price prevailing at the time goods were ready for delivery differed from what it was when the purchase money was originally paid, in which case adjustments between buyer and seller had to be made.[54]

In addition to acting as commodity-brokers for the *ummeânû* of Assur, the representatives abroad could be directors of their own commercial networks, and frequently are seen to be financing *tamkârû* and *šamalla'û* in their own right. To be sure, the picture of commercial activities presented by our sources shows that the participants in Cappadocian trade reserved to themselves the privilege of engaging in strictly private deals above and beyond the enterprise required of them under the terms of their contractual obligations.

If the powerful merchant lords of Assur and their regional representatives living in Anatolia were the catalysts of Cappadocian trade, the *tamkârû* were its expediters. These men made careers of itinerant trading, and employed a host of lesser functionaries, including *šamalla'û* in their activities. Always concerned with the smooth operation of the caravan trade, they might advance fares on behalf of their principals, receive pledges against any loans their employers had made, or represent the latter in legal cases. They are seen, furthermore, to take charge of liquidating the assets of deceased traders, and generally served to facilitate the transport of goods and monies from place to place. Should opportunity arise, the *tamkârum* could also do business on his own.[55]

It remains to say a word about the *šamalla'û* and other small, but indispensable, functionaries. The *šamalla'û* usually traveled in pairs, for as Prof. Landsberger has pointed out, an *ummeânum* or *tamkârum* would subsidize two, so that one would assume responsibility for the investment capital should the other default payment for any reason.[56] To the *šamalla'û* fell the task of winning profit, selling goods, of scouring the countryside for needed commodities, and of seeking out new sources of supply when old ones failed. Often required to travel for years in the

[54] The technical term for such an adjustment is *nipiltum*, for which see *EL*, I, p. 219a (219-222).

[55] The reference to the *tamkâri rabi* ("Head Merchant") in *TC*, III, 44, Rev.: x +3, seems to suggest that the *tamkârû* of the Cappadocian Period were organized into an association of some sort, but the reference is enigmatic.

[56] Cf. Landsberger, *AHK* (1925), 12, and *idem.*, "Solidarhaftung von Schuldnern ...", *op. cit.*, 33f.

hope of realizing some small gain from the money invested with them, their lives were lonely and hard, but highly enterprising. Such also were the lives of the guides, drivers, the loaders and others without whose efforts the steady operations of Assyrian caravans would have been impossible.[57]

The trade goods carried by these caravans present a formidable array. Metals and clothing in great variety passed back and forth between Anatolia and Mesopotamia. From Assur, the principal exports were the metal *annâkum*, wool, and various types and manufactures of clothing,[58] while copper and Anatolian cloth-stuffs formed the chief imports from across the Taurus.[59] A chief aim of Cappadocian trade appears to have been the procurement of copper for the Assyrian government, and many texts testify to the large quantities which were moved by the caravans.

We can but touch on the vast catalogue of Cappadocian trade goods.[60] Of the metals *annâkum* was shipped from Assur in bulk containers which either bore the seals of private shippers or of the city-assembly.[61] Al-

[57] Among the more important of the functionaries connected with the caravan operations were the "freighter", (*qaṣṣârum*), discussed briefly by J. Lewy, "Studies in Akkadian Grammar and Onomatology", *Or ns*, 15 (1946), 385, n. 4; the "donkey driver", or "pack-master" (*sarridum*), for which cf. B. Landsberger, "Zu Driver's Übersetzungen ...", *op. cit.*, 277, and J. Lewy, "Studies in the Historic Geography of the Ancient Near East, II ...", *op. cit.*, 272, n. 1. (Gelb, *OIP*, 27 (1935) 52, n. to line x +4 of Text 50 translates (harnesser"); and the *ṣuhârum* (fem: *ṣuhârtum*), who were "helpers" or "dependents" of the merchant-entrepreneurs (*KTBl*, p. 24-25, n. to line 22 of Text no. 5).

[58] Although there has been controversy over which goods were exported from, which imported to, Assur, and although there has been no special study of the question, our own studies of the sources allow us tentatively to agree with Prof. Lewy that the *luqûtum*, comprising the metal *annâkum*, wool and clothing, formed the principal exports of Assyria to Anatolia. Cf. J. Lewy, "*Ḫatta, Ḫattu, Ḫatti, Ḫattuša* and 'Old Assyrian' *Ḫattum*", *ArOr*, 18, 3/4 (1950), 419, n. 294.

[59] The question is complicated because of the many stages through which a single shipment passed before it reached its destination. One carrier would meet another, and transfer to him the goods which he had brought, to be conveyed to yet a third transfer point, etc. There is no doubt, however, about the large lots of copper which were collected by the Assyrian trading agents.

[60] Almost every study of Cappadocian texts, or article about the historical or cultural significance of the Old Assyrian settlements contains some mention of the goods which were carried by the traders. The reader is directed to Appendix A, especially the articles cited under XI A, C, E, F and G.

[61] *Annâkum* is translated by some as "lead", by others as "tin", the confusion arising because both the Babylonians and Assyrians used the term in different periods to designate either metal. E. Bilgiç, "Asurca Vesikalara Gore Etilerden Once Anadolu'da Maden Ekonomisi", *Dil ve Tarih-Coğrafya Fakultesi, Sumeroloji Enstitüsü Nesriyati No.* 1 (1941) 913-950 (abstracted by H. G. Güterbock, "Türkische Beiträge zum Studium des Alten Orients", AfO 15 (1945-51) 128f.) came to the conclusion that "tin" was meant on the basis of a study of bronze finds from Mesopotamia and Anatolia,

though forming an important export when shipped in talent- and mina-weights, it also served as a medium of exchange for traveling expenses of the caravaners, who were supplied with small quantities for expenses.[62] It is interesting to note that on a single journey expenses might be paid in lead, copper or silver, depending upon the monetary preferences prevalent in any particular area.[63]

Silver seems to have served only as a means of payment and a standard of value.[64] It appears in our texts in a variety of qualities.[65] Like *annâkum*, it was also shipped in containers, rings and bars.[66] Copper, too, is known in a great variety of qualities, and although it appears primarily as a trade export from Anatolia to Assyria, it could also serve as a means of payment and as investment capital.[67] Other metals include gold, which is frequently used as investment capital, and as such interchanges with silver,[68] and *amûtum* and *ḫusârum*, which appear to have been among the most precious.[69]

Most of the clothing mentioned in our sources is designated by place of origin, and a great variety of styles, designs and qualities is evident, although precise understanding of many of the individual types of garments is not possible at the present time.[70] A frequently-mentioned export from Assur was the *kutânu*-garment, which Gelb has seen as connected to the *chiton* of the Greek, and *tunica* of the Roman Period.[71]

---

and of alloy-data appearing in cuneiform and other sources. Against this stand the views of R. Campbell-Thompson, *DACG* (1936) 121-122 and J. Lewy, "Apropos of a Recent Study ...", *op. cit.*, 13, n. 2, and *idem*, "Studies in the Historic Geography ... II", *op. cit.*, 422, n. 1, who, among others, translate "lead". A most recent work which argues that *annâkum* = 'tin' is B. Landsberger, "Tin and Lead: The Adventures of Two Vocables", *JNES* 24 (1965), 285-296.

For the sealing of *annâkum* shipments by the city-authorities of Assur cf. n. 86, below.

62 Cf. the phrase *annâk qâtim* (lit: "lead of the hand", i.e., "loose lead") in contrast to *annâkum kunûkum* ("lead under seal"), *passim* in the sources.

63 Cf. the text OIP 27:54, which mentions payments in all these media for a single trip.

64 Silver is consistently mentioned as the payment for, or measure of the value of goods purchased in Assur. It never appears as a trade good, in the sense that, e.g., *annâkum* is.

65 For a survey of these, as of other metals, cf. Bilgiç, "Asurca Vesikalara ...", *op.* cit.

66 *Ibıd.*

67 *Ibid.*, and *EL* I, *passim.*

68 Cf. H. Lewy, "Marginal Notes ...", *op. cit.*, 309, no. 21.

69 For *amûtum*, cf. B. Landsberger, "Kommt *Ḫattum* 'Hettiterland' ..." *op. cit.*, 331, n. 14 (332). For *ḫusârum*, cf. J. Lewy, "Old Assyrian *ḫusârum* ...", *op. cit.*, 155-160.

70 Cf. the remarks in n. 60, above. The listing in the text is merely suggestive.

71 Cf. OIP 27 (1935) 29, n. to line 11 of Text n. 7; also B. Landsberger, "Zu Driver's Übersetzungen ..., *op. cit.*, 277.

Others, though not necessarily Assyrian exports, include the Talhadian ephods,[72] the *biriqani*-garments[73] and *šitrum*,[74] among a host of others.

Our texts, finally, mention many small products and manufactured items like barley (*aršâtum*),[75] oil (*šamnum*),[76] straw (*tibnum*),[77] hides (*maškû*)[78] and honey (*dišpum*),[79] and the like, which appear to have been traded locally in Anatolia, and do not from part of the export stocks to Assyria.

The transport of all these items was accomplished through the use of donkey caravans, which frequently included waggons (*eriqqâtum*) for heavy hauling.[80] Our sources also report the use of boats by these caravans at river-crossings, and perhaps of different routes according to season.[81]

It cannot be stressed enough that the appearance of Old Assyrian traders in Anatolia wrought a remarkable economic effect upon the region. The presence of resident Assyrian trading emporia and of a highly-organized Assyrian long-distance caravan operation so stimulated the mining of precious metals, especially copper, and so created a sense of economic unity in an area that previously had been relatively quiescent, that we strongly feel the full-fledged emergence of the Old Hittite Kingdom, only a short period after the end of the Old Assyrian, is in great measure due to the groundwork prepared by the Semitic traders.

While our sources show that many of the transactions between traders belong to the sphere of private dealings, the Assyrian government retained supervisory powers over the traders' activities and over the operations of the caravans. Thus the hand of the Assyrian government is clearly to be seen in such areas as taxation of goods in transit, auditing of individual merchant's accounts, as well as in supplying rare metals to

[72] Cf. e.g., OIP 27 (1935) 69, etc., and J. Lewy, "On Some Institutions ...", *op. cit.*, 34, n. 117.

[73] Cf. E. Bilgiç, "Die einheimischen Appellativa der kappadokischen Texte und ihre Bedeutung für die anatolischen Sprachen", *DTCFY*, No. 96 (1954), 56.

[74] *Ibid.*, 82f., and J. Lewy, "On Some Institutions ...", *op. cit.*, 33, w.n. 116.

[75] For this and other kinds of grain mentioned in the Cappadocian texts, cf. H. Lewy, "On Some Old Assyrian Cereal Names", *JAOS*, 76 (1956), 201-204.

[76] Cf. e.g., *BIN*, IV 81:7-8; *KTHahn*, 6:22; *TTC*, 1:17-18.

[77] Cf. e.g., *EL*, II, p. 155, n. (b); *EL*, 236.

[78] Cf. OIP, 27 (1935), 57, n. to line 18 of Text no. 55.

[79] Cf. e.g., *EL*, 64; *KTBl*, 14:34.

[80] Cf. the citations in *CAD*, 4 (1958), 296.

[81] Cf. Lewy, "Studies in the Historic Geography ... II" *op. cit.*, 274-276, though we cannot accept the identifications there made. For the different routes, cf. Chapter One, n. 34, above.

prospective sellers, and in the guaranteeing of the weights and standards of shipments leaving Assyria.

In Assur, the "City-house" or *Bît Âlim*[ki] was the institution through which the government acted to oversee the commerce.[82] The head of the *Bît Âlim*[ki] appears to have been the eponym-official, or *lîmu*.[83] In the "City-house", which no doubt also served as the meeting-place for the city assembly or *âlum* (for which see below), commercial accounts for the traders were kept.[84] Beyond this, it appears to have had warehouse facilities, since it was capable of supplying the metals *amûtum* and *ḫusârum* for enterprising traders.[85] On shipments of *annâkum* leaving Assur for Anatolia, it frequently affixed its seal, probably as a guarantee of weight and quality.[86]

It is, however, through the operations of the *Kârum*-house, the *Bît Kârim*, which stood at the center of the commercial and administrative life of the *kârum*-settlements in Anatolia, that the dependence of the Assyrian trader on his government can most fully be seen.[87] Here it was that shipments of goods were received and the amounts and value credited to the individual accounts of the traders who had deposited them for

[82] For the *Bît*, *Âlim*[ki] cf. *TC*, 21, 19, 25; *TC*, 29, 44; *TC*, II, 43, 23; *BIN*, IV, 220, 20; *BIN*, VI, 56, x +1, 14; 197, x +11f; *ICK*, I, 17, 27. The *Bît Âlim* of Assur finds its parallel in the *Bît Kârim* of the Assyrian *kârum*-settlements abroad.

[83] J. Lewy, "Old Assyrian *husârum* and Sanchunyaton's Story About Chusor", *IEJ*, 5 (1955), 156, n. 4, points to the virtual identity of the *Bît Âlim* and the *Bît Lîmim*. Further references to the latter are: *TC*, II, 9, 4 and *BIN*, VI, 159, 6f. For the *lîmu*-official and problems connected thereto in the Old Assyrian period, cf. n. 125, below.

[84] In *TC*, II 43, 22-25 a question about a debt owed to the *Bît Âlim* is raised by a trader writing to his associates. For other sums paid to the *Bît Âlim* cf. *TC*, 21, 18-19, 24-25; *TC* 29:43-45.

According to such passages as *BIN*, VI 21, 6, *TC*, 21, 18-25 and *TC*, III 29, 4-9, the Bît Âlim received charges or payments called the *nisḫatum* and the *šaddu'âtum*; the former was a kind of duty on shipments of goods, usually taken in kind (cf. KTHahn 21 for its general meaning in Anatolia), while the latter represented another kind of fee, as yet not precisely known (cf. *CSQ*, II [1925], 53, n. 25). These payments, and others to be noted below, were also made to the *Bît Kârim*. The payment of these charges by the traders for the privilege of doing business testifies to the financial interest in, and the formal control over, Cappadocian trade by the Assyrian government.

Additionally, *TC*, III, 42, 13-16 points to the function of the *Bît Âlim* in supervising the establishment of business portions or shares (*qâtum*) for individual traders According to *EL*, 310, *inter alia*, these shares could be bought and sold.

[85] Cf. Lewy, "Old Assyrian *ḫusârum* ...", *op. cit.*, 156, n. 4. On *amûtum* and *ḫusârum* cf. n. 69 above.

[86] Cf. e.g., *BIN*, VI 192, 8-9; *CCT*, V, 25b, 1-5; 29a, 9; *ICK*, 124, 14-15; *TC*, III, 2, 3-8; 92, 7-8; 270, 4f.

[87] Cf. the list of *kârum*-settlements in Chapter One for the citations.

further distribution and delivery.[88] Here, also, various kinds of tolls and charges were levied upon goods in transit.[89]

In all, the functions of the *Bît Kârim* were those of a warehouse, accounting office, bank and commercial taxing agency.[90] It could borrow money from affluent members of the merchant community, and appears to have been given favorable interest rates when it did so.[91] The business of the *Bît Kârim* is somewhat obscure at the present time, but some evidence exists to show that it had thriving commercial relations with the local administrations of cities wherein it was situated.[92]

Having briefly sketched an account of Cappadocian trade, we may fill out the necessary background by presenting a view of the relationships of Assur to its dependencies in Anatolia, and of the Assyrian settlements to each other. It will be seen that very clear and formal ties existed between the government at Assur and the governments of the *kârû* and *wabârâtum*, and that we are justified in referring to an Assyrian "colonial

[88] Goods are frequently said to be "deposited" (*nadâ'um*), "registered" (*lapâtum*), 'given' (*nadânum*), 'paid' (*šaqâlum* or *napâlum*) to the *kârum*-house. The *Bît Kârim* was the central depository of commercial debt tablets. In addition, traders are said to "settle accounts" (*nikkassî šasâ'um*) there. Apparently the "caravaners' treasury" (*mîšittum ša ellâtim*) was located therein (*ICK I*, 157, 1-9), although *CCT*, 38b, 1-16, given in *EL*, II, p. 103 n. (a) (104), seems to suggest that the *Bît Kârim* and the *mîšittum ša ellâtim* were separate organizations. For *mîšittum*, cf. *EL*, I, p. 100, n. (b) (101).

[89] These were the *nisḫatum*, the *šaddu'âtum* (for both of which cf. n. 84, above); the *išratum* (10% tax: cf. Lewy, "On Some Institutions ...", *op. cit.*, 38; the *metum-ḫamšat* (5% tax: *ibid.*, w.n. 133); the *ṭa'tum*, var: *ṭa'tum ša ḫarrânim* ("road tax": *ibid.*, 68, w.n. 289-290, and *KTHahn*, p. 32, n. to line 23 of text 18). Other types of charges paid by the traders were the *tassi'âtum* ("transportation costs": Landsberger, "Zu Driver's Übersetzungen ...", *op. cit.*, 279), and the *waṣitum* ("export-toll", Lewy, "On Some Institutions ...", *op. cit.*, 32, n. 113. For other taxes such as the *gamrum*, the *ṣîttum šarri* and the *erbum* ("audience-gift to a prince"), cf. later notes.

[90] Cf. generally Landsberger, *AHK* (1925), *passim*.

[91] The classic example is *EL*, 225, 1-14, and 23-38a. In these two sections of a *Sammelurkunde*, which records four debts, *Kârum Kaniš*, as represented by various individuals, is the debtor to Enlil-bani, an affluent member of the Kaniš community of traders. From 11. 1-14 it appears that the *kârum* could purchase goods, since it was for this purpose that the loan was taken, but the circumstances surrounding the purchase are hidden from view. In 11. 23-38a, the *kârum* borrows for an unknown purpose. For both loans an interest penalty of 15% per mina per month is set should payment be overdue. Compare this to the 40% per m. per mo, which the *kârum* charges one of its debtors (11. 14-22), and 30% per m. per mo. imposed by one trader upon another (11. 38-47) — all recorded in the same tablet. Further, compare *TC*, III, 213, 32-44, where the *kârum* borrows refined silver measured by its own mina-standard (*MA.NA-im ša kârim*, 1. 33) at its apparently favorable and regular interest rate of 15% per m. per mo. For the mina of the *kârum*, cf. J. Lewy, "*Ḫatta, Ḫattu, Ḫatti, Ḫatttuša* and 'Old Assyrian' *Hattum*", *ArOr*, 18, 3/4 (1950), 418, n. 289.

[92] Cf. Chapter Six, below.

system" when we consider the distribution of power and pattern of allegiances characterizing the whole.[93]

A view of the administrative structure of the government at Assur during the Old Assyrian period shows that the chief official was the *rubâ'um*, or "prince",[94] Officially, the *rubâ'um* preferred to call himself *iššî'akkum*, or "earthly vicar" of the god Assur.[95] The strange phraseology which occasionally appears in his titularies — "Aššur is king, NN (the ruler) is the *iššî'akkum* of Aššur; or, "The City (*Assur*[ki]) is king, NN is the *iššî'akkum* ..." — may perhaps be explained to indicate that the titular deity of the Assyrians was always considered to be the real ruler, while the earthly prince was merely his representative.[96] Yet it seems clear that in at least one instance the Assyrian *rubâ'um* thought of himself as a *šarrum*, or "king", and several references in the Cappadocian

[93] We use this designation here merely to suggest the formal degree of power exerted by Assur over the settlements of its own traders abroad. We do not wish to imply that Assur ruled Anatolia.

[94] This usage is directly attested in *OIP*, 27, 58 where Puzur-Aššur (II) is called *mera' rubâ'im*, 'son of the Prince'. The *rubâ'um*, then, must allude to *Šarru-kîn II*, in whose reign the most prosperous period of Assyrian activity at Kültepe falls (Level II). It is a matter of dispute whether the isolated reference to *rubâ'um* in line 27 is to Šarru-kîn or not. Additional occurrences of "*rubâ'um*" as the designation of the rulers of Assur appear in numerous phrases which link the term with the "city-assembly" (*âlum*) of Assur (for which see n. 103, below).

[95] Four examples of a royal seal impression found on Cappadocian tablet envelope cases confirm this. Cf. K. Balkan, *TTKY* VII Seri — No. 28, 51-54. As for the identity of the person alluded to in these exemplars — usually assumed to be Šarru-kîn II —: Balkan reads *Il(um)-šar* (*ibid.*, 53, to which J. Lewy, "On Some Institutions ...", *op. cit.* 78, n. 332, offers rebuttal). Further examples of the *iššî'akkum* (*ENSI*) title used by members of the Old Assyrian Dynasty come from the so-called "Irišum-Inscription", published by K. Balkan and B. Landsberger, "Die Inschrift des Assyrischen Königs Irišum, gefunden in Kültepe, 1948", *Belleten*, 14 (1950), 219-268. Lines 1-4 of the longer of two variants there published (*kt a/k*, 315), show that Irišum's three predecessors on the throne of Assur also used the title.

[96] The royal seal impressions published by Balkan, and cited in n. 95 show that both the Old Assyrian ruler, Ikunum, and his son Sargon (or Il(um)-šar?), are styled *iššî'ak* (*ENSI*) *[d]Aššur*, "City-ruler of (the god) Aššur", while the rulers cited in the "Irišum-Inscription", cited in n. 95, are styled *iššî'ak* (*PA*: = abbrev. for *PA.TE.SI* = *ENSI*) *Assur*, "City ruler of Assur". In light of the interchange between *âlim*[ki] *[d]Aššur* in *EL*, 230, and *âlim*[ki] *Assur* in *EL*, 102, both used to designate the Assyrian capital during the period of Cappadocian trade, it is evident that the presence or absence of the divine determinative in the royal titulary carries with it no especially troublesome implications. In kt a/k 315, 36-6 (the longer variant of the "*Irišum*-Inscription"), the phrase "(The god) Aššur is king, Irišum is the city-ruler of Assur", *[d]Aššur šarrum* (*LUGAL*) *Irišum iššî'ak* (*PA*) *Ass*[*ur*], indicates a theoretical distinction between the god as the divine ruler, Irišum as the earthly ruler, of the capital. Cf. Balkan and Landsberger, *loc. cit.*, 230f. for further discussion. For the phrase *Assur*[ki] *LUGAL*, "The city of Assur is king", etc. cf. Balkan, *TTKY*, VII, Seri — No. 28, 54f.

texts show that the Assyrians, themselves, used this term for their ruler.[97]

The prince of Assur worked hand-in-hand with a city-council called the *âlum*.[98] This council was composed of the free citizens of the city, and naturally included the influential merchant entrepreneurs of the capital. Wherever we observe an official action of the Assyrian government, the prince and the assembly are the instrumental figures. This might suggest that there was an elementary division of power, but in no sense was the *âlum* a mere figurehead. We have already seen that its agency, the "City-House", or *Bît Âlim*^{ki}, was an effective controller of imports and exports, as well as supervisor of accounts and other business.[99]

The effective pleaders in the *âlum* were the elders, called *šîbûtum* in our sources. It seems probable that the *âlum* of Assur had its smaller, more specialized assembly, a *puḫrum*, but this cannot presently be documented.[100]

On the whole, our sources show that the *rubâ'um* and the *âlum* had two main types of functions, executive and judicial. Under the first category appear those having to do with the administration of the Anatolian settlements, while under the second, those which made of the ruler and his assembly a court of appeal in litigation involving the Assyrian traders.

The chief evidence showing the executive power of the Assyrian government over the Anatolian settlements is seen in the ability of the *âlum* to impose a tax levy on them for construction of a fortification in Assyria, the money to be collected by the chief of the settlements, *Kârum Kaniš*.[101] But beyond this, the Assyrian government also kept a check on

[97] Cf. kt a/k 315:20 (in Balkan and Landsberger, *loc. cit.*), where Irišum clearly thinks of himself as a *šarrum* (LUGAL), although the term is not an official stylization of the titularies. Cf. Balkan and Landsberger, *loc. cit.*, 252f. J. Lewy, "On Some Institutions ...", *op. cit.*, 14, n. 64, for citations in the Cappadocian tablets.

[98] The term means literally, "The City", and should not, of course, be confused with the use of *âlim*^{ki} "The City (as a physical place)", a synonym for Assur, the capital. On the writing of *âlum*^{ki} *Assur*, cf. Lewy, "On Some Institutions ...", *op. cit.*, 28, n. 111a.

[99] Cf. n. 82-86, above.

[100] The *šîbûtum*, "elders", are cited in *TC* 1 as having imposed a *gamrum* ("levy", "tax") on *Kârum Kaniš* for the building of a wall (*dûrum*^{ki}), perhaps at Assur. For discussion cf. Levy, "On Some Institutions ...", *op. cit.*, 65f. with n. 274f. Whether the *šîbûtum* formed only a special assembly within the larger gathering of the townsmen, or whether the term is exactly synonymous with *âlum* is not known. To our knowledge the term *puḫrum*, which can connote a smaller, specialized assembly within a larger one, does not appear in our sources except in reference to the assembling of the authorities in a *kârum*.

[101] Although *gamrum* bears the general meaning of "expenditure" for the caravans

the activities of its settlements by sending official envoys, called the *šiprû ša âlim*[ki], or "Envoys of the City", to consult with, and advise, the officials of *Kârum Kaniš*.[102]

In a broader sense, the sovereignty of Assur is to be seen in the realm of law. Assyrians in all the Anatolian colonies were bound by the judgements of the prince of Assur and the assembly. These judgements were issued on documents called *ṭuppum* (sg.), and altogether reflected the law of the City.[103]

The application of this law is most fully seen in disputes between traders which came to the attention of the *âlum*. Litigants in cases which originated in a *kârum* or *wabârtum* had the right of appealing to the City as a last resort if no accaptable decision in their behalf was made by settlement officials. In any of the Anatolian settlements a litigant was called upon to swear the oath of "the City and the Prince", *nîš âlim*[ki] *u rubâ'im*.[104] As visible symbols of Assur's authority stood the dagger (*paṭrum*), or the hook-shaped emblem (*šugari'aum*), before which decisions of *kârum* and *wabârtum* judges were given.[105] In circumstances

(cf. e.g., *KTS*, 14a:21), it also is used in the sense of "administrative impost", "assessment". The ten mina *gamrum* imposed by the city-assembly of Assur upon *Kârum Kaniš* in *TC*, I (cf. n. 100, above), was expected to be collected from all of the other *kârum*-establishments. There is no doubt, then, that Assur had the power of taxation over its settlements in Anatolia, nor that *Kârum Kaniš* was responsible for seeing that such taxes as were imposed by Assur were collected promptly. (In this connection, *TC* I reports that *Kârum Kaniš* would perhaps have been charged the expense of a messenger to it from Assur had its representatives not prevailed upon the *âlum*, 9f.).

102 It is quite clear from numerous references in our sources that the *šiprû ša âlim*[ki] were not only the highest-ranking official legates from Assur to the Anatolian settlements, but also that they seemed, at least part of the time, to have maintained residence at *Kârum Kaniš*, and have taken a direct hand in the administration of the various *kârû* and *wabârâtum*. For their role in diplomatic relations with local Anatolian princes as representatives of Assur, cf. Chapter Four, below.

103 The *âlum* was the author of the highest binding law over the Assyrian traders — the *dîn âlim*. This was issued under the further authority of the prince (*rubâ'um*). The documents commonly refer to the "tablet of the city (assembly) and the prince" (*ṭuppum* ša *âlim*[*ki*] *u rubâ'im*), or merely to the "tablet of the city (assembly)", (*ṭuppum ša âlim*[*ki*]). Much rarer is the usage "tablet of the prince", (*ṭuppum ša rubâ'im*), for whose identity with *ṭuppum ša âlim* Lewy has cited evidence in "On Some Institutions ...", *op. cit.*, 67, n. 282.

104 Together the *âlum* and *rubâ'um* constituted a final court of appeal in disputes between Assyrian traders, or between a trader and a government agency, such as the *kârum*. Dissatisfied litigants in a *kârum*- or *wabârtum*-court might request that their cases be brought "to the City and my Lord (i.e., the prince)", (*ana âlim*[ki] *u bêlia awâti bîla*), and ask to appear before the city-assembly (*âlam mahârum*); cf. also the phrase, "Let the city-assembly judge me" (*âlum lidîni*).

105 Cf. J. Lewy, "Studies in Old Assyrian Grammar and Lexicography", *Or ns*, 19 (1950), 15-31, and E. Bilgic, *DTCFY*, No. 96, *op. cit.*, 39-40, and 83-84.

where appeal was made, the litigant would journey to Assur to appear before the City-Assembly. It also appears in our sources that the City had the right to order the extradition of a trader to answer charges before it.

Both the *âlum* and the *rubâ'um* had judicial assistants at their disposal. The most important of these were the *waklum*, the *laputtâ'um* (NU.-BANDA), who was a high-ranking member of the *waklum*'s staff, and the *râbiṣum*.

There has been considerable controversy over the interpretation of the term *waklum* in the Old Assyrian period, as well as over who the officials bearing this title were likely to have been. While it now seems clear that the ruler of Assur, himself, used the title, it is possible that people not in the royal succession may have, also. It is safe to assume only that the *waklum* was a very high-ranking judicial officer.[106] Similarly, the *laputtâ'um*, about whom all too little is known, is safely seen also in a vaguely-defined judicial capacity.[107]

Perhaps the most ubiquitous official attached to the administration at Assur was the judicial commissioner, or attorney, called *râbiṣum*. Most likely a member of the palace staff, the *râbiṣum* of the City (*râbiṣ âlim*), could be sent by the Assembly to any of the Anatolian settlements to make on-the-spot investigations in complicated and long drawn-out legal cases. Usually he appeared in a colony-court at the request of one of the litigants, and bore an official commission inscribed on a tablet. Once in Anatolia, he required the cooperation of the officials at the settlement to which he had come, before he could proceed with his investigations. He had the power to interrogate litigants, to subpoena witnesses, and to demand the extradition of reluctant defendants to Assur.[108]

106 For a detailed discussion of *waklum* cf. Lewy, "On Some Institutions ...", *op. cit.*, 26, n. 109, and *idem*, "Some Aspects of Commercial Life ...", *op. cit.*, 100, w.n. 72.

107 Cf. Lewy, "On Some Institutions ...", *op. cit.*, 33, n. 115 for this official.

108 Line 55 of the synthesized versions of the "Irišum-Inscription" published by Balkan and Landsberger, *loc. cit.*, 228, directly attests the existence of a *râbiṣum* (MASKIM) of the palace (*ša E.GAL^{lim}*), while in the Cappadocian tablets such an official dispatched from Assur to Anatolia is called a *râbiṣum ša âlim^{ki}* (cf. e.g., *EL*, 335, 336, 338, 339, 340, and Balkan and Landsberger, *loc. cit.*, 266). The *râbiṣum* appears often in the service of a merchant in an action against a debtor, etc., but it is not clear whether he always receives his commission through an act of the *âlum* in Assur (or of the *kârum* in Anatolia; cf. below). Usually a petitioner has requested that a *râbiṣum* be sent out to the Anatolian settlements (cf. e.g., *EL*, 327, 6-7). The *râbiṣum* is often said to be in possession of a firm mandate from the city (*ṭuppum ša âlim^{ki} dannam râbiṣum ukal*, e.g., *TC*, II 21, 3-6).

It was required, however, that the *râbiṣum* function through the offices of the settlement to which he was sent, the terminology for this being "the *kârum* is the authority

If the Assyrian capital was the financial center and legal sovereign of the Assyrian settlements,[109] *Kârum Kaniš* was the colony which exercised direct and immediate practical supervision over them. In cooperation with the messengers of the City, the *šiprû ša âlim*^{ki}, it sent directives to "each and every *Kârum*",[110] and it received letters from individual settlements requesting aid and advice in particular matters.[111] Its own messengers, the *šiprû ša Kârim Kaniš*, traveled back and forth between Kaniš and individual colonies on official business.[112] Beyond this, as will be discussed in a later chapter, it was empowered to enter diplomatic negotiations with Anatolian princes.[113]

Kârum Kaniš had its own assembly, as, similarly, did the other *kârû* in the Assyrian system of colonies.[114] While the *kârum*-assembly appears to have included all the adult males of the community, it appears not to have sat in continual session.[115] Rather, the "great men" of the *kârum*

(or "the authorizing agency") of the *râbiṣum*" (*kârum emûq râbiṣim*, e.g., *EL*, 327, 10-12). It would appear that the *râbiṣum* simply initiated proceedings, or acted as a "friend of the court", for although litigants acknowledged the authority of this official, they still could request hearings by higher courts (e.g., *EL*, 338, *EL*, 326, *EL*, 298).

109 One further body which appears to have had judicial authority in Assur may be mentioned. This was the Temple of Aššur in Assur (*Bît Aššur*), whose judicial role is but hinted at. According to the "Irišum-Inscription", Balkan and Landsberger, *loc. cit.*, 232, the "monumental entrance hall" (*mušlâlu*) of the temple served as a place where litigation was heard. Apparently the *râbiṣum* of the palace functioned here, as well as a judge (*daianum*), for which see lines 54-59 of the synthesized version of the variant inscriptions.

110 Cf. e.g., *BIN*, VI, 120, referred to by Lewy, "On Some Institutions ...", 69, n. 295.

111 Cf. e.g., Lewy, *ibid.*, 20, n. 85.

112 Cf., *inter alia*, *TC*, 32, 1f.; 35, 12, 17; *CCT*, IV, 16c, 26; *BIN*, IV, 58, 11; *KTP*, 3, 9f.; 6, 8; 14, 1; *KTS*, 7b, 2f. The list is not intended to be exhaustive. That the *wabârtum*-type of settlement also had its own official *šiprû* is demonstrated by *KTP*, 10, 28, a letter in which the *wabârtum* of Šalatuwar (erroneously written *Ša-lá-ar-ma*, 1. 4), writes to the *Kârum Waḫšušana*, and mentions its messengers, 1. 28.

113 Cf. Chapter Four, below.

114 By reasonable conjecture, the *kârum*-assembly must have embraced the entire adult male population of the settlement. The terminology which designates the *kârum*-assembly acting as a whole (as opposed to committees appointed for special purposes) is *ṣaḫir rabi* (TUR.GAL), which appears in apposition to the name of the particular *kârum* in question in formal legal documents, etc. Limitations of time and space here prevent a long, technical discussion and the citation of the many pertinent references. The reader is directed to G. Evans, "Ancient Mesopotamian Assemblies", *JAOS*, 78 (1958), 7-9, especially 9 (top), Th. Jacobsen, "Primitive Democracy in Ancient Mesopotamia", *JNES*, 2 (1943), 161, w.n. 12, and *idem*, "Early Political Development in Mesopotamia", *ZA*, N.F. 18 (1957), 102, n. 14, with the further references there cited.

For a proposed restoration of *OIP*, 27, 40, in which Prof. Lewy reads: *wu-ba-ra-*[*tim*] *ṣaḫer rabi* to mean "all the *wubârâtum*", (11. 4-5a), cf. "On Some Institutions ...", *op. cit.*, 71, w.n. 304.

115 Cf. *EL*, 290, x + 3 – x + 9. Only the *âwîli rabi'ûtim*, 'the great men', from their

(or perhaps, "senior men"), the *âwîli rabi'ûtim*, seem to have managed its affairs. These men, meeting as a body, may have composed the *namedum*, or "executive committee".[116]

However, the assembly was to be convoked if the members of the *namedum* could not agree in a particular case, and then only by a call from the clerk, or scribe, of the assembly, upon specific instructions from the *namedum*.[117] One badly damaged document appears to show that in the *namedum*, itself, the scribe was responsible for polling the members, a task which he performed by dividing the group into three parts.[118]

The functions of the *kârum*-assembly were, like those of the *âlum*, executive and judicial. Its role in the commercial life of the Assyrian trader has already been alluded to in the previous chapter, where its agency, the *Bît Kârim*, was seen to provide warehouse and accounting facilities, as well as to collect tolls and charges from the caravans. Additionally, the *kârum*-assembly had the power to fix rates of interest on loans contracted by traders.[119] Of its other executive functions, its administrative relationships to the other settlements have already been mentioned, while its negotiations with the Anatolian princes will be examined in a later chapter.

The judicial functions of the *kârum* are clearly and fully to be seen in our sources. Frequently they consist in appointing referees or arbiters

---

namedum, '*multitude*' = '*collegium*?' may authorize the calling of the entire assembly, the *ṣahir rabi*. The terminology is difficult. Cf. the articles of Evans and Jacobsen, cited in n. 114, above; the comments in *EL*, I, p. 336f.; and n. 116f., below.

116 *EL*, 289, when considered with *EL*, 290, seems to shed some light on the procedure of the *namedum* of the *âwîli rabi'ûtim*. For one, the precise language of *EL*, 290, x +4—x +5, seems to suggest the equation *namedum* = *puḫrum*, hence that the *âwîli rabi'ûtim* comprised a smaller assembly within the larger one called the *ṣahir rabi*. On *puḫrum* and its implications, cf. especially the articles of Jacobsen cited in n. 114, above.

117 The assembling of the *ṣahir rabi* is achieved in strict parliamentary fashion. Only the clerk (*ṭupšarrum*, lit: "scribe", *EL*, 290, x +3—x +6a) might assemble it. So important is this provision that the clerk faced a stiff fine of 10 shekels of silver should he issue the call to assembly alone (*EL*, 290, x +11—x +14a). Lines x +7—x +10 of the same document have received significantly different translations and interpretations, for which cf. G. R. Driver and J. C. Miles, *The Assyrian Laws* (Oxford: 1935) 378; *EL*, I, 338f. w. notes to *EL*, 290 in *EL*, II, pp. 191-192 (followed by Jacobsen, "Primitive Democracy ...", *op. cit.*, 161, n. 13); and *CAD*, 4 (1958), 37, sub. *êdu*.

118 Cf. *EL*, 289:1-5. For a discussion of voting in the assemblies of ancient Mesopotamia, and perhaps at *Kârum Kaniš*, cf. Evans, "Ancient Mesopotamian Assemblies", *op. cit.*, 5-7f., and *idem*, "Ancient Mesopotamian Assemblies — an Addendum", *JAOS*, 78 (1958), 114-115.

119 The usual terminology for this is: "They shall add interest according to the decree of the *kârum*": *kîma awât kârim ṣibtam uṣab*, e.g., *TC*, III, 224, 9-10, etc.

to hear disputes and take testimony,[120] but a litigant might request that his case be taken before the entire *kârum*-assembly for trial, in which case the judgement of the *kârum*, or *dîn kârim*, was issued.[121] We have already pointed out that the litigant had the right of appeal to Assur.

Our sources show that the *kârum* also appointed committees of three, called *šalištum*,[122] and five, called *hamištum*,[123] to hear disputes. A

[120] Much of the legal activity reported in our sources took place without the special attention of duly-constituted courts. The main requirement of Cappadocian business transactions was that any type of goods or monies entrusted to traders, or borrowed for the purpose of doing business had to be fully acknowledged before witnesses, quite in accordance with the spirit of Article 7 of the Hammurabi Code of Old Babylonian times, which affirms that without valid proof of ownership or authority of possession, a man is to be considered a thief. (We do not here wish to imply that the same penalties applied to the Old Assyrian traders). While normally the terms of these contracts were fulfilled without incident, occasions frequently arose when the services of a *kârum*- or *wabârtum*- court were required.

Accordingly, one of the chief activities of the *kârum* as a judicial agency was to appoint referees or arbiters to conduct a hearing and take evidence. The plaintiff is said "to seize" one or more of the referees against a defendant. Sometimes the documents begin with the statement of the referees that they have "solved" the case (*awâtim nigmur*). The text *EL*, 332 suggests that these kinds of proceedings took place within the *kârum*-chambers, for the disputants are said to have caused the referees to enter the *kârum*, after which the arbiters report that they arbitrated the case. The closing formula on most of the tablets which record such transactions is "in this case *Kârum GN* (or *wabârtum ša GN*) gave us, and before the dagger (or *šugaria'um*-emblem, cf. n. 105) of Assur we gave our deposition" (*ana awâtim aniatim Kârum/wabârtum ša GN idîniatima mahar paṭrim/šugaria'im ša Aššur šibutini nidin*).

[121] Cf., e.g., *EL*, 338, 21-23. The decision of the entire *kârum* in a legal case would be formally expressed as "*Kârum, GN* has rendered a decision", *Kârum GN dînam idinma* (cf. *EL*, I, p. 306f.). That the *wabârtum*-type of establishment was also able to issue formal decisions of this type is attested, e.g., in *EL*, 282. Several documents appear to show that when a case was heard by the entire *kârum*, a person acting, perhaps, as president of the court, and called "solver of the case" (*pâšer awâtim*: cf. *EL*, 275) gave the decision. For the phrase "Ender of the case" (*gâmir awâtim*: cf. *EL*, 332 and 335).

The *dîn kârim* and the *dîn wabârtim* here noted were the highest local law of the Assyrian settlements, but both were subordinate to the *dîn âlim*^{ki}.

[122] The *šalištum* appears to conduct more or less formal questionings of a defendant by a plaintiff. By a comparison of *OIP*, 27, 57, 3 with *EL*, 319 and *EL*, 320, it would seem that the *kârum* first authorized such a hearing and then set up either a formal committee like the *šalištum*, or appointed specific referees.

[123] According to *EL*, 244 it is mentioned that the *ḫamištum* has made a decision according to (the rules of?) the Temple of Aššur in Assur (*ḫamištum šimtam warki Bît Aššur ina âlim*^{ki} *išimniatima*, II. 5-8). The *ḫamištum's* action seems to have been taken according to a judgement of the *kârum*. (For the *Bît Aššur* of Assur, cf. n. 109, above). In *EL*, 283, the *ḫamuštum* gives a judgement before *bêlum*, which may mean the god Bel, or simply the master of the slave who figures in the judgement. A third possibility is that the *rubâ'um* of Assur is meant. The *ḫamuštum* also figures in *EL*, 289 as an important member of the *kârum*, but here is probably meant the eponym-official. Cf. *EL*, I, p. 141, n. (b), 255, n. (a) and 302, n. (c), and *OIP*, 27 (1935), 59-61.

group of ten, called an *eširtum*, may also have been appointed by the *kârum*, but the presence of two of these groups in towns not boasting a *kârum* is mystifying.[124]

Little can be said about the officials of the *kârum* with certainty at the present time. Some evidence seems to show that the heads of the *kârum*-settlements were called *lîmu*, but whether these were eponym-officials in the sense that the *lîmu* of Assur were, is not known.[125] Beyond this, our sources speak of a *hamuštum*-eponym, an official who served for a five-day period of time, but his functions are not clearly seen in our sources.[126]

[124] The *eširtum*-committee, unlike the *šalištum* and the *ḫamištum*/*ḫamuštum*, seems to have had important functions not limited to intra-*kârum* affairs. There is some question whether it was not even a special kind of administrative organization of Assyrians which could reside permanently in places which did not boast the presence of a *kârum* or *wabârtum*. Four of the *eširtum* are known — at *Burudum* (*CCT*, III, 36a, 1), at *Ḫaḫḫum* (*CCT*, IV, 30a, 4), at *Niḫria* (*An Or*, VI, 15, 102) and at *Šimala* (*CCT*, *III*, 36a, 3). The characteristic phraseology referring to these organizations is *eširtum ša* ("Ten-man Committee of") *GN*, just as is the case with designations of the various *wabârtum*-settlements, though the special meaning of this distinction as opposed to the typical designation for *kârum*-establishments, *Kârum GN*, is not precisely known. The *eširtum*-organizations of *Ḫaḫḫum* and *Niḫria* exist in towns which also boast a *kârum*, but the other two do not. Of special importance is the action of the *eširtum* of *Ḫaḫḫum* in going with certain Assyrian traders to interview the ruler of *Ḫaḫḫum*, reported in *CCT*, IV 30a, and discussed in Chapter Four, below. Was the *eširtum* perhaps a traveling (circuit) court? The possibility of its being an *ad hoc* group also exists.

[125] At the present time approximately eighty holders of the *lîmu*-office are known from the Cappadocian tablets (cf. *PNC*, 96, and Balkan, *TTKY*, VII Seri — No. 28, 79-101). Of these three have been found in, or assigned to, Kültepe Ib, five come from Alishar Hüyük tablets, and four from Boğazköy. All the rest originate from Kültepe Level II tablets, and serve along with other chronological indications to confirm the long-held opinion that the Assyrian settlement of that period endured for at least three generations.

The institution of the *lîmu*, itself, was a distinguishing feature of Assyrian (as opposed to Babylonian) culture. Its origin is lost in the dimness of early Assyrian history. During the Old Assyrian period it may have been more meaningful than in later times, for under the Assyrian Empires of the First Millennium, it was essentially honorary, while the equation of *Bît Âlim* with *Bît Lîmim* indicates its vitality during the former period.

At *Kaniš* the *lîmu*-official appears to have been important, for according to *EL*, 298, one (or three? cf. 1. 1 and 1. 8f.) authorizes the sending of a sealed tablet-container in which were deposited four messages written by the *kârum*, four tablets of a trader sealed with the *kârum*'s seal, and two other debt tablets. The destination of the container is the city-assembly of Assur and the prince (*mahar âlim*^{ki} *u bêlini išakunu*, 11. 35-36.

Whether the *lîmu*-official was considered to be the chief political officer of *Kârum Kaniš* is doubtful, as is, in our view, the postulation of an official called the *wêdum* as the *kârum*-chief (*CAD*, 4 [1958], 37, *sub. êdu*). It is most pertinent to note that in all the correspondence of an official nature sent to Kaniš, it is the *kârum* (including often the *šiprû ša âlim*^{ki}) which is addressed, and not any particular individual.

[126] Cf. n. 123, above. The existence of the *ḫamuštum*-eponym official is a unique

Further, there exist several officials whose functions are too infrequently seen for close definition. One of these, the "Treasurer" (?), "Treasury Official" (?) (*awîlum ša nikkassî*) was certainly attached to the *kârum*-administration, though his precise activities are unknown.[127] Another, the clerk (or scribe) of the *kârum* (*ṭupšarrum*) is cited in n. 117, above. There are also infrequent references to judges (*daianû*).[128]

If Assur stationed its envoys, the *šiprû ša âlim*^{ki}, in *Kârum Kaniš*, it appears also that the latter had its special representative in the capital whose function may have been to represent it before the city-assembly. Such an envoy was the *nibûm*,[129] though there are instances in which the *waklum*-official without the intercession of the *nibûm*, wrote directly to *Kârum Kanis*.[130]

Lastly, our sources acquaint us with the *g/kaššum*-official,[131] as with two enigmatic officers, the *šâqil-ṭatim* and the *bîruttum*,[132] both of whom were located at Šalatuwar, but is is entirely possible that these three types of officials were not exclusively Assyrian.

feature of the Cappadocian tablets. Like the *lîmu*-eponyms, who gave their name to their year of service, the *hamuštum*-eponyms seem to have served for five-day periods, and like the former, they could serve in pairs. Cf. Balkan, *TTKY*, VII Seri — No. 28, 79f. To all indications the *ḫamuštum*-eponym was essentially a judicial officer.

127 Cf. *EL*, 290, x +8, x +16, with the translation there offered, as well as *CAD*, 4 (1958), 37, *sub. êdu*.

128 Cf. e.g., *TC*, III, 50, 36, etc.

129 Cf. *TC* 1, and Landsberger, *AHK* (1925), 10, Gelb, *OIP*, 27 (1935), 39, note to line x +1 of Text no. 23.

130 Cf. *ICK*, 182. For other letters of the *waklum*-official at Assur to individuals at *Kaniš*, cf. Lewy, "Some Aspects of Commercial Life ...", *op. cit.*, 100f.

131 The q/*kaššum*-official has been interpreted in *EL*, II, p. 73, w.n. 1, as "Altester", "Ortsaltester", "Altester Sohn", according to the several contexts in which it appears. These interpretations follow, on the one hand, from the fact that the q/*kaššum*- official appears frequently in cities passed through by Assyrian caravans as a kind of local "mayor" to whom payments are made (e.g., *TC*, III, 165, 6, 16f., and *TC*, III, 166, 14-16), and on the other from the use of *kaššum* in the following formula: *ḫamuštum ša* q/*kaššim ša qâti PN*, where the sense requires something like a translation of "altester Sohn" (?). There is great difficulty in seeing the *kaššum* as an exclusively Assyrian official, for he is often coupled with Anatolian administrations, as in *TC*, III, 165 and 166, cited above. K. Balkan and B. Landsberger, "Die Inschrift des assyrischen Königs Irišum ...", *op. cit.*, 233, w.n. 25, see *kaššum* as the "courtyard of a temple", which indicates an association of the meanings offered by Lewy with the idea of a place wherein an administrative organization, or representative of such, normally functioned.

132 For references and discussion cf. Lewy, "On Some Institutions ...", *op. cit.*, 67-68, w.n. 283-290, and Bilgiç, *DTCFY*, No. 96 (1954) 76-77, w.n. 188.

PART TWO

POLITICAL RELATIONSHIPS BETWEEN THE ASSYRIAN SETTLEMENTS AND THE ANATOLIAN PRINCES

III

THE ANATOLIAN RULERS AND THEIR PRINCIPALITIES

The first part of this study offered a rapid survey of the Old Assyrian settlements in order to provide the background necessary for an examination of their political character. We saw that the network of these settlements was tightly integrated, the whole being legally dependent upon the governing institutions of Assur. We spoke of this network as an "Assyrian system", by which we mean only, for the moment, that it was unified and self-sufficient enough to merit its being regarded as a single entity.

So described, the "Assyrian system" forms one of two major contributors to the political environment of central Anatolia during the Old Assyrian Period. The other is what may loosely be called the "system of local town governments", each headed by an indigenous prince. There was no single administration over all these local governments; rather, all represent small, city-state types of principalities, each more or less independent of the others. Naturally some principalities were more important and powerful than others, and as such were able to control large regional territories [*mâtum*], but until Anitta, King of *Kuššara* and *Neša*, there was no single suzerain.[1]

From the Cappadocian tablets we learn of about thirty rulers of Anatolian towns or regions, to whom the Assyrians referred by several different titles. The usual title is *rubâ'um*, "prince",[2] but frequently the gentilic is employed for the same purpose.[3] The impersonal designation, *bêl âlim*, "Lord of the City", also appears.[4] In several instances rulers

[1] The Assyrians sometimes referred to Anatolian Princes as "uncultivated", *nuâ'um* cf. I. J. Gelb, *OIP*, 27 (1935) 46; B. Landsberger, given in *EL*, I, p. 251, n. (b); *idem*, "Kommt *Ḫattum* 'Hettiterland' und *Ḫatti'um* 'Hettiter' in den Kültepe-Tafeln vor?" *ArOr*, 18, 1/2 (1950) 346, n. 79, with the further references there given.

[2] Cf. e.g., *KTP*, 4:12-13, 26; kt f/k 183:7 (in K. Balkan, *TTKY*, VII Seri — No. 28 [1955] 73f.); *TC*, III, 85:6-7; *OIP*, 27, 1:1, Rev. x +1 — x +3, etc.

[3] Cf. e.g., *CCT*, II, 48:32; *EL* 150:1-2; *TC*, III, 166:10, etc.

[4] Cf. *TC*, III, 165:15 (12-22).

are called *šarrum*, "king", but this title appears simply to be a synonym of *rubâ'um* during the period of Level II at *Kârum Kaniš*, and even to denote a vassal of a *rubâ'um* during the period of Ib.[5] Finally the title *rubâ'um rabî'um*, or "great prince", is attested of the ruler of *Burušḫattum*, as later it is of Anitta the conqueror. It must be assumed that the sovereigns who bore this title merited it because they controlled far more significant systems of vassals, or far more territory, than the ordinary *rubâ'um*.[6]

While most of the rulers who appear in the sources are contemporary with the period of Level II, a number post-date this period. It is at present impossible to determine an accurate chronology for the pre-Hittite Anatolian kings. At best they can be assigned to either the first [Level II] or the second [Level Ib] phase of Assyrian trading activity in Anatolia. In a few instances information has been recovered which allows contemporary rulers to be noted, or successors, as when a father and his son are mentioned. It remains a desideratum of the future to attempt to assign the reigns of these kings to corresponding *lîmu*-dates from the Assyrian tablets, and ultimately, if possible, to fix the *lîmû* within the reigns of the Old Assyrian kings known to be contemporary with the Assyrian trading settlements.[7]

A survey of the towns in which a prince, a palace administration, or indigenous officials are directly attested shows that many were places in which the Assyrians maintained a *kârum* or a *wabârtum*, while the rest were towns within which the traders normally did business, but apparently maintained no permanent residence quarters or business organization. In order to allow the reader a comprehensive view of the references, as well as provide a convenient guide to the source material, we present a chart of the Anatolian towns and the political organizations or institutions associated with them. The figures in the chart refer not to footnote-numbers but to the entries under the name of each town giving textual references. These entries follow immediately after the presentation of the chart, below. The following abbreviations are used in the column headed "Regional Location":

[5] Cf. *CCT*, IV, 30a:13. For the Old Assyrian equation *rubâ'um* = *šarrum*, cf. Chapter Two, n. 97, above, also *TTKY*, VII-31a, 25f.

[6] A *rubâ'um rabî'um* is attested at *Burušḫattum* during the most flourishing period of Cappadocian trade (cf. *TTC*, 27: 6-7). Another bearer of this title is Anitta, the well-known conqueror of central Anatolia who appears to have been contemporary either with the last days of Level II, or of Ib at Kültepe (cf. *OIP*, 27, 49A:24-25; B:27-28).

[7] Cf. *Appendix B.*

CA: Central Anatolia [when not otherwise more closely definable]
E: Eastern Anatolia
HB: Halys River Basin
K: Plain of Kayseri
NE: North East Anatolia
NSy: North Syria
SC: South Central Anatolia
SE: South East Anatolia
SW: South West Anatolia
?: Location unknown

Kingdom	Regional Location	*Rubâ'um*	*Rubâtum*	*Šarrum*	*Rubâ'um Rabî'um*	*Êkallum*	Indigenous Officials	Assyrian *Kârum*-Site	Assyrian *Wabârtum*-Site	Assyrian *Ešîrtum*-Site
Amkuwa	HB[1]	x[2]	x[3]		x[4]	x[5]	x[6]		x[7]	
Badna	NSy[8]						x[8a]		x[9]	
Mât Burušḫattum	SW[10]	x[11]			x[12]	x[13]		x[14]		
Dadania	HB[15]	x[16]								
Durḫumit	HB[17]							x[18]		
Ḫaḫḫum	E[19]	x[20]		x[21]		x[22]		x[23]		x[24]
Ḫanakna (k)	?								x[25]	
Ḫarkiuna	HB[26]									
Hattuš (a)	HB[27]			x[28]				x[29]		
Ḫudurut	?						x[29a]			
Ḫurama	SE[30]	x[31]				x[32]		x[33]		
Mât Kaniš	K[34]	x[35]	x[36]			x[37]	x[38]	x[39]		
Kapitra	?	x[40]								
Karaḫna	HB[41]								x[42]	
Kuššara	HB[43]	x[44]		x[45]	x[46]	x[47]	x[48]		x[49]	
Luḫuzadia	SE[50]	x[51]	x[52]			x[53]				
Mama	SE[54]	x[55]							x[56]	
Naduḫtum	?	x[57]					x[58]			
Nenašša	SW[59]	x[60]				x[61]	x[61a]			
Neša	K[62]	x[63]		x[64]	x[65]	x[66]				
Niḫria	NSy[67]							x[68]		x[69]
Paḫatima	CA[70]						x[71]			
Puruttum	NSy[72]						x[73]			x[74]
Qatara	NSy[75]						x[76]			
Šalaḫšua	SE[77]					x[78]	x[79]			
Šalatuar	SC[80]	x[81]							x[82]	
Šamuḫa	NE[83]					x[84]			x[85]	
Sibuḫa	SE[86]	x[87]		x[88]						
Šiḫwa	?	x[89]								
Šimala	NSy[90]									x[91]
Širmuin	?	x[92]								
Širun	NSy[93]						x[94]			
Taišama	K[95]	x[96]		x[97]						
Tamnia	HB[98]	x[99]						x[100]		
Tarakum	NSy[101]	x[102]					x[102a]			
Tawinia	HB[103]							x[104]		

Kingdom	Regional Location	*Rubâ'um*	*Rubâtum*	*Šarrum*	*Rubâ'um Rabî'um*	*Êkallum*	Indigenous Officials	Assyrian *Kârum*-Site	Assyrian *Wabârtum*-Site	Assyrian *Ešîrtum*-Site
Tegarama	E[104a]					x[105]				
Tilimria	?	x[106]								
Timilkia	E[106a]	x[106b]	x[106c]			x[106d]	x[106e]			
Tuḫpia	NE[107]	x[108]							x[109]	
Ulama	SW[110]	x[111]					x[112]		x[113]	
Uršu	SE[114]							x[115]		
Ušša	SC[116]						x[117]			
Wašḫania	SC[118]	x[119]				x[120]	x[121]		x[122]	
Mat Waḫšušana	SC[123]	x[124]	x[125]			x[126]	x[126a]	x[127]		
Zalpa	HB[128]	x[129]		x[130]		x[131]	x[132]	x[133]	x[134]	

Fig. 1. Chart showing political references associated with Anatolian towns (1).

AMKUWA (written also *AKKUWA* and *a-lim*[ki] *A-ku-wa* [cf. Bilgiç, *AfO*, 15 (1945-51), 32-37 here and below for citations of place-names in the Old Assyrian texts].

1. *Amkuwa* has been equated with Alishar Hüyük [e.g. Gelb, *OIP*, 27 (1935), 9-10] or with a town in its near vicinity [e.g. Garstang and Gurney, *Geog. of the Hitt. Empire*, 4-5 (hereafter cited in this section as *GHE*)]. See also *AfO*, 15 (1945-51), 30-31 and Lewy, *HUCA*, 27 (1956), 60-61.

2. *rubâ'um* (unnamed): *OIP*, 27, 17:4, 6 [Period Ib, pre-Anitta] Ḫarbatiwa (untitled); *OIP*, 27, 53:14, with note [Period Ib, pre-Anitta].
Anitta, *rubâ'e*, *OIP*, 27, 1:1 and rev. x + 2. [Period Ib].

3. *rubâtum* (princess); *OIP*, 27, 5:12 [Period Ib, pre-Anitta].

4. Anitta, *rubâ'um rabî'um* (Great Prince): *OIP*, 27, 49A:24-25; B:27-28 [Period Ib].

5. *êkallum* (palace): as residence of the *rubâtum* [No. 3, above], *OIP*, 27, 5:17-21 (without association, in *Amkuwa*?): *OIP*, 27, 25: rev. 13 with ll. 19-20.

6. *Officials:*

a. *rabi simmiltim* (Chief of the Citadel), in service of the *rubâtum* [No. 3, above]: *OIP*, 27, 5:12.
r.s. (without association): *OIP*, 27, 46A:y + 4.
r.s. in service of Anitta, *rubâ'um rabî'um* [No. 4, above]: Peruwa, *OIP*, 27, 49A:25; B: 27-28.

b. *Pu/burullum rabûm* (Mayor? Police Chief?), in service of Anitta *rubâ'um rabî'um*: Ḫabuala, *OIP*, 27, 49A:9-10, 15-16; B:11-12, 15-16.
c. *Nibûm* ("The Appointed One?") (without association): *OIP*, 27, 23:x+1.
d. *GA-šu-um* (Magistrate? Elder?) (without association): *OIP*, 27, 23:x+2.

7. Assyrian *wabârtum*: perhaps *OIP*, 27, 17:x+6. [Cf. J. Lewy, *HUCA*, 27 (1956), 61, w.n. 257].

BADNA

8. Located by A. Goetze [*JCS*, 7 (1953), 66] at present-day Sürüc, between Urfa and Birecik.

8a. *Officials:*
a. *Pu/burullum*-officials (written *Ba-ru-li*): *KTHahn*, 3: 25f. [Cf. J. Lewy, *HUCA*, 27 (1956), 61, n. 257].

9. Assyrian *wabârtum: KTHahn*, 3:14, with II. 23f.

BURUŠḪATTUM (Attested as *Mât Burušḫattum: KTHahn*, 1:3).

10. To be located in the region of the Plain of Konya [cf. Ch. I, nn. 37f.].

11. *AMÊL* *[alu]Pu-ru-uš-ḫa-an-da:* "the Man of Burušḫanda" [= synonym for "ruler of *GN*"]: *Anitta Inscription*, ll. 74, 77 [Period Ib].

12. *rubâ'um rabî'um* (unnamed): *TTC*, 27:6-7.

13. *êkallum: CCT*, II, 8-10:64-65; *ibid.*, 13:6-7; *ICK*, I, 190: 8-9; *ICK*, II, 127:x+24; *VAT*, 9276: rev. 8-11 [cf. J. Lewy, *HUCA*, 27 (1956) 38, n. 132]. Possibly *CCT*, III, 4:32-34, and *ICK*, I, 189:34-35, also refer to this palace. Further, cf. Lewy, *AHDO*, II, 129, n. 1 and *ArOr*, 18 3/4 (1950), 432, n. 378.

14. Assyrian *kârum:* cf. citations in Ch. I, above.

DADANIA

15. Located by A. Goetze [*JCS*, 7 (1963), 68] as a possible Euphrates river-crossing site near Birecik.

16. Cited in gentilic form: *Da-da-na-i-um*, *TC*, III, 166:10.

DURḪUMIT

17. To be located in the north-eastern part of the Halys Basin. See Ch. I, n. 48, above, and further, *GHE* (1959), Index, with Map 2, p. 15.

18. Assyrian *kârum:* cf. citations in Ch. I, above. For reference to this *kârum* in Period Ib cf. kt f/k 183:5-6 [*TTKY*, VII, Seri — No. 28, p. 73f.].

ḪAḪḪUM

19. To be located in the area of Harput [cf. Ch. I, n. 53, above].

20. *rubâ'um:* unpublished Ankara text b/k 612:18, communicated by Balkan, *TTKY*, VII, Seri — No. 31a, p. 28.

21. *šarrum* (king): *CCT*, IV 30a:13 [perhaps, but not necessarily the same ruler cited in No. 20, above].
In *CCT*, IV, 30a:5, a reference is made to the *rubâ'û*, or "princes". Are these the sons of the *šarrum*?

22. *êkallum: CCT*, IV, 30a:5; 18a:26-27; possibly also 42a:14.

23. Assyrian *kârum:* cf. citations in Ch. I, above.

24. Assyrian *eširtum* ("Ten-man Committee/Board): *CCT*, IV, 30a:4.

ḪANAKNAK Location unknown.

25. Assyrian *wabârtum:* cf. citations in Ch. I, above.

ḪARKIUNA

26. In the *Anitta Inscription* [1l. 17, 23] this town appears as an enemy of Anitta, and may perhaps be counted as part of the larger coalition of Halys Basin kingdoms led by the King of *Ḫatti* [Period Ib].

ḪATTUŠ(A)

27. Positively identified with present-day Boğazköy in the Halys Basin.

28. *šarrum:* ^{m}*Bi-i-u-uš-ti-iš ŠÀ*[*R* ^{al}]^{u}*Ḫa-at-ti*, "Pijuštiš, king of the city of *Ḫatti*", *Anitta Inscription*, l. 36; cf. also, l. 14, 44, 50 [Period Ib].

29. Assyrian *kârum:* cf. I. J. Gelb in R. S. Hardy, *AJSL*, 58 (1941), 179, n. 6, J. Lewy, *ArOr*, 18, 3/4 (1950), 371ff., B. Landsberger, *ArOr*, 18, 3/4 (1950), 321-329, and Lewy, *ibid.*, 435-440.

ḪUDURUT Location unknown.

29a. *Officials:*

a. *rabi sikkitim: BIN*, IV, 45:9. Perhaps normal Old Assyrian writing for *rabi sikkatim*, "general?" but Garelli, *Les Assyriens en Cappadoce*, p. 217 w n. 4, sees this official as being in charge of distribution of metals.

ḪURAMA

30. To be located in the general area of the approaches to the Anti-Taurus west of the Euphrates and somewhat to the east and north of *Uršu* [cf. Ch. I, nn. 61 and 54.]

31. Reference to the ruler of this town appears in the gentilic: [*Ḫu-ra*]-*ma-im*, *CCT*, II 48:32. [Cf. J. Lewy, *ArOr* 18, 3/4 (1950), 422f., esp. 430 w n. 353, for an extended treatment of the context.]
Inferentially *ATHE*, 62:33-35 [33] contains a reference to the ruler of *Ḫurama*, or at least his administration.

32. *êkallum: TC*, II, 27:11; *VAT*, 13535 [*EL*, 252]:6.

33. Assyrian *kârum:* Cf. citations in Ch. I, above.

KANIŠ (Attested as *Mât Kaniš*: *TC*, 18:42).

34. Positively identified with present-day Kültepe, about 20 km. northeast of Kayseri.

35. *rubâ'um: ru-ba-um* [*Kà*]-*ni-ší-im*, "the Kanishean Prince", *KTP*, 4:12-13, also 1.26.
Kà-ni-ší-im: ATHE, 66:10 [9-13].
Perhaps *TC*, 130:x+5 refers to the Prince of *Kaniš* [cf. J. Lewy, *ArOr*, 18, 3/4 (1950), 399, n. 163].
Warpa/ba, *ru-ba-im: TC*, 122 [*EL*, 3]:x+9—x+10; *KTP*, 43 [*EL*, 189]:19-20. [For arguments supporting the idea that Warpa/ba was a prince of *Kaniš* see the Excursus to Ch. III].
Waršama, *ru-ba-im Kà-ni-ší-im:* g/t 35:2-3 [Period Ib].
Inar [father of Waršama]: g/t 35:29-30 [Period Ib].
Labarša, who is said to have "seized the kingdom" in *ICK*, I, 178: x+2—x+4, may be a Prince of *Kaniš*.
Assuming that *Kaniš*=*Neša* [cf. *Appendix C*], we may also add:
Pitḫana, King of *Kuššara: Anitta Inscription*, 4-9, with the further citation of his name as *rubâ'um* in *TC*, III, 214A:19-20, though without connection to *Kaniš* attested in the text [Period Ib].
Anitta, son of Pitḫana, *Anitta Inscription*, 10ff., with the further citation of his name as *rubâ'e* in *OIP*, 27, 1:1 and rev. x+2, though without connection to *Kaniš* attested in the text [Period Ib].

36. *rubâtum: ICK*, I, 13:6-7, to be read with II. 10-11; perhaps also *ATHE*, 62:35 [32-35 in the context of the entire letter].

37. *êkallum: ICK*, I, 189:20-rev. 23; *Jena*, 287 [*EL*, 247]:4-6[5] = *Jena*, 334+331 [*EL*, 248]:4-7 [6]; *TC*, III, 213:11-27.

38. *Officials:*

a. *rabi simmiltim:* Ḫalkiašu, in service of Warpa/ba, *rubâ'um: TC*, 122 [*EL*, 3]:x+10−x+11; *idem*, *KTP*, 43 [*EL*, 189]:21-22.

Turupani (without association): *TTKY*, VII, Seri — No. 31a, p. 4 [= g/t 36:30-31] [Period Ib].

Anitta, in service of Pitḫana (see above), *TC*, III, 214A:21-22 [Period Ib].

Perhaps the Peruwa, Anitta's *rabi simmiltim* of *OIP*, 27, 49A:25; B:27-28, should also be tentatively counted here [Period Ib].

b. *rabi huršâtim* (Chief of the Storehouse): Ḫalkiašu, g/t 36 and 42, communicated by Balkan, *TTKY*, VII, Seri — No. 31a, p. 4 [Period Ib].

The reader is referred to the *Excursus* of Ch. III for a discussion of possible officials during the Period of Level II at *Kârum Kaniš*.

39. Assyrian *kârum:* Cf. citations in Ch. I, above.

KAPITRA Location unknown.

40. *rubâ'um:* (in gentilic): *Ga-bi-id-ra-i-um*, *BIN*, VI, 193:19.

KARAḪNA

41. Located by Garstang and Gurney, *GHE*, northeast of present-day Boğazköy and east of Çorum in the Upper Halys Basin [p. 25].

42. Assyrian *wabârtum:* Cf. citation in Ch. I, above.

KUŠŠARA

43. Although most scholars place *Kuššara* in the Halys Basin area, no uniformity of opinion exists about its location. Garstang and Gurney, *GHE*, locate it at Alishar Hüyük [p. 63]. Bilgiç, *AfO*, 15 (1945-51), p. 30 puts it in the close vicinity of *Ḫattušaš* [Boğazköy], while Balkan, *TTKY*, VII, Seri — No. 31a, p. 58, prefers a location closer to *Kaniš* than to *Ḫattuš*. See further J. Lewy, *HUCA*, 33 (1962), 45-57.

44. [*rubâ'um*]: hypothetical restoration by J. Lewy, *HUCA*, 27 (1956), 59, n. 251 [60].

45. *šarrum:* Pitḫana, *Anitta Inscription*, 1, 5; by implication, Anitta, son of Pitḫana, *Anitta Inscription*, 1 with ll. 10ff. [Period Ib].

46. *rubâ'um rabî'um:* By implication Anitta, now king of *Neša* and (presumably) *Kuššara*, *Anitta Inscription*, l. 41 [Period Ib].

47. *êkallum: ICK*, I, 1:48, 52, 56.

48. *Officials:*
rabi simmiltim: By implication Anitta, in service of his father Pitḫana, cf. *Anitta Inscription*, l. 1 and *TC*, III 214A:21-22. Similarly, Peruwa in service of Anitta, *OIP*, 27, 49A:25; B:27-28 [Period Ib].

49. Assyrian *wabârtum:* Cf. Ch. 5, n. 95, below.

LUḪUZADIA

50. To be located in the region in or around Eastern Cilicia. *Luḫuzadia* is associated with *Ḫurama* and *Šalaḫšua*, all generally to be sought in the south-eastern border lands of the Central Anatolian Plateau [cf. *GHE*, 52-53, and Ch. I, n. 61, above].

51. *rubâ'um: CCT*, II, 48:36.

52. *rubâtum: CCT*, IV, 19c:20 [17-20].
By implication *ATHE*, 62:32-35 contain a reference to the ruler of *Luḫuzadia* (prince or princess?), or to the administration.

53. *êkallum: CCT*, II, 43:24-27 [cf. J. Lewy, *ArOr*, 18, 3/4 (1950), 432, n. 375]; *CCT*, IV, 19c:18 [17-20]. There is a possibility that the palace listed as being at *Ḫurama* [*VAT*, 13535 [*EL*, 252]: 6, cf. above], may belong to *Luḫuzadia*.

MAMA

54. To be located on the Göksun-Maraş or the Elbistan-Maraş routes, between *Kaniš* and *Uršu* [cf. Bilgiç, *AfO*, 15 (1945-51), 25, and Balkan, *TTKY*, VII, Seri — No. 31a, 31-33.

55. *rubâ'um: ru-ba-um Ma-ma-i-u-um*, "the Mamean Prince", = Anum-Ḫirbi, g/t 35:1-2 [Period Ib].

56. *ru-ba-*im Ma-ma-i-im*, kt g/k 51:20-21 [Cf. *TTKY*, VII Seri — No. 31a, p. 32.

56. Assyrian *wabârtum:* Cf. the citations in Ch. I, above.

NADUḪTUM Location unknown.

57. *rubâ'um: TC*, III, 75:6, 24.

58. *Officials:*
a. *Sinaḫilum* (Second-in-command): *TC*, III, 75:7 [cf. Friedrich, *Hethitisches Wörterbuch* (Heidelberg, 1952), 324b (*sub*: "Churritische Wörter")].

NENAŠŠA

59. To be located at, or perhaps near, Aksaray, in the approach area to the Plain of Konya [cf. Ch. I, n. 40, above].

60. *rubâ'um: ru-ba-im Ni-na-ša-i-im*, "the Ninaššian Prince", *TC*, 72:20. Perhaps also *TC*, III 10:7 [*Ni-na-ša-i-um*].
In *TC*, III, 165:15 [12-22], the ruler of *Nenašša* is called *bêl âlim*[ki], "Lord of the City".

61. *êkallum: TC*, III, 165:14-15 [12-22].

61a. *Officials:*
 a. *GA-šu-um: TC*, III, 165:11-18 [16].
 b. *bêl ha-*[*tí*?]*-tim* (reading unclear): *TC*, III, 165:17
 c. x-x-*ru-um*: *TC*, III, 165:17
 d. *râbiṣum* [here probably an indigenous official]: ("Commissioner"): *TC*, III, 165:18.

NEŠA

62. On one set of assumptions *Neša* = *Kaniš* [cf. *Appendix C*, below]. Opposed to this hypothesis is the opinion of H. Lewy that *Neša* is to be located either at Akçadag, or at Darende, or Gürün, all to be located east-south-east of *Kaniš* [cf. *JCS*, 17 (1963), 104].

63. *rubâ'um:* on the assumption that *Kaniš* = *Neša*, see entries under *Kaniš*.

64. *šarrum: Anitta Inscription*, 4, 7
Pitḫana, *idem*, 5-9. [through conquest] [Period Ib]
Anitta, *idem*, 10ff. [through succession] [Period Ib]

65. *rubâ'um rabî'um:* Anitta, *Anitta Inscription*, l. 41 [Period Ib].

66. *êkallum:* Winkenbach 7:3 [cf. H. Lewy, *JCS*, 17 (1963), 103].

NIḪRIA

67. To be located approximately in the triangle of land formed by connecting lines between Mardin, Siverek and Diyarbekir at the North Syrian approaches to the Anti-Taurus. Cf. Ch. I, n. 64, above.

68. Assyrian *kârum:* Cf. citations in Ch. I, above.

69. Assyrian *ešírtum: EL*, 1, p. 255, n. a.

PAḪATIMA

70. To be located generally in Central Anatolia, but no further precision

is possible [cf. *GHE*, p. 118, ll. 32-33, where the *milieu* is definitely Central].

71. *Officials:*
 a. *Pu/burullum: CCT*, 29:8, 14.

PU/PARUTTUM

72. Generally to be located in the region of Gaziantep [Goetze, *JCS*, 7 (1953), 68].

73. *Officials:*
 a. The payment of *sika šarri/u* [=*ZI.GA šarri/u*? or *ṣît šarri/u*?] "(a kind of) tax-payment to the king?", suggests the possible presence of indigenous officials, even a *šarrum*, in *Pu/Paruttum*. [Cf. *EL*, I, p. 288, n. a and e; *EL*, II, p. 187 and n. 1; Bilgiç, *Appellativa*, *DTCFY*, 96 (1954), 70].

74. Assyrian *eširtum: CCT*, III, 36a:1.

QATARA

75. Located by Goetze between Assur and the Ḫabur River in Syria [*JCS*, 7 (1953), p. 66].

76. *Officials:*
 a. *GA-šu-um: PSBA*, VI, 1883-84, 18f. [Cf. Or ns 21 (1952), p. 271, n. 4.]

ŠALAḪŠUA

77. To be located in or around the region of Eastern Cilicia. *Šalaḫšua* is associated with *Ḫurama* and *Luḫuzadia*, all generally to be sought in the south-eastern border lands of the Central Anatolian Plateau [cf. *GHE*, 52-53].

78. *êkallum:* According to J. Lewy, *AHDO*, II (1938), 128f., the Alishar text *OIP*, 27, 5:9-10 is a reference to the palace in *Šalaḫšua*.
By implication, *ATHE*, 62:32-35 [34] contains a reference to the ruler or the administration of *Šalaḫšua*.

79. *Officials:*
 a. *ATHE*, 62:32-35 [34] by implication.

ŠALATUAR

80. To be located somewhere in the south-central area of the Anatolian Plateau, perhaps between Nigde and the Plain of Konya [cf. Ch. I, n. 42, above].

81. *rubâ'um: AMÊL* [alu]*Ša-la-ti-va-ra:* "the Man of Šalatiwara" [= synonym for "ruler of S."]: *Anitta Inscription,* l. 65 [Period Ib].

82. Assyrian *wabârtum:* cf. the citations in Ch. I, above.

ŠAMUḪA

83. To be located in the area between the Upper Halys and the Upper Euphrates Rivers [cf. Ch. I, n. 61, above, and *GHE,* pp. 32-36].

84. *êkallum: VAT,* 6209:6-8 (unpublished) [cf. Lewy, *HUCA,* 27 (1956), p. 70, n. 301, for a transliteration of this text].

85. Assyrian *wabârtum:* cf. the citations in Ch. I, above.

SIBUḪA

86. This town was a vassal of the Prince of *Mama,* hence within Mamean-controlled territory, probably close to the border of *Mât Kaniš* [cf. Balkan, *TTKY,* VII, Seri — No. 31a, pp. 30-32].

87. *rubâ'um:* in the gentilic, *Si-bu-ḫa-i-am/um:* g/t 35:7, 13 [Anum-Ḫirbi Letter] [Period Ib].

88. *šarrum:* [= vassal by implication, g/t 35:13-15].

ŠIḪWA Location unknown

89. *rubâ'um:* kt c/k 441:17 [communicated by Balkan, *TTKY,* VII, Seri — No. 31a, p. 60, n. 98].

ŠIMALA

90. Perhaps to be located at Zencirli [ancient *Šam'al*] south-west of present-day Maraş [cf. *EL,* I, p. 35, n. b, and Goetze, *JCS,* 7 (1953), p. 68].

91. Assyrian *eširtum: CCT,* III, 36a:3.

ŠIRMUIN Location unknown.

92. *rubâ'um: ru-ba-im Ší-ir-me-a-im, KTP,* 6:2.

ŠIRUN

93. Located by Goetze about halfway or more between Assur and the Ḫabur River in Syria [*JCS,* 7 (1953), p. 66.]

94. *Officials:*
   a. *GA-šu-um: VAT,* 9260:18-19 [cf. *Or,* ns 21 (1952), p. 265].
   b. *râbiṣum: VAT,* 9260:20-21, *ibid.*

TAIŠAMA

95. According to g/t 35 [Anum-Ḫirbi Letter], *Taišama* was a vassal kingdom of *Mât Kaniš*, sufficiently close to the territory of the Prince of *Mama* to cause the latter anxiety [ll. 5, 9, 15, 19f.]. It should be looked for near the border between *Mât Kaniš* and the territory of *Mama*, perhaps between Kayseri and Göksun or Elbistan. [Cf. Balkan, *TTKY*, VII Seri — No. 31a, p. 30]. [Period Ib].

96. *rubâ'um: ru-ba-um Ta-i-š* [*a-ma-i-u-um*]: g/t 35:15 [Period Ib].
Ta-i-ša-ma-i-um: g/t 35:5, 9, 19. [Period Ib].
Tí-ší-ma-i-im ru-ba-im [= Prince of *Taišama*?]: Oxford, 1933, 1053:22 [cf. Kennedy and Garelli, *RHA*, 66 (1960), pp. 37-44].
If this reference is in fact to the Prince of *Taišama*, it would attest such a ruler for Period II, in addition to Ib of the Anum-Ḫirbi Letter.

97. *šarrum:* [= vassal by implication, g/t 35:8-13, yet the Prince of *Mama* fears that the Prince of *Taišama* will raise his status to that of a "third prince" *a-na ša-al-ší-ni ru-ba-um*, ll. 16-17 with himself and the Prince of *Kaniš*]. [Period Ib].

TAMNIA [See also *Tawinia*/*Tawnia* for separate entries].

98. If this town is the same as *Tawinia*/*Tawnia*, then it is to be located near Boğazköy-*Ḫattuša* in the Halys Basin [cf. *GHE*, = *Tavium*, and Bilgiç, *AfO*, 15 (1945-51), 31, who supports Goetze's localization of *Tawinia* between Boğazköy and Merzifon].

99. *rubâ'um: ru-ba-im ša Ta-am-ni-a:* kt f/k 183:7 [cf. transliteration of this text in Balkan, *TTKY*, VII, Seri — No. 28, pp. 73f., and Lewy, *Or*, ns 26 (1957), p. 27, n. 1] [Period Ib].

100. Assyrian *kârum:* kt f/k 183:3-4 [Period Ib].

TARAKUM

101. Located just west of the Ḫabur River in Syria by A. Goetze [cf. *JCS*, 7 (1953), 67].

102. *rubâ'um: mera' ru-ba-im: CCT*, 26b:7, with ll. 4 and 11.

102a. *Officials:*

a. *GA-šu-um: CCT*, 26b:14-15 with ll. 4 and 11. *TC*, III, 163:20-22.

TAWINIA/*TAWNIA*

103. See above, No. 98.

104. Assyrian *kârum:* Cf. the citation in Ch. I, above.

TEGARAMA

104a. Most likely to be associated with Assyrian *Tilgarimmu,* the present-day Gürün [cf. Goetze, *JCS*, 7 (1953), p. 69, n. 140, and *GHE*, p. 38].

105. *êkallum: CCT*, V, 30a:14-16 [15].

TILIMRIA Location unknown.

106. *rubâ'um:* attested in the gentilic, *a-tí-li-im-ra-i-im* "to the Tilimraium [Prince]: *TC*, III, 158:7.

TIMILKIA

106a. To be located in the east-south-east region of the Anatolian Plateau, perhaps somewhat east of Kommagene [cf. Goetze, *JCS*, 7 (1953), p. 69, and Ch. I, n. 51, above].

106b. *rubâ'um:* (gentilic) *Ti-mì-il$_5$-kà-i-im*, *TC*, III, 162:9;
ru-ba-im Tí-mì-il$_5$-ki-a-i-im: Jena 442:2-3;
ru-ba-im ... i-na Tí-mì-il$_5$-ki-a: TC, III, 211:47-49.

106c: *rubâtum: TC*, III, 211:45.
dowager queen: Jena 442:5.

106d. *êkallum: TC*, III, 211:44.

106e. *Officials:*
a. *mâlikim ša rubâ'im: TC*, III, 211:47 [perhaps not a proper title].

TUḪPIA

107. To be located in the general region of the north-eastern Halys Basin, in the vicinity of *Durḫumit* [cf. Ch. I, nn. 48 and 49, above].

108. *rubâ'um: TC*, 39:8, with l. 4.

109. Assyrian *wabârtum:* cf. citation in Ch. I, above.

ULAMA

110. To be located somewhat south of the Tuz Gölü, "The Salt Lake" at the approaches to the Plain of Konya [cf. Ch. I, n. 41, above].

111. *rubâ'um:* perhaps the gentilic [*Ú*]*-la-ma-i-im*, *TC*, 118:x+5.

112. *Officials:*
a. *ra-bi sí-kà-tim ša Ú-lá-ma: TC*, III, 271:24-25.

rabi sí-ki-tim ša Ú-lá-[*ma* ...]: *Ibid:* 27.
b. *râbiṣum: TC*, III, 165:25.
c. *GA-šu-um: TC*, III, 165:22-24 [24].

113. Assyrian *wabârtum:* Cf. the citations in Ch. I, above.

URŠU

114. To be located between the Amanus Mt. and the Euphrates River, north of present-day Cerablus [ancient *Carchemiš*, cf. Ch. I, n. 54, above].

115. Assyrian *kârum:* Cf. the citations in Ch. I, above.

UŠŠA

116. Located by *GHE* in the region of the southern shore of the Tuz Gölü ["Salt Lake], in the area of Aksaray [p. 74].

117. *Officials:*
a. *rabi sí-ki-tim: BIN*, IV, 45:8.

WAŠḪANIA

118. To be located a short distance south of Kayseri [cf. Ch. I, n. 38, above].

119. *rubâ'um: KTP*, 14:5.
ru-ba-um [*Wa-á*]*š-ḫa-na-i*(!)*-um: CCT*, V, 15b:x+4 —x+5.
idem, kt g/k 185:4-5 [cf. Balkan, *TTKY*, VII, Seri — No. 31a, p. 60, n. 98.

120. *êkallum: TC*, III, 165:6.

121. *Officials:*
a. *GA-šu-um: TC*, III, 165:5-12 [6].
b. *râbiṣum: TC*, III, 165:5-12 [9].

122. Assyrian *wabârtum:* Cf. the citations in Ch. I, above.

WAḪŠUŠANA (Attested as *Mât Waḫšušana: KTHahn* 1:3-4; *KTP*, 10:23).

123. To be located in the area of present day Niğde [cf. Ch. I, n. 36].

124. *rubâ'um:* (gentilic), *Wa-aḫ-šu-ša-na-im: ATHE*, 66:9. *Wa-aḫ-šu-ša-*⟨*na*⟩*-i-i*[*m*]*: TC*, III, 143:x+2.

125. *rubâtum: ru*(!)*-ba-tum Wa-aḫ-ša-na-i-tù: KTS*, 50c [= *EL*, 150]:1-2.

126. *êkallum: ATHE*, 63:21-24 [22]; *BIN*, VI, 186:5-6f.; *CCT*, II, 46b and 47a:27-28; *TC*, III, 271:10, 13, 31.

126a. *Officials:*

a. *rabi sí-ki-tim: KTHahn*, 14:14-15.

127. Assyrian *kârum:* Cf. citations in Ch. I, above.

ZALPA

128. To be located in the general vicinity of Boğazköy-*Ḫattuša* [cf. Ch. I, nn. 45 and 48]. A. Goetze locates a second *Zalpa/Zalpaḫ* a day's march from the Euphrates (east), near Birecik [cf. *JCS*, 7 (1953), p. 68, and further, *Kleinasien* (1957), p. 74, n. 12]. We assume that *Kârum Zalpa* is the Halys Basin, *wabârtum ša Zalpa*, the North Syrian town.

129. *rubâ'um:* (gentilic), *Za-al-pá-i-im*, *TC*, III, 85:6 *ru-ba-um*, *Ibid:* 7; *ru-ba-im* ... *i-na Za-al-pá: TC*, III, 166:13-16 [13], perhaps North Syrian *Zalpaḫ*.

130. *šarrum:* *ᵐU-uḫ-na-aš ŠÀR ᵃˡᵘZa-a-al-pu-va*, *Anitta Inscription*, l. 39 [Pre- or Early Period Ib].
[*ᵐḪ*]*u-uz-zi-ia-na ŠÀR ᵃˡᵘZa-a-al-p*[*u-va*]: *Anitta Inscription*, l. 43 [Period Ib].

131. *êkallum:* Jena 285+383 ⌊*EL*, 267]:8, with l. 13. Is this the palace of *Zalpa/Zalpaḫ* in North Syria, as appears to be suggested by the fact of its citation in a document issued by the *wabârtum ša Zalpa* [l. 13]?
TC, III, 166:22; the *êkallum* of Zalpa here referred to is in the town which is apparently close to *Dadania*, hence, North Syria?
TC, III, 85 reports an encounter in the palace of Zalpa.

132. *Officials:*

a. *GA-šu-um: TC*, III, 166:15-16.

133. Assyrian *kârum:* Cf. the citations in Ch. I, above.

134. Assyrian *wabârtum: ibid.*

THE KINGDOM OF KANIŠ: THE BACKGROUND CONTROVERSY

It is now clear that *Kaniš* was in existence from early in the third millennium B.C. and was probably also one of the important small city-states of central Anatolia by the turn of the second. The events which form the record of her early history are lost to us, and what we can infer about it is based at present on the barest archaeological soundings on the city-mound at Kültepe (see Appendix B). From a small mud village whose pottery styles suggest only local and regional influence during the Early

Bronze I period, the site gradually grows until by the end of Early Bronze III the architecture has developed to impressive size (including a temple with a megaron-style room in *EB*, IIIb), and *Kaniš* has established permanent contacts, to judge by the pottery, with Cilicia and North Syria. There can be little doubt that by the Early Bronze III period *Kaniš* was a commercial center well known to the dynasts and traders of Syria and Mesopotamia, although the question of Mesopotamian political and military contact with Anatolia is still open. At least it can be said that the climate of opinion is less rigidly exclusive of admitting such contacts than was the case a decade ago.

Early Bronze III on the City-Mound comes to a close through some sort of violence attested by a burned level. Was the burning evidence of a defeat to an outside conquerer or simply the result of a disturbance within the Plateau? Nothing can presently be known about it. However, the onset of Middle Bronze I brings evidence of the first inhabitation on the *Kârum*-terrace. *Kârum* Levels IV and III represent perhaps a century of occupation by unknown people before the first Assyrian settlers arrive and begin to keep the archives which have been found in such abundance in Level II. It would be fruitless to speculate overmuch about who these people may have been. Perhaps they were native Anatolian merchants, residents of *Kaniš*, who lived in what may even then have been the commercial quarter of the city, though no pre-Assyrian records have been found. In any event, it seems clear from the current state of the excavations at Kültepe that there is an unbroken development of life from the beginning of the *Kârum* levels through the end of Level II, which appears to have suffered a violent catastrophe. The first Assyrian level (II) seems peacefully to have succeeded upon its two predecessors, and this speaks strongly against any idea of Old Assyrian conquest as the reason for the establishment of the Assyrian trading network in Anatolia.

It is Level II, then, that has given us our first substantial evidence of Anatolian Dynasts and their political interests, for some names of these rulers and their activities may occasionally be recovered from the Assyrian tablets. Later chapters are devoted to a survey of relations between the Assyrian traders and the local rulers, but here we must present a picture of the indigenous political situation, and especially that which appears to have prevailed at *Kaniš*.

As is to be expected where early evidence is built up slowly over the years and is incomplete, differences of scholarly opinion tend to polarize around the possibilities suggested at the time of study. The Old Assyrian settlements are no exception to this, and substantially different opinions were developed about the entire nature of the trading settlements, which in themselves included interpretations of the status and the role of the rulers of *Kaniš*. It is therefore most necessary to review what was thought about the Old Assyrian presence in Anatolia before reviewing the latest evidence on the matter.

At the present time, two major lines of interpretation hold the day. One of these sees the Anatolian princes as vassals of an Assyria which had conquered their home regions,[8] while the other proposes that the Assyrian settlements had the status of "guest enclaves" which were entitled to pursue commerce in central Anatolia under some sort of mutual arrangements with the various local administrations.[9] The force of the first interpretation is that the Anatolians are subject peoples; of the second, that Assyrians and Anatolians enjoyed a peaceful, symbiotic relationship.

Beyond the differences of opinion about interpreting particular bits of evidence in the sources which exist between proponents of each theory, there is another sort of difficulty which has tended to confuse the issue considerably. This difficulty appears in the casual and vague terminology which has been used to describe the status of the Assyrian *kârum*. This vital institution has been defined or alluded to in such a wide variety of ways that almost every writer who addresses himself to the question has something different to say about it. Were we to prepare a random listing of these definitions as in the form of a dictionary entry, they would appear as follows:

Karum: (1) *Kolonie, Handelskommune;*[10] (2) *einer organisierten assy-*

[8] The chief supporters of this position are: E. Meyer, *Geschichte des Altertums*, I², 3rd. Ed. (Stuttgart and Berlin, 1913) 612; B. Hrozný, "Assyriens et Hittites en Asie Mineure vers 2000 B.C.", *ArOr*, 4 (1932), 112f.; and J. Lewy, *passim*, most especially "Zur Geschichte Assyriens und Kleinasiens im 3. und 2. Jahrtausend v. Chr.", *OLZ*, 26 (1923), 533-544, "Der *karrum* der alt-assyrischen-kappadokischen Stadte und das alt-assyrischen Grossreich", *ZA*, N.F. 2 (v. 36) (1925), 19-28, "'Kappadokische' Tontafeln und Frühgeschichte Assyriens und Kleinasiens", *OLZ*, 29 (1926), 750-761; 963-966, "*Ḫatta, Ḫattu, Ḫatti, Ḫattuša* and 'Old Assyrian' *Ḫattum*", *ArOr*, 18, 3/4 (1950), 414f., "On Some Institutions of the Old Assyrian Empire", *HUCA*, 27 (1956), 1-79 and "Apropos of a Recent Study in Old Assyrian Chronology", *Or*, *ns*, 26 (1957), 12-36.

[9] The chief supporters of this position are: B. Landsberger, "Über die Völker Vorderasiens im dritten Jahrtausend", *ZA*, N.F. 1 (v. 35) (1924) 225f., *AHK* (1925), 4f.; E. Forrer, *RLA*, 1 (1928), 232; M. David, Review of *EL*, I in *ZSS*, 52 (1932), 501-503 and "Beiträge zu den altassyrischen Briefen aus Kappadokien", *OLZ*, 36 (1933), 209, n. 3; I. J. Gelb, *OIP*, 27 (1935), 11-13; J. Klima and L. Matouš, "Les tablettes 'cappadociennes'". *RAI*, 2 (1951) 59; A. Goetze *Kleinasien* (1957) 72.

[10] Cf. B. Landsberger, *AHK* (1925), 9.

rischen Handelskolonie;[11] (3) foreign commercial colony;[12] (4) Assyrian trading colony, fort;[13] (5) *colonie de négociants assyriens;*[14] (6) *florissantes colonies sémitiques;*[15] (7) *Provinzhauptstadt, Marktstadt, Gerichtstadt, Regierung, Regierungstadt;*[16] (8) principal quarter of a city [(here, specifically *Kaniš*)] as well as its governing body, which, *inter alia*, functioned as a law-court;[17] (9) a sort of Chamber of Commerce controlling the mechanism of trade between Assyria and the cities of Anatolia;[18] (10) *en quelque manière une chambre de commerce et en meme temps un tribunal de commerce;*[19] (11) *chambre de commerce;*[20] (12) *une sorte de chambre de commerce ou Bazar;*[21] (13) communal court of a city in Asia Minor;[22] (14) commercial settlement, station, judicial power.[23] The list could be elaborated, but the point is already clear.

Even within the two main types of theories about the nature of the Assyrian settlements, there is a discernible lack of precision. For example, those who deny that the *kârû* and the *wabârâtum* were imperial outposts of Assyria have never attempted to discuss the political class to which these settlements belong beyond suggesting in a general way that they were analogous to the merchant colonies of the Venetians and the Genoese of a much later date; they have never discussed the particular characteristics of a *Handelskommune* or *Handelskolonie*, or the type of colonialism they are specifically talking about.[24] On the other hand,

11 Cf. *idem*, "Kommt *Ḫattum* 'Hettiterland' und *Ḫatti'um* 'Hettiter' in den Kültepe-Tafeln vor?" *ArOr*, 18, 1/2 (1950), 329.

12 Cf. S. Lloyd, *Early Anatolia* (Baltimore, 1956), 32.

13 Cf. G. R. Driver and J. C. Miles, *The Assyrian Laws* (Oxford, 1935), 2.

14 Cf. J. Klima and L. Matouš, "Les tablettes 'cappadociennes'", *RAI*, 2 (1951), 49.

15 Cf. E. Cavaignac, *Les Hittites* (Paris, 1950), 16.

16 Cf. J. Lewy, *KTBl* (1929), 18-19.

17 Cf. *idem*, "On Some Institutions ...", *op. cit.*, 35-36, w.n. 123.

18 Cf. S. Lloyd, *Early Anatolia, op. cit.*, 115.

19 Cf. L. Delaporte, *Les Hittites* (Paris, 1936), 49.

20 Cf. *idem, Les peuples de l'orient méditerraneen*, 1 (Paris, 1948), 115.

21 Cf. G. Contenau, *La Civilisation des Hittites et des Hurrites du Mitanni* (Paris 1948), 42.

22 Cf. S. Smith, *Early History of Assyria* (New York, 1928), 162.

23 Cf. I. J. Gelb, *OIP*, 27 (1935), 12, w.n. 141.

24 In seeking to describe the nature of the relationship between the *kârum*-establishment of Anatolia and the government of Assyria at Assur, B. Landsberger, e.g., used the following descriptive statements: "Das *kârum*, etwa mit Kolonie oder Handelskommune wiederzugeben, war das Ein und Alles der kolonialen Selbstverwaltung" (*AHK* [1925], 9), while he also is able to say, "... die Kolonisten bleiben auch in ihren neuen Wohnsitzen Bürger der Stadt Assur, ihre *kârum* ('Kolonien') sind hinsichtlich der politischen Organisation exponierte Teile des *âlum* [i.e., Assur]" (*ZA*, N.F. 1 [v. 35] [1924], 223). Although the two quotes appear to supplement each other, in fact they do not. For if the *kârum* is the epitome of a self-governing "Kolonie" or "Handelskommune", in what sense is it to be understood as "der politischen Organ-

those who believe that Assyria had conquered Anatolia at some time before the period roughly defined by the extant sources fail to acknowledge that a conquering power may treat a subject region in various ways, not all of which require it to display itself visibly in all pomp and power, and with all the imperial trappings.[25] Partly because the idea of "colony" has been so loosely applied to the Assyrian *kârum*, and partly because we feel that the interpretation of an Assyrian conquest of Anatolia is but loosely suggested by the available evidence, we feel it necessary to re-open the question of Assyrian political status *vis à vis* the Anatolian princes. As a preliminary step we must make some distinctions of a theoretical nature about the kinds of possible conclusions our study might lead to.

In attempting to characterize a situation in which members of one ethnic group or "state" are seen to be substantially settled and actively pursuing economic objectives in regions indigenously settled by another, we may understand two general possibilities — indeed those which have already been proposed for the Assyrian settlements. Either the settle-

---

isation exponierte Teile des *âlum*?" Prof. Landsberger never appears to answer this question satisfactorily, although he stresses that *kârum* and *âlum* are parallel types, both belonging to the same category of communities with their own political structures: the *kârum* is "nicht eine Behörde von Kaniš", but "Kaniš selbst ist ein *kârum*", (*ZA*, N.F. 1, *loc. cit.*, 223). Yet if this is so, how can the circumstance that the *kârum* can be taxed by the government of Assur (which Landsberger himself points out, *AHK* (*loc. cit.*, 10) be understood? For the power to tax as well as the evident legal subordination of the Anatolian settlements to Assur, indicates that *kârum* and *âlum* are not political equals *as far as the exercise of decision-making is concerned.*

If we point out this difficulty, we do not, nevertheless, fail to admire the importance of the early articles of Landsberger, which represent more brilliant summary insights than closely-argued final conclusions. Our only regret is that Prof. Landsberger has not issued a fuller synthesis of his views than has appeared to date.

[25] Prof. Lewy has done the most to call attention to the legal dependence of the Old Assyrian settlements of Anatolia upon Assur, yet we cannot but feel that his theory of an Old Assyrian Empire in Anatolia is based upon assumptions which are less flexible than they might be. Although his more recent and highly valuable articles concern themselves with elucidating the textual evidence for this position, it nevertheless remains that the theoretical basis for it was clearly established by 1926 in such remarks as: "... die Möglichkeit wirtschaftlicher Expansion, insbesondere auch die Anlage geschlossener Handelsniederlassungen, auch im Alten Orient in erster Reihe eine Folge militärischer Stärke zu sein pflegte ...", (*OLZ*, 29 [1926], *loc. cit.*, 756), and "Die Möglichkeit der plötzlichen Bildung eines altassyr. Grossreiches vom Tigris bis zum Halys aber wird nur leugnen, wem das Entstehen und Vergehen altorientalischer Herrschaften, etwa derjenigen des Lugalzaggisi, des neubabylonischen oder des medischen Reiches, nicht gegenwärtig ist". (*ibid.*, 757). The argument that empires are built only by the sword is fallacious, as indeed Gelb remarks in *OIP*, 27 (1935), 11. While we do not contest Prof. Lewy's extremely valuable and pertinent demonstrations of the legal connections between Assur and its settlements across the Taurus Ranges and in North Syria, we do not think that Assur had sovereignty over any but her own citizens abroad. Cf. our arguments in Chapters Four through Six.

ments came into being as a consequence of the use of force, or they were founded in some other way. Considering the first alternative, had Assyria conquered Anatolia, thereby expanding and annexing contiguous territory, then roughly four courses of action were open to it which may be called "imperial".[26] Assyria might have accorded the subject peoples full autonomy controlled only by, perhaps, token forces. At the other extreme, it might have annihilated or expelled the inhabitants, and settled the area as an integral part of itself. It might, thirdly, have permitted the indigenes to remain, but in a permanently inferior status. Or again, fourthly, it might have accorded full citizenship to the individuals of the conquered area and attempted to submerge their "nationhood" into a large nation. In practise, all of these "imperial" solutions — each assuming the annexation of contiguous territory — imperceptibly shade into one another. There is, however, a fifth solution, which can in a distinct sense be called "colonialism". By this is meant a relationship created when one nation establishes and maintains political dominion over a geographically external political unit inhabited by people of any race and at any stage of national development.

A feature common to all these alternatives, including "colonialism" as we accept the use of this term, is that the conquering state holds *political dominion* over the conquered peoples, in no matter what form or through what agencies it appears. It may, if it has annexed contiguous territory, treat the natives harshly or mildly, or with some degree of both at various times. It may maintain a full military occupation and allow its subjects no autonomy at all, or by contrast maintain only token forces. Applying these alternatives to the Assyrian settlements of Anatolia, assuming for the moment that Assyria had conquered and annexed the area, we could say that they were *provincial outposts*, although the *kinds* of political domination they exercised could vary. Continuing to assume an Assyrian conquest, but that Assyria chose to administer Anatolia as a geographically external unit rather than annex it, we would then be justified in speaking of Assyrian *imperial colonies*. The difference here exists in whether the conquering power attempts to make the conquered region a part of itself by occupying and administering it as if it were an integral part of the homeland, or whether it is content to provide token control in order to protect its interests, whether strategic or commercial, in the area conquered.

[26] The following theoretical material is taken from H. Kohn, "Reflections on Colonialism", in R. Strausz-Hupé and H. Hazard, eds., *Idea of Colonialism* (New York, 1958), 3-4.

All this assumes an act of conquest lying behind the political dominion; but we must also inquire into the alternatives which emerge from the assumption that Assyria *did not* have political dominion over Anatolia and its numerous princely administrations. The possibilities here are either that the Assyrians held the status of guest foreigners, engaged in trade, but with little coercive power over the Anatolian rulers; or, that they had considerable power which was granted them for reasons other than conquest. In either case, some types of treaty arrangements must be sought which would explain arrangements under which Assyrians had the right to occupy quarters in important Anatolian cities, and to maintain their own system of law and administration. We should also be allowed to speak of the Assyrian settlements as "colonies", but of a vastly different order than if they had been founded through acts of conquest.

It therefore becomes most imperative to examine whether the Assyrians maintained *political dominion* over Anatolia during the Cappadocian Period, and if so, what kind, if we hope to define the class of political organization to which the Assyrian settlements belong. It cannot be overlooked that relations between Assyrians and Anatolians might appear to be most friendly and co-operative and yet be based upon an imperial or "imperial colonial" policy of the Mesopotamian state; but neither can it be overlooked that such relations might prove not to require such an interpretation, and that a colonialism of another type is operating. We may conveniently begin by inquiring into the position of those who believe that force played a part in the establishment of the Assyrian settlements.

As developed chiefly by Professor Julius Lewy, the "empire" view maintains that during the Cappadocian Period there existed an Old Assyrian Empire consisting of Assyria proper and its dependency, a vassal state in Asia Minor, which Lewy calls "Halys Assyria".[27] The capital of this Empire was Assur, while the provincial capital of "Halys Assyria" was *Kaniš*, itself tributary to the ruler of Assur.[28] In *Kaniš* a viceroy of Assyrian nationality bearing the title *iššiʾakkum* (= *rubâʾum*, 'prince'), represented the home government.[29]

The alleged conquest of Anatolia took place before the period defined by the bulk of the Cappadocian tablets now known from Kültepe (Level II, which is generally contemporaneous with the reign of Sargon I, and

[27] Cf. J. Lewy, "Apropos of a Recent Study in Old Assyrian Chronology", *op. cit.*, 23. Earlier references: "Zur Geschichte Assyriens und Kleinasiens ...", *op. cit.*, 538, 543; "Der *karrum* der alt-assyrischen-kappadokischen Stadte ...", *op. cit.*, 19.

[28] Cf. *idem*, "On Some Institutions ...", *op. cit.*, 65-68f.

[29] Cf. *idem*, "Apropos of a Recent Study ...", *op. cit.*, 23.

his son, Puzur-Aššur II).[30] This conquest, Prof. Lewy thinks, was made by an unknown successor of Ilušumma (the great-grandfather of Sargon I), who transferred Assyrian nationals to numerous town across the Taurus Ranges and settled them there in the *kârû* and *wabârâtum* in order to secure his newly-won possessions.[31]

The existence of this Old Assyrian Empire is an entirely expected feature of early Near Eastern history, Lewy thinks, because Assyria was not the first Mesopotamian state to conquer Anatolia.[32] Before her the Dynasty of Akkad had already penetrated into Asia Minor under its illustrious kings, Sargon of Akkad and Narâm-Sîn.[33] These conquerors are alleged to have subdued the areas of *Kaniš* and of *Burušḫattum*, far to the south-west. They even must have reached *Hattuš* (Boğazköy) in the Halys Basin.[34]

The alleged Old Akkadian Empire, extending as it did into the heartland of Anatolia, lasted for a considerable period, even retaining its form after the fall of Akkad to Gutium.[35] Following the interlude of Gutian reign in Mesopotamia, the Third Dynasty of Ur which had risen to ascendancy began a new series of penetrations into Anatolia. Under Ur-Nammu and Šulgi, its first two kings, Ur III is alleged to have conquered and annexed the old state of *Kaniš*, though to what extent they conquered areas of Anatolia to the west and north of *Kaniš* Lewy leaves as an open question.[36] However, he feels that the Sumerian conquerors regarded *Kaniš* as a starting point for further campaigns in Asia Minor.[37] At *Kaniš* they organized an administration whose duties, among others, included exercising control over Sumerian possessions south of the Taurus Ranges in North Syria.[38] In the very same period Assur was also a vassal of Ur, and there, as at *Kaniš*, were stationed administrative officers of the Kings of Ur.[39]

30 Cf. *idem*, "On Some Institutions ...", *op. cit.*, 53, 65, w.n. 273, and "Some Aspects of Commercial Life ...", *op. cit.*, 99 (bottom), 101.

31 Cf. *idem*, "On Some Institutions ...", *op. cit.*, 53, 65.

32 Cf. *idem*, "'Kappadokische' Tontafeln und Frügeschichte ...", *op. cit.*, 756-761, 963f.

33 Cf. *idem*, "Lykier Syrer und Choriter Syrer", *ZA*, N.F. 1, (v. 35) (1924), 147-148; "'Kappadokische' Tontafeln und Frühgeschichte ...", *op. cit.*, 756 w.n. 3, 963; "*Ḫatta, Ḫattu, Ḫatti, Ḫattuša* and 'Old Assyrian' *Ḫattum*", *op. cit.*, 407, w.n. 215, 415.

34 Cf. *idem*, "'Kappadokische' Tontafeln und Frühgeschichte ...", *op. cit.*, 756, w.n. 3.

35 We take this inference from the source references cited in n. 32-34, above, and further from Lewy, "Lykier Syrer ...", *op. cit.*, 147-148.

36 Cf. Lewy, "*Ḫatta, Ḫattu, Ḫatti, Ḫattuša* ...", *op. cit.*, 416-418, w.n. 286-288.

37 *Ibid.*

38 *Ibid.*

39 *Ibid.*, 416. For Lewy's remarks on officers of the King of Ur at Assur, cf. "Zur Geschichte Assyriens ...", *op. cit.*, 538.

After the fall of Ur III Assur became independent. In Anatolia the old "Sumerian" vassal state of *Kaniš* is alleged to have dissolved into a number of small principalities.[40] It was during this period that Assur seized the opportunity to gain her independence of Ur and re-invade Anatolia.[41] Thus she would have embarked on a re-conquest of the old imperial provinces that had existed under Akkad as well as Ur. The unknown successor of Ilušumma who campaigned in Anatolia was therefore allegedly guided by precedent in making the city of *Kaniš* the chief provincial capital of his newly-won possessions.[42] Professor Lewy further believes that the Assyrians allowed the rulers of the many small principalities in the area to keep their thrones. These were expected to give oaths of allegiance to their Assyrian overlords, and accordingly were governed from *Kaniš* as vassals.[43]

To complete the picture drawn by Prof. Lewy, the alleged Old Assyrian Empire in Anatolia lasted on until the reign of Šamsi-Adad I, or that of his son, Išmê-Dagan.[44] Some of the Old Assyrian settlements, however, lived on as important centers of Assyrian culture into the period of the Hittite Empire.[45]

From the preceding sketch we select two points for special emphasis. First, Professor Lewy believes that Assyria effected a more or less permanent occupation of Anatolia through conquest; that it provided a great number of occupying garrisons which were administrative agencies of the Assyrian government; and that it designated an occupation governor and stationed him at *Kaniš*. Second, Prof. Lewy alleges that the Assyrians maintained control over the local princes through oaths of vassalage — which bears witness to Assyrian political domination in the imperial sense.

Precisely these two points are the crux of the "Empire" theory, and also the only points that can be examined from the Old Assyrian sources themselves. The notion that early empires were carved out in Anatolia by Akkad and Ur III is highly controversial though theoretically interesting. We take up the question in *Appendix C*. The first indisputable evidence for an indigenous line of rulers at *Kaniš*, the so-called "Anum-Ḫirbi Letter", came to light relatively recently, and is presented imme-

[40] Lewy, "*Ḫatta, Ḫattu, Ḫatti, Ḫattuša* ...", *op. cit.*, 418-422.
[41] *Ibid.*, 421, w.n. 309; 422, w.n. 314.
[42] *Ibid.*, 417-418, w.n. 288.
[43] Cf. the references in n. 41-42, above, and also, Lewy, "La chronologie de Bitḫana et d'Anitta de Kuššara", *RHA*, 3 (1934-36), 2, n. 14 (3).
[44] Cf. Lewy, "Apropos of a Recent Study ...", *op. cit.*, 27, n. 2, and 32f.
[45] Cf. *idem*, "Zur Geschichte Assyriens und Kleinasiens ..., *op. cit.*, 543-544.

diately below. It speaks, however, only for the political situation at *Kaniš* during the period of *Kârum* Level Ib. Since a hypothesis has been proposed and argued that the Kanishean rulers during the Level II period were *Assyrian* viceroys, this hypothesis will be taken up and analyzed after the Anum-Ḫirbi Letter, following which the evidence for a line of indigenous and autonomous rulers of *Kaniš* will be surveyed and a synthesis attempted [*excursus* to this chapter].

THE ANUM-ḪIRBI LETTER

In 1957 Kemal Balkan published a monograph — *TTKY*, VII, Seri — No. 31a — on the then but recently discovered letter sent by a certain Anum-Ḫirbi, King of *Mama* to a King of *Kaniš* called Waršama which had come to light on the City-Mound of Kültepe. It was an outstanding find because it represented the first documentary evidence of a political nature emanating from an indigenous Anatolian royal court, though written in Old Assyrian, and also the first which gave us direct evidence of relations between Anatolian principalities. Until the recovery of this letter, such information was rarely available, and then chiefly by inference from the letters and other documents of the Assyrian traders themselves. For the convenience of the reader I shall present Balkan's transliteration and translation of the text, whose catalogue number is G/T 35:

G/T 35

Obv. (1) um-ma A-nu-um-ḫi-ir-bi ru-ba-um
(2) Ma-ma-i-ú-um-ma a-na Wa-ar-ša-ma
(3) ru-ba-im Kà-ni-ší-im qí-bi-ma
(4) ta-áš-pu-ra-am um-ma a-ta-ma
(5) Ta-i-ša-ma-⟨i⟩-ú-um ur-dí-i
(6) a-na-ku ú-ša-ba-šu ú a-ta
(7) Sí-bu-ḫa-i-a-am IR$^{ra\text{-}ad}$-kà
(8) a-ta ša-bi-šu iš-tù-ma
(9) Ta-i-ša-ma-i-ú-um kà-lá-áb-kà-ni
(10) a-mì-nim iš-tí ša-ra-ni-e ša-ni-ú-tim
(11) i-dá-ba-áb
(12) ša-ni-ú-tim i-da-ba-áb
(13) Sí-bu-ḫa-i-ú-um kà-al-bi

(14) iš-tí ša-ra-ni-e ša-ni-ú-tim
(15) i-da-bu-ub ru-ba-um Ta-i-š[a-ma-i-ú-um]
(16) a-na ša-al-ší-ni ru-ba-im
(17) i-tù-wa-ar ki-*ma be-el (*Text = *NA*)
(18) nu-ku-ur-tí-a i-du-kà-ni
(19) ù Ta-i-ša-ma-i-ú-um
(20) a-na ma-tí-i-a im-qú-ta-ma
(21) 12 a-lá-ni-e-a úḫ-ta-li-iq
(22) al-pí-šu-nu ú ṣé-ni-šu-nu
(23) il$_5$-tí-qí um-ma šu-ut-ma ru-ba-um
(24) me-it-ma ḫu-ḫa-ra-am
Edge (25) al-tí-qí ki-ma ma-tí-i-ia
(26) na-ṣa-ri-im ú li-bi-im
Rev. (27) ta-da-nim ú ma-tí-i
(28) iš-ta-ra-áp ú qú-ut-ra-am
(29) ub-ta-i-iš i-nu-mì a-bu-kà
(30) I-na-ar a-lam Ḫa-ar-sá-am-na
(31) MU 9-ŠÈ il$_5$-wi-ú ma-tí-i
(32) a-na ma-tí-kà im-qú-tám-ma
(33) al-pá-am ú-lu ṣé-na-am
(34) iš-gi$_5$-*iš (Text: IT) u$_4$-ma-am ta-áš-pu-ra-am
(35) um-ma a-ta-ma a-mì-nim ḫa-[ra-nam]
(36) lá tù-ša-ra-am ḫa-ra-nam
(37) lu-ší-ir ša *pá-e-ma (Text: MA)
(38) li-[traces] a-lá-am x[xx]
(39) ú [xxxx] ḫa-ra-n[am xx]
(40) i[š-tù xxx ha-r]a-na-am
(41) lu-[ší-ir xxx a-n]u-um-ma
(42) l[i-xxx xx iš]-tí 17 a-wi-li
(43) š[u xxxxx] x
(44) x[xxxxxx]-y- šu-nu
(45) [xxxxxx]-nim
(46) [xxxxxx]-ma-tí-kà
(47) [xxxxxx-t]ám ša ú-bi-lu-nim
(48) [xxxxxx]-y-ma
(49) [xxxx ta-áš-pu-ra]-am
(50) um-ma a-ta-ma lu ni-it-ma
(51) ma-mì-tum pá-ni-tum e-ṣa-at
(52) DUMU ší-ip-ri-kà
Edge (53) a-na ṣé-ri-a li-li-kam

(54) ù DUMU ší-⟨ip⟩-ri-a a ṣé-ri-kà
(55) li-ta-lá-kam
left E (56) Ta-ri-ku-ta-na ki-ma KÙ.BABBAR áb-na-tim *ik-mu-uk-ma (*Text = ku)
(57) e-tí-zi-ib a-ni-a-tum a-na DINGIR^{li} dam-qá-a

(1) Thus says Anum-Ḫirbi (2) The Mamean (1) *rubâ'u* (2) To Waršama, (3) the Kanišean *rubâ'u* say: (4) "You wrote me: (5) 'The Taišamean is my slave; (6) I shall take care of him. But do you (8) take care of (lit: "and appease (imp) the Sibuḫean your slave") (7) the Sibuḫean, your slave?' (8) Since (9) the Taišamean is your dog (10) why (11) does he argue (10) with other *šarrus*? (13) Does the Sibuḫean my dog, (15) argue (14) with other *šarrus*? (15) Is a Taišmean *rubâ'u* to become (16) the third *rubâ'u* with us? (17-18) When my enemy 'killed' (i.e., defeated) me, (19) the Taišamean (20) invaded my country and (21) 12 of my cities he destroyed and (22) their cattle and sheep he carried away. (23) He said thus: "the *rubâ'u* (24) is 'dead', (25) so I have taken (24) (my) fowlers snare'. (25-26) Instead of protecting my country and (27) giving (me) heart' (i.e., encouraging me) (28) he not only burned up (27) my country, (28) but (29) created evil-smelling smoke. (29) while your father (30) Inar (31) was besieging for nine years (30) the city of Ḫarsamna, (32) did my land (i.e., people) invade (32) your land and (34) did it kill (33) an ox or a sheep? (34) Today you wrote me (35) as follows: 'why (36) do you not free (35) the road (36) for me?' (37) I will free (36) the road. (37) Witnesses (38) may [xxxx]. The city [xxxx] (39) and [xxxx] the road [xxxx] (40) F[rom xx the ro]ad (41) I may [free ...] (42) may [come here wi]th seventeen men. (43) [xxxxxx]
(44) [xxx] your [xxx]
(45) [xxxxxx] here
(46) [xxxxxx] your country
(47) [xxx] which they brought here
(48) [xxxxxx] and
(49) [xxxx you wrote] to me (50) as follows: 'let us take an oath.' (51) Is the former oath insufficient? (52) Let your messenger (53) come to me (54) and let my messenger (55) come regularly (54) to you (56) Tarikutana, instead of silver, sealed stones, and (57) deposited (them here). Are these (things) good to (i.e., in the sight of) the gods?'

The chief importance of G/T 35 is that it shows not only that two rulers of towns where the Assyrians maintained residence quarters could conduct diplomatic negotiations on their own, but also that they controlled vassals in their own right, fought petty wars and could make alliances with each other, all at a time when the Assyrians are alleged by the proponents of the "Empire" school to have ruled Anatolia. The date of Waršama at *Kaniš* is contemporaneous with *Kârum* Level Ib.

The information presented by G/T 35 fits meaningfully into the picture to be drawn in Chapters Four through Six, following, to the effect that the Assyrians at no time ruled the Anatolian princes as a military or political overlord, nor did they gain the right to establish residence areas in Anatolian cities as the result of conquest.

The letter originates from the town of *Mama*, seat of an Assyrian *wabârtum*. As we noted in Chapter One, *Mama* was on the southern route of Assyrian trade, leading from *Kaniš* to *Assur* by way of northern Syria. It must be sough for west of *Uršu*, which is in the area north of modern Cerablus (ancient *Carchemish*) and close to the western bank of the Euphrates. The prince of *Mama*, Anum-Ḫirbi, controls a number of lesser princes as vassals, all, we may assume, located within a resonable distance of his dynastic seat. For his part Waršama, the ruler of *Kaniš*, is also seen to be at the head of a number of vassal city-states. The puppet prince of one of these, the city of *Taišama*, has aggressed against the Mamean ruler's territory on an earlier occasion. Apparently he has been a source of continual unrest and potential danger to *Mama* because Waršama has had to reassure Anum-Ḫirbi that the Taišamian prince is indeed under Kanišean control. In making this assurance, Waršama takes the opportunity to accuse Anum-Ḫirbi of failing adequately to control his own vassal, the Prince of *Sibuḫa*. After further references to events involving Waršama's father, Inar, the letter alludes to a cessation of normal communications between *Kaniš* and *Mama*, and the interruption of diplomatic relationships between the two princes, although a treaty exists as the basis for such relationships.

The letter G/T 35 demonstrates the independence of the Kingdom of *Kaniš* for at least the reigns of two individuals, Waršama, and his father Inar. The general attribution of their reigns to the last period of Assyrian activity at *Kaniš* (Level Ib) allows an inference to be made about the independence of *Kaniš* at that time, but has not been taken to apply to the political situation of Level II, and therefore it is necessary to review the evidence of royal names associated with *Kaniš* either directly or indirectly for this period, as well as an examination of the reasons which have been put forward for denying that it was a kingdom independent of Assyrian rule. We reserve for a later chapter a reconstruction, within the limits of probability, of the position of *Kaniš* within the Anatolian system of city-states.

THE HYPOTHESIS OF AN ASSYRIAN RULER AT KANIŠ

The opinion that the ruler of *Kaniš* was an Assyrian is chiefly drawn by Prof. Lewy from three sources, the most important of which is a group of seal-impressions on Cappadocian tablets, while the remaining are statements in two texts emanating from Kültepe. We may begin our analysis by discussing the problems connected with an interpretation of the so-called "Ṣilûlu-seals".

A number of examples of a seal-impression bearing the name of a certain Ṣilûlu, who is styled on several as *iššiʾakkum* (ENSI), or "city-ruler" of Assur, have been collected from tablets emanating from Level II at Kültepe.[46] The reconstructed legend of these impressions declares that Ṣilûlu was the son of a certain Dakiki, who himself was a "city-herald" (NIMGIR.URU) of Assur.[47] The impressions were obviously made from a seal which was cut in much earlier times and re-used by someone during the Cappadocian period.[48] Who was its original owner?

Kemal Balkan came to the conclusion that this Ṣilûlu must have been an independent ruler of Assur some time prior to Puzur-Aššur I, who founded the Old Assyrian dynasty.[49] He was, thinks Balkan, more or less contemporary with the last years of Ur III, an opinion which he bases on certain epigraphical features of the seal-impressions, themselves.[50] In style, the Ṣilûlu- impressions are markedly similar to seal impressions of rulers of Eshnunna, who came to power after the fall of Ur III.[51] Balkan supposes, then, that the Ṣilûlu, son of Dakiki, ruled in the years before the Old Assyrian Dynasty filled the power vacuum left by the disappearance of Ur from the Mesopotamian political scene.[52]

Prof. Lewy, for his part, agreed that the Ṣilûlu-seal must have been re-used, but rejected the idea that the son of the city-herald, Dakiki,

46 Cf. K. Balkan, *TTKY*, VII Seri — No. 28, *op. cit.*, 54f., w.n. 51, for the documents upon which the impressions appear.

47 *The best preserved copy of the legend of the Ṣilûlu seal reads:* (1) *A-šùr*[ki] (2) *LUGAL* (3) *Ṣi-lu-lu* (4) *ENSI A-šùr*[ki] (5) *DUMU Da-ki-ki* (6) *NIMGIR.URU A-šùr*[ki] (7) (*blank*). Cf. K. Balkan, *ibid.*, 54-55, w.n. 52-55.

48 Cf. K. Balkan, *ibid.*, 55, and J. Lewy, "On Some Institutions ...", *op. cit.*, 29.

49 Cf. K. Balkan, *ibid.*, 55.

50 Cf. *ibid.*, 55-56.

51 Cf. *ibid.*, 55.

52 Cf. *ibid.*, 55-57.

preceded the establishment of the Old Assyrian Dynasty in time.[53] Rather, he believes that he must have been a contemporary of one of the early Assyrian successors of Puzur-Aššur I. Accordingly, since this *iššiʼakkum* could not have occupied the throne simultaneously with any of the early rulers listed as successive members of the Old Assyrian Dynasty by the Assyrian King List, he must have fulfilled the role of *iššiʼakkum* of Assur somewhere else.[54] "One of Ilušumma's successors", thinks Lewy, "entrusted him with the administration of a conquered country over which he was to rule in the name of Aššur, the divine king".[55] Such a country "is likely to have been Halys Assyria, and ... accordingly, Ṣilûlu can be supposed to have been *iššiʼakkum* at *Kaniš* ...".[56] The full elaboration of this argument appears in Prof. Lewy's reasoning that a certain Ṣilûlu who apparently lived at *Kaniš* during the reign of Sargon I at Assur, and who is styled "son of Uku", used the seal of the older Ṣilûlu, was his grandson, and also was the Assyrian provincial governor of *Kaniš* during the period of Level II.

The basis of this argument is to be found in that the text *ICK* 29 bears the impression of the older Ṣilûlu's seal, while the tablet, which records the sale of two slaves characterized by their names as Assyrian by a certain Uṣuranum to a certain Amur-Šamaš, bears the name of a Ṣilûlu as a witness.[57] Now two unpublished texts recently excavated at Kültepe, and on which the seal impression of the older Ṣilûlu appears (although fragmentarily) begin by mentioning the name of a Ṣilûlu son of Uku.[58] Hence it is proposed that the Ṣilûlu who witnessed the slave sale recorded in *ICK* 29 was this very son of Uku, who came into possession of his earlier namesake's seal, and who therefore used it at the later date.[59]

Prof. Lewy rightly argues that "many an Assyrian of *Kaniš* possessed and used a seal cylinder which he had inherited from his father or grandfather", and also that boys were often given the names of their grandfathers.[60] Thus he permits himself to see in the Ṣilûlu, son of Uku, a grandson of the Ṣilûlu, son of Dakiki, who was an *iššiʼakkum*.[61] But

[53] Cf. "On Some Institutions ...", *op. cit.*, 28-29.

[54] Cf. *ibid.*, 30.

[55] Cf. *ibid.*

[56] Cf. *ibid.*, 31.

[57] The text *ICK* 29 is transliterated by Prof. Lewy, *ibid.*, 24, n. 105 [25].

[58] Cf. kt b/k 27la:1 and kt b/k 683a:1, referred to by K. Balkan, *TTKY*, VII Seri — No. 28, *op. cit.*, 55.

[59] The Ṣilûlu, son of Uku, appearing in the texts cited in the previous note, is doubtless the same as the Ṣilûlu, son of Uku, of *KTS*, 31:5. Cf. also J. Lewy, "On Some Institutions ...", *op. cit.*, 28.

[60] J. Lewy, *ibid.*, 29.

[61] Cf. *ibid.*, 29-30.

beyond this, Prof. Lewy argues that "deals involving the sale of slaves who belonged to the same ethnical element as the dominant population of the country used to be closed before the king's highest local representative ...", and therefore he concludes that the presence of the Ṣilûlu of *ICK* 29 as witness to the sale of Assyrians by a compatriot can only indicate that the Ṣilûlu in question was the *iššiʼakkum* (= *rubâʼum*) of *Kaniš*.[62]

Our critique of this position begins with the observation that although Prof. Lewy has made several pertinent criticisms of Balkan's stylistic analysis of the older Ṣilûlu's seal and hence takes the opportunity to deny that the latter necessarily ruled at Assur before the establishment of the Old Assyrian Dynasty, he does not thereby justify his attribution of Ṣilûlu as a ruler of *Kaniš after* this dynasty came to power in Assyria.[63] For this attribution depends upon: (a) the assumption that Ṣilûlu, son of Dakiki, was in fact the grandfather of Ṣilûlu, son of Uku because some boys at Kültepe are known to have borne their grandfather's names and inherited seals and the like from their forebears; and (b) the further assumption that since the older Ṣilûlu does not appear in the Assyrian King List, nor could he have ruled as an independent *iššiʼakkum* of Assur before Puzur-Aššur I, he must therefore have ruled elsewhere.[64]

As for the alleged family relationship between the older and the younger Ṣilûlus, it must be pointed out that the possibility of it is indeed most tenuous; there is no proof whatsoever that the younger Ṣilûlu benefited in the way described, nor is it any more than convenient to solve the problem by using the relationship to make the older Ṣilûlu a contemporary of one of the successors of Puzur-Aššur I. For it is only by asserting the grandfather-grandson relationship that a place needs to be made for the older man as *iššiʼakkum* somewhere besides Assur. And beyond this it cannot be completely ruled out that the older Ṣilûlu may have been a ruler of Assur between the reigns of Ilušumma and Puzur-Aššur II, and omitted in the King List, despite the objections of Prof. Lewy.[65]

[62] Cf. *ibid.*, 24-25; 31.

[63] The chronological argument which Prof. Lewy uses seems unconvincing. Cf. n. 65 below.

[64] Prof. Lewy offers some interesting technical criticisms of Balkan's epigraphical analysis of the Ṣilûlu-seal impressions in denying that the Ṣilûlu, son of Dakiki, predates the Old Assyrian Dynasty. But these criticisms ("On Some Institutions ...", *op. cit.*, 29, n. 111b) are not less inconclusive as an argument for placing Ṣilûlu after the O. A. Dynasty than Balkan's appear to Prof. Lewy.

[65] On the basis of his acceptance of the information given by the synchronisms of the Babylonian Chronicle, Prof. Lewy finds the period between Ilušuma and Puzur-

Yet these are lesser objections compared to those which must be offered against the interpretation drawn from the circumstances recorded in *ICK* 29. First it is implied that there was an Assyrian ruler at *Kaniš* for essentially circumstantial reasons, and then that the Assyrians were the "dominant population" of Anatolia precisely because such a ruler could be affirmed. But if anything, Prof. Lewy's proposal about the role of high officials in the sale of slaves could also be applied to the non-Assyrian population. For in at least one instance Anatolian slaves are sold by their compatriots under the authority of an indigenous prince, Warpa, and his Chief-of-Citadel, Ḫalgiašu;[66] while in at least two others, court officials of an Anatolian administration supervised similar transactions.[67] And furthermore, it is hardly likely that a deal in which two Assyrians settled a sale-transaction involving their fellow-countrymen required the official notice of the alleged Assyrian *iššiʾakkum* in light of the fact that Assyrians could and did become debt-servitors of Anatolian creditors.[68]

Nor should it be supposed that the name Ṣilûlu is as rare as Prof. Lewy suggests it is. One person bearing this name appears as an ordinary trader, and another is an eponym-official, who must have lived at *Kaniš* during the same time as the alleged *iššiʾakkum* who supposedly bore this name.[69] It seems entirely possible that Ṣilûlu, son of Uku, could have

---

Aššur II too short to accommodate an additional ruler (cf. "On Some Institutions ...", *op. cit.*, 30, n. 111f.). The information derived from Assyrian sources and the King List, on the contrary, provides sufficient possibility of this. As is well-known, the data derived from the Assyrian and from the Babylonian sources are incompatible, so that a choice between the two must be made. On the basis of B. Landsberger's recent studies in "Assyrische königsliste und 'dunkles Zeitalter'", *JCS*, 8 (1954), 31-45; 47-73, with Exkurs 1 and 2, 120-133, it would appear that the Assyrian tradition is essentially sounder than the Babylonian. We do not hereby wish to argue that the Ṣilûlu, son of Dakiki, *ought* to be inserted in the King List, but only that the possibility is still viable. We believe, with Balkan, that Ṣilûlu is anterior to the Old Assyrian Dynasty.

66 Cf. *EL*, 189.

67 Cf. *TC*, III 253 and 254.

68 Cf. the redemption of the Assyrian Anina from the house of the *nuâʾum* in *OIP*, 27, 12.

69 For Prof. Lewy's opinion, cf. "On Some Institutions ...", *op. cit.*, 29, and also 31, n. 111k, where it is stated that "no Selulu is found among the various contemporary caravan-leaders and minor employees known to have continually journeyed from Assur to Cappadocia and back ...". But a trader named Ṣelûlu receives a loan in silver for business in *ICK*, 187: 57, while for the eponym-official of the same name, cf. List A of the eponyms given in Balkan, *TTKY*, VII Seri — No. 28, *op. cit.*, 94, sub. no. 53, to which should now be added *CCT*, V 19a: 7-8; 22b:19-20; 23a:11-12.

A comparison of the names appearing in the published tablets with those of well-

been the eponym-official, who employed the seal of an earlier namesake in official functions as witness or the like. This conclusion still would account for the fact that the younger Ṣilûlu appeared to have friends in high places in *Assur* and *Kaniš*, as proposed by Lewy, but we cannot agree that he was the Assyrian provincial governor of *Kaniš*.[70]

Now in addition to the interpretation of the seal-impressions just discussed, Prof. Lewy has also argued that the texts *OIP*, 27:58 and *CCT*, III, 44b attest the presence of such an official. In the former he has seen a piece of evidence to the effect "that a member of the court at Assur, namely the future king Puzur-Aššur II, sent gifts to the ruler of Halys Assyria".[71] For in this memorandum of a list of goods apparently sent from Assyria to Anatolia appears the mention of "5 garments of Puzur-Aššur, the son of the prince (*rubâ'um*)", and also, "5 veils of clothing, 3 *išratum*, 2/3 minas of copper for (to) the prince".[72] Prof. Lewy interprets that the designation of the veils of clothing, the *išratum* and the copper "for the prince"[73] indicates that they are destined to be delivered to the *rubâ'um* of *Kaniš*. But even should this be feasible (and nothing appears to show that the destination of the shipment is *Kaniš*), we have absolutely no reason to believe that the *rubâ'um* in question is an *Assyrian* official. Indeed, Prof. Lewy refers to the second of our texts, *CCT*, III, 44b, for proof that the prince (of *Kaniš*?) commanded an armed force which was ready to help Assyrian caravans in danger, but (a): all proof that the action of the prince either took place at *Kaniš*, or (b) was the action of an Assyrian official, or (c) that the *rubâ'um* in question dispatched troops, is wanting.[74]

---

known Kanisian traders of Level II, establishes the contemporaneity of the Ṣilûlus cited.

70 Cf. J. Lewy, "On Some Institutions ...", *op. cit.*, 31.

71 Cf. *ibid.*, 35.

72 Cf. *OIP*, 27, 58: Rev. 11. 24-27a. *Išratum* is translated "tithes" by Gelb, *loc. cit.*, 63, but "belts" by Lewy, "On Some Institutions ...", *op. cit.*, 33 and 34, n. 117.

73 Cf. J. Lewy, *ibid.*, 34. The phrase is: *ana rubâ'im* (*OIP*, 27, 58:27a).

74 Cf. *ibid.*, 21-23, w. 21, n. 91f. The text, *CCT*, III, 44b, may be summarized briefly. The Assyrian Asanum, writing to an associate, Anina, who is en route to the former with a shipment of goods, first reminds Anina of a previous instruction he has issued to leave behind (in an unnamed place) ninety of the fine garments he has in his possession. Then he further instructs Anina to leave behind one-hundred, either in the town of Tegarama or in Baradum. He goes on to say (after asking Anina not to cause him any anxiety in the matter): (14) *a-na-kam ru-ba-um* (15) *ú-ma-nam a-na* (16) *pá-ni-ku-nu i-tá-ar-dam*. Prof. Lewy translates this: "here, the prince dispatched troops to meet you", *loc. cit.*, 23, w.n. 100.

One may raise several points about this interpretation. First, does *ú-ma-nam* (1. 15) justify a translation of "troops", especially since Gelb has pointed to this term

THE EVIDENCE FOR ROYAL PERSONAGES AT KANIŠ

If there is no compelling reason to assume the presence of an *Assyrian* ruler at *Kaniš* during the period of Level II, then we may present the evidence for a line of indigenous rulers in the city. This evidence is derived from four texts which attest such rulers without, however, mentioning their names; from two additional texts which mention the palace of *Kaniš* directly; and finally, from several which mention the names of rulers, but whose association with *Kaniš* is a matter of inference rather than certain knowledge.

A. Texts mentioning Kanishean rulers without their names:

(1) One badly damaged tablet, *KTP* 4, mentions a Prince of *Kaniš* certainly (ll. 12-13), and perhaps a second time (l. 26). The tablet is badly broken and yields no clear context, though it seems to be a letter to the *Kârum Kaniš*.[75]

(2) A second tablet, *ATHE* 66, refers to the Kanishean ruler in an interesting diplomatic context. The Assyrian trader, Puzur-Aššur, writing to his colleagues Idi-abum and Kulumaa, mentions that he has heard that messengers have not been freed to travel to *Wašḫania*, hence he will send a report and his trade goods only after he has heard that the rulers of *Kaniš* and of *Waḫšušana* have concluded a treaty guaranteeing the safety of commerce between their realms (ll. 9-14).[76]

---

as a contraction for *ummeânum*, 'creditor"? (cf. *OIP*, 27 [1935], 35, n. to 1. 33 of text no. 15). Second, there is no compelling reason to think that the location of the *rubâ'um* of our text was *Kaniš*, especially since Prof. Lewy, himself, has said that when Asanum was not present at *Kaniš*, he "served his principals as caravan leader and as buyer of goods to be imported from *Assur*" (*loc. cit.*, 21, n. 92). There is no real indication that Asanum was in *Kaniš* when he sent the letter. Third, and most important, there is no indication that the caravan which Anina is conveying is in any sort of danger.

Assyrian caravans frequently sought to conceal their goods in order to avoid paying "lawful" taxes imposed upon them by the various palaces. Yet in his interpretation of *CCT*, III 44b, Prof. Lewy seems to imply that Assyrian traders were willing to be escorted by the alleged royal troops. Even if it be argued that rather than risk losing a valuable shipment they would have preferred to pay the necessary charges that the palace would impose upon them, we cannot understand why the alleged troops would have been dispatched from Kanis to help a caravan which was, at the time of Asanum's writing, so far away. Should we not expect an "endangered" caravan to call for assistance from any of the *kârû* along the way, if the Assyrians had military control of Anatolia? For in that case, troops would not have been based at *Kaniš* exclusively.

[75] Cf. also Bilgiç's restoration of 1. 2 as [*ru-ba-u*]*m Tu!-uḫ-p*[*í-a-ú*]*ma*, *AfO*, 15 (1945-51), p. 36, sub. *Tuḫpia*.

[76] Discussed by B. Kienast, *ATHE*, p. 95, note to 11. 9-13. Cf. H. Hirsch, *WZKM*, 57 (1961), p. 57, and P. Garelli, *AfO*, 20 (1963), p. 169.

(3) According to a third tablet, *ICK* 13, a *rubâtum*, or "princess" is attested at *Kaniš*. The document, a letter from an Assyrian trader to several of his superiors, mentions a debt of grain and silver of a certain Anatolian named Ḫabuala, who is called "the princess's shepherd" [*rêi'um ša rubâtim*, ll. 6-7]. The locale of *Kaniš* as her residence is established by the stipulation that after the fourth year the debt is to yield interest "according to the decree of the city of *Kaniš*".[77]

(4) In *ATHE* 62, a business letter sent by the Assyrians Imdîlum, Ennam-bêlum and Aššur-ṣulûlî to Puzur-Aššur, the writers inform the adressee that the well-known Kanishean entrepreneur, Pûšukîn, had been thrown in jail by a palace administration, and that the princess had written to the [rulers?] of *Luḫuzatia*, *Ḫurama*, *Šalaḫšua* and had also informed "her land" to beware about Assyrian smuggling activities (ll. 28-35 [31-35]). The possibility exists that the princess referred to here is the princess of *Kaniš*, though it is an inference, and not supported by a specific statement in the text.[78]

B. Texts referring to the palace of Kaniš:

(1) The texts which refer to the residence or "palace" of the rulers of *Kaniš* report, on the one hand, that a shipment of goods is to be brought down from the palace in this city after the *nisḫatum*-tax has been paid to the local authorities and then sent on to *Burušḫattum*,[79] and on the other, that an Assyrian trader who is to travel for five months with goods imported from Assur should claim them and take them from the palace of *Kaniš* after their arrival from Assyria.[80]

C. Texts naming rulers who must be thought of as Kanishean:

(1) Two tablets refer to a ruler named Warba/pa, each of them documents of what may be called Anatolian family law.[81] The first is a divorce

[77] Cf. 11. 10-11, and also *TC*, III, 239:10-11.
[78] Cf. P. Garelli, *AfO*, 20 (1963), pp. 168-169.
[79] *ICK*, I, 189:20-rev. 23.
[80] *TC*, III, 213:11-27. Also in *EL*, 247:4f. [= *EL*, 248:4f.], the Palace of *Kaniš* is seen ordering back some Kanishean traders from *Sis/zum*, doubtless present-day Sis.
[81] Cf. *EL*, Nos. 1-11 for examples.

decree, the second a slave sale each involving persons whose names are exclusively Anatolian. Each is notarized by the formula: *iqqâti Warba/pa rubâ'im, Ḫalgiašu rabi simmiltim*, "By the authority [lit., "by/under the hand of"] Warba/pa, the Prince, Halgiašu [being] the "Citadel Chief".[82]

(2) One text, *ICK* 178, dates a loan to an Assyrian trader of *Kaniš* by the phrase: *inûmi Labarša rubâ'utam iṣbutûnî*, "when Labarsa seized the kingdom".[83]

The texts cited above cannot be harmonized to produce a picture of Kanishean royalty which is clear and certain; yet by and large it is possible to build from them a line of reasoning which justifies the conclusion that at *Kaniš* there was a line of autonomous rulers during the period of *Kârum* Level II. From *ATHE* 66 [= A. 2, above], we recognize that the continuation of Assyrian trade depended upon an internal *Anatolian* system of treaty-relations between the powerful city-states of the region. This texts recalls the circumstances of another, *KTHahn* 1, in which the Assyrian trader Idi-Ištar informs his colleague, Assur-nada, that since the kingdoms of *Burušḫattum* and *Waḫšušana* were in unsettled (turbulent) state, he would not go to *Waḫšušana* and could not make disposition of a supply of copper which had been laid up there until he received a report that it was safe for him to do so.[84] From *ATHE* 63:[21-25], a letter written in *Waḫšušana*, we learn of the permission the ruler of that land grants to Kanishean traders to come to *Waḫšušana* with stocks of Zalpaean clothes and Ḫuramaian copper. To these should be added the many texts reporting that either the roads had been "freed" by one ruler or another for trading journeys, or that individuals had been given permission by the officials of one or another kingdom to proceed with their caravans [see Chapters Four and Five, below].

From *ICK* 13 [= A. 3, above], we see that the debt of a minor official of the Princess of *Kaniš's* court is governed by a "decree of the [indigenous] city [administration] of *Kaniš*, and not by the usually-stated "decree of *Kârum Kaniš*", which is invoked for interest-stipulations on loans owed by Assyrians to each other. The concern of the indigenous administration about the affairs of its subjects who entered financial and legal arrangements with the Assyrian traders is clearly documented in other texts [see Chapter Five, below].

[82] *TC*, 122 [*EL*, 3]:x+9 — x+11; *KTP*, 43 [*EL*, 189]:19-22. K. Balkan's attempt to emend the name of Warpa/ba to Waršama [*TTKY*, VII, Seri — No. 31a, pp. 43-46, w. nn. 65-66] is not reasonable [cf. P. Garelli, *Les Assyriens en Cappadoce*, pp. 62-63].

[83] Cf. 11. x+2 — x+5. Further, J. Lewy, *Or ns*, 26 (1957), p. 20, n. 3.

[84] Cf. 11. 1-12.

DURING THE PERIOD OF KÂRUM LEVEL II

EXCURSUS

The hypothesis of this *Excursus* is that it is highly probable that Warpa/ba, the *rubâ'um*, and Halkiašu, his *rabi simmiltim* [*EL*, 3 and 189], were resident at *Kaniš*, and that a number of officials mentioned in the Old Assyrian tablets without reference to place belong to the administration of *Kaniš*. The arguments are prosopographic in character, and for the convenience of the reader we place the involved technical data in the notes.

We mention briefly first that in 1956 Prof. J. Lewy pointed to the strong possibility that the god An(n)a was patron deity of *Kaniš*.[85] Prof. Lewy subsequently modified this opinion,[86] and it is clear that An(n)a is attested both as an Anatolian and a Semitic deity.[87] While it is further true that the texts in which An(n)a is cited fail to mention *Kaniš* (or any other place) as the god's cult-center, they do mention some Assyrian creditors and witnesses, one of whom, Ahatum, does appear to have resided in *Kaniš*.[88] While we need surely not regard An(n)a as *patron deity* of *Kaniš*, it does not strain credulity to regard this god as perhaps *one of a number of cult-deities worshipped there*.[89] We suppose, therefore, that two individuals of *TC*, III, 254 characterized as officials or high-ranking members of an administrative circle: Kuraa, *rabi nappâhî* [Chief Smith], and Tarḫuala, *ahu rabi simmiltim* [brother of the Citadel-Chief], resided in *Kaniš*.[90]

Another official who must have belonged to the Kanishean population is Washuba, *rabi mahîrim* ["Chief of the Market"], who through the appearance of his name on tablets in which the Kanishean native, Enišru, functions in his customary dealings in slaves and money-lending,[91]

[85] Cf. *HUCA*, 27 (1956), pp. 10-11.
[86] Cf. *HUCA*, 32 (1961), pp. 37-38.
[87] Cf. H. Hirsch, *Untersuchungen zur altassyrischen Religion* [*AfO*, Beiheft 13/14 (1961), p. 27, n. 131, and P. Garelli, *Les Assyriens en Cappadoce*, pp. 322-323.
[88] Cf. Hirsch, *op. cit.* for the An(n)a citations. For Ahatum/tim at *Kaniš*, most likely *ICK*, I 12b.
[89] One need not jettison Prof. Lewy's proposal in its entirety. We feel only that An(n)a's status as *Patron Deity* of *Kaniš* need be questioned.
[90] Kuraa: *TC*, III 254:1; Tarḫuala: *ibid*:2. These high-ranking individuals seal a document involving the afore-mentioned Ahatum/tim as a principal in a slave sale. Note also that the debt contracted has a payment date *a-na ša A-na*, "at the [feast-day] of An(n)a", 11. 13-14.
[91] For Enišru [var: Enašru] and his activities in *Kaniš*, cf. J. Lewy, *HUCA*, 27 (1956), p. 8, w.n. 36, and *idem*, *AHDO*, I (1937), p. 96f.

is thereby shown to be a contemporary of the latter at *Kaniš*.[92]

The argument that Warpa/ba the *rubâ'um*, and *Halkiašu*, his *rabi simmiltim* belonged to the Kanishean administration depends upon the validity of a line of reasoning which links a certain Humadašu, whose divorce is the subject of a decree issued by the authorities mentioned above [*TC*, 122 = *EL*, 3], and a man named Šarabunuwa, cited as son of Ḫumadašu in *TC*, 99, and who also appears in a text as debtor to a man who is also cited as a witness to a transaction involving Enišru, the Kanishean. The names of the individuals involved are rare, and the likelihood of the individuals being the same in the texts to be discussed is therefore very high. The group of texts follows:

1. *TC*, 68 [*EL*, 86]: Enišru (creditor), Kigaršan (witness).[93]
2. *CCT*, 8b [*EL*, 64]: Kigaršan (creditor), Šarabunuwa (debtor), Dunumna (witness).[94]
3. *TC*, 99 [EL, 236]: Šarabunuwa, son of Humadašu (debtor).[95]
4. *TC*, 122 [*EL*, 3]: Humadašu, party to his divorce, Warpa/ba, *rubâ'um*, Halkiasu, *rabi simmiltim*, authorities.[96]

The contemporaneity of Kigaršan with Enišru at *Kaniš* is established,[97] therefore Kigaršan with Šarabunuwa, the discovery of whose archive in Level II of *Kârum Kaniš* makes his residence in *Kaniš* certain.[98] Admit-

[92] Two texts, *BIN*, VI 226 and *CCT*, V 26A establish the contemporaneity at *Kaniš* of Enišru and a certain Wašhuba, who bears the *rabi mahîrim* title. In both these documents Enišru is seen in his customary business; in the former he is a witness to a transaction by which Wašḫuba and two other Anatolians receive one-half mina of silver, the price of Šubiaḫšu, from a certain Šakriuman; in the latter, Enišru, himself, purchases a certain Ḫuziri, the transaction itself noting [1. 2] that Wašḫuba, the market chief with (others) affixed his seal. It now appears that the slave-sale recorded in *TC*, III, 253, analyzed by J. Lewy in *AHDO*, I (1937), p. 102f., is to be connected with the above-mentioned *BIN*, VI, 226, since it deals with the completion of the transaction begun in the latter. As in *BIN*, VI, 226, Wašḫuba the *rabi mahîrim* appears, here as a witness (1. 1].

[93] Enišru: 1. 9; *bît*$^{bi\text{-}it}$ *Enišru*, "the House of Enišru", 1. 14. Kigaršan [son of Šubunaḫšu], 1. 1 (seals tablet). In this text an indigenous couple is mentioned as endebted to Enišru [11. 6-10].

[94] Kigaršan, 1. 5; Šarabunuwa, 1. 3; Dunumna, 1. 15. The text is a promissory note registering the debt of Šarabunuwa and a partner, Peruwa, to Kigaršan [11. 1-6].

[95] Cf. 11. 12-13. Šarabunuwa, son of Ḫumadašu, owes a quantity of straw to an unnamed creditor.

[96] Cf. 1. 1, and x+2.

[97] This is seen especially in that *TC*, 68 [*EL*, 86] mentions that if the indigenous debtors fail to pay Enišru their debt at term, they must enter "the House of Enišru". The *Bît Enišru* must have been in *Kaniš*.

[98] Cf. K. Balkan, *Belleten* 82, p. 344, and T. Özgüç, *TTKY*, V, Seri — No. 19, p. xxii for discovery-site at Kültepe.

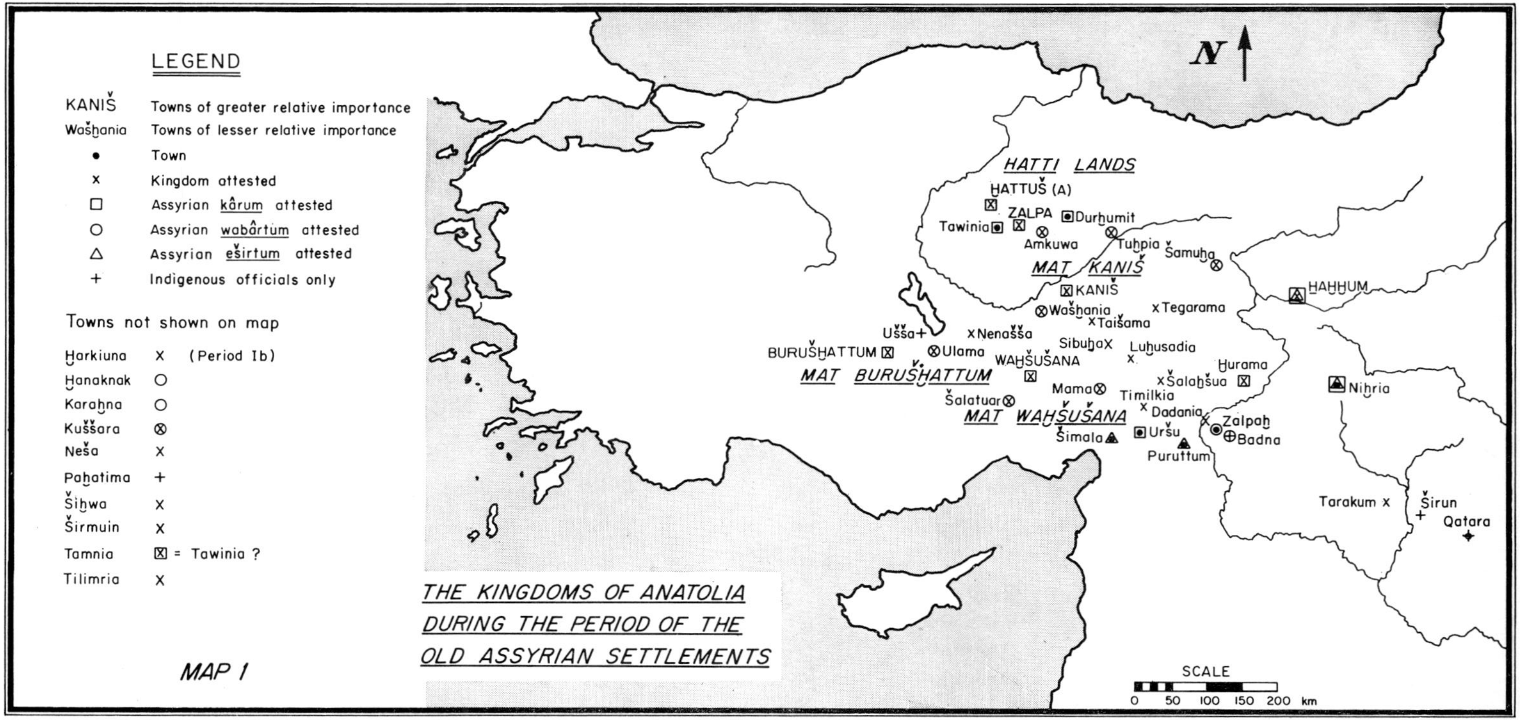

LEGEND
KANIŠ Towns of greater relative importance
Wašḫania Towns of lesser relative importance
• Town
x Kingdom attested
□ Assyrian kârum attested
○ Assyrian wabârtum attested
△ Assyrian ešîrtum attested
+ Indigenous officials only
Towns not shown on map
Ḫarkiuna x (Period Ib)
Ḫanaknak ○
Karaḫna ○
Kuššara ⊗
Neša x
Paḫatima +
Šiḫwa x
Širmuin x
Tamnia ☒ = Tawinia ?
Tilimria x
MAP 1
THE KINGDOMS OF ANATOLIA
DURING THE PERIOD OF THE
OLD ASSYRIAN SETTLEMENTS
N
HATTI LANDS
ḪATTUŠ (A)
ZALPA
Durḫumit
Tawinia
Amkuwa
Tuḫpia
Šamuḫa
MAT KANIŠ
KANIŠ
ḪAḪḪUM
Wašḫania
Taišama
Tegarama
Uššša
Nenašša
Sibuḫa
Luḫusadia
BURUŠḪATTUM
Ulama
WAḪŠUŠANA
Ḫurama
MAT BURUŠḪATTUM
Šalaḫšua
Niḫria
Mama
Timilkia
Šalatuar
MAT WAḪŠUŠANA
Dadania
Zalpaḫ
Šimala
Uršu
Badna
Puruttum
Tarakum
Širun
Qatara
SCALE
0 50 100 150 200 km

tedly the most vulnerable link is the connection between the Ḫumadašu of *TC*, 122 and the man who is cited as Šarabunuwa's father in *TC*, 99. Yet we proceed to make the assumption that they are the same man[99] and that therefore the divorce action authorized by Warpa/ba, Ḫalkiašu being *rabi simmiltim* took place in *Kaniš*.

To proceed further, *CCT*, 8b [*EL*, 64], listed above, cites a certain Dunumna as a witness. He is probably the same man who appears as a witness also in Chantre 2 [*EL*, 219][100], a text which attests three individuals bearing official titles: Aludḫuḫarša, *rabi E-zi*;[101] Šulia, *rabi paššure*;[102] and Kulakula, *rabi alpâtim*.[103] These men are witnesses, as is, among several others, a man named *Luḫraḫšu*.[104] The citation of Dunumna on this tablet, considering the rarity of this name in the Cappadocian onomastica, strongly suggests that the individuals mentioned in context with him are Kanisheans, therefore officials of the Kanishean administration. Support for this appears to be given if we note that on a third text, *KTHahn* 28, which can be strongly argued to emanate from *Kaniš*, a man named Luḫrahšu appears [as the father of an Anatolian named Ašid].[105]

To sum up to this point, we believe it possible to affirm that:

1. Warpa/ba, *rubâ'um*
2. Ḫalkiašu, *rabi simmiltim*
3. Wašḫuba, *rabi mahîrim*
4. Aludḫuḫarša, *rabi E-zi*
5. Šulia, *rabi paššure*
6. Kulakula, *rabi alpâtim*

are residents of *Kaniš*. If the preceding arguments are valid, these officials also belong to the same milieu of individuals having business dealings to which they are party or witnesses.

Other Anatolians who must be counted as residents of *Kaniš* during the same period and in the same milieu are Ušḫuba [= Wašḫuba], son of a man named Ḫalkiašu, and Abeziašu, also cited as the son of a Ḫalkiašu.[106] The former appears in *KTHahn*, 28, already noted as a

[99] The identification cannot be more than a suggestion now. New evidence of texts in which he may appear, future prosopographic studies of relationships of individuals with whom he is associated in presently-known tablets, must eventually be relied upon beyond the connection cited in the text above.

[100] Cf. 1. 15.

[101] Cf. 11. 17-18. For this title see now Garelli, *Les Assyriens en Cappadoce*, pp. 216-217, w.n. 1 [217].

[102] Cf. 11. 19-20; *ibid*, 216.

[103] Cf. 11. 21-22; *ibid.*

[104] Cf. 11. 14.

[105] Cf. A:4; B:6, 10, 13-14, 21-22.

[106] For Ušḫuba, son of Ḫalkiašu, *KTHahn*, 28A:3, 6, 12; B:5, 9, 12-13, 20-21. For Abeziašu, son of Ḫalkiašu, *TC*, III, 252:1.

Kanishean tablet [cf. n. 19a], the latter in *TC*, III, 252, where he seals (with others) a record of a slave sale involving Enišru, the Kanishean entrepreneur.[107] A third individual cited as son of a Ḫalkiašu is Tamuria, in *ICK*, I, 129, whose origin as a Kanishean tablet is assured by the presence of a well-known Assyrian trader's name as witness.[108] All that can be asserted from the above is that one, two or three men bearing the name Halkiašu, are attested as having sons during the Period of Level II at *Kârum Kaniš*. We do not dare to assert that such are all sons of the same man. Yet it is interesting to recall that a Wašḫuba, *rabi mahîrim*, as well as Abeziašu (no title), seal documents of slave sales among the Anatolians of *Kaniš* as witnesses, and also to recall that indigenous administrations and officials usually functioned in these matters involving natives. Is it possible that the Ušḫuba, son of Ḫalkiašu in *KTHahn* 28, and the Wašḫuba, *rabi mahîrim*, are the same person? And that Ḫalkiašu, Warpa/ba's *rabi simmiltim*, is his father? Also that Abeziašu is a brother to Wašḫuba and a son to the *rabi simmiltim*? Similarly, can we now think of Tarhuala, "brother of the *rabi simmiltim*" in *TC*, III, 254 as brother of Halkiasu, *rabi simmiltim*, and also of Kuraa, the *rabi nappâhî* of *TC*, III, 254, as belonging to Warpa/ba's administration?[109]

If we may reasonably assume the existence of *rubâ'um* Warpa/ba at *Kaniš* during the time of Enišru and his contemporaries, we are justified in asking whether the *rubâtum* mentioned in *ICK*, I, 13 may have any association to him. That *ICK*, I, 13 belongs to the Kanishean milieu of Pûšukîn's time is affirmed by the names of the Assyrian traders cited in it.[110] The same is true of Gol. 11 [*EL*, 188], where the Assyrian Itur-ili and his son, Ḫanu [relationship established by comparison with *CCT*, 49a [*EL*, 249]:2] are principals in a transaction where an Anatolian's outstanding debt is arranged to be paid through the personal intervention of an unnamed *rubâ'um* and *rubâtum*.[111] An official named Šubunahšu,

[107] Cf. 11. 6-10, 15-17.

[108] For Tamuria, son of Ḫalkiašu, cf. 11. 3-4; the Assyrian witness, Uṣur-ša-Aššur, son of Dan-Aššur, 11, 19-20. Further support comes from the reference to Šadaḫšu, son of Šaktunuwa, as a creditor along with Tamuria and Enišru, son of Kunzat [II. 2-3]. The discovery of Šaktunuwa's archive in the *Kârum Kaniš* is cited in Balkan, *TTKY*, VII, Seri — No. 28, p. 61, and *Belleten* 76, p. 453. See further *TTKY*, V, Seri — No. 19, p. xxii.

[109] Other individuals who very probably lived in *Kaniš* during the same period and belonged to the official milieu are: Ḫabu(w)ašu, *rabi ṣabim* ["General"]: *CCT*, II, 30:9-10, and Nakilid, *rabi šarîqî* ["Chief of the temple-slaves"]: *LC*, 242 [*EL*, 5]:5; the discussion is reserved for a future article.

[110] Inaa: 1. 1; Aššur-taklaku, 1. 2.

[111] Cf. 11. 1-4 [3].

titled *rabi alaḫḫinim ša rabi sikkitim*,[112] agrees to pay half the debt to Itur-ili in two installments, while for the remainder of it, Šubunahšu obligates the original Anatolian debtor and his family to Itur-ili's son, Ḫanu.[113] Through a comparison of several documents, it seems abundantly clear that Itur-ili and his son, Ḫanu, were residents of *Kaniš* during the same period as the traders of *ICK*, I, 13 mentioned in n. 24, and therefore quite likely during the time of the *rubâtum* of *ICK*, I, 13.[114] If the texts *ICK*, I, 13 and Gol. 11 [*EL*, 188] are established for the same general milieu of trading activity at *Kaniš*, the conclusion seems warranted that the *rubâtum* of the one and the *rubâtum* of the other were perhaps the same person, even that the unnamed *rubâ'um* may have been Warpa/ba.[115]

112 Cf. 11. 6-7, w. 8-14.

113 Cf. 11. 15-18f.

114 For Itur-ili and Ḫanu as residents of *Kaniš* and in the same period as Inaa and Aššur-taklaku, compare the texts *CCT*, 49a [*EL*, 249]: 2 and rev. x+2; *TC*, 82 [*EL*, 250]:17, 22 and 27; and *CCT*, 4 [*EL*, 225]:36-37 + 42-43.

115 Further, the unnamed *rabi simmiltim* of Gol. 11 [*EL*, 188]: 23, may be Ḫalkiašu.

IV

INDICATIONS OF DIPLOMATIC RELATIONSHIPS BETWEEN ASSYRIANS AND ANATOLIANS

Whereas many of the cuneiform tablet funds excavated from ancient Near Eastern sites amply document the political and diplomatic conditions of the time in which they were written, the Cappadocian fund, by contrast, is singularly poor in this respect. There are no official documents, properly speaking — no treaties or royal edicts, no annals or chronicles. On the other hand, from the many reports to be found in the business documents and letters emanating from Kültepe and Alişar Hüyük, it is possible to put together a comprehensive picture of the political contacts which existed between the Assyrian settlements and the Anatolian rulers during the Cappadocian period in central Anatolia.

We may begin by treating two letters which give information about diplomatic encounters between Assyrians and particular indigenous princes. The first, *KTP* 14, belongs to the environment of Level II at Kültepe, while the second, kt f/k 183, is contemporary with Level Ib at the same site. Although each letter has been transliterated and translated elsewhere, it will be convenient to reproduce them again as we come to discuss their implications.

KTP 14[1]

(1) *[a]-na ši-i[p-ri ša a-lim*^{ki}*]* (2) *ú kà-ri-[im Kà-ni-iš]* (3) *[q]í-bi-ma um-ma kà-ru-[um]* (4) *[W]a-aḫ-šu-ša-na-ma* (5) *[r]u-ba-um ša Wa-ás-ḫa-n[i]-a* (6) *[iš]-pu-ra-am um-ma šu-ut-ma* (7) *[ku-sí]-a-am ša a-bi*$_4$*-a* (8) *[aṣ]-ba-at ma-mì-tám*(!) (9) *[ta]-mì-a-ni um-ma ni-nu-[ma]* (10) *[kà]-ru-um Kà-ni-iš* (11) *[be-lu]-ni*[2] *ni-ša-pár* (12) *[šu-nu] ú-ul a ṣé-ri-[kà]* (13) *[i-š]a-pu-ru-nim* (14) *[ú-ul a ṣé]-ri-ni* (15) *[i-š]a-pu-ru-[ni]m* (16) *[š]í-na ša [m]a-ti[m]* (17)

[1] The text-copy appears in *JSOR*, 11 (1927), 119. It was studied by B. Landsberger, *TTAED*, 4 (1940), 26f., and J. Lewy, "On Some Institutions ...", *op. cit.*, 18-20. The transliteration and translation here presented is Lewy's, *loc. cit.*

[2] Cf. Lewy, "On Some Institutions ...", *op. cit.*, 18, w.n. 74.

of commerce and legal disputes arising therefrom, but here its control over what may be called "international" negotiation on the part of its subsidiary corporations is manifest. Nor can it be denied that the interests of the Assyrian government at Assur in such negotiation is reflected in the participation of the *šipru ša âlim*^{ki}, who act in coordination with the Assembly of *Kaniš*.

This being granted, we may further observe that the Prince of *Wašḫania* voluntarily requested to be sworn to an oath upon becoming the ruler of his town. It is he who originates the request (cf. ll. 5-9), and we may therefore infer that it was a normal procedure for a newly-acceded prince to enter into some type of formal oath-agreement with the Assyrian corporations. *We must stress that we have no information from the text itself about what kind of oath the Prince of Wašhania expects to take.* This is an all-important consideration because of the temptation to assume *a priori* that the oath is one binding the prince to vassalage merely because the Assyrians are invited *to administer it.* Professor Lewy rightly points out that the phrase *mâmîtam tammu'um* — the verb having factitive force — means "to make someone swear an oath".[15] However, he also understands this to mean, "to make someone swear an oath *of allegiance*" (my italics).[16] The basis for this interpretation as applied to the circumstance in *KTP* 14, the letter under discussion, he finds in certain texts of Tukulti-Ninurta I and Tiglath-Pileser I — Assyrian conquerors of a later period — which use similar phraseology to report that the kings in question were placing an oath of servitude on the heads of conquered princes. However we must guard against applying insights gained from the study of texts belonging to different periods to the situation reflected in *KTP* 14, which was written many centuries earlier than those mentioned above, especially since we wish to discover from a study of *KTP* 14 and other relevant documents precisely what the political situation during the Cappadocian period may have been. We know that Tukulti-Ninurta I and Tiglath-Pileser I scored military and political successes, and therefore we may define the oaths they administered to conquered victims, but in the absence of any evidence that the Old Assyrian kings conquered Anatolia, we must rather reserve judgement on the meaning of the oath in question.

This is all the more important when we consider that the desire of newly-acceded kings to renew oath-relationships concluded by their

[15] This was first stated by Fr. Thureau-Dangin in "Notes assyriologiques", *RA*, 24 (1927), 83, and cited by Lewy, "On Some Institutions ...", *op. cit.*, 17, n. 73.
[16] Cf. Lewy, "On Some Institutions ...", *op. cit.*, 19, n. 78.

predecessors is well-documented in ancient Near Eastern history, especially during the Hittite Empire Period in Central Anatolia. It is noteworthy, to be sure, that in circumstances involving the great king of the Hittites, the oath-agreement is considered to be offered by him *to* vassals *or allies*, and that such agreements had to be renewed with individual princes each time a new one succeeded to the throne, whereas our *KTP* 14 merely suggests the possibility that the Assyrians are following this practice with the Prince of *Wašḫania*.[17] Nor can another possibility inherent in the situation be overlooked — namely, that this prince had status other than that of a vassal *vis à vis* the Assyrians. Should he have been an *ally* of the Assyrians he might still have legitimately expected to renew agreements continuing that arrangement. However this point must be reserved for later discussion. We reiterate simply that *KTP*, 14 establishes a firm basis for the belief that relations between the Assyrians and individual princes were formal, based on oaths, and were of such a kind as to require confirmation of the highest Assyrian authorities of *Kaniš* and Assur — at least in the instance of the Wašḫanian prince.

Quite fortunately, we have for examination the contents of another Cappadocian letter reporting a diplomatic encounter between Assyrian envoys of *Kârum Durḫumit* and the Prince of *Tamnia*, although the missive itself is sent to *Kârum Kaniš* by the *Kârum* of Tamnia. The text, catalogued as kt f/k 183 by the excavators of Kültepe, where it was found, reads as follows:

kt f/k 183[18]

(1) *a-na kà-ri-im* (2) *Kà-ni-iš qí-bi-ma* (3) *um-ma kà-ru-um* (4) *Ta-am-ni-a-ma* (5) *ší-ip-ru-ú ša kà-ri-im* (6) *Tur*$_4$*-ḫu-mi-it* (7) *a-na ru-ba-im ša Ta-am-ni-a* (8) *a-na ta-mu-im* (9) *ir-ba-am*[19] *ub-lu-ni-šu-ma* (10) *um-ma*

[17] Cf. J. Pirenne, "La politique d'expansion hittite envisagée à travers les traités de vassalité et de protectorat", *ArOr*, 18, 1/2 (1950), 373-382 (381).

[18] This tablet was discovered in 1954 in Level Ib. A text-copy of this important document remains to be published. A transliteration and translation of its contents appears in K. Balkan, *TTKY*, VII, Seri — No. 28 (1955), 72, n. 14 (73-74), and J. Lewy has included Balkan's transliteration in his "Apropos of a Recent Study ...", *op. cit.*, 27, n.l. The translation offered here is that of Balkan, *loc. cit.*, with appropriate comments.

[19] Lewy makes the logical assumption that an *irbum* is to be rendered "gift for admittance", to a royal personage (from *erâbum*, "to enter", *loc. cit.*, 28, n. 2. Balkan, *loc. cit.*, 74, note to 1. 9, translates "present", and rightly distinguishes between it and a commercial tax).

For examples of the giving of an *irbum* to Anatolian princes cf. the following: to the Prince of *Zalpa*, *TC*, III, 85: 6-7; the Prince of *Tuḫpia*, *TC*, 39:4f.; the prince of

šu-ut-ma a-na (11) *ší-ip-ri-ma* (12) *a-li ší-ip-ru* (13) *ša a-ba-e-a* (14) *ša kà-ri-im Ka-ni-iš* (15) *šu-nu li-li-ku-nim-ma* (16) *iš-tí-šu-nu* (17) *ma-mì-tám a-lá-qí-ma* (18) *ú-ma-zà-aḫ-ni-a-tí-ma* (19) *um-ma šu-ut-ma* (20) *a-lá-am e-pá-áš* ... (26) *ir-ba-am ni-ší-šu-um* (27) *ú-za-ku-nu ni-ip-tí* (28) *a-li-kam e ú-ma-zi-ḫu.*

"(1) To the *Kârum* (2) *Kaniš* speak: (3) Thus (said) the *Kârum* (4) *Tamnia:* '(5) The envoys of the *Kârum* (6) *Durḫumit* (went up) (7) to the Prince of Tamnia (8) for swearing. (9) They brought him a gift, and (10) thus (said) he to (11) the envoys: '(12) Where (are) the envoys (13) of my fathers (14) of the *Kârum Kaniš*?[20] (15) Let them come to me and (16) from them (17) I shall take an oath.'[21] '(18) He insults (?)[22] us, and (19) thus (said) he (further): '(20) I shall build a city ...'[23] ... (26) We carried up to him a gift. (27) We have opened your ear.[24] (28) Let them not insult (?) the messenger'".

A preliminary comparison of this text with *KTP*, 14, previously discussed reveals several important differences between the two. Just as the Prince of *Wašḫania* in the preceding text appears to have ignored the *wabârtum* in his own town in favor of contacting the *Kârum Wahšušana*, the Prince of *Tamnia* similarly is seen not to have dealings with the *Kârum Tamnia,* but with envoys (*šiprû*) of *Kârum Durḫumit; Kârum Tamnia* is simply acting as a reporter of the incident to *Kârum Kaniš.* Beyond this, our text reveals that it is the Assyrian envoys who gain an audience with the Tamnian prince, whereas in *KTP*, 14, the Prince of *Wašḫania* originates the contact. Furthermore, *Kârum Tamnia* addresses its letter to *Kârum Kaniš* alone, and not also to the Envoys of the City. There are further differences, to be sure, but we must stop for the moment to consider the circumstances just mentioned.

While the precise location of *Tamnia* (var: ?*Tawinia*) is unknown, it appears to have been situated in the close vicinity of Boğazköy, Old Assyrian *Hattuš*, wherein an Assyrian *kârum* was located.[25] In the same

Mama, BIN, IV, 201:1-9. Also cf., e.g., *CCT*, IV, 1b:7f., *OIP*, 27, 23: x +8f., etc., for the mention of an *irbum* without the recipient being named. The *irbum* should perhaps be distinguished from the kinds of payments ("bakhshish"?) which the Assyrian caravaners made to the local princes and their officials as they passed from town to town (cf., e.g., *TC*, III, 165; 166, etc.).

20 Cf. n. 31 and 32, below.

21 Cf. n. 35 through 37, below.

22 Cf. n. 38 and 39, below.

23 Cf. n. 40 and 41, below.

24 I.e., "we have informed you."

25 On the location of *Tamnia*/*Tawinia* cf. Chapter One, w.n. 44, above.

general region, the Kizil Irmak (*Halys*) Basin, but further to the East, lay *Durḫumit*.[26] Since both *Tamnia/Tawinia* and *Durḫumit* were seats of Assyrian *kârû*, we have a situation in which the members of one important Assyrian settlement come to negotiate with a prince of a town wherein was established an Assyrian settlement of equal rank. Furthermore, although in *KTP*, 14, the prince of *Wašḫania* was informed by *Kârum Waḫšušana* that *Kârum Kaniš* alone had charge of a diplomatic negtiation involving an oath, kt f/k 183 reports that the envoys of a subordinate *kârum* (*Durḫumit*), were quite ready to enter into an oath ceremony with the Prince of *Tamnia*. Finally, *Kârum Tamnia* reports to *Kârum Kaniš* in such a way as to suggest that nothing was amiss in the original arrangement until the prince objected.[27]

Professor Lewy has characterized the resemblances between the two texts under consideration as follows: "... *KTP*, 14 and kt f/k 183 resemble each other in two respects only; either text relates to the question as to who has the power to administer an oath to the prince of an Anatolian town, and in either text one of the parties concerned implies that only representatives of the authorities in Kaniš have this power".[28] However, we believe this view over-simplifies the state of affairs observable in kt f/k 183 since it tacitly assumes that the Prince of Tamnia is to be the *recipient* of the oath in question. A detailed examination of the contents is in order.

Our first observation is that the envoys from *Kârum Durḫumit* show the Tamnian prince the respect due his station by bringing him a gift, or *irbum*, which is a usual gesture Assyrians made when they sought an audience with an indigenous prince.[29] The text goes on to reveal the purpose of the visit — the Assyrians expected to participate in an oath-ceremony. The phrase, *a-na ta-mu-im*[30] says nothing about who is to administer an oath or who is to be sworn. The Prince, however, is dissatisfied with the envoys who have come up to him, and requests that others come instead.

At this point several cruxes require discussion. The first part of the speech made by the prince to the envoys — "Where (are) the envoys of my fathers of the *Kârum Kaniš*?" (ll. 12-14) — has been interpreted in two radically different ways. Kemal Balkan, who first presented a transliteration and translation of the text, understands this to mean:

[26] On the location of *Durḫumit*, *ibid.*, w.n. 48.
[27] Cf. 11. 10-17.
[28] Cf. J. Lewy, "Apropos of a Recent Study ...", *op. cit.*, 27.
[29] On *irbum*, cf. n. 19, above.
[30] Cf. 1. 8.

"Where are the messengers of the *Kârum Kaniš* who came to the previous kings, my fathers?"[31] Professor Lewy understands: "Where are the envoys of *my superiors* — (my italics) — of the *Kârum Kaniš*?"[32] In point of fact, there are important reasons underlying each interpretation. For Balkan's interpretation the recollection that newly-acceded kings had to renew oaths previously concluded by their predecessors is of great pertinence.[33] It would be entirely relevant that the Prince of *Tamnia* appeal to a practice under which his ancestors concluded agreements with *Kârum Kaniš* when faced with envoys of what he obviously might have considered an inferior negotiating body — the *Kârum Durḫumit*. In its turn, Lewy's interpretation finds a reasonable authority in the fact that very frequently the term *abu*, or "father", in the Cappadocian texts means "superior", as, for instance, when an Assyrian trader addresses his employer in requesting favors and the like.[34] On this point, therefore, nothing can be asserted dogmatically for either view. It is true, however, that whichever interpretation be accepted, the status of *Kârum Kaniš* as the legitimate sender of diplomatic envoys is affirmed.

But granting this, one does not also automatically grant that the Assyrians are necessarily the *administrators* of an oath to the Prince of *Tamnia* in the letter under examination. The second part of the prince's remarks to the envoys of *Durḫumit* therefore requires comment in its own right. We see that the prince desires that envoys from Kaniš come to him so that, in his words: (16) *iš-tí-šu-nu* (17) *ma-mì-tám a-lá-qí*, "(16) from them (17) I shall take an oath". Balkan interprets this to mean: "I will bind them also (sic) to myself by an oath".[35] Lewy interprets this to say, in effect, "I am willing to accept the oath from X" and translates, "... they shall administer the oath to me".[36] In light of the evidence Lewy has cited for the meaning of the idiom in question,[37] we are persuaded that the Prince of Tamnia was willing to enter an oath-relationship with envoys from *Kârum Kaniš*, yet *this is not to say anything about the kind of oath which is involved, or the circumstances which surround the oath-taking ceremony.* For a consideration of lines 18 through 28 of the text seems to allow a conclusion that the Prince of Tamnia, far from

[31] Cf. K. Balkan, *TTKY*, VII, Seri — No. 28, *op. cit.*, 74 (n. to 1.12 of kt f/k 183).

[32] Cf. J. Lewy, "Apropos of a Recent Study ...", *op. cit.*, 28, w.n. 4.

[33] For this practice during the period of the Hittite Empire in Anatolia cf. the remarks of A. Goetze, *Kleinasien* (1957), *op. cit.*, 98f.

[34] Cf. the references given in n. 32, above.

[35] Cf. K. Balkan, *TTKY*, VII Seri — No. 28 *op. cit.*, 74 (n. to 1.17 of kt f/k 183).

[36] Cf. J. Lewy, "Apropos of a Recent Study ...", *op. cit.*, 28, w.n. 5.

[37] Cf. *Ibid.*

being a weak and subservient "vassal", was in fact confident enough to act defiantly, even aggressively, toward the Assyrians. This follows from a consideration of the implied meaning of the verb in lines 18 and 28, and of the expression *a-lá-am e-pá-áš* in line 20.

Since the Old Assyrian syllabary does not distinguish between voiced and voiceless consonants, it is not possible to know whether the verb in lines 18 and 28, which appears with its pronominal suffix as *ú-ma-zà-aḫ-ni-a-tí-ma* in Balkan's transliteration, should be read as the II 1 form of *mazâ'um*, or of *masâḫum*. Balkan translates: "to squeeze juice from" (*mazâ'um*), and interprets that the Prince of *Tamnia* "squeezes" the Assyrians for presents (l. 18), and further that in line 28 the Assyrians of *Kârum Tamnia* are requesting their colleagues at *Kârum Kaniš* to be alert so that the Tamnian prince "not squeeze" the messenger who will be sent out from *Kaniš* to *Tamnia* for presents.[38] Lewy, in contrast, translates the verb: "to disregard" or "to insult (a person)" (*masâḫum*), and accordingly interprets that the prince "insults" the Assyrians, etc.[39]

Even though this difference of interpretation exists, it seems clear that the Prince of *Tamnia* is acting haughtily or contemptuously toward the Assyrians, whichever translation is adopted. This is all the more apparent in the statement of the prince: *a-lá-am e-pá-áš*, "I shall build a city (l. 20)". Balkan interprets this to mean that the Prince of Tamnia "intended to build a fortified town, probably to protect the merchants".[40] But the criticisms of this interpretation by Lewy deserve consideration. In speaking of the idiom in question he asserts:

> ... we do not doubt that it describes the prince's intention to refuse allegiance to the Assyrian magistrates of Kaniš. For there is ample evidence from various periods of Ancient Oriental history (1) that, when used in respect to a town already in existence, "to build" signifies "to consolidate" (the town), "to erect fortifications", (2) that the building of fortifications used to be one of the first actions of potentates who were about to rise against their overlords or had just done so and (3) that the overlords saw in the unauthorized construction of fortifications by a vassal an unmistakable sign of rebellion. Consequently, we learn from *kt f k 183* that even during the "late period" of "Kültepe I b" the Assyrian population of Central Anatolia claimed for themselves the traditional right to demand of "native" rulers an oath of allegiance and that they met with difficulties when trying to assert this right.[41]

Professor Lewy is certainly right in questioning whether a prince who "squeezed" presents from the Assyrians (cf. Balkan's reading of *mazâ'um*,

[38] Cf. K. Balkan, *TTKY*, VII, Seri — No. 28, *op. cit.*, 74 (n. to 1.18 of kt f/k 183).
[39] Cf. J. Lewy, "Apropos of a Recent Study ...", *op. cit.*, 29, w.n. 1.
[40] Cf. K. Balkan, *TTKY*, VII, Seri — No. 28, *op. cit.*, 74 (n. to 1.20 of kt f/k 183).
[41] Cf. J. Lewy, "Apropos of a Recent Study ...", *op. cit.*, 30-31, w.n. 2-5.

cited above) would be eager to build for them a fortified town, and his remarks about the implications of "fortifying a town" appear to be justified. Yet we must argue that the meaning of the idiom *âlam epâšum* in the Cappadocian tablets is entirely uncertain. To our knowledge its appearance in *kt k/f 183* is unique, and in light of other texts which appear to show that the indigenous princes were capable of a great deal of individual action *vis à vis* the Assyrians and which will be discussed in this and later chapters, we must hold in abeyance any judgement on this point.

We may, however, make a preliminary summation of the implications yielded by *KTP* 14 and *kt f/k 183*. The former, we saw, depicted a situation in which the Prince of *Waḫšušana* desired to be sworn to an oath of unspecified nature by representatives of the Assyrians. We learned here that *Kârum Kaniš* and the *šiprû ša âlim*^{ki} were expected by the *Kârum Waḫšušana* to send properly authorized envoys to participate in the oath-ceremony. In *kt f/k 183* the Prince of *Tamnia* refused to participate in an oath-ceremony unless envoys from *Kârum Kaniš* appeared to participate. As in *KTP* 14, the nature and the contents of the oath are unknown. There can be no doubt on the basis of these texts that formal oath-relationships between the Assyrians and the Anatolian princes existed, but before we can conclude anything about the types of oaths involved, we must make a detailed examination of a series of texts which seem to shed more light on the subject. The texts in question all belong to the period of Level II at Kültepe, the period which witnessed the most flourishing activity of Assyrian enterprise in Anatolia.

The first of these texts to be discussed is the letter *CCT*, IV, 30a, which reports an encounter between a party of Assyrians at *Ḫaḫḫum* and the rulers of that city. The letter reads as follows:

CCT IV 30a

(1) *a-na I-na-a qi-bi-ma* (2) *um-ma E-la-ni-ma iš-tù* (3) *a-li-kà-ni I-dí-ku-bu-um* (4) *ù ella-*(*ILLAT*)*-sú eširtum* (*U*)^{tum} *ša Ḫa-ḫi-im* (5) *ù a-na-ku a-na êkallim* (*E.GAL*)^{lim} (6) *ni-ta-na-li-ma ru-ba-ú* (7) *ki-ma i-ta-pu-lim i-ta-na-*[*pu*]*-lu-ni-a-tí* (8) *a-ma me-eḫ-ra-at* (9) *ma-mì-tim ša* [*ú*]-[*bi*]*-lu-ni-a-tí-ni* (10) *a-na kà-ri-im lá-pu-ta-nim* (11) *ù ší-*[*pá-ar*]*-ni im-*gu_5*-ur-šu-nu-ma* (12) *a-wi-lu-ú i-ta-ba-al-ku-tù* (13) ⌈*šarrum*⌉[42] *da-me e-ta-pá-áš-ma* (14) *ku-sí-šu lá ta-aq-na-at* (15) *ší-ik-na-tum a-ḫu-ra* (16) [*ru*]*-ba-ú i-na ba-ri-šu-nu* (17) [*i*]*-ta-ṭù-lu a-bi a-ta* (18) *be-li a-ta ki-ma* (19) *ṭuppam*$^{pá\text{-}am}$

[42] So, though with some question, according to Sidney Smith's copy.

kà-ru-um (20) *iš-me-ú-ni mu-ḫu-ur-šu* (21) *té-ir-tí kà-ri-im* (22) *ù té-ir-ta-kà li-li-kam-ma* (23) *lá tal-kam a-ma-kam-ma* (24) *ta-ta-wa* [...]-*ma a-dá-šu* (?) (25) *e-lá*-[......]-*id* (26) *a-na-ku a-na* [...]-*šu-a*(?) (27) *ù a-dì* u_4-[*me-im a*]-[*ni-im*(?)] (28) *na-ak-zu-tí-a* [...] (29) *a-ni-tám aḫ*-[*ta*]-*aḫ*-[bi_4-...] (30) *a-ta a-lá-nu*(?)-*kà ma*-[...] (31) *i-šu* u_4-*me-e ma-ší*-[*el*(?)] (32) *a-ta-ša-ab a-na kà-ri*-[*im*] (33) *i-ḫi-id-ma lá ma-ku*(?) [...] (34) *lá tal-kam-ma* ... (rest [6 *lines*] *illegible*).

"(1) To Inaa speak: (2) Thus (said) Elani: 'When (3) I came here Idi-Kubum (4) and his colleagues, the 'Ten-Man Committee' of *Ḫaḫḫum* (5) and I (6) continually kept going up (5) to the palace. (6) The princes (7) in place of (directly) answering, repeatedly answered us (evasively?)[43] (8) Here is a copy (9) of the oath which they [brou]ght us (10) for writing down (registry?) in the *kârum* (11) and (concerning which) our envoy gave them satisfaction![44] For (12) the citizens have revolted.[45] [The

[43] This translation follows the sense of that offered for *CCT*, IV, 30a:3b-7, in *CAD*, IV (1958), 119b (*sub. elû*, 1c). It is not likely that the verb of 1.7 is *napâlum*, "to make a compensatory (or equivalence) payment", rather than *apâlum*, "to answer", though this remains, nevertheless, a slight possibility.

[44] The meaning of 11. 8-11 is not completely clear. Alternative translations and interpretations include:

(a): "Here (i.e., in the palace of *Ḫaḫḫum*) is a copy of the oath ...", etc. (11. 8-9).

(b): "Herewith (i.e., 'included with this letter for delivery to *Kanis*') is a copy of the oath ...", etc., (*ibid.*).

(c): The restoration of [*ú*]-[*bi*]-*lu-ni-a-tí-ni* (1.9) is based on clear traces of the *bi* sign in Smith's copy, contra Balkan, *TTKY*, VII, Seri — No. 31a, p. 26; cf. Garelli, *Les Assyriens en Cappadoce*, p. 349, n. 6, for report of his collation, which supports our reading.

(d): Line 10 may perhaps also be translated, "on (matters) touching on the *kârum*". But since *lapâtum* is used so often in the Cappadocian texts to mean "to write down, register, book (an account)" in a *Bît Kârim* or other fiscal agency, we interpret from its appearance in our text that an oath, which had been concluded between the rulers of *Ḫaḫḫum* and *Kârum Kaniš* was sent by the former to be deposited in the document file of the latter, a copy having been retained in the palace of *Ḫaḫḫum*. Continued excavation of Kültepe-Kaniš may indeed uncover just such types of oath-documents.

(e): The restoration of 1.11 depends upon the fact that the *šiprû*, or "envoys" of *Kârum Kaniš* or other Assyrian settlements, usually made diplomatic contacts with local Anatolian rulers. Cf. especially the texts *KTP*, 14 and kt f/k 183 in the present chapter. The reading *ší*-[*pá-ar*]-*ni*, "our envoy", is in harmony with the singular aspect of the verb *magâru*. Of the latter, while "to be willing, to favor, to satisfy", is the usual meaning, *magâru* may perhaps also mean here "to come to an agreement with", as in *OIP*, XXVII, 49A:17, B:16, discussed by J. Lewy, "Old Assyrian Documents ... II", *op. cit.*, 131, n. 6. Indeed, our context seems to require this coloring.

Balkan reads: (11) *ù ší*-[*k*]*i*-[*tám*] *nimguršunûma*, and translates: "But upon a ... we agreed with them, ..." [*TTKY*, VII, Seri — No. 19a, p. 26.

Garelli reads: (11) *ù ší*-[*ki-tám*] *ni-im-gu*$_5$-*ur-šu-nu-ma*, and translates: "et nous nous sommes entendus avec eux (sur) les dis[positions] (?);" [*Les Assyriens en Cappadoce*, p. 350, n. 1 with p. 349, n. 7].

king] has spilled blood and (14) his throne (i.e., reign) is unstable. (15) Conditions are lagging! (16) [The pr]inces (17) are consorting (conspiring?)[46] (16) among themselves. You are my father! (18) You are my lord! When (19) the *kârum* (20) has heard (read) (19) the tablet (i.e., 'this letter'), (20) go before it (i.e., 'make an appeal to it'). (22) Let (21) the advice of the *kârum*, (22) and your advice, come to me. (23) Don't you come! (Instead) (24) you should talk it over (23) there (i.e., at *Kaniš*). (24) [...] I shall give him (or 'it'?). (25) [...] (26) I to [...]-šua (Šalaḫšua?) [(will go?)] (27) and to ⌈this day⌉ (28) my finances (?) [...] (29) this (acc.) [...?...]. (30) As for you — your *allanum* (perhaps the plant: *Peganum harmala*)[47] [...] (31) is (here?). (32) I shall stay (here?) (31) for [hal]f-a-day (longer?). (33) Take heed (32) of (what) the *kârum* (advises you)! (33) ... (34) Don't you come! ... (rest [6 lines] illegible).

To our knowledge a full translation and critique of this most important letter has never appeared in print although the text was published over thirty years ago.[48] Yet a careful study of its contents yields data which are highly pertinent to an understanding of the political climate in Anatolia during the most flourishing period of Old Assyrian activity. Accordingly we must analyze the contents of *CCT*, IV, 30a in considerable detail.

It appears certain that the destination of our letter was *Kaniš* since Inaa, the addressee, was usually resident there;[49] also, there can be little doubt but that the letter was written in *Ḫaḫḫum* shortly after the events described in lines 3-17 took place. When we recall that *Ḫaḫḫum* is to be sought in the region of modern Harput, east of Kültepe-*Kaniš*, we are again vividly reminded of the authority which the businessmen of *Kaniš*

45 This seems to be the only acceptable translation in light of the context of our letter, especially the following lines, 13-15. A translation: "The gentlemen have changed (their minds)", or any such, would yield no sense.

46 The verb is *naṭâlu*, "to look at, towards, about". Lines 16-17a say literally: "The princes are looking about among themselves", which indeed carries the overtones of conspiracy. For the root *nṭl* in a business context cf. J. Lewy, "On Some Institutions ...", *op. cit.*, 75, w.n. 323.

47 For the tentative equation of *allanum* and *Peganum harmala*, cf. I. J. Gelb, *OIP*, XXVII (1935), p. 25, n. to 1.4 of text no. 5.

48 Prof. Lewy cursorily alludes to *CCT*, IV, 30a in his "On Some Institutions ...", *op. cit.*, 53, n. 217, where he transliterates 11. 13-14. Balkan offered 11. 2-17 in *TTKY*, V, No. 31a, p. 26. See now also Garelli, Les Assyriens en Cappadoce, 350, n. 1.

49 For Inaa, cf. *ibid.*, 26, n. 109 [27], and J. Lewy, "*Ḫatta, Ḫattu, Ḫatti* ...", *op. cit.*, 376, n. 52, and 424.

and the *Kârum* itself were capable of exercising over the Assyrian trader in no matter what town he happened to be.[50]

Our letter begins with a notice to Inaa that not only the writer (Elani) and his companions (Idi-Kubum and company), but also the *eširtum* of *Ḫaḫḫum* have "gone up" to the palace of *Ḫaḫḫum* time and again.[51] Elani is characterized as a subordinate business associate of Inaa's by the phraseology of lines 17-18 (*a-bi a-ta* (18) *be-li a-ta*), and we may reasonably surmise that Idi-Kubum and his business colleagues as well as Elani were looking after some business interest of Inaa's in *Ḫaḫḫum*. That the *eširtum* accompanied them to see the local ruler seems to confirm this, for the board or committee of ten men which went by this name appears in other texts to act primarily as a commercial group.[52] That they were constituted by the *Kârum* of *Ḫaḫḫum* to assist Elani, Idi-Kubum, *et. al.* in their representations before the indigenous ruler of *Ḫaḫḫum* indicates that whatever the matter might have been, the audience which the Assyrians "continually sought" (cf. line 6: *ni-ta-na-li-ma*, "We went up time and again") was one backed by an official interest of *Kârum Ḫaḫḫum*. We may even suggest that the matter at hand was serious enough for Inaa's representative at *Ḫaḫḫum* to enlist the aid of a delegation from the local *kârum*.

According to lines 5-7, on several different occasions the *rubâ'û* had seen them but had put them off by being evasive, even perhaps diverting the issue. It is because Elani has failed to gain any sort of satisfaction for his petition that he is led to appeal to Inaa, and ultimately *Kârum Kaniš*. The nature of the appeal, which, most significantly, mentions an oath concluded between the rulers of *Ḫaḫḫum* and *Kârum Kaniš*, indicates to what extent formal diplomatic relations governed affairs between Assyrians and individual Anatolian principalities.

The appeal of Elani is an indignant one. He seems to be saying something like: "Look here, how we are treated despite the existence of an oath which they (messengers of the rulers of *Ḫaḫḫum*) brought us!"; or again, "We are treated this way even though there is a copy of the oath they brought us right there in the palace, itself!"[53] In either case, Elani feels he is justified in calling Inaa's and *Kârum Kaniš*' attention to the *violation* of some provision of an agreement which ought to have been honored. But especially interesting is line 11, which suggests that the

50 Cf. Chapter One w.n. 53, above.

51 The verb *elâ'um* is typically used in the Cappadocian tablets in the sense of: "to go up to a higher authority" (*viz.*, a prince, palace, high official, etc.).

52 Cf., e.g., *CCT*, III, 36a and *AnOr*, VI, 15.

53 Cf. n. 44, above.

Kanisian envoy sent to negotiate with the ruler of *Ḫaḫḫum* "came to an agreement" with him, and therefore the ruler's present disinclination to treat the petitioning Assyrians under the terms of the implied treaty in question appears to place the latter in a very awkward position, as a discussion of lines 12-17 will demonstrate.

The information contained in lines 12-14 appears to deal a direct blow against the idea that the Assyrians exercised political and military dominion over Anatolian towns, since it characterizes a highly unstable local situation at *Ḫaḫḫum* in terms that nowhere suggest the Assyrians are able to intervene or influence the outcome in any way, as they assuredly would were they masters of Anatolia. Elani, the writer of our letter, does not appear to be concerned with any actual or potential danger to himself or his companions, or to the position of the Assyrian *kârum* at *Ḫaḫḫum*, but only with the circumstance that the position of the king of *Ḫaḫḫum* is threatened. In the revolt of the citizens of *Ḫaḫḫum* we see ample proof of the ability of alleged "subjects" of "foreign conquerors" to defy their own rulers, who would have had all the authority of the occupying power to support them in such a dangerous situation. In other words, the mere fact of a revolt in so important a city as *Ḫaḫḫum* is reason enough to doubt that any Assyrian military occupation ever existed in Anatolia during the Cappadocian period.

If Elani does not show any unusual concern for his own or his companion's safety, what then is his interest? Line 15 seems to supply the answer. "Conditions are slumping", he reports, and thereby we may understand that the revolt at *Ḫaḫḫum* has dealt a severe blow to Assyrian commercial activity in that city. In his appeal to Inaa at *Kaniš*, then, Elani is chiefly concerned not only about his inability to settle a grievance in the palace at *Ḫaḫḫum*, but equally much with the possibility that the king, with whom an earlier agreement has been reached, may perchance be dethroned, a circumstance which would terminate relations until new ones could be concluded with the successful rebels.

How then are we to interpret Elani's words in lines 16-17, viz: "The princes are consorting together.[54] Why, in other words, should the fact of a revolt in *Ḫaḫḫum* have been accompanied by such haughty and lordly behavior? It would make no sense to see in *rubâ'û* of lines 6 and 16 a term designating the king of *Ḫaḫḫum* and his consort, as Professor Lewy has done, for their unstable position as a result of the revolt would serve to have the opposite effect from making them highly independent.[55]

[54] Cf. n. 46, above.

[55] Cf. J. Lewy, "On Some Institutions ...", *op. cit.*, 53, n. 217.

Nor can it be argued that the revolt in *Ḫaḫḫum* gave the king and his wife a chance to "lord it" over the Assyrians, since such behavior would be meaningless in light of their own predicament. Accordingly, we are led to make a distinction between the *rubâ'û* (*loc. cit.*) and the *šarrum*, or "king", of line 13, and to see in the former the sons of the latter. It seems quite possible that our letter reports a palace conspiracy, and that the difficulty Elani writes about in connection with being "answered evasively" by the *rubâ'û* is due to their ascendancy as rivals to the ruling *šarrum*. Hence it might be thought that the instability of the *šarrum's* reign is due to the threat posed by the *rubâ'û*. However we cannot insist on this interpretation, but merely call attention to it as a possibility.

If the situation at *Ḫaḫḫum* was such as has been described in the preceding pages, the appeal of Elani to Inaa and through him to the *Kârum Kaniš* can only be an appeal for advice, and not for the use of force or anything similar. For in consideration of the seriousness of conditions at *Ḫaḫḫum*, it is noteworthy that a *private individual* like Elani writes to his business superior about a deteriorating political situation, and hopes that the superior can raise the issue at hand before the *kârum*-assembly. There is nothing in the letter to suggest that the oath-agreement to which Elani alludes in lines 8-11 was one *granted by Kârum Kaniš* to the *šarrum* of *Ḫaḫḫum*, and therefore nothing to suggest that Elani was urging Inaa and the *Kârum Kaniš* to "take action" against the non-Assyrian administration of *Ḫaḫḫum*. Rather the situation appears to be one in which businessmen who expected fair treatment under the terms of a formal agreement were rebuffed, and therefore sought some kind of support from the executives of their home *kârum*, which happened also to be the chief Assyrian *kârum* in Anatolia. It is especially interesting that Elani asks Inaa to "go before" the *kârum* — that is, to make an appeal to it — and also to be sure to send *his own* advice along with the advice the *Kârum* happened to give him.[56] If *Kârum Kaniš* were the political superiors of the rulers of *Ḫaḫḫum*, would its advice in such a crucial matter as the rebuff of Assyrians there be transmitted through the agency of the entrepreneur Inaa? Should we not expect so potentially dangerous a situation to call for official *action*, rather than advice? This becomes more than merely an academic question when we consider that Elani urges Inaa *not to come himself* to *Ḫaḫḫum*, but rather to talk the matter over at *Kaniš*.[57] Perhaps Elani has reason to fear for the safety of Inaa — we cannot know. But by and large, *CCT*, IV, 30a appears to

[56] Cf. 11. 21-22.
[57] Cf. 11. 23-24a.

show that in addition to formal agreements existing between *Kârum Kaniš* and the king of *Ḫaḫḫum*, individual Assyrian businessmen might be placed in awkward situations *vis à vis* their anticipated rights, and that in such cases they sought instructions from their superiors rather than claimed military protection from them. Unfortunately we do not know the outcome of Elani's appeal to Inaa about his treatment at *Ḫaḫḫum*.

At this point in our treatment we may pause to summarize what has been learned from the only three texts in the Cappadocian fund which allude to a *mâmîtum*, or "oath", between individual Anatolian princes and Assyrian officials.[58] In no case is the kind of oath specified, and in no case can we assert more than that relations between the interested parties were formal. The status of *Kârum Kaniš* as the chief Assyrian negotiator of diplomatic agreements appears to be affirmed in each of the documents discussed to this point, and in the one encounter between Assyrians and the King of *Ḫaḫḫum* which placed the Assyrians at a disadvantage, there is absolutely no evidence to support the idea that *Kârum Kaniš* was expected to retaliate against this ruler, nor (as we have stated in the previous chapter) is there any reason for believing that the Assyrians had the ability to do so. However, these are but preliminary appraisals, and will be further called into play as we continue to survey what our sources can tell us about the political climate of central Anatolia during the Cappadocian Period.

The letter *CCT*, IV, 30a, just discussed, was a communication from a business subordinate of Inaa, the Kanišian entrepreneur, to his principal, concerning evasive and contemptuous treatment afforded him at *Ḫaḫḫum*, and by the greatest good fortune we have another letter, similarly addressed to Inaa by yet another business subordinate, which reports an encounter which took place between the latter and the prince of *Naduḫtum*. This encounter actually involved the detention of Assyrians in the town of *Naduḫtum*, and therefore is most pertinent to our analysis. The text of this letter, catalogued as *TC*, III, 75, reads as follows:

TC III 75

(1) *a-na I-na-a qi-bi-ma* (2) *um-ma Da-da-a-ma* (3) *a-di ša a-na-kam* (4) *kà-al-a-ku-ni i-na* (5) *Na-du-ùḫ-tim wa-áš-ba-ku* (6) *a-di 10 a-na ru-ba-im* (7) *ú ší-na-ḫi-li-im ni-li-ma* (8) *um-ma a-na-ku-ma*[59] (9) *be-lí a-ta ḫa-ra-nam*

[58] Add now *ATHE*, 66:9-13, which appeared in 1960, after my original study. Cf. Chapter Three, above.

[59] Lines 4b through 8a are given in J. Lewy, "On Some Institutions ...", *op. cit.*, 46, n. 173; lines 24 through 28, *ibid.*, 70, n. 303 [71]. Passing reference to the text as a

(10) *dí-nam um-ma šu-ut-ma* (11) *ki-ma qá-ta-tim* (12) *ší-ip-ru êkallim* (*E.GAL*) (13) *i-dí-nu-ni-kà* (14) *wa-ar-ki-ta-ma* (15) *um-ma a-na-ku-ma* (16) *a-na* [...]-*ni* (*6 lines almost completely illegible*) (23) *lá-at-bi*$_4$*-ma lá-ta-lá-ak* (24) *um-ma ru-ba-ú-ma* (25) 3 *ku-nu-tí A-šur-ni-im-ri* (26) *A-šur-mu-ta-bi*$_4$*-il*$_5$ *ú ku-a-tí* (27) ⟨*la*⟩ *ú-ša-ar a-dí tí-er-tum* (28) *iš-t*[*ù Kà*]*-ni-iš i-lá-kà-ni.*

"(1) To Inaa speak: (2) Thus (said) Dadaa: '(3) As long as (4) I have been held back (3) here, in (5) *Naduḫtum* I have been dwelling. (6) Up to ten times (7) we went up (6) to the Prince (7) and the Second-in-Command.[60] (8) Thus (said) I: '(9) You are my lord! (10) Grant me (permission) (9) to leave!' (10) (But) thus (said) he: '(12) The Palace-Envoys (13) have turned you over to me (11) as a (security-) pledge (hostage).' (14) Afterward (15) thus (said) I: '(16) to ...... (6 lines almost completely illegible) (23) May I be up and going!?' (24) Thus (said) the Prince: '(25) The three of you — Aššur-Nimri, (26) Aššur-mutabil and you — (27) I shall not free until information (28) comes to me fro[m *Ka*]*niš*.[61]

Although our text relates that the three Assyrians — Dadaa, Aššur-Nimri and Aššur-Mutabil — were detained in the town of *Naduḫtum*, they appear to have had freedom of movement to some extent. For "up to 10 times" they "went up" to the palace, and sought to be allowed to leave, but were refused. Before we examine the reason, we may dwell for a moment on the implications of lines 9-10, where Dadaa quotes his own remarks to the Prince of *Naduḫtum*. "You are my Lord", he says, "Give me (permission to go on) a journey". Not only do we single out the phrase, *bêli atta*, which suggests Dadaa's acknowledgement of the Prince of *Naduḫtum* as his superior, and seems in this situation to be more than a merely courteous remark, but also the *pro tem* authority which the Prince appears to have over the Assyrians, a feature which would not be expected if he were a vassal.

whole was made by Prof. Lewy in "La chronologie de Bitḫana ...", *op. cit.*, 2, n. 14. See now Garelli, *op. cit.*, p. 343, n. 6, and 344, n. 1.

[60] For this translation of *šinaḫila* cf. J. Friedrich, *Hethitisches Wörterbuch* (Heidelberg, 1952), 324b (*sub.* "Churritische Wörter").

[61] The insertion of *lá* before *ú-sa-ar* in 1.27 was made by Prof. Lewy in his rendering of 11. 24-28 (*loc. cit.* in n. 58, above), and we have followed him in our translation. In the autograph copy of *TC*, III, 75 done by Lewy in 1935, there is space at the beginning of 1.27 for one sign, which may have been omitted by the scribe in the original. On the other hand, should there be no missing sign, we may perhaps read 11. 24-28 as a rhetorical question without appreciably altering the sense, *viz*: "Thus (said) the Prince: 'Shall I free the three of you — Aššur-Nimri, Aššur-Mutabil and you — until (= before) information comes to me from *Kaniš*?'"

Noteworthy it is that the three Assyrians in question were handed over to the prince *ki-ma qá-ta-tim* (l. 11) by the palace-envoys of *Kaniš*. How are we to understand *qá-ta-tim*? In legal and economic usage it signifies "guarantors" of a loan, or "security pledges".[62] In the circumstance related in *TC*, III, 75, we might interpret that the three Assyrians were delivered as "pledges" against some promise concluded between the prince of *Naduḫtum* and the officials of *Kaniš*, and thus we feel justified in translating, "hostages", without necessarily implying that the prince had seized the Assyrians and were holding them as a threat of any sort. For the information contained in the concluding lines of our letter strongly suggests that the men were held "legally", that is, as a result of a prior negotiation; and that the Prince shows his willingness to release Dadaa and his companions upon receipt of information as to their disposition from *Kaniš*.

We see no reason to accept the view that the Prince of *Naduḫtum* is waiting for an *order* from *Kaniš* to release the men, as Professor Lewy interprets.[63] For one thing, there is no question but that the Assyrians were "handed over" to the prince, and this point is made by the prince, himself, to explain to Dadaa why he is being held.[64] Nor is there any question about the intention of the prince to keep the Assyrians until his business is settled with the authorities of *Kaniš*. Hence to see in the prince of *Naduḫtum* a subordinate indigenous ruler wanting, as it were, to please his alleged *Assyrian* superiors at *Kaniš*, is untenable.[65] Nor should we fail to point out for *TC*, III, 75, as we did in discussing *CCT*, IV, 30a, that the appeal to Inaa at *Kaniš*, to an influential private person, in other words, — adds some small light to the matter. For Dadaa appears to be *explaining* to his superior why he has been held up, and

[62] Cf. P. Koschaker, *Babylonisch-assyrisches Bürgschaftsrecht* (Leipzig and Berlin, 1911) 15-24. The use of the verb *waššûrum*, "to let go of a person", in 1.27, strengthens the idea that the Assyrians may have been hostages. For the implications of this usage cf. J. Lewy, "Old Assyrian Documents ... II", *op. cit.*, 132, w.n. 1.

[63] Cf. Prof. Lewy's translation of *têrtum* with this specific coloring, *loc. cit.* in n. 58, above.

[64] Cf. 11. 11-13.

[65] Prof. Lewy's interpretation of this text depended on two assumptions, viz: (a). that 1. 12 of the text was to be read: *ší-ip-ru-ú GAL*, "the Chief Envoys", [i.e., perhaps either those of *Kârum Kaniš*, or of Assur]; and (b). that the text appeared to represent a transaction in which the Prince of *Naduḫtum* awaited disposition of the matter by a decision of *Kârum Kaniš*, the foremost representative of that part of the Assyrian Empire Prof. Lewy called "Halys Assyria" [Cf. *HUCA* 27, (2956), p. 70]. However, Garelli, who collated the tablet, reads line 12 as *ší-ip-ru E.GAL*, 'Envoys of the palace.' On the basis of this collation, the negotiation appears to be between the indigenous administrations of *Naduḫtum* and of *Kaniš*, and recalls *EL*, 247 and 248, in which the palace of *Kaniš* acted to recall certain Assyrian traders from *Siz/sum*.

having learned the reason from the Prince of *Naduḫtum*, seems to imply that the faster some kind of decision is taken at *Kaniš*, the faster he and his companions will be released. May he not hope that Inaa use his influence at *Kaniš*? And may we not conclude that perhaps some unknown action of Inaa's subordinates has precipitated their delivery to a non-Assyrian potentate, and that their release depends upon the satisfactory termination of negotiations between the latter and the indigenous administration of *Kaniš*?

If *TC*, III, 75 shows us a situation in which an indigenous prince was granted the right to detain Assyrians in his town, another text from the Louvre Collection, *TC*, III, 85, reveals to us the steps which were taken to reclaim Assyrian caravan-goods seized by the palace officials at Zalpa. In this text we have perhaps the fullest account yet received of an interview held between an indigenous prince and an Assyrian. The contents of the document, a letter, are as follows:

TC III 85

(1) *a-na A-šur-*[*i*]*-mì-*[*tí*] *qí-bi-ma* (2) *um-ma Ì-lí-a-lúm-ma* (3) *a-na šu-mì ḫu-lu-qá-i-kà* (4) *a ma-lá tí-er-tí-kà ší-ip-ra-am* (5) *e-bi-ru-ni-ma 9 šiqlî* (*GÍN*) (6) *ḫurâṣam* (*KÙ.GI*) *er-ba-am a-na Za-al-pá-i-im* (7) *ni-ší-e um-ma ru-ba-um-ma* (8) *ḫurâṣ* (*KÙ.GI*)*-kà qá-tí ú-kà-al* (9) *kaspum* (*KÙ.BABBAR*) *ḫa-lá-aq sí-pá-ri* (10) *ú sá-ḫi-ir-tù-šu ša*![66] *a-na ša* (11) *wardim* (*IR*)^{dim}

[66] Lines 8-12 present difficulties. In the transcription of Prof. Lewy, they should read as follows: (8) *ḫurâṣ* (*KÙ.GI*)*-kà qá-tí ú-kà-al* (9) *kaspum* (*KÙ.BABBAR*) *ḫa-lá-aq sí-pá-ri* (10) *ú sá-ḫi-ir-tù-šu šu a-na ša* (11) *wardim*^{dim} *iṣ-bu-tù-*[*x*] (12) *ak-bu-us* ... The second *šu* of line 10 might seem to be a simple dittography on the part of the scribe, and is so taken by Garelli in his transliteration of 11. 8-11 in *Les Assyriens en Cappadoce*, p. 345, n. 1. His translation of these lines is:

(8) "je (lit. ma main) détient ton or. (9) L'argent est confisqué, (car) mon bronze (10) et son anneau, pour (l'affaire) de (11) l'esclave, ils (les Assyriens) ont pris".

However, Garelli does not include line 12 in the unit he treats. The first word of this line is *akbus*, spoken by the prince, and meaning "I have curtailed, [suppressed, clamped down upon]" [cf. n. 67 below]. I believe that we are to read 11. 9-12 therefore as containing a relative clause, and that the second *šu* of line 10 is meant to be a *ša*, and which was left uncompleted by the scribe. Support for this conclusion comes first from the fact that there appears in Lewy's copy after the *iṣ-bu-tù* of line 11 some traces of a sign — one expects a *ni* [but this cannot be judged to have been there from the copy], and second that the entire passage seems to make better sense if we include *akbus* of line 12 as the main verb of the unit beginning with *sá-ḫi-ir-tù-šu* of line 9. Hence:

(12) "I have curtailed (9) the bronze object (10) and its encircling cover which! (11) they seized (10) relative to the affair of (11) the slave" ..., etc.

My understanding of the text therefore differs significantly from that of Garelli.

iṣ-bu-tù-[*ni*?) (12] *ak-bu-us*[67] *tí-er-ta-kà* (13) *a-na kà-ri-im li-li-ik* (14) *iš-tù tí-er-tí a kà-ri-im* (15) *i-li-ku* [*a*]-*dí ma-lá* (16) *ú ší-ni-*[*šu*] *ni-li-ma*[68] (17) *20 u₄-me-e ú-sá-as-ḫi-ir-ni-a-tí-ma*[69] (18) *i wa-ar-ki-tim um-ma* (19) *šu-ut-ma a-tal-kà be-el* (20) *ḫu-lu-qá-e li-li ar-gám-ma-ni*[70] (21) *šu-wa-tí-ma* (22) *a-da-šu-um um-ma* (23) *ni-nu-ma ik-ri-bi ša i-lim* (24) *lá tù-kà-al a-na ší-ip-ri-im* (25) *dí-in-ma a kà-ri-im lu-ub-lu* (26) *um-ma šu-ut-ma a-na-ku* (27) *ḫu-lu-qá-i-ku-nu ú-ta-ra-ku-nu-tí* (28) *i-a-tum tí-er-tí a-dí ma-lá* (29) *ú ší-ni-šu a kà-ri-im* (30) *i-li-ik-ma a-wa-tám-ma* (31) *lá i-dí-nu-nim*[71] *2/3 manâ'e* (*MA.NA*) [*x*] *šiqlî* (*GÍN*) (32 *ḫurâṣam* (*KÙ.GI*) *i-a-ma ù* (33) *Bu-ur-nu-nu ḫa-b*[*u*]*-lu-nim* (34) *um-ma* [*šu-ut-ma a-n*]*a* (35) *kaspi* (*KÙ.-BABBAR*)^{pl}-*ku-nu ḫa-al-qi wardam* (*IR*) (36) [*a*]-*tù-ra-ma i ḫa-ar-pí* (37) *a-wi-li ta-me Bît* (É) *Ša-ša-nim*[72] (38) *ḫu-lu-qá-um ib-ší-ma ú-kà-al*[73] (39) 1/2 *manâ'e* (*MA.NA*) 5 *šiqlî* (*GÍN*) *kaspum* (*KÙ.BABBAR*) *gám-ru-um* (40) *ik-šu-ud-kà.*[74]

(1) To Aššur-[i]mi[tti] speak: (2) thus (said) Ili-Alum: (3) Concerning the matter of your lost goods — (4) according to your full instructions,

[67] For *kabâsum* in the sense of "curtail", cf. *EL*, I, p. 162, n.c.

[68] For the phrase *a-dí ma-lá ú ší-ni-*[*šu*], cf. n. 71, below.

[69] In a modern vein one might translate quite literally, "he gave us the run-around".

[70] On Prof. Lewy's copy of this text, line 20, the signs looks as arranged in the transliteration immediately following:

(20) *ḫu lu qá e li li ar*
kám ma ni

Garelli, *op. cit.*, p. 345, n. 2, reads: (20) *ḫu-lu-qá-e li-li-kám-ma ar-ni*, which he gets by twice reading between the main line and the appended signs below it, rather than in normal sequence from left to right, which produces: *ḫu-lu-qá-e li-li ar-kám-ma-ni.* The word *ark/gammani* signifies a deep-red or purple material, manufactured either as a robe or a mantle, or as wool. In Hittite our word appears as *arkammaš* (N sg.), with a meaning equivalent to Akkadian *irbu*, "gift to royalty", or simply "tribute". [Cf. J. Friedrich, *Hethitisches Wörterbuch*, 30a-b, and Delitzsch, *HWB*, 129a]. The presence of *argammani* in our text as part of a lot of temple goods cited as *ikribu* [1. 23] is not surprising.

[71] Cf. Prof. Lewy's discussion of 11. 26-31a in "Studies in Akkadian Grammar ...", *op. cit.*, p. 405, w.n. 6.

[72] The sixth sign of line 37 in Prof. Lewy's copy is clearly the *É* or *bîtu* sign, and is quite different from the signs for *u* as drawn in the text-copy elsewhere. Hence I differ with Garelli's reading of it as *u*, to judge only by the copy before me. For *šaššânum* as perhaps a small "sun-ornament" see Bilgiç, "Die Einheimischen Appellativa ...", *op. cit.*, p. 58.

[73] For Garelli's different translation and understanding of 11. 34-38, cf. *Les Assyriens en Cappadoce*, p. 345, n. 4.

[74] Cf. the translation of these lines in *CAD*, V (1956), 38, sub. *gamru* (2). There it is interpreted that the silver, the expenditures, have been debited against "you", i.e., the addressee of the letter, Aššur-imitti. Does this mean the expenditures entailed in providing for the messengers who undertook the twenty-day attempt to negotiate with the Prince of *Zalpa*? It does not seem to refer to the sum of silver which the latter had detained and later released.

(5) they chose an (4) envoy (5) for me and (7) we brought (6) a gift of (5) 9 shekels of (6) gold to the Zalpaian [prince]. (7) The prince said as follows: (8) "My hand detains your gold [= I am holding back your gold]. (9) The silver is lost. The bronze object (10) and its encircling cover which![75] (11) they seized (10) relevant to the matter of (11) the slave (12) I have curtailed.[76] (13) Let (12) your report (13) go to the *kârum*". (14) After my report (15) went (14) to the *kârum* (15) once (16) and twice we went up[77] [= "again and again we went up (to get an audience)], but (17) he made us go round in circles [= tarry] for 20 days.[78] Then (18) later on thus (19) said he: "Go! (20) Let (19) the owner (20) of the lost goods come up! (21) To *him* (22) I shall give (20) the red-dyed wool!"[79] (22) Thus (23) we said: (24) "Don't detain (23) the property of the god! (25) Give it (24) to the messengers (envoys) (25) that they might bring it to the *kârum*". (26) Thus he said: "As for me, (27) I shall return to you your lost goods. (28) My communication (30) went (28) once (29) and twice to the *kârum* [= "again and again I sent word to the *kârum*], but (30)-(31) they did not enter into negotiations.[80] (31) The 2/3 mina, [x] shekels (32) of gold are mine, for (33) Bur-Nunu owes (it) to me!" (34) Thus [said he (further): "Relevant to] (35) your lost silver, (36) they shall free (35) the slave and (37) make the men take an oath (36) at the harvest festival. (37) The House of the *Šaššanum*[81] ...? (38) There were "lost" goods ["confiscated" goods of Assyrian traders] and he detained [them].[82] (39) One-half mina, 5 shekels of silver, the expenditure (40) has "reached" you.[83]

As in other texts we have examined so far, the events leading up to the actual encounter between representatives of the Assyrians and a particular Anatolian prince are somewhat obscured, but it is possible to fill in some of the background from the contents of the letter. The Prince of *Zalpa* has seized a shipment of goods specified as over two-thirds of a mina of gold[84] an unspecified quantity of silver, bronze and

[75] Cf. 11. 31-32f. Line 8 appears to refer to the special gift, the *irbum*, carried up to the Prince. However, it is possible that the gold mentioned in 1.8 is the same as that which is allegedly owed to the prince by Bur-Nunu (11. 32-33).

[76] Cf. 11. 9-10, with 11. 35-36, and 11. 20-22.

[77] Cf. 11. 28-30.

[78] On *šiprum*, cf. Chapter Two, n. 110-113, above.

[79] Cf. 11. 2b-6a of *CCT*, IV, 30a, discussed in the present chapter, above.

[80] Cf. 11. 4-7a.

[81] Cf. 11. 9-13.

[82] Cf. 11. 12-13.

[83] Cf. 11. 15b-17.

[84] Compare *TC*, III, 75:6-7, and *CCT*, IV, 30a:6, both discussed in the present chapter.

red-dyed wool.[85] The owner of the goods is the addressee of the letter, Aššur-imitti, a resident of *Kaniš*, while Ili-âlum, the writer, appears as the former's business associate and subordinate. There is no doubt that the Prince of *Zalpa* has held the goods in question for a period of time prior to the events narrated in *TC*, III, 85, for he states that he has contacted the *kârum* (i.e., *Kârum Kaniš*) on more than one occasion about them.[86]

The first point of interest appears in the protocol which characterizes the beginning of negotiations for recovery of the confiscated valuables. Ili-alum receives a *šiprum*, or "messenger" (also, "envoy"), to accompany him on his mission. This *šiprum* may have come from *Kaniš*, but since Ilialum appears to be informing Aššur-imitti at *Kaniš* of facts presumably unknown to him until the letter was sent, it is likely that Ili-alum gains his companion in *Zalpa*.[87] This would agree with the action noted in *CCT*, IV, 30a in which the Assyrian, Elani, was accompanied by the *eširtum* of *Ḫaḫḫum* on a visit to the rulers of that city.[88] After the messenger was chosen, the two Assyrians gained an interview with the ruler of Zalpa by bringing up a rather substantial gift to him.[89] The audience gained by Ili-alum and his companion appears, then, to represent an official negotiation, in which the potential interests both of a private entrepreneur and of the *Kârum Kaniš* are at stake.

The interview begins with a completely frank, if not bold, assertion by the Prince that he has, indeed, seized and confiscated the goods in question, and has informed the *kârum* that he has done so.[90] His biting remark to the petitioners, that the latter, themselves, should get in touch with their own executives of *Kârum Kaniš*, indicates the indignant anger the Prince felt at the tardy response to his own act of good faith, and also his scorn at the presumption taken by the two Assyrians in appearing suddenly, as it were, to reclaim goods which were the proper object of more official negotiation. This explains sufficiently, to our view, why he let the Assyrians "cool their heels" for twenty days before he chose to grant them another interview. We have already seen in *CCT*, IV, 30a and in *TC*, III, 75 that the rulers of Anatolian cities were adept at

[85] Cf. 11. 18b-22a.

[86] Cf. 11. 22b-25.

[87] Cf. 11. 26-30f.

[88] On the general characteristics of the Hittite treaties cf. J. Pirenne, "La politique d'expansion hittite ...", *op. cit.*, 373-382, and A. Goetze, *Kleinasien* (1957), *op. cit.*, 95f. That one possible connection may be pointed out does not, of course, mean that further connections or parallels should automatically be assumed.

[89] Cf. 11. 31-33.

[90] Cf. 1. 25.

keeping Assyrian petitioners waiting until they were ready to receive them, and the experience of Ili-alum and his companion at *Zalpa* is yet another example of this show of independence on the part of an indigenous prince.

Later, when the Assyrians again are received by the ruler of Zalpa, they are taunted by him. In effect the prince is saying: "No, I won't deal with *you*, but come now, send up the owner of the things I have confiscated, and then we shall debate this matter, just he and I, and *then* I'll hand the goods over, but to *him*". Now this is clearly an ironic speech, and in it we have no doubt but that the Prince is playing a bit of "cat and mouse" with Ili-alum and the *šiprum*, but in the answer of Ili-alum to this sortie we enter upon a most serious and significant phase of the negotiation.

The Assyrian reveals, and obviously for the first time in the talks, that the *huluqqâ'ê*, or "lost goods" are temple property. The effect on the Prince is startling, for whereas earlier he had adamantly refused to return them, now he acquiesces, with only a bitter repetition of the fact that he had shown his good faith by contacting the *kârum*, but had received no reponse in the matter. Why should the mention of "temple-goods" (*ikribi ša ilim*, l. 23), have precipitated such a response? Only, we feel, because of the impressive sanctions against violation of divine prerogatives everywhere known and honored in the ancient Near East. What is strongly suggested to us is that between the Prince of *Zalpa* and the Assyrians at *Kaniš* there existed a treaty which would have been sanctioned by the deities of the respective parties, very much as were treaties concluded by Hittite kings of a later period in Anatolia and their vassals or allies. It is the appeal against a possible religious violation that secures for Ili-alum and the *šiprum* at *Zalpa* that which no other kind of appeal could achieve: the release of goods which obviously the Prince of *Zalpa* recognized were being held by him contrary to diplomatic agreement.

Now it is quite possible that Ili-alum may have acted rather resourcefully in the face of repeated refusals on the part of the prince, and may have used this kind of appeal as a last resort. We cannot know. We can, however, point out that the prince refuses to turn over what is rightly his (from his point of view), and so keeps a large amount of gold which he claims the Assyrian, Bur-Nunu, owes him. Nor does he allow the matter to rest there, but demands that an oath-ceremony at the forthcoming harvest-festival be undertaken.

It would appear, though we cannot insist on this, that the Prince of *Zalpa* does not wish to be branded as a trespasser against holy things, and as violator of a treaty perhaps witnessed by the very deities whose property he might be accused of mishandling. In all, his actions as seen in *TC*, III, 85 do not display him as a timorous or guilt-ridden vassal, but rather as a ruler who seems fully conscious of his own sovereignty and powers. He, it was, who initiated correspondence with the *kârum* after feeling confident enough to interfere with the transit of goods through his territory, in order (if we are to believe him), to collect a bad debt. He, it was, further, who was not at all impressed with the arrival of Ili-Alum and the *šiprum*. Finally, he, it was, who *still* retained the gold allegedly owed him, even after he was willing to release the temple-goods.

Nor can it be overlooked once more that *Kârum Kaniš* appears to play a most passive, if not enigmatic role. We cannot know why it ignored the prince's oft-sent communications, but surely this does not reflect any Assyrian contempt of, or disdain for, the ruler of *Zalpa*, especially when we consider the difficulties experienced by Ili-Alum in trying to get a satisfactory disposition of the issue. It is impossible to think that the Assyrians felt they could retrieve the lost goods as a matter of course and at their own convenience, else why the repeated petitions of Ili-Alum and his *šiprum*? We cannot help but feel that at base, the "affair of the lost goods" is a private one. Aššur-Imitti, we recall, is keenly interested as owner or guardian of them. Ili-Alum is acting on Aššur-Imitti's instructions, and it is to the latter, not to the *kârum*, that the report of the interview goes. We acknowledge the implied existence of a treaty between *Zalpa* and *Kârum Kaniš*, which appears to have said nothing about restricting the Zalpaian ruler's police powers, for the latter exercised precisely such powers in holding up the movement of goods that were proceeding to the *kârum*. And we further acknowledge the solemn sanctions of such a treaty, and appeal to which was instrumental in gaining the release of the *huluqqâ'ê* of *TC*, III, 85. But the prince's willingness to satisfy his Assyrian petitioners is not based on fear, but rather, we feel, on his unwillingness to be branded a violator of an agreement that would bring divine reprisals upon his head.

With the discussion of *TC*, III, 85 we bring to a close the first series of textual examples which show Assyrian diplomatic contacts with individual Anatolian princes. The five texts presented in this chapter stand in the forefront of political documents from the Cappadocian fund, and when taken together strongly support the idea of formal and mutually binding treaty-relationships between the Assyrian settlement communities, as represented in diplomacy by *Kârum Kaniš*, and the governments of the indigenous principalities. There remain other texts which shed light on political matters, and these may more easily be discussed now that the most important have been introduced. In our concluding chapter we shall inquire into the meaning of *Kârum Kaniš*'s position as chief diplomatic executive for the Assyrians, and attempt to reach conclusions about the nature of Assyrian "colonization", but for the present we shall simply deny the presence of coercion in the political encounters between Assyrian and Anatolian, and affirm, rather, a measure of regulation which limits the interests and activities of either side. To further test the viability of this hypothesis in the sphere of the political relationships which characterize the period of Kültepe Level II will be the task of the following chapter.

V

SURVEY OF ASSYRIAN-ANATOLIAN POLITICAL ENCOUNTERS DURING THE MAIN PERIOD OF ASSYRIAN ACTIVITY IN ANATOLIA

The five texts introduced in the previous chapter show that there is a basis for the belief that relations between Assyrian corporations or individuals and one or another Anatolian prince were defined by formal diplomatic protocol sustained by oaths, and that the indigenous rulers had considerable freedom of action in confiscating Assyrian goods and detaining Assyrian personnel. One of the texts, kt f/k 183, which reports the interview between the envoys of *Kârum Durḫumit* and the Prince of *Tamnia/Tawinia,* belongs to the chronological mileu of Kültepe Level Ib; the other four, however, owing to their presence in the collections of the British Museum, the Louvre and the Museum of the University of Pennsylvania, respectively, must be attributed to the period of Kültepe Level II. Since the latter were shown to lend little support to the theory of an Old Assyrian Empire, it is pertinent to continue our inquiry by surveying other information offered by Level II texts about political contacts between Assyrians and Anatolians throughout the entire area in which the Assyrian settlements are found. We may conveniently begin by discussing the letter *TTC*, 27, which reports the intention of an Assyrian trader, who feels he has been rather summarily dealt with by an unnamed *kârum*, to consult with the "Great Prince" of *Burušḫattum.*[1]

[1] The text *TTC*, 27 reads as follows:

(1) *um-ma Im-*[*tí*]*-ilum-ma* (2) *a-na A-šùr-na-da qí-*[*bi$_4$-ma*] (3) *i-na ṭuppi^{pí} ší-ta-pu-*[*ri-im*] (4) *a-ta-aḫ-da-ar a-*[*na-kam*] (5) *A-šùr-ta-ak-la-ku a-*[*ḫu-kà*] (6) *a-na Bu-ru-uš-ḫa-tim* (7) *a-ṣí-ir ru-ba-im rabî'im* (*GAL?*) (8) *i-ša-pár šu-ma iš-ti* (9) *kà-ri-im e-na-na-tim* (10) *e-ri-iš-ma um-ma šu-ut-ma* (11) *a-na a-lim^{ki} ḫa-ra-ni e-na-nim* (12) *ù ku-a-ti a-na kà-ri-im* (13) *um !-ma-ša-aḫ-kà um-ma* (14) *šu-ut-ma A-šùr-na-da kaspam* (*KÙ.BABBAR*) (15) *ma-dam ú-kà-al-ma* (16) *a-šu-mì na -pá-áš-ti-a* (17) *e-tá-ru lá a-li-a* (18) *ù a-na kà-ri-im* (19) *um-ma šu-ut-ma ṭuppam$^{pá-am}$ ša ma-lá* (20) *lu-qú-tam ú-kà-lu* (21) *lu-šé-ṣí-a-ma am-ra kà-ru-um* (22) *ú-lá e-ta-na-an-šu-um* (23) *a-na Bu-ru-* ⟨*us*⟩ *-ḫa-tim i-lá-ak* (24) *i-na ša-am-ší ṭuppi^{pí} ta-ša-me-ú* (25) *iš-ti Ì-lí-áš-ra-ni tí-ib-a* (26) *a-tal-kam-ma a-bi-iš a-ḫu-kà* (27) *a-na-kam la-šu ú a-šar kaspam* (*KÙ.BABBAR*) (28) 1 *šiqlam* (*GÍN*) *i-ṣé-ri-kà lá-qá-im* (29) *lu-ni-im-lik-ma te$_4$-em-ni* (30) *lu ni-iṣ-ba-at a-ḫu-kà e-na-šu* (31) *ek-lá a-sú-ri iš-tù iš-ti* (32) [*r*]*u-ba-im a-wa-sú i-lá-qí-ú* (33) *a !-ma-nu-ma a-na ṣé-ri-a* (34) *e !-ti-qám-ma a-ma-kam e ú-ni-*[*kà*]*-ma* (35) [*be-ú*]*-lá-tí-kà e it-*[*ba-a*]*l-*[*ma*]

The city of *Burušḫattum*, it will be recalled, was the most westerly of Anatolian localities in which the Assyrians maintaned a *kârum*, and is to be located somewhat south-west of the modern Tuz Gölü, in the approaches to the Plain of Konya.[2] The largest city of a region bearing its name (*ma-at Bu-ru-uš-ḫa-tim:*[3] *KTHahn*, 1:3), its ruler bore the title of "Great Prince" (*rubâ'um rabî'um:*[4] *TTC*, 27:6-7). Its palace administration is alluded to in several Cappadocian tablets,[5] while its *kârum* was one of the most flourishing of all the Assyrian settlements. It is, then, all the more interesting that although there existed an Assyrian assembly and court at *Burušḫattum*, a member of a trading firm with ties to the great houses of *Kaniš* and *Assur* felt he could take counsel with a powerful native potentate in the hope of bypassing an adverse decision of his compatriots.

The text we are to consider — *TTC*, 27 — was freely translated by B. Landsberger in *AHK*, but without accompanying transliteration or textual commentary; and with the exception of several lines which Prof. Lewy has recently communicated and studied, the text has escaped notice by scholars.[6] The copy done by Contenau shows that the original is damaged in a few key places,[7] while it will be seen further that the contents report a final stage in a sequence of events which is presently hidden from view. It must remain for a later study to collect the correspondence of the traders in question, so as to determine why the "Great Prince" of *Burušḫattum* was approached but nevertheless, certain features of the text are noteworthy.

The writer of our letter, the trader Imtîlim, reports to his correspondent and business associate, Aššur-Nada that a third colleague, Aššur-taklaku, who was originally located in the same unnamed place as Imtîlim, was sending a message (or a messenger?) to the "Great Prince" of *Burušhattum*.[8] We learn from the writer that Aššur-taklaku had appeared before

(36) *e ú-ḫa-li-kà šu-ma lá ta-ḫi-id-ma* (37) *lá ta-ta-al-kam ḫa-al-a-ti ki-ma en-*[...] (38) *a-ḫu-kà sà-aḫ-ru-um ú-ni-ú-kà*.

[2] Cf. Chapter One, w.n. 37.

[3] Cf. *KTHahn*, 1:3.

[4] Cf. *TTC*, 27 (above, n. 1), 11. 6-7.

[5] Cf. the list of rulers of towns having a *kârum*, Chapter Three, above, sub. *Buruš-ḫattum*.

[6] For Prof. Landsberger's translation cf. *AHK* (1925), 12, where, however, the text is erroneously cited as *TC*, 23. For Prof. Lewy's references to this text cf. "Grammatical and Lexicographical Studies", *Or ns*, 29 (1960), 34-35, w.nn.

[7] Cf. *TTC*, (1919), pl. 14.

[8] Cf. *TTC*, 27:3-8. The restoration of *a*-[*na-kam*] in line 4 and *a*-[*ḫu-kà*] in line 5, is based upon text indications in 11. 26b-27a. Contenau's copy shows slight damage to the text at the ends of 11. 6-8; whether any signs are missing is questionable.

an unnamed *kârum* to petition it for a favor.[9] The letter states that his caravan is going to the City (i.e., *Assur*), and that Aššur-taklaku asks that the *kârum* make Aššur-Nada relinquish a debt-tablet for goods imported from *Assur* which he is now holding.[10] Apparently, Aššur-taklaku is on the verge of bankruptcy because of Aššur-Nada's failure to square accounts with him, and he is reported as having accused Aššur-Nada of holding back much silver — perhaps, then, of not having paid Aššur-taklaku for his part in the entire transaction.[11] The unnamed *kârum* does not see fit to grant the petition, however, with the result that Aššur-taklaku decides himself to go to *Burušḫattum*. And he expects not only to take counsel with the Great Prince of that city, but also to gain some meaningful decision or advice from him.[12] It is noteworthy that Aššur-taklaku is said to have "denounced" Aššur-Nada before the *kârum*.[13] Also, Aššur-taklaku is characterized as having sinister intentions,[14] which produces an emergency call for Aššur-Nada to come to Imtilim's side at once.[15]

That Aššur-taklaku felt that he could challenge the authority of the unnamed *kârum* by appealing to a native potentate of high rank seems to show that he expected this ruler to act independently of any Assyrian authority, not then as a bound-vassal. For otherwise, what solace would Aššur-taklaku hope to gain, since it would be expected that a political inferior support the actions of the legally-constituted courts and assemblies of the superior power? We cannot, unfortunately, know what the outcome of Aššur-taklaku's appeal was, but we are entitled to feel that in the ruler of *Burušhattum*, an outraged Assyrian may have found at least a protector. It is a moot point whether this ruler had any power to force a reversal of a *kârum's* decision. But further to the point, it should be noted that the action of the unnamed *kârum* took place not in *Burušḫattum*, but somewhere else.[16] Actually, then, the trip of Aššur-taklaku represents an attempt even to bypass the *Kârum Burušḫattum* in favor of the non-Assyrian city-administration there.

[9] Cf. 11. 8bf., translated in *CAD*, 4 (1958) 164b (sub. *enênu C*, b.) as: "he demanded a favor of the *kârum*, thus he (said), "My caravan is going to the City, do (imp. pl.) me the (following) favor".

[10] Cf. 11. 19b-21a.

[11] Cf. 11. 13b-17.

[12] Cf. 1.23, and 11. 31b-32: *iš-tù iš-ti* (32) [*ru*]-*ba-im a-wa-sú i-lá-qí-ú*, "when from (32) the prince he takes his word" (i.e., "when he gets either advice or a decision from the prince".)

[13] Cf. 11. 12b-13a.

[14] Cf. 11. 30b-31a, and 1.38.

[15] Cf. 11. 29-30, and 33b-34a.

[16] Cf. Imtîlim's statements in 11. 6, 23 and 26b-27a.

Isolated as is the information contained in *TTC*, 27, its interpretation is strengthened by further allusions in the Cappadocian texts to interference of Anatolian princes in the affairs of Assyrian businessmen. The influence of the palace-administrations on the movement of caravans is discussed in the next chapter, but here it is pertinent to note that the Princes of *Ḫurama* and *Luḫusatia*, according to the British Museum tablet *CCT*, II, 48, appear to serve as restrictive influences upon a group of Assyrians interested in obtaining the metal *aši'um* (iron?) in the regions of these cities.[17] Although this text, which must be considered in company with several others dealing with phases of the same commercial transaction, has been differently interpreted by Professors Landsberger and Lewy, it seems a valid inference that the Assyrians involved in the joint enterprise to obtain the precious metal attempted to bypass the authority of the rulers in question, and smuggle out supplies of it to their superiors in *Kaniš*.[18] Professor Lewy stresses that "... as a rule, the native princes were most desirous to obtain iron ...",[19] which seems highly likely in light of the further known rights of preemption they enjoyed, which "compelled the Assyrian merchants to submit by the 'palace' all incoming goods".[20] It is not possible to say, for instance, whether the *Kârum Ḫurama*, which was located in the midst of the area of operations described in *CCT*, II, 48, et. al., was aware of any illegal attempts to move "restricted" trade goods, but the concern of the principals in the group of interrelated texts cited in footnote 18, would seem to indicate that the possibility of arrest, and the confiscation of contraband, were of real concern to them.

Quite pertinently, another text — *EL*, 252 — the record of a legal hearing conducted before a referee from *Kârum Ḫurama* in the neighboring city of *Luḫuzatia*, appears to throw light on the process by which a non-Assyrian could be summoned to an interrogation concerning a transaction he had undertaken with an Assyrian.[21] It should be said at

[17] Since this long and rather involved text has been published in transliteration by J. Lewy in "*Ḫatta, Ḫattu, Ḫatti* ...", *op. cit.*, 430, w.n. 356, we refer the reader thereto. Cf. also *ATHE*, 62.

[18] The group of texts in question includes with *CCT*, II, 48 the texts *ICK*, 1, *TC*, II, 29 and *CCT*, II, 43. The differences of interpretation appear between J. Lewy, "*Ḫatta, Ḫattu, Ḫatti* ...", *op. cit.*, 422-441, and B. Landsberger, "Kommt *Ḫattum* 'Hettiterland' ...", *op. cit.*, 331-336, and *idem*, "Hettiterland und Hettiter in den Kültepe Tafeln ...", *op. cit.*, 321-329. A transliteration of *CCT*, II, 43:1-27 appears in Lewy, *loc. cit.*, 432, n. 379; and of *TC*, II, 29, *ibid.*, 431, n. 358. A transliteration of *ICK*, 1 appears in Landsberger, "Kommt *Ḫattum* ...", *loc. cit.*, 331, n. 13.

[19] Cf. "*Ḫatta, Ḫattu, Ḫatti* ...", *op. cit.*, 430, n. 355.

[20] Cf. *ibid.*

[21] For the convenience of the reader we reproduce from *EL*, I, pp. 273-274, the

the outset that instances of Anatolians appearing before Assyrian judicial bodies are rare. From a survey of the limited number of Cappadocian texts which concern themselves with legal matters, it is possible to affirm that by and large it is the Assyrian trader, himself, whose disputes are arbitrated, and who is subject to the judgement of his compatriots. The Assyrian courts are primarily concerned with Assyrian civil and commercial affairs. Therefore the hearing recorded in *EL*, 252, and involving the Anatolian Šarnikat is of paramount interest.

Although the context is not entirely clear, and the text requires restoration in places, a brief summary of the matter at hand may be given. Šarnikat, the Anatolian, who apparently lives in the city of *Luḫuzatia*, has lent the Assyrian Šamaš-taklaku (almost certainly a resident of the neighboring city of *Ḫurama*), a sum of money in silver, as security for which Šamaš-taklaku has given a slave in pledge.[22] Apparently, though not certainly, Šamaš-taklaku had previously assigned the slave in question to another Assyrian, Šalim-Aššur, perhaps as collateral in a financial agreement between them.[23] The issue, then, is one of deciding whose claim to the slave is valid.

Šalim-Aššur, the plaintiff, has petitioned *Kârum Ḫurama* for a referee to accompany him to *Luḫuzatia* to question Šarnikat.[24] Šamaš-taklaku was brought along as a material witness.[25] Our text states that both Šalim-Aššur and Šarnikat "seized us" in *Luḫuzatia* (i.e., "Came before

transliterated copy of *EL*, 252:

(1) *Ša-ar-ni-ga-ad* (2) *ù Sál-ma-A-šur i-na* (3) *Lu-ḫu-sá-dí-a iṣ-bu-tù-ni-a-tí-ma* (4) *um-ma Ša-ar-ni-ga-⟨ad⟩ -ma* (5) *a-na Ša-lim-A-šur-ma mì-šu-um* (6) *êkallam*$^{lam}_{4}$ *ta-al-pu-ta-ma* (7) *ra-bi-ṣa-am a-na bîti*^{ti}*-a* (8) *ta-ar-dí-am 18 šiqlî kaspam* (9) ^{d}*Šamaš-ta-ak-la-ku ḫa-bu-lam* (10) *um-ma Ša-ar-ni-ga-⟨ad⟩-ma* (11) [*a-n*]*a Šál-ma-A-šur-ma 18 šiqlî* (12) [*kaspa*]*m dí-na-ma wa-ar-dí* (13) [*ù a*]*m-tám ta-ru* (14) [^{d}*Šamaš-ta*]*-ak-lá-ku* (15) [*ni-iš-ta-na*]*-a-al-ma* (16) [*um-ma n*]*i-nu-ma kaspam* (17) [*18 šiqlî ha-bu-l*]*a-tí um-ma šu-ut-ma Rev.* (18) [*18*] *šiqlî kaspam k*[*i-n*]*a* (19) [*ḫ*]*a-bu-lá-ku* [wa-ar-dam] *e-zi-ib* (20) *Šál-ma-A-*[*šur a*]*mtam ú-lá* [*ú*]*-ta-er* (21) *18 šiqlî kaspam ḫu-bu-ul* (22) ^{d}*Šamaš-ta-ak-lá-ku* la iq-bi (23) *amtam ú-šé-ṣí a-na a-wa-tim* (24) *a-ni-a-tim kà-ru-um Ḫu-ra-ma* (25) *i-dí-ni-a-tí-ma maḫar paṭrim ša A-šur* (26) *ṭup-pá-am ší-bu-tí-ni ni-dí-in* (27) *maḫar A-šur-rê'im mêr I-dí-da maḫar Ku-bi*$_4$*-na-da* (28) *maḫar Da-da-a A-šur-rê'um mêr Ki-sí-ma-nim* (29) *Pì-lá-aḫ-A-šùr ù E-ra-dí* (30) *ta-pá-ú-ni a-wi-lu paṭram* (31) *ša A-šur iṣ-bu-tù-ma* (32) *ša-sú-ḫu a-ta* (33) *ma-lá-kà ṭup-pu-um* (34) *a-ni-um ša ší-bu-tí-šu-nu* (35) *me-eḫ-ru-um*.

For the Anatolian name, Šarnikat, cf. E. Bilgiç, "Die Einheimischen Appellativa ...", *op. cit.*, 20, n. 45.

[22] Cf. 11. 8b-19.

[23] Cf. *EL*, I, p. 272.

[24] This inference is taken from the combination of 11. 1-8a and 24f., especially 1. 32, for which cf. *EL*, I, p. 275, n. (b).

[25] Cf. 11. 14f.

us to have us take testimony or affidavits in a dispute").[26] But we learn that Šalim-Aššur has contacted the palace of *Luḫuzatia* and acquired the services of a *râbiṣum*, who then came to the residence of Šarnikat and summoned him to the hearing.[27] We interpret this action to mean that an Assyrian had formally to contact the non-Assyrian palace adminstration and secure the assistance of a legal officer attached to that administration before an Anatolian could legally be obliged to appear as a party to litigation before an Assyrian board of inquiry.

The grounds for our interpretation require extended discussion, since their implications go to the heart of our belief that Assyrian-Anatolian political relationships presuppose the existence of agreements or treaties which define the rights of either on a *parity* basis, and do not reflect an Assyrian superiority. To begin with, it is apparent from our sources that in addition to the Assyrian system of courts represented by the various *kârum* and *wabârtum* assemblies, there were also tribunals attached to the Anatolian administrations.[28] The Cappadocian fund contains a small number of tablets recording the disposition of cases involving indigenous persons by courts composed entirely of indigenous officials.[29] Usually a decision in such a court is given under the authority of a particular prince, and the case may be heard before high-ranking secular or religious officials.[30] Certain legal formulas used in the records of these indigenous courts differ from those used in the *kârum* and *wabârtum* tribunals;[31] and the fact that the legal records of the Anatolian courts are composed in Assyrian strongly suggests that native scribes made use of writing techniques introduced by the Assyrian traders.[32]

It was inevitable that instances arise in which Anatolians and Assyrians together required the services of legal officials to settle disputes and conflicts which sprang up through their mutual engagement in commerce or through intermarriage. It is noteworthy that because the Assyrian trader was normally far more affluent than his Anatolian neighbor, he was in a position not only to loan money or goods to him against the pledge of debt-servitude of the latter and his family, but also to claim

26 Cf. 11. 1-3.

27 Cf. 11. 4-8a.

28 Cf. J. Lewy, "Old Assyrian Documents from Asia Minor (about 2,000 B.C.) II", *AHDO*, 2 (1938), 111-125.

29 A special study of these is a primary requisite for future Cappadocian tablet studies. The reader is referred both to the texts cited in n. 28-33, and the books and articles listed in Section F of the bibliography in *Appendix A*, below.

30 Cf., e.g., *EL*, 3; 188; *OIP*, 27, 1; 49A and B; 53, etc.

31 Cf. J. Lewy, "Old Assyrian Documents ... II", *op. cit.*, 111.

32 Cf. *ibid.*, 111-125, and "On Some Institutions ...", *op. cit.*, 8, n. 37.

such servitude in default of payment.[33] That many indigenous individuals, and frequently whole families, appear to be in bondage to Assyrian creditors reflects nothing but the operation of the commercial law of the intruding group, in our opinion. The Anatolian rulers of towns through which Assyrian caravans passed garnered to themselves financial reward from the operations of Cappadocian trade,[34] and this is reason enough to argue that they were likely to have granted the Assyrians certain rights over their subjects, where the latter chose to have financial dealings with the former. Nor can it be overlooked that it was possible for Assyrians, themselves, to fall into debt-servitude to their own compa-triots, and even more significantly — to Anatolian creditors, as well.[35] Both Anatolian and Assyrian were eager to be redeemed from such bondage, to be sure, and we have evidence, on the one hand, of a native prince and his wife redeeming an indigenous family from an Assyrian creditor,[36] and on the other, of Assyrians reclaiming an associate from an Anatolian, styled *nuâ'um*.[37]

To return again to the text we have been discussing — *EL*, 252 — the lack of a clear context for the events therein described prevents us from saying anything about the identity of the slaves whose possession is the subject of the altercation between Šarnikat of *Luḫuzatia* and Šalim-Aššur, but the fact that the palace of *Luḫuzatia* (as we think) and a *râbisum* attached to it appear in the same record of proceedings as a referee from *Kârum Ḫurama* illustrates one of those instances in which law must interest itself in a conflict of interest between members of different political allegiances, who nevertheless are parties to a joint financial transaction. There is no question but that the palace of *Luḫuzatia* was the seat of an indigenous administration. The prince of this town figures in the British Museum tablet *CCT*, II, 48,[38] where it appears that a group of Assyrian traders attempting to obtain the precious metal *aši'um* (iron?) in the contiguous regions of *Ḫurama* and *Luḫuzatia* are instructed by their principal to avoid transactions in *Luḫuzatia*, possibly for fear of having to surrender their supplies to the ruler.[39] In another text it is reported that a number of *kutânu*-garments of an Assyrian

[33] Cf. the discussion and citation of texts in J. Klima and L. Matouš, "Les tablettes 'cappadociennes'", *op. cit.*, 55-58.

[34] Cf. Chapter Six, below.

[35] Cf. n. 37, below.

[36] Cf. *EL*, 188.

[37] Cf. *OIP*, 27, 12.

[38] Cf. 11. 34-36. For transliteration-notice of this text, cf. n. 17.

[39] Cf. n. 17 and 18, above.

shipment have been seized by the palace-administration of that city, a fact which the princess of *Luḫuzatia* reiterates in response to an Assyrian petition about them.[40] But despite the fact that the rulers of *Luḫuzatia* interfere with the passage of Assyrian goods, or intimidate traders who may be attempting to smuggle contraband, there is reason to believe that even in the normal course of events they, as well as other princes, kept an interested eye on financial relationships between their subjects and the Assyrian traders. We learn from two documents, for example, that the palace administrations sometimes involved themselves in these relationships by overseeing the terms to which people heavily in debt were subjected by their creditors. One document deals entirely with persons bearing Anatolian names, including the witnesses.[41] The second is of greater pertinence, for it shows that an unnamed palace administration has helped to negotiate the terms by which a debtor, who must have been Anatolian, was obliged to pay a particularly large debt to eleven Assyrian creditors.[42] Here, then, appears to be a strong indication that while the administrations of the local princes generally followed a "hands-off" policy in financial dealings between their subjects and the Assyrians, they nevertheless could use their right of influencing the terms of those dealings to prevent unusual hardship for the obligated Anatolian.

To return once again to *EL*, 252 — the affair of Šalim-Aššur and Šarnikat at *Luḫuzatia* — it seems reasonable to affirm that when the plaintiff, Šalim-Aššur, sought to clarify a matter which involved a non-Assyrian, he took formal steps to have Šarnikat summoned with the full knowledge and consent of the highest legal authority over the latter. That the legal arbiter from *Kârum Ḫurama* returned to *Ḫurama* after the proceedings in *Luḫuzatia* indicates, to be sure, that the Assyrians felt they had the right to exercise their jurisdiction over persons belonging to their own group even in places which did not have a *kârum* or *wabârtum*-court.[43] But it should not thereby be thought that were *Luḫuzatia* to have

[40] The text *CCT*, IV 19c, reads as follows:
(1) *a-na A-šùr-Na-da* (2) *qi-bi*$_4$*-ma um-ma Ú-ṣú-ur-ša-A-šùr-ma* (3) *ù A-šùr-ta-ak-lá-ak-ma* (4) *2 manâ'ê kaspam* [*KÙ.BABBAR*] (5) *ku-nu-ki-ni Da-a-a* (6) *ù Tâb-ṣí-la-A-šùr* (7) *na-áš-ú-ni-kum* (8) *a-na-kam kà-ra-am* (9) *am-ḫu-ur-ma* (10) *ta-ta-lá-kà-nim* (11) *i-na ú-me-im* (12) *ša ṭuppam*$^{\text{pá-am}}$ (13) *ta-ša-me-a-ni* (14) *té-ib-a-nim-ma a-tal-kà-nim* (15) *a šu-mì 25 ṣubâtê ku-ta-ni* (16) *ša šé-bi*$_4$*-lá-ni-ni* (17) *i-na Lu-ḫu-sa-dí-a* (18) *ṣa-áb-tù a-na êkallim*^{lim} (19) *ni-li-ma um-ma* (20) *ru-ba-tum-*⟨*ma*⟩ *ṣa-bi*$_4$*-it* (21) *ṣubâtê*$^{\text{HI[A]}}$. *a-na annâkim* (22) *i-la-kam šu-ma ṣubâtê ku-ta-nu* (23) *i-ba-ší-ú li-qí lá-šu* (24) *šu-ma lá-áp-tù kaspam li-qí.*

[41] Cf. *EL*, 209.

[42] Cf. *EL*, 217.

[43] Cf. the closing lines of *EL*, 252 (above, n. 21), 30b-32a, and *EL*, I, p. 275, n. (b).

been the seat of an Assyrian settlement, the palace would not have been involved at all. For even in places where the Assyrians were well-established, the palaces could act to protect their own subjects, or to inhibit Assyrian actions.

In this regard, for example, Professor Lewy alludes to an unpublished fragment which records the experiences which an Assyrian named Buṣuttaa once had in *Burušḫattum:*

The fragment relates, inter alia, that he was kept in jail (cf. *AHDO*, II, 1938, p. 129, note 1), that iron (*amûtum*) and cloths had to be surrendered and that he was compelled to "go up to the palace" and to "pay silver", to all appear, ances because he was held responsible for the imprisonment of a non-Assyrian(?). Significantly enough, this letter begins with a passage from which it follows that Buṣuttaa subsequently lodged complaints at Aššur.[44]

Our purpose in citing this is to show that even in a city such as *Burušḫattum*, which had a *kârum*, and where (as we have seen) a Great Prince could be appealed to by a disgruntled Assyrian — under other circumstances an Assyrian could be jailed by the palace. Professor Lewy, no doubt, intends the implication that the complaints Buṣuttaa may have made to *Assur* were complaints to the alleged imperial overlord of "Halys Assyria", and further, that *Assur* would be in a position to overturn a decision of the palace of *Burušḫattum*, yet we need not acquiesce in this.[45] For it follows from our discussion of Chapter Four, above, that the release of Assyrians detained by Anatolian princes was obtained through negotiation. Beyond this, Prof. Lewy has himself pointed to the arrest and detention of the Assyrian merchant Inaa by the *non-Assyrian administration of Kaniš* (my italics), and to the fact that the local administrations were careful observers of the caravan traffic, and even held merchants suspected of irregular activities under close surveillance.[46]

Despite these instances of the exercise of authority by local Anatolian administrations, relations between them and the *kârû* and *wabârâtum* were essentially cordial and cooperative. Instances of loans by Assyrians to Anatolian officials appear in our sources. According to one document, an unnamed *kârum* issues an injunction against any Assyrian who would give anything whatsoever to a *rabi simmiltim*, or "citadel chief", until the latter pays his earlier-contracted debt to the Assyrian Ikunum. The penalty for disobedience is that the violator of the *kârum*'s decree shall

[44] Cf. "*Ḫatta, Ḫattu, Ḫatti* ...", *op. cit.*, 432, n. 378.

[45] We take this inference from the general outlines of Prof. Lewy's position, for which cf. Chapter Three, w.n. 27-45, above.

[46] Cf. "*Ḫatta, Ḫattu, Ḫatti* ...", *op. cit.*, 433, n. 381-385; 434, n. 386-387; 435, n. 388-389; 436, n. 392.

be himself required to pay the amount of the debt in question. The *kârum* here appears to have absolute authority to restrain its own members from acting against the interests of their fellows, but it cannot extend its authority to the actions of the *rabi simmiltim*, and apparently cannot even institute legal action to secure repayment.[47]

In another document we learn of a debt (in gold) which perhaps the same Ikunum as in *EL*, 273 (discussed above) now owes a palace, and of its payment by two Assyrians, representing him, to a third Assyrian, who appears to represent the palace's interest as an assignee of the loan.[48] If, in fact, this *wabârtum* was located in the same place attested as having a prince and palace in *TC*, III, 85 (for which cf. Chapter Four, above), then we might tentatively point to yet another instance of financial dealing involving a high-ranking Anatolian official — here a prince — and an Assyrian trader at *Zalpa*.[49] For in *TC*, III, 85, the ruler of *Zalpa* makes a point of saying that a certain Assyrian named Bur-Nunu owes him more than 2/3 of a mina of gold.[50]

While relations between Anatolian officials and individual Assyrians were usually cordial, it was not always so between the Anatolian administrations and the trading companies of the various Assyrian settlements, for the palaces appear to have had the right of confiscating certain goods from the warehouses and residences of the traders. Most likely, as Prof. Lewy suggests, the goods in question were contraband of some sort. According to the text *TC*, III, 271, which is the record of a hearing involving the Assyrians Alaḫum and Kuzizia at *Kaniš* (and which may have been authorized by an order of the city-assembly of *Assur*), the former requests the latter to accompany him to *Waḫšušana*, where the palace administration has denounced and confiscated a quantity of *aši'um* belonging to Alahum.[51] This metal had been stored in the house

[47] Cf. *EL*, 273.
[48] Cf. *EL*, 267.
[49] Cf. 11. 12-14.
[50] Cf. *TC*, III, 85: 31b-33, in Chapter Four, above.
[51] The text of *TC*, III, 271 reads as follows:

(1) *A-la-ḫu-um a-na Ku-zi-zi-a* (2) *i-na Kà-ni-iš*^{ki} (3) *iṣ-ba-at-ni-a-tí-ma um-ma* (4) *A-la-ḫu-um-ma a-na Ku-zi-zi-a-ma* (5) *i-na bîti*^{tí}*-kà i-na Wa-aḫ-šu-ša-na* (6) *lu kaspi*^{pí} *lu ḫurâṣi*^{ṣí} (7) *lu kà-sà-tum ša ik-bi*(*sic!*)*-ri-a* (= *ik-ri-bi-a*) (8) *lu ṭuppu*^{pu} *lu sà-ḫi-ir-ti* (9) *lu ki-ta-a-tum ib-ši-ú* (10) *ba-a-am šu-ma a-ši-i êkallum*^{lúm} (11) *i-na bîti*$^{\text{bi-tí}}$*-kà im-šu-úḫ* (12) *a-na Wa-aḫ-šu-ša-na iš-tí-a* (13) *a-lik-ma êkallam*^{lam} [......] (14) *a-ši-i i-na bît* [......] (15) *lu-šé-ṣí um-ma Ku-z*[*i-zi-a-ma*...] (16) *ú-lá a-la-ak* [.........] (17) *ba-al-*[............] (18) *i-tù-*[............] (19) *šu-ma a-n* [*a*............] (20) *a-na e-ra-*[............] (21) *pá-al-ḫa-tí* [......]. *Rev.* (22) *a-na Wa-lá-ma iš-*[.........] (23) *lá-ar-dí-kà-ma i-n*[*a*......] (24) *iš-tí ra-bi sí-kà-tim* (25) *ša U-lá-ma ra-bi-ṣa-am* (26) *li-ri-ša-ku-ma ra-bi*$_4$*-ṣú*[...] (27) *ša rabi sí-ki-tim ša U-lá-*[*ma*......] (28) *a-na Wa-aḫ-šu-ša-na*

of Kuzizia.[52] Obviously Alahum desires to recover his supply of this valuable commodity, and his formal action in petitioning for a referee in *Kaniš* further indicates that an Assyrian had recourse to the authority of the law of his own group in attempting to force a colleague to enter into potentially unpleasant, even dangerous negotiations with an indigenous administration. It is significant that Alahum appears to be protecting his own interests by making Kuzizia legally blameworthy in the Assyrian community should his *aši'um* not be recovered. Furthermore, it is enlightening that Assyrian traders, who may have been trafficking in a contraband commodity — against the implied provisions of Assyrian treaties with the local administrations — could have their "misdeeds" recognized through the vehicle of a legal action undertaken before the dagger of Assur — the very symbol of Assyrian law in the trading settlements![53]

A close look at *TC*, III, 271 shows that Kuzizia's initial response to Alahum's demand is that he will not go to *Waḫšušana* with the latter.[54] Alahum then appears to take cognizance of Kuzizia's fear of facing a hostile prince, and offers to conduct him to the city of *Ulama*, where he will ask the *rabi sikkatim* of that city for an attorney (*râbiṣum*) to accompany them, and serve as protection for Kuzizia.[55] Alahum evidently believes he can regain possession of his *aši'um* from the palace of *Waḫšušana* if Kuzizia appears, though it also seems clear that the latter, who seems to have been a permanent resident of *Kârum Wahšušana*, would no longer be welcome to stay in *Waḫšušana*, for Kuzizia is offered safe-conduct from *Waḫšušana* to the town of *Mama*, seat of a *wabârtum*.[56]

Kuzizia is unmoved by these promises, however. He refuses to go under any circumstances, but appears also to be implying that Alahum could make things very difficult for him if he wanted to.[57] He goes on to say: "I swear to you that I did not take any of your *aši'um*!"[58] While acknowledging that he is in a touchy position, Kuzizia wishes to make it

(29) *lu-šé-ri-ib-ni-a-tí-ma* (30) *li-ip-qí-id-kà-ma a-*[...] (31) *iš-tí êkallim*^{lim} *lá-al-q*[?...] (32) *ù a-na Ma-ma iš-tù* (33) *Wa-aḫ-šu-ša-na lu-šé-ṣí-a-kà* (34) *um-ma Ku-zi-zi-a-ma ú-lá* (35) *a-lá-ak šu-ma ta-pá-li-lá-ni* (36) *bi-lá-ni-ma lá-at-ma-a-kum* (37) *mì-ma i-na a-ší-i-kà a-na-ku* (38) *ú-lá al-qé ú*? *a-lik-ma* (39) *a-ší-a-kà ší-e a-na ma-lá* (40) *ṭup-pim*$^{pí-im}$ *ša dí-in* (41) *a-lim*^{ki} *maḫar paṭrim ša A-šur* (42) *ší-bu-ta-áš-nu ša eqlim*^{lim} (43) *Im-dí-ilum ú Pu-šu-ki-in i-dí-nu.*

52 Cf. 1. 5f.

53 Cf. 11. 39b-43.

54 Cf. 11. 15b-16.

55 Cf. 11. 21-30.

56 Cf. 11, 31-33.

57 Cf. 11. 34-36a.

58 Cf. 11. 36b-38.

perfectly clear that he did not appropriate to himself any of the goods which the Palace of *Waḫšušana* has confiscated. He ends by saying, "Look after your (own) *aši'um*!"[59]

Not only, then, does our text show us that a palace-administration could enter a *kârum*-area to search an Assyrian's house and seize certain of his goods, but also it informs us that a fugitive, such as Kuzizia must certainly be considered, might acquire aid from a friendly Anatolian official who resided in a neighboring city. We must inquire further into this aspect of our text, especially in light of the geographical implications of the situation of *Waḫšušana* relative to *Ulama*, and of the meaning of the *rabi sikkatim's* proposed concern. From the discussion presented in Chapter One, the city of *Ulama* was seen to be the last station before *Burušḫattum* according to the itinerary given in *TC*, III, 165, which describes a road leading south-west from *Kaniš*.[60] It was probably a short journey for a caravan, though not less than three days march away. The city of *Waḫšušana*, it will be recalled, lay more directly south of *Kaniš*, perhaps the same distance away from it as *Ulama*, but on a different road.[61] Thus while *Ulama* may generally be described as neighboring to *Waḫšušana*, it actually lay much closer to *Burušḫattum*. Since *Waḫšušana* is characterized as a *mâtum*, or "land", even as is *Burušḫattum*,[62] it might be supposed that *Ulama* was part of the jurisdictional area of the ruler of *Waḫšušana*, yet this does not satisfy the geographical data. Nor, it should be stressed, would a city situated so close to the region ruled by a Great Prince of *Burušḫattum* be likely to belong to the sphere of influence of a ruler bearing a less grandiose title. Hence the possibility of an official of *Ulama* providing protection for an Assyrian against whom the threat of punishment existed in *Waḫšušana* seems not to emerge from any direct jurisdiction responsibility owed to the palace of *Waḫšušana* by the *rabi sikkatim*.

It is also possible to interpret that the *rabi sikkatim* of *Ulama* was a personal friend of the Alaḫum of *TC*, III, 271, and one to whom an appeal for a legal assistant would have been the equivalent of a request for a favor to help a friend in distress. This deserves some consideration especially because our sources report that the Assyrian caravaners were used to making small payments to the officials of cities through which they passed, sometimes in payment of services rendered, but sometimes,

59 Cf. 1. 39a.

60 Cf. Chapter One, n. 41, above.

61 Cf. *ibid.*, n. 36.

62 For *mât Waḫšušana*, cf. *KTP*, 10:25, and *KTHahn*, 1:3-4; for *mât Burušḫattum*, cf. *KTHahn*, 1:3.

no doubt, as "bakshish".[63] One itinerary text reports, for example, that on a trip between *Kaniš* and *Burušḫattum*, the *gaššum* and a *rabiṣum* of *Ulama* "took" sums of copper from the stocks of a caravan passing through the city.[64]

Finally we may point out that the *rabi sikkatim*-officials in the service of various local administrations not only made business arrangements with individual traders, but also could occasionally exert pressure upon them to supply valued commodities.[65] In this light it seems entirely possible that the Assyrian Alaḫum, of *TC*, III, 271, may have had a business relationship with the *rabi sikkatim* of *Ulama*, — one in which he could have expected his influence to result in the grant of assistance to Kuzizia and himself.

If in cities where both *kârum*-establishments and palaces existed side by side there is no indication of Assyrian political domination, then the same conclusion must be drawn from a study of relationships in cities having both *wabârtum*-settlements and cities. In the city of *Kuššara*, for example, if indeed the Assyrians maintained a *wabârtum* there, the palace administration is autonomous enough to be able to compel an Assyrian trader to pay a sum of gold to it, perhaps (as Lewy conjectures) so that he could regain a certain freedom of movement after arrest.[66] In the cities of *Mama* and *Tuḫpia* gifts are brought to the rulers as *erbum*,[67] but at *Šamuḫa* an altercation between the *wabârtum*, itself, and the local palace, is attested. We need pause to consider this encounter, contained in *VAT*, 6209.[68]

63 Cf. e.g., *TC*, III, 165; 166; 211:46-47, etc.
64 Cf. *TC*, III, 165:18b-25.
65 Cf. the texts *BIN*, IV, 45:8f., which reports the pressure placed upon an Assyrian for delivery of quantities of *aši'um* by the *rabi sikkatim* officials of Ušša and Ḫuduru-tum, and *KTHahn* 14, which reports an instance in which an Assyrian and the *rabi sikkatim* of Waḫšušana have agreed to cooperate in a business deal, but later came to a disagreement.
66 Cf. J. Lewy, "*Ḫatta, Ḫattu, Ḫatti* ...", *op. cit.*, 434, w.n. 386.
67 For an *irbum* to the Prince of Mama, cf. *BIN*, IV, 201: 1-9; to the Prince of Tuḫpia, cf. *TC*, 39:4-13f.
68 The text *VAT 6209* reads as follows:
(1) *a-na ší-ip-ri ša a-lim*^{ki} (2) *ù kà-ri-im Kà-ni-iš* (3) *qí-bi-ma um-ma wa-bar-tum* (4) *ša Ša-mu-ḫa-ma a-na-kam* (5) *a šu-mì ša emârî* (6) *ša êkallum*^{lúm} *iṣ-bu-tù-*[*ni*] (7) *êkal-lam* $^{lam}{}_4$ *nu-*⟨*ma*⟩*-ḫir-ma* (8) *um-ma êkallum*^{lúm}*-ma* (9) *šu-ma mì-iš-lá-am* (10) [*t*]*a-lá-qí-a li-*[*qí-a*] (11) [...*l*]*á-qí* [...] (12) [.........] (*rev.*) (x +1) *lu-ni-ir-*[*dí*] (*x* +*2*) *16 bilâtim 30 m*[*anâ'ê annakam*] (*x* +*3*) *ù 3 emârî*$^{H[IA]}$, (*x* +*4*) [*ṣa-lá*]*-mì i-dí-*⟨*nu*⟩*-ni-a-*[*tí-ma*] (*x* +*5*) [*a-na*] *ší-ip-ri-ku-nu* (*x* +*6*) [*ni*]*-ip-qí-id-ma* (*x* +*7*) *i-*[*ra*]*-dí-ú-ni-ku-nu-tí* (*x* +*8*) *ší-ip-ru-ku-nu ù* (*x* +*9*) *ni-nu ni-zi-iz-ma* (*x* +*10*) *ší-bi*$_4$ *ni-iš-ku-šu-nu-tí.*

Prof. Lewy has published a transliteration of this text in "On Some Institutions ...", *op. cit.*, 70, n. 301.

The text itself is a letter sent by the *wabârtum* of *Šamuḫa* to the Envoys of the City and *Kârum Kaniš*, hence represents an official communication. From it we learn the following: the palace at *Šamuḫa* has seized a number of donkeys, presumably with their loads.[69] Hence we are to be concerned with a situation in which an Assyrian caravan has been detained. The *wabârtum* reports that it "approached" the palace so as to discuss the matter, and that the palace replied that if it wished to take half of the detained caravan's load it could do so.[70] At this point the text is damaged, but several lines later the *wabârtum* reports that the palace gave them three donkeys and sixteen and one-half talents of lead.[71] The *wabârtum* entrusted these to the messengers from *Kaniš* for delivery to *Kaniš*.[72] The letter ends with the significant statements that the *wabârtum* and the *Kanišian* messengers "stood" (i.e., were representatives) and that they established their testimony before the palace.[73]

Once again we are confronted with a situation in which a formal negotiation is carried on because a ruler has, for one reason or another, interfered with the progress of an Assyrian caravan.[74] We cannot know whether the Assyrian petitioners succeeded in regaining their goods entire; the palace offers only half, and the number of donkeys and talents of lead mentioned in the text may, in fact, represent only this portion. But most important of all, the Assyrians are represented as having been required to "establish their testimony (or witnesses)", which would normally include swearing oaths before the appropriate and legitimate divine symbols of the tribunal where the discussions took place.[75] When we recall from *TC*, III, 85 that in a similar situation the Assyrians were required to take an oath in an altercation with the Prince of *Zalpa*, we can again affirm that negotiations between high-ranking Assyrian functionaries and individual princes were conducted in an atmosphere of legality in which the implied sovereignity of the rulers is everywhere manifest.[76]

In another instance, this time to report that an Assyrian has been robbed of some garments while in the vicinity of *Badna*, the *wabârtum* of this town "goes up" to a *burullum* official, hence to a palace functionary

[69] Cf. 11. 1-6.
[70] Cf. 11. 7-11.
[71] Cf. rev. x +2 – x +4.
[72] Cf. rev. x +5 – x +7.
[73] Cf. rev. x +8 – x +10.
[74] For others, cf. e.g., *TC*, III, 85 and *CCT*, 30a in Chapter Four, above.
[75] This follows from many records of affadavits ending with such allusions. Cf., e.g., *EL*, 238-290, *passim*, etc., and Chapter Two, n. 120, above.
[76] Cf. *TC*, III 85:36b-38, Chapter Four, above.

of that city, and is told that if the goods are not discovered — hence are lost — they shall nevertheless be restored.[77] Prof. Lewy points to this text as an indication that the local palaces were responsible for police functions in their areas, and we further stress that this is fully in line with indications elsewhere that the Anatolian palaces supervised the trade routes and generally provided guard-services.[78] No doubt the *burullum* of *Badna* was acting under the terms of existing agreements in offering to search for, and if necessary make good, the stolen property. That these agreements were likely to have been concluded with a *kârum* of the neighborhood instead of the *wabârtum* of *Badna* seems probable in light of the fact that the ruler of *Wašhania*, a city which boasted a *wabârtum*, negotiated with *Kârum Wahšušana* and then *Kârum Kaniš* according to *KTP*, 14.[79]

At *Amkuwa*, which may have been the seat of a *wabârtum*, several indications exist that its rulers were substantially autonomous during the tenure of Assyrian inhabitation.[80]

The documents from that site contain references to three rulers,[81] who seem likely to have ruled the city. The text *OIP*, 27, 53 records the freeing of apparently indigenous slave girls under the authority of a prince named [Har]-batiwa, who may have ruled either *Amkuwa* or one of the neighboring cities.[82] The action here recorded is fully in harmony with the fact that transactions involving native slaves or debtors at Kültepe are similarly completed, under the aegis of a prince or high court officials.[83]

Another aspect of the activities of indigenous princes and their officials comes to light in *OIP*, 27, 5, where an Assyrian Enna-Aššur, writes to his

[77] Cf. *KTHahn*, 3. For the convenience of the reader we present Prof. Lewy's transliteration of this text:
(1) *a-na A-šur-na-da* (2) *qí-bí-ma um-ma* (3) *Pí-lá-ḫi-Ištar-ma* (4) *iš-tù Ba-ad-na* (5) *A-gu$_5$-a Tá-bi-A-nu-um* (6) *ú Ili$_5^{li}$-ba-ni ú-wa-šé-ru-ni-ma* (7) *um-ma Tá-bi-A-nu-ma* (8) *ba-am iš-tí-ni ṣubâtî ^{hi}* (9) *ú-qá-i-ú iš-tí-šu-nu* (10) *iš-tù Ba-ad-na* (11) *na*-ba-*ta-am* (12) *nu-ṣí-ma iš-tí-šu-nu* (13) *a-na bît wa-áb-ri* (14) *ú-lá ú-šé-ru-ni* (15) *a-ḫa-ma bît al-pí* (16) *a-bi-id bîtám^{tám}* (17) im-*lu-šu-ma* 6 *ṣubâtî^{hi}* (18) *i-ta-áb-ku* (19) *ib-ra-ra-am a-na qá-qí-dí-a* (20) *áš-pu-⟨kà⟩-kum-ma* (21) *a-na Ba-ad-na* (22) *a-na ṣé-er A-lá-bi-im* (23) *a-tù-ra-ma wa-ba-ar-tum$_6$* (24) *ša Ba-ad-na* (25) *a-na ṣé-er Ba-ru-li* (26) *e-li-ú-ma um-ma* (27) *um-ma* (*dittography*) *šu-nu-ma lu ni-iš-ma*[*r*] (28) *ú šu-ma i-ḫa-li-qú* (29) *ni-nu nu-ma-lá*.

[78] For Prof. Lewy's opinion, cf. "Old Assyrian Documents from Asia Minor, II", *op. cit.*, 138-139.

[79] Cf. the discussion in Chapter Four, above.

[80] On the assumption that *Amkuwa* (= Alishar Hüyük?) was a *wabârtum*, cf. J. Lewy, "On Some Institutions ...", *op. cit.*, 61, n. 257.

[81] Cf. Chapter Three, citations under *Amkuwa*.

[82] Cf. I. J. Gelb, *OIP*, 27 (1935), 54, n. to 1.14 of text no. 53.

[83] Cf. Chapter Three, above, nn. 66 and 67.

colleague, Nabi-Enlil, who may have lived at *Amkuwa*-Alishar Hüyük. Enna-Aššur asks that the latter petition a princess and her Citadel-Chief (in *Amkuwa*?) to discover whether they will either return outright or accept ransom money for some *habiri* ("mercenaries") who have come from the city of *Šalaḫšua*, and who now appear to be languishing in jail.[84] Why Enna-Aššur is so interested in behalf of the *habiri*-men, who are also styled *âwîli*, or "gentlemen", (i.e., as opposed to slaves) is unknown. But it is noteworthy that an Assyrian here waits upon a decision of a princess and her citadel-chief as to whether he must ransom them or not, so as to obtain their release.

Much the same kind of information comes to us from *OIP*, 27, 49A and B, where the release of six captives seized during a war is accomplished through the intervention of a relative.[85] The men had been detained at *Amkuwa* under the charge of the *Great Burullum* of that city, and their release follows upon this identification by the relative and an agreement with the Great *Burullum*.[86] The document itself is issued under the authority of Anitta, the great Prince, and Perruwa, Citadel chief.[87] Thus in the days of the Assyrian quarter at Alishar-Hüyük there existed princes in the palace or in the near vicinity who give every indication of having had full competence and authority in dealing with important matters, which included the release of slaves, and other, higher-ranking, captives from neighboring cities.

We see then that in political and legal encounters between local princes and *wabârtum*-establishments or in the activities of rulers in *wabârtum*-towns the same kind of legal atmosphere prevails as between the ruler and the *kârum*-establishments — namely one in which formal notice is taken of conflicts, and negotiations of equals take place. We would also point out that the situation is not different in the contacts between the Assyrians and rulers whose towns were *not* the seats of Assyrian settlements.

The chief documentary source of interest reporting such contacts in addition to the encounter between Assyrians and the Prince of *Naduḫtum* discussed in Chapter Four (*TC*, III, 75) is the tablet *KTP*, 6, a letter from

[84] This is Prof. Lewy's interpretation in "Old Assyrian Documents ... II", *op. cit.*, 128-131.

[85] Cf. *ibid.*, for an interpretation by Prof. Lewy, 125-142.

[86] On the *burullum*-official, cf. J. Lewy, Review of *OIP*, 27 (1935) in *JAOS*, 57 (1937), 434-435; *ibid.*, Old Assyrian Documents ... II", *op. cit.*, 138-139, w.n. 5; I. J. Gelb, *OIP*, 27 (1935), 51; E. Bilgiç, "Die einheimischen Appellativa ...", *op. cit.*, 75.

[87] Cf. *OIP*, 27, 49A:24b-25; 49B:26b-28.

Kârum Kaniš to the Prince of *Širmiya*.[88] This text reports that two envoys of the *Kârum* are bringing the prince a sum of silver and gold, which appears to have the character of a special gift, though it is not stated that an *erbum* is involved.[89] Apparently the prince has contacted the *Kârum* earlier, and the *Kârum* appears to be exhorting the prince to carry out some decision he has informed them of.[90] Little can be learned from the context of our document, but the *Kârum* has occasion to write to the Širmiyan prince: "You are our son (and) our lord!"[91] Prof. Lewy cites this usage to argue that "while extending to the 'native' princes all the courtesies normally accorded royalty, the Assyrian magistrates of *Kaniš* did not hesitate to call these princes their 'sons', thus indicating that they saw in them proteges supposed to comply with their orders with the deference with which a son accepts and obeys his father's wishes".[92] We suppose, on the other hand, that the phrase incorporates the idea of equality, by which the *Kârum Kaniš* recognizes that the Širmiyan prince is both superior and inferior to it at the same time — hence the *Kârum* is equally both superior and inferior to the prince. Thus they would appear to be parties of equal sovereignty and status *vis à vis* each other.[93]

We cannot conclude this general survey of the political situation during the most active days of Assyrian trade in Anatolia without referring to the so-called "Anitta-Inscription", which gives an account of the military conquests of Anitta and his father, Pitḫana, two early Anatolian rulers who definitely belong within the chronological limits of the Old Assyrian Period.[94] According to our text, Pitḫana originally ruled the city of

[88] The text *KTP*, 6, transliterated and translated by J. Lewy, "Apropos of a Recent Study ...", *op. cit.*, 31-32, reads as follows:

(1) *a-na ru-ba-im* (2) *Ši-ir-mì-i-a-im* (3) *qí-bi-ma um-ma* (4) *kà-ru-um Kà-ni-iš-*[*ma*] (5) *1 manâ'um* (*MA.NA*) *kaspum* (*KÙ.BABBAR*) *ṣa-ru-pu-um* (6) *ù 3 šiqlû* (*GÍN*) *hurâṣum* (*KÙ.GI*) (7) *A-bi-a-a ù A-gu-a* (8) *ší-ip-ru-ni* (9) *na-aš-ú-*[*ni*]*-kum* (10) *ṭup-pì-kà ni-iš-me-ma* (11) [...] *Kà*(?)*-ni*(?)*-iš*(?) (*lower edge and beginning of reverse lost*) (*x* + *2*) [... *a ma*]*-la* [*ša*] (*x* + *3*) [*ta*]*-aš-pu-ra-ni* (*x* + *4*) *e-pu-uš-ma* (*x* + *5*) *ta-aq-bi-ta-kà* (*x* + *6*) *i li-bi₄-ni* (*x* + *7*) *i-ba-ší me-ra-ni be-el-ni a-ta* (*x* + *8*) *ma-la ší-ip-ru-ni* (*x* + *9*) *i-qá-*[*bi₄*]*-ú-*[*ni-ku-ni*] ... (*x* + *14*) *mêr* (*DUMU*) *A-šùr-*[......] (*upper edge and beginning of left edge lost*) (*y* + *1*) *ša a-na ṣé-ri-*[*kà* ...] (*y* + *2*) *i-lá-kà-ni* [......]

[89] Cf. 11. 1-9.

[90] Cf. 11. 10— x +4.

[91] Cf. 11. x +7b.

[92] Cf. J. Lewy, *loc. cit.*, 31.

[93] We strongly infer this not only from the practice alluded to in II Kings 16. 7- where "son" bears the overtone of "protege", as Prof. Lewy notes (*loc. cit.*, 31, n. 3), but just as much from the counter-practice of weak or vassal kings referring to their superiors as "my Lord", as, for example, in I Kings 20. 4, 9.

[94] *VAT*, 7479, transliterated and translated in B. Hrozný, "L'invasion des indo-

Kuššara, which is the seat of a palace in the Cappadocian texts.[95] The date of Pitḫana's reign is uncertain; he appears on a Louvre document as a *rubâ'um* (prince),[96] but this tablet antedates Hrozný's discovery and first excavation of Kültepe as the chief distribution center of Cappadocian tablets in Turkey. Until evidence to the contrary appears, we would assign Pitḫana to the period of Kültepe Ib.[97]

Assuming the rule of Pitḫana at *Kuššara* during the days of Level Ib, it is noteworthy that he was able to attack the city of *Neša* and capture its king at a time when the Assyrians are alleged by the "Imperial" school to have ruled Anatolia as a province.[98] Furthermore, Anitta followed in the path of his father. Whereas Pitḫana had been but a *rubâ'um*, Anitta, who had first served his predecessor as *rabi simmiltim*, was able to claim for himself the title of *rubâ'um rabî'um*, "Grat Prince", as a result of his military prowess.[99] Among the towns and princes who appear as his adversaries are *Zalpa*,[100] *Ḫatti*[101] and *Burušḫattum*,[102] all of which were host cities to Assyrian *kârû*, and *Šalatiwara*,[103] Old Assyrian *Šalatuwar*, which was the seat of a *wabârtum*.

All of these conquests must have taken place during the time when the Assyrians are supposed to have been powerful enough to dictate to vassal princes. Yet are we not surprised to find such vigorous internecine warfare on the part of these "vassals"? The successes of Pitḫana and Anitta are all the more astonishing if we here note an assertion that the Assyrians forbade the native rulers to acquire bronze and collect weapons.[104] What could be more ironic in the face of this proposal than the

---

europeens en Asie Mineure vers 2000 av. J-C", *ArOr*, 1 (1929), 273-281 f. Its historical value is discussed by R. S. Hardy, "The Old Hittite Kingdom", *AJSL*, 58 (1941), 182, n. 18. See now also *Appendix C* below, and Otten, *MDOG*, 83 (1951), pp. 40-42.

95 Cf. *VAT*, 7479:1. For the palace of *Kuššara* in the Cappadocian texts, cf. *ICK*, 1:48. *Kuššara* may have been the seat of an Assyrian *wabârtum*, cf. E. Bilgiç, "Die Ortsnamen ...", *op. cit.*, 30.

96 Cf. *TC*, III, 214A:19-20.

97 Cf. T. Özgüc, *TTKY*, V, Seri — No. 10, *op. cit.*, 154, and Balkan, *TTKY*, VII, Seri — No. 31 a, pp. 38-44.

98 Cf. *VAT*, 7479:1-9.

99 For Anitta as *rabi simmiltim*, cf. *TC*, III, 214A:21-22; as *rubâ'um*, *OIP*, 27, 1:1 (*ru-ba-e*), rev. x +2 — x +3 (*ibid.*); as *rubâ'um rabî'um*, *OIP*, 27, 49A:24b-25; B:27.

100 Cf. *VAT*, 7479:31, 38-43; 78.

101 Cf. *ibid.*, 36, 44-51.

102 Cf. *ibid.*, 73-77.

103 Cf. *ibid.*, 52-54; 64-72.

104 Cf. Lewy, "Some Aspects of Commercial Life ...", *op. cit.*, 94-95. There it is proposed that the existence of an official bearing the title *rabi kakke*, 'Chief of the weapons', indicates that the alleged Assyrian government had supervision over the possession and use of weapons all over Anatolia, and similarly the existence of a *rabi*

presence of Anitta's bronze dagger lying in the ruins of *Kaniš*, itself?[105] For the conqueror ranged all over central Anatolia and sacked that great city, destroying the palace of the indigenous Kanisian ruler. It cannot be doubted, in light of the present discussion, that the individual Anatolian cities maintained full-fledged armies during the Cappadocian Period. The official cited as a *rabi ṣâbim*, "General" in the British Museum text *CCT*, II, 30, must have headed one such armed force.

A possible objection to the line of argument developed in the last few pages might be: whereas Assyria was strongly in control of Anatolia during the period of Kültepe Level II, its power was weakened *after* the karum-community of that period, and that the political situation was substantially different during the days of Kültepe Level Ib. There is a hint of this in Prof. Lewy's remarks about the meaning of the encounter between the Assyrians and the Prince of *Tamnia*, recorded in the Level Ib tablet kt f/k 183 we discussed fully in the last chapter. Although insisting that it was the Prince of *Tamnia* who expected to be sworn to allegiance by the envoys of *Kârum Kaniš*, he nevertheless states that "my conclusions as to the might and extension of the Old Assyrian Empire ... were based exclusively upon the contents of the Kültepe tabets from level 2. Consequently, they cannot be undermined by a single text from level 1b ..."[106] And there is a further hint of this in Kemal Balkan's notion that the Assyrian commercial position in Anatolia during Kültepe Ib was substantially weakened by contrast to what it had been earlier, although Balkan does not support the idea of Assyrian overlordship during the period of Level II.[107] However, we must reject any contention

siparrim, 'Administrator of Bronze', suggests government control of the metal. In Prof. Lewy's words:

> "... it appears that, when conquering and colonizing parts of Asia Minor, the Assyrians took precautions to prevent the natives from acquiring new weapons. It goes without saying that such a policy was certainly accompanied by regulations which made it unlawful for Assyrian merchants established in the conquered lands to engage in the bronze trade". *Loc. cit.*

If this be true, then the Anatolian palaces were not only powerless puppets, but also subject to Assyrian commercial restrictions. But first, wherever men bearing official titles are met with they bear Anatolian names, except, of course, those who obviously belong to a *kârum*-administration; there is little reason to believe that the *rabi kakke* official is an Assyrian. Nor, secondly, when we recall that the ruler of *Ḫaḫḫum* was engaged in meeting a rebellion of his citizens, as discussed in Chapter Four, or that areas such as *Burušḫattum* and *Waḫšušana* were disturbed by commotion at one time or another, can we accept Prof. Lewy's theory that the Assyrians maintained a tight control over weapons in Anatolia.

105 Cf. *Appendix B*, below.

106 Cf. J. Lewy, "Apropos of a Recent Study ...", *op. cit.*, 26.

107 Cf. *TTKY*, VII Seri — No. 28, *op. cit.*, 42f.

that the political situation of Ib is radically different from II, first because, as we have been attempting to show throughout this study, the Assyrians appear never to have had military and political superiority over Anatolia during the days of Level II; and second, from the evidence of archaeology, the Assyrian *kârum* at *Kaniš* during the period of Ib was still large and prosperous, even though the previous settlement phase had been destroyed and the site abandoned for at least a generation.[108] Should it be argued, moreover, that the conquests of Pitḫana and Anitta were possible only *after* Assyrian power had been weakened at some time toward the end of Kültepe II, then we must ask: what is assumed to be the cause of such weakness? And if it be answered that the rise in strength of small Anatolian principalities is responsible, then we remain mystified, because of the stress which has been placed on the alleged Assyrian monopoly of weapons and control of bronze by Prof. Lewy.

The fact appears that there was no significant reversal of the Assyrian position in Anatolia between the period of Kültepe II and Ib because Assyria never had the control it is alleged to have had over the small principalities of the central Plateau. The previous chapters, in discussing those texts which bore on the diplomatic and other encounters of a political nature between Assyrians and Anatolians, allowed the conclusion that a number of formal agreements, certainly treaties, governed affairs between the various Anatolian administrations and the Assyrian *kârû* and *wabârâtum*. The discussion presented in this chapter has attempted to show that the Anatolian principalities were capable of exercising the kind of initiative which argues against their having been Assyrian vassals.

[108] Cf. *Appendix B*, discussion of Kültepe Level I, below.

PART THREE

CONCLUSIONS

VI

THE ASSYRIAN "COMMUNITY" AND THE ANATOLIAN COMMUNITIES: TOWARD A DEFINITION OF ASSYRIAN "COLONIZATION"

Our inquiry has, to this point, prepared the way for an attempt to answer the central question of this study: who, if any one group at all, has ultimate sovereignty in Anatolia during the period of Assyrian trading activity? And should authority be divided in some way, what is the relation of Assyrian administrative power to that of the Anatolian administrations? We have already observed many instances in which Assyrian settlement-corporations were politically engaged with one or another of the Anatolian local governments, and have suggested that fixed treaty relationships existed between the Assyrians and their Anatolian neighbors. But since we have continually denied that any significant evidence of Assyrian imperial power exists, we are free to construct a definition of the Assyrian settlements which is based upon other than coercive considerations.

By reviewing the structure of Assyrian political institutions we may conveniently prepare the background for this definition. Recalling that in Assur the Assyrian prince and the City-Council together hold the positions of highest authority, we see them as the law-givers and chief judicial officers of Assyria. They are the actual rulers of Assyria, but hold their offices under the aegis of the god Assur, who is the nominal sovereign. As such, they define policy and administer it, and act to protect the state against external threat or internal deterioration as far as possible. They are supreme over the Assyrian citizen, who dutifully obeys Assyrian law. All this is true for the geographical region of Assyria, itself. But our chief concern must be with the range and effectiveness of Assyrian law *in Anatolia* during the Cappadocian Period.

By "law" in this context we mean the total of administrative and judicial acts which affect the liberty of the individuals who may be subject to them.[1] We concentrate to be sure, on the force of Assyrian jurisdiction over the Assyrian trader, and the position of the *kârû* and *wabârâtum* in

[1] Cf. H. D. Lasswell and A. Kaplan, *Power and Society* (New Haven, 1950), 196-197.

the entire structure of Assyrian decision-making institutions; but we need also examine whether Assyrian policy has such effects upon *Anatolians* as to allow us to define them as Assyrian citizens. Equally important, we should not overlook the effects of policy-making by Anatolian administrations upon the Assyrian traders and their settlements. In this way we can arrive at a concept of effective rule, or government, in a milieu where two different ethnic groups interact closely with each other.

Since the Assyrian trader in Anatolia belonged to one or another of Assyrian political agencies — the *kârum* or *wabârtum*, etc. — which themselves represent authority-structures, we may define him as an Assyrian subject.[2] Not only did he share a common language, religion and system of mores with his fellows, but he also paid public homage to Assyrian authority, as is to be seen, for example, by his taking the usual oaths before the symbols of Assur's power — the dagger or the hook-shaped emblem of the protecting deity. His values, his attitudes, were Assyrian values and attitudes, and his entire perspective was oriented toward maintaining himself as a member-in-good-standing of his group. His practices thus represent an attempt to fulfill Assyrian political and commercial interests.

In the *kârum* or the *wabârtum* the Assyrian trader found an organizational focus for the many diversified acts which characterize Cappadocian trade. He, himself, functioned as but one worker in the vast division of labor, which effectively exploited a whole region for economic advantage. His immediate loyalties were to his caravan leader, his financial backers, or to his company and its directors. He worked together with his fellows, who largely depended upon his vitality and trustworthiness for the success of their own functions. But he had a sense of the whole, a sense of solidarity, because of which he thought and felt himself to be an Assyrian subject. The organization of Cappadocian trade merely gave pattern to the solidarity and cooperation the individual trader experienced as a member of a closely-knit ethnic and religious group.

This organization may be studied as an aggregate of groups, each of whose functions meshed with those of its partners.[3] At bottom appear the demigroups, the small clusters of trading partners linked to caravans, which themselves are but lesser forms of organization within larger associations. In commerce, the key large association is the patriarchally-dominated trading house, which at times joined with its equals to form trading partnerships. In these commercial associations we find a con-

[2] On authority structures cf. *ibid.*, 133f.

[3] Cf. *ibid.*, 29-31.

siderable degree of diversification, integration of operations and solidarity. No matter how complex and rigid the division of labor, the operations and perspectives of each house are smoothly integrated with those of the others. In the larger scheme of organization, these commercial associations are superseded by the *kârum* or *wabârtum*, which draw from the trading houses a new aggregate of members that functions administratively and judicially. Within the unified perspectives of the Assyrian community, special business relationships are contractual, whether the contracts are of the small *commenda*-type known in Medieval trading, or represent large combinations of entrepreneur-investors. Underlying these contractual relationships, however, are those feelings of ethnic and political unity which are given effective function by the emergence of supervisory associations that serve to guarantee private contracts under law, and minimize the difficulties of private parties in obtaining valuable objectives.

Within the Assyrian organization there exists a pattern of reciprocally-shared religious faith, political loyalties and commercial interests. Little conflict exists between the group perspectives and the predispositions of individuals. Continuance of the economic operation is seen in the easy transfer of responsibility from one generation of traders to the next. Although class loyalties and national loyalties often are seen to clash in the history of communities, the Assyrian organization was sustained by the peaceful perpetuation of established group membership. Within the whole, no new economic groups or classes arose because of any failure of the established commercial and political associations to fulfill the legitimate expectations of their members.[4]

The Assyrian trader participated actively in Cappadocian trade both for national and for personal reasons. The first found him serving an economic motive of the state; the second, his own purse. Consequently his morale was high, a reflection of the solidarity of the entire organization. But this solidarity was not inflexible. Non-Assyrians could function within the operation of Cappadocian trade, although they usually held inferior and peripheral jobs.[5]

Our interest now shifts to the domain, the scope, weight and coerciveness of Assyrian power, as well as its forms. If a *decision* is a policy involving severe sanctions or deprivations, then *power* may be defined as participation in the making of decisions.[6] Hence a decision represents

[4] Cf. *ibid.*, 33f.

[5] Cf. *ibid.*

[6] On power and decision-making cf. *ibid.*, 74-75.

an effective determination of policy, and the decision-making process includes the application as well as the determination of policy, which means that those who are affected by decisions contribute to the decision making insofar as they conform to, or disregard, the policy involved.[7] To the extent that the Assyrian traders came completely under the aegis of Assyrian law, and to the furhter extent that they helped promulgate that law through the *kârû* and *wabârâtum*, they effectively shared in the decision-making processes of the Assyrian government.

By discussing *power* in terms of *decision-making*, we recognize an element which distinguishes it from simple *influence*, for if decision-making carries with it the threat of sanctions for non-obedience, then power becomes a special case in the exercise of influence, "the process of affecting policies of others with the help of (actual or threatened) severe deprivations for nonconformity with the policies intended".[8] But power need not always, or even generally, rest on violence, for other values also play a part.[9] To distinguish between the influence the Assyrians exerted in Anatolia and the power *cum* sanctions they exercised in the same region is a necessary analytical operation.

The weight of Assyrian power may be apprehended first through an attempt to measure its distribution throughout the system which sustained it.[10] In Assur, the institutions of government represent integrated patterns of practice; their functions are describable in terms of sovereignty and supremacy, the "maxima of formal and effective power".[11] Nominal sovereignty, or the highest degree of authority, rested with the national god, Aššur, and is no doubt reflected in the old political formula, "Aššur is king, NN (the reigning sovereign) is the *išši'akkum* of Assur". The theoretical basis of power is religious, a harking back to the idea that the patron deity is the real ruler of an ethnic group. Such a motif is also to be seen, for example, in the history of the Israelitic tribes. In the *rubâ'um* of Assur, who styles himself by the various formulae showing his role as vicar of the titular deity, and in the *âlum*, the council of elders, we find the secular agencies for the expression of divine power. The *dîn âlim^{ki} u rubâ'im*, "Judgement of the City and the Prince", whose efficacy is acknowledged through the Assyrian practice of oath-swearing "by the City and Prince (*nîš âlim^{ki} u rubâ'im*), represents the highest expression of Assyrian law.

[7] Cf. *ibid.*, 74.
[8] Cf. *ibid.*, 76.
[9] Cf. *ibid.*
[10] Cf. *ibid.*, 77.
[11] On sovereignty, cf. *ibid.*, 177-181.

In addition to being the chief political and judicial officer, the Old Assyrian *rubâ'um* was responsible for maintaining the temples of various gods and for improving the city. There could be no appeal beyond the *rubâ'um* in private or public affairs, though the *âlum* appears to have carried through much routine business in the name of the state. No extant inscription left by an Old Assyrian king claims for the ruler more stature than that of *iššì'ak Assur*, "city-ruler of Assur". It remains for Samsi-Adad I later to take for himself the epithet *šar kiššâtim*, "king of totality", a specifically "imperial" designation.[12] This does not mean that Old Assyrian kings were, on this criterion, incapable of having been conquerors of extensive land areas, but rather reflects the immediate sense of obligation to the titular deity, which they felt primarily as a personal relationship.

The *dîn âlim^{ki} u rubâ'im*, representing the effective symbol of Assyrian decision-making, was the legal instrument of control not only in Assur, but over the *kârû* and *wabârâtum* and their members. It brought the sovereignty of the *rubâ'um* and the *âlum* to the least as well as the greatest among the Assyrians. It was the standard which supported the existing Assyrian political institutions and officials. But first and foremost it was law over Assyria proper.

Our sources do not help us to define the precise land area which comprised the territory effectively governed by Assyrian officials in northern Mesopotamia. Yet we may postulate the existence of Assyria as a state, a sovereign territorial group. It represented an organized aggregate of persons inhabiting a common territory, and contained within itself supreme authority. Everyone having authority over the group *in Assyria* is in the group.[13]

There are important senses, too, in which the Assyrian settlements of Anatolia belonged to the Assyrian "community" as a whole. The Assyrian trader's actions were clearly organized about a given territorial base — his foreign residence — which was a specific physical "dwelling unit" located in a specific physical place,[14] whether at *Kaniš*, *Burušḫattum*, *Waḫšušana*, or elsewhere. To be sure, he could and did move about freely as his business required of him, and could also retire to Assur after his trading days in Anatolia were over, but he was still essentially "at home" in a particular *kârum* or *wabârtum*. This residence area, as we

[12] Cf. *IAK*, VIII, 1:2; 5:2; 6:2. In other instances Šamši-Adad I styles himself *iššak ^{d}Assur*, *IAK*, VIII, 3:2-3; 4:3; 5:5.
[13] Cf. H. D. Lasswell and A. Kaplan, *Power and Society*, *op. cit.*, 181.
[14] Cf. Talcott Parsons, "The Principal Structures of Community: A Sociological View", in Carl Friedrich, ed., *Community* (= *Nomos*, II) (New York, 1959), 154.

have seen, was also part of an area in which Assyrian jurisdiction was enforced. And furthermore, in his Anatolian residence, the Assyrian trader fully participated as a member of the Assyrian social organization, since he had the same status and rights as he would have enjoyed in Assyria. To this extent the population of the Assyrian settlements represent an extension of the population of the homeland.

In that the residence areas were also work areas, and were devoted to sustaining commercial operations that benefited the homeland, they appear to us further to provide an environment in which the typical occupational patterns practised in the Assyrian community of Mesopotamia could be reduplicated abroad.[15] Thus the Anatolian *kârû* and *wabârâtum* functioned primarily to sustain a complex network of economic relations, which had its focal point in Assur. All the evidence seems to support the idea that these settlements were work districts populated by entrepreneurs, and not primarily residential districts. As physical locations they were, to be sure, not always exclusively used by the people who lived in them, nor as work places by people who had regular employment therein, for under the requirements of Cappadocian trade, only part of a trader's activities was carried out in one specific location. But as the trader visited one or another settlement, he still felt himself to be within the limits of the Assyrian community as a whole.

And in still another sense we may include the Anatolian settlements under the idea of the Assyrian "community" writ large — by calling attention to what the sociologist Talcott Parsons calls "the communicative complex".[16] Parsons writes that "Communication as an aspect of the structure of community may ... be defined as the processes involving on the one hand the physical media by which messages and objects are transferred from one person in location to another, and on the other hand the physical aspects of change of location of persons themselves when this takes place as meaningfully related to communicative performance in a social role".[17] Not only do the Assyrian traders participate in exchanging goods and information, but also act to fulfill the expectations of their colleagues for their common good. In this sense Parsons seems right in further asserting that "... communication always implies a common culture".[18] The transfer of physical objects such as trade goods and money by means of caravan, and of information and requests

[15] Cf. *ibid.*, 156-160 [158].
[16] Cf. *ibid.*, 167-176.
[17] Cf. *ibid.*, 167-168.
[18] Cf. *ibid.*, 169.

through the medium of a commonly-used language, clearly was the means through which the Assyrian anywhere in Anatolia affirmed his membership in the Assyrian community of Mesopotamia.

Finally, the jurisdiction which Assur exercised over its settlements confirms most impressively that the network of *kârû* and *wabârâtum* were an integral part of the concept of an Assyrian community extending across the Taurus Ranges.[19] In considering the position and role of the Anatolian settlements of Assyrian traders in the scheme of Assyrian organization as a whole, we must see deeper than the surface manifestations of Assyrian law and administrative operation. The city of Assur made certain demands on its far-off communities. It demonstrated its control over *Kârum Kaniš* by imposing an official tax on it, and expecting such an impost to be collected from the other *kârû* if necessary. It also sent the *šiprû ša âlim*[ki] to participate in executive decision-making at *Kârum Kaniš*, and could authorize such functionaries as the *râbiṣum*, "attorney", to investigate disputes in any settlement. To this extent the power of Assur as a controlling political center is formal, and not to be discounted. Further, the individual Assyrian living and working abroad was a compulsory member of a *kârum* or a *wabârtum*, and could not throw off his membership except by returning to Assur or by expatriation. For the Assyrian, the Anatolian settlements were necessary associations; they possessed the legal power of coercion over him, and far from being, themselves, simply subject to control and regulation by Assur, they were extensions of the Assyrian community. But Assyrian power was limited both in scope and domain, as we shall see.

Within the structure the power of the *rubâ'um* and *âlum* of Assur is not directly perceived at all times in the affairs of the Assyrian communities. Infrequently (beyond the imposition of a tax on *Kârum Kaniš*), are the acts of a *kârum* or other agency subject to the personal directives of the sovereign or the assembly of the capital. To be sure, each Assyrian settlement accepts the authority of duly-appointed Assyrian officials in extraordinary matters, but nevertheless retains a large measure of original jurisdiction. The envoys of Assur may or may not be consulted in negotiations with indigenous princes, but *Kârum Kaniš* is, without exception. The envoys have the power to direct all the *kârû*, but in our sources they appear to act solely in business matters, or affairs related thereto. When a legal case is tried, it is usually before the entire membership of the *kârum* or *wabârtum* in question. No envoy from Assur interferes in the interests of the City unless it be the *râbiṣum*,

19 Cf. *ibid.*, 160-167.

whose degree of authority is much less than that of the *šiprû ša âlim*^{ki}, and appeals to the *âlum* of Assur are undertaken without the envoys' help. The *šiprû* of Assur are therefore limited to occasional participation in diplomatic negotiations with Anatolian princes, or to the appointment of subordinates who visit the settlements at large.

It is *Kârum Kaniš* which retains first place as an interested party in diplomatic negotiation. By its participation, it served to represent the *rubâ'um* and *âlum*, of course, but it is noteworthy that encounters of whatever nature and difficulty between Assyrians and Anatolian princes require its advice or consent even to the exclusion of explicit orders from Mesopotamia. In fact, there is no extant appeal or report from *Kârum Kaniš qua kârum* to Assur. If the *šiprû sa âlim*^{ki} are kept informed, it is the *kârum* which must initiate action, or forward instructions. This apparently has been overlooked in that theory which postulates the existence of an Assyrian viceroy at Kanis. Had such an official existed, he should certainly have been approached in diplomatic affairs, and his actions would have been observable.

Granting the hand of the *rubâ'um* and *âlum* in Assyrian settlement affairs through the implied action of the Envoys of Assur at *Kârum Kaniš*, we observe that the ties between the settlements and Assur are less than rigid. The individual Assyrian could well feel the power of Assyrian law were he summoned to account for violations before *kârum* or *wabârtum* courts, but the Assyrian community *qua* community does not stand in the same kind of relationship to the sovereign officials of Assur. While paying its taxes and subjecting itself to governmental paternalism, it also governs itself, subject only to the fiat of *Kârum Kaniš*, in most matters of importance. Yet even here, much of the activities of the individual *kârum* or *wabârtum*, as well as those of the traders who passed to and for between them, are independent of dogmatic or coercive regulation. The force of Assyrian law exists to sustain a pattern of equity between individual merchants, to define who is in good standing and who is not for purposes of participating in Cappadocian trade; but it is the commercial association which pays homage to the law without being unnecessarily interfered with by it that sustains the entire operation, and makes of the *kârum* and other Assyrian political agencies auxiliary and cooperating units, rather than primarily *police* institutions. In pointing this out we do not deny the power of the Assyrian community over its member-individuals, but rather stress that the Assyrian *kârum* was fully able to run its own affairs — even was expected to do so — without persistent and uncalled-for interference by the political institutions of the home city. The power of the *rubâ'um* and *âlum* could indeed be felt when it was necessary for it to be felt, but otherwise the role of Assur in the affairs of its Anatolian settlements was relatively quiescent.

As regards their presence in Asia Minor, it is clear that the Assyrians did not constitute a coercive force, or attempt to annihilate or expel the settled inhabitants of Anatolia. There is hardly a reference to Assyrian military forces or officials, while on the other hand, it is manifest that the local princes maintained their own soldiers and constabularies, which in part had the task of policing the trade routes in their own territories.

Nor in the legal sphere is it to be seen that the Anatolians held an inferior position. To be sure Assyrian cultural superiority is reflected in the cuneiform script which the traders brought with them, yet this does not speak to the political question at all. For a dual system of courts prevailed and the Anatolian palace-administrations were careful to protect the rights of their subjects in cases where Assyrians and Anatolians together figured in litigation. If there is superiority at all, it is economic, a direct result of the financial position of the Assyrian.

Similarly the religious situation does not show that the Assyrian gods took a paramount position in the consciousness of the non-Assyrian inhabitants. The individual gods of the Anatolian pantheon were actively worshipped; debts contracted by indigenous persons were usually to be paid at the harvest festival of a particular deity; and in no way does there appear to have been an imposition of Assyrian deities upon the religious life of the Anatolian. Hence one does not find what one would expect to find if the Assyrians had conquered Anatolia and annexed it as an imperial province — the raising of the conqueror's gods to pre-eminent position over the conquered peoples.

Thus the legal situation as discussed in earlier chapters, and the religious situation, do not support the idea that the Anatolians were Assyrian citizens. The existence of individual indigenous tribunals making decisions in cases involving non-Assyrians, and of joint supervision in cases involving Assyrians and non-Assyrians shows clearly enough that Assyrian law is not paramount in Anatolia. Even if it be argued that the Assyrians granted the Anatolian principalities full autonomy after an alleged conquest, there is no evidence that *tribute* was paid them.[20] In fact, where Assur is seen to exercise its powers of taxation, it is either over the Assyrian caravans and their personnel, or over the Assyrian settlements, themselves. *Kârum Kaniš* is expected to pay an impost to

[20] This must be considered especially significant, since tribute payment by vassals to overlords is a standard feature of ancient Near Eastern imperial relationships.

Assur which it may collect from the other *kârû*. In no instance is a formal tax collected from an Anatolian administration, as one would expect were the Assyrians even titular overlords. Beyond this we have already seen in earlier chapters that the rulers of these administrations not only act as autonomous sovereigns in political and commercial matters, but also the Assyrians could even seek advice from them against the apparent interests of their own group.

In other words, there is no significant evidence that the Assyrians annexed the region of Anatolia and ruled it as contiguous territory. The character of the *kârû* and *wabâratum* as settlements overwhelmingly concerned with trade speaks once again to this conclusion, as does the essentially limited application of *âlum* and *kârum* decision-making to Assyrian traders alone. Furthermore, the weakness of the case for an Assyrian ruler at *Kaniš*, coupled with the knowledge that the individual principalities maintained standing armies and could have powerfully-designated rulers, solidifies this conclusion.

If no annexation of Anatolia appears valid, if no military occupation, is it possible that the Assyrians dominated the various principalities across the Taurus by other means? Is it possible that even if there was no Assyrian ruler with an army at *Kaniš*, the Assyrian settlements represent foundations of veterans which could call upon Assyria in times of danger?

It has indeed been argued that the Assyrians come into possession of their Anatolian residences in this way.[21] Is it possible that a conquest may originally have been made, but that once the country was subdued, treaties were made which not only kept the peace, but stimulated economic activities to the mutual benefit of the resident aliens and the indigenous populations? Could an alleged conquest have produced a situation not requiring continual military concern, but only observation from afar — implied and easily marshalled force to cope with danger, but no necessity of permanent military occupation?

Arguments in favor of this interpretation are possible. On the one hand, the extent and distribution of the Assyrian settlements must be considered. We have said that the *kârû* and *wabâratum* appear not to be randomly situated or temporary encampments. Also, it might be pointed out that caravans made regular and generally undisturbed trips between Anatolia and Mesopotamia. Beyond this, the tightness of organization which characterizes the entire network of settlements appears to argue for some sort of calculated settlement pattern.

[21] Cf. J. Lewy, "On Some Institutions ...", *op. cit.*, 56f.

However attractive such an interpretation might seem, it remains that the hey-day of Assyrian activity in Anatolia was interrupted by the overwhelming destruction of the Level II settlement at *Kaniš*, and again by the final destruction visited upon Level Ib. That the Assyrian traders returned to *Kaniš* after at least a generation of absence following the first catastrophe indicates a persistence not usually associated with temporary and lightly-held objectives. But the nagging question returns: would the destruction of the chief Assyrian settlement in Anatolia by an indigenous prince have been possible at all if the Assyrians could marshall help when needed? And even if it be suggested that the attack came quickly and without notice, how is it to be explained that the *re-occupation* of *Kaniš* was not carried out so as to insure against a repetition of the event? Perhaps the homeland was itself being weakened by strife at this later date, yet the reappearance of Assyrians at *Kaniš* with a fully re-built residence quarter indicates that the new settlement was not a casually-approached task. And if the settlement lasted into the reign of Išmê-Dagan I, then there was time and purpose enough to reorganize the basis of alleged Assyrian control in Anatolia. The first setback should have alerted the Assyrian government for future difficulties. Yet if anything is true, the foundation appears to have been laid in Anatolia for the emergence of ever-greater *indigenous* hegemony, culminating in the rise of the Old Hittite Kingdom and later in the Hittite Empire. And all this, when considered with the evidence for the autonomy of the individual princes during the period of Level II at *Kaniš* forces us to reject the notion that the Assyrians had even a tempered, moderated limited power with which they governed a subject area leniently from without, but with the threat of force. Even more is this reasonable if we note the methodological difficulties inherent in analyzing the Cappadocian fund for the military practices of late Assyrian rulers.

Was it destroyed by an Anatolian prince?

Our first major conclusion, then, is that the Assyrian *kârû* and *wabâ-râtum* were not colonies in the imperial sense — not, that is, the settlements of a conquering power which *annexed* Anatolia as contiguous territory; nor of a power, which having originally conquered, maintained politically influential domination over a geographically external unit through the implied threat of its power from afar.[22]

If the Assyrian establishments were not *imperial* colonies, may they be described as *colonies* at all? We think they can, but a proper answer to the question will entail a consideration of the ways in which non-imperial foreign settlements are formed. Some help must be gotten from evalua-

[22] Cf. Chapter Three, w.n. 26.

ting the motivations which produce such establishments, and these are as often economic and sociological, as they are political.

One of the major stumbling blocks in the history of speculation about the Old Assyrian settlements has been the effortless assumption that colonization is a consequence of conquest. As early as 1908, A. H. Sayce casually assumed that *Kârum Kaniš* was "in fact, the last outpost of Assyria in the north-west, at the end of the *military road* (my italics) which led along the valleys of the Euphrates and Tokhma-Su to the metal-bearing districts of Asia Minor", and this at a time when the number of Cappadocian tablets known and studied was insignificantly small.[23] The distinguished historian, Eduard Meyer, made a similar appraisal with but slightly more justification;[24] and Prof. Lewy, who, as we respectfully feel, has been one of the very few outstanding pioneers of Cappadocian research, continued in this spirit of interpretation from the early 1920's to this day.[25] The identification of *colonization* and *conquest* is but a stereotype, but the terms are not necessarily synonymous. Similarly some of the major and explicitly stated "first assumptions" of the imperial school appear fallacious in the light of cold logic. Does trade always follow the flag in the ancient Near Eastern experience? And because "empire-building" appears in the political activities of dynasties which were previous to, and also followed upon, the Old Assyrian, does it follow that the Old Assyrians were *ipso facto* "empire-building" themselves? Indeed not. Therefore we require a more judicious set of first principles.

[23] Cf. A. H. Sayce, "The Cappadocian Cuneiform Tablets", *Babyloniaca* 2 (1908), 2.

[24] In 1911, Fr. Thureau-Dangin published a Cappadocian debt tablet on whose envelope face appeared the inscription of a cylinder seal identified as belonging to a certain Ur-Lugal-banda, a scribe in the service of Ibi-Sin, last ruler of the Third Dynasty of Ur. Despite the fact that there were good reasons for believing that the seal was re-used, Professor Meyer made the following remarks:

"Mithin hat sich die Oberherrschaft dieses alten babylonischen Reiche bis in diese Gebiete [i.e., Kültepe] ausgedehnt. Besiedelt aber sind sie von Assyrern, die hier inmitten einer fremden Bevölkerung eine Kolonie gegründet haben, deren Überreste der Hügel Kültepe bedeckt. So sehen wir, dass schon damals, ... die Herrscher von Assur, Vassalen Babyloniens, durch das obere Tigristal und über Malatia (Melitene) am Euphrat ins östliche Kleinasien vorgedrungen sind, um sich den Weg ans Schwarze Meer zu bahnen, eine Strasse, die später ihre Nachfolger immer von neuem gezogen sind; so erklärt es sich auch, das in der alteren griechischen Geographie die Küstenlandschaft an der Mundung des Halys und Iris bis nach Sinope hin den Namen Assyrien trägt. Durch diese Funde an einer Stätte, wo niemand derartiges gesucht hatte, fernab von Assyrien, erhalten wir so Kunde von der Geschichte und Kultur Assyriens aus einer Zeit, aus der sich in Assyrien selbst auch nicht ein einziges schriftliches Dokument erhalten hat" (*Reich und Kultur der Chethiter* [Berlin, 1914], 51-52).

[25] Cf. Chapter Three, w.n. 27-44, above.

We would propose first that "occupation, but not necessarily fighting, must precede colonization", of whatever type.[26] If it is not necessarily true that expansion demands conquest, then "expansion can be arrived at in two other ways: by *occupation* and by acquisition".[27] Occpuation in this sense takes place when hitherto uninhabited territory — virgin territory — is occupied without conflict.[28] Acquisition, by contrast, occurs when "the new arrivals, coming up against the 'earlier occupiers', make an agreement or treaty with them, and thus obtain with more or less good will, the right to settle:" hence acquisition by contract.[29]

Now it is clear, that the Old Assyrians did not occupy their Anatolian residence areas by coming to them as the first settlers. The excavation of *Kârum Kaniš* shows that Levels IV and III had already been settled before the great Assyrian settlement of Level II. It is conjectural whether Level III represents a tabletless phase of Assyrian activity; but certainly Level IV seems decisively earlier, and prior to the arrival of the Semites. And, indeed, the presence of the *kârum*-area next to a city inhabited by a non-Assyrian population and ruled by a non-Assyrian prince, speaks for a late founding.

But the possibility of acquisition by contract is a real one. Admittedly, this mode of settlement is not the rule, but its occurrence "disposes of the contention that there is an inevitable connection between colonization and violence".[30] And we shall attempt to test this possibility as meaningful for an explanation of the Old Assyrian settlements.

Colonization, at base, involves a contact of peoples, the emigration of the newcomers, and their reception by the established population of the area in question. Now "emigration" consists both of the emigration of persons and an exportation of goods — or emigration of capital. The persons involved in such an enterprise may be adventurers, expatriates, and the like, or persons following some special aims, such as explorers or, to be sure, traders, etc. And the peopling of new countries may be intensive and rapid, or not, depending upon purposes, conditions, and the like.[31]

There was obviously an emigration of persons to Anatolia, though we should note that it was not an overwhelming one. For example, the area of the *kârum* at *Kaniš*, the largest of the Assyrian settlements, was of

[26] Cf. R. Maunier, *The Sociology of Colonies*, I (London, 1949) 3.
[27] Cf. *ibid.*, 4.
[28] Cf. *ibid.*
[29] Cf. *ibid.*
[30] Cf. *ibid.*, 5.
[31] Cf. *ibid.*, 5-6.

moderate size compared to the area of its host city, and this proportion must have been true at other sites. The Assyrian emigrant was a specialized emigrant — an entrepreneur-trader, and the population of his residence quarter consisted chiefly of men like himself and personnel attached to caravan operations. In other words, our sources consistently picture a commercial population; as we have elsewhere noted, the characterization of the settlement at Alishar Hüyük as agricultural is highly conjectural.

It is further manifest that there was a huge emigration of capital and goods to Anatolia. If any purpose for Assyrian emigration appears, it is not to be found in what might be called "habitable colonies" — where the colony appears merely to foster an extension of residence patterns of the motherland;[32] rather it is actively and continually to exploit a region rich in desirable goods for economic gain, and to provide a permanent market area for Assyrian surpluses. Were the settlements of the "habitable" type, emigration would appear to be rather intensive so as to accommodate the excess population of the motherland.[33] But the residents of the Assyrian settlements were not randomly selected. They are fully and calculatedly concerned with one major objective — to keep their caravans moving in the interests of their trading companies. They do not exploit native labor. We do not see in our sources that the majority, the indigenous, are worked for the benefit of the minority Assyrians. Rather, the latter include financially qualified non-Assyrians in their own operations, and work deals to insure the build-up of their own economic potential.

Now in non-military contacts between peoples, the settlement patterns appear first to be intermittent. Original intermittent contacts are usually made through explorations or expeditions, and only later comes permanent settlement.[34] No doubt the first contacts are as much reconnaissance as deliberate movement toward an objective. No area of the world illustrates the power of the trader to bring peoples into contact as well as the Near East in ancient times, where even in pre-historic times, rare goods brought in from a distance, already appear in Mesopotamian villages. The professional merchant as an auxiliary to foreign policy stands in the forefront of expanding relationships between peoples and areas, and if it be argued that "trade follows the flag", it is also abundantly true that "the flag follows trade". The Assyrian traders, we

32 Cf. *ibid.*, 8.
33 Cf. *ibid.*, 9.
34 Cf. *ibid.*, 10.

feel, at first made contact with the cities beyond the Taurus, and brought with them a trading apparatus which they had already developed highly in Assyria. They came at first looking for new commercial vistas.

Later came permanent and diffused settlement, and it is at this stage we may speak of actual "colonization" if both emigration and some type of motivating political impetus occur. The idea of "colony" includes the notion that emigration should be accompanied and endorsed by government. Hence the occupation of new residence areas by administration.[35] Note that there might be "transplantations", but not governments, actual but not legal settlements. The difference between a transplantation so-called, and a colony, is that the former do *not* have legal jurisdiction of any kind in the new country, nor do they have legislation or administration of their own. They exist as homogeneous groups, but recognize their subjection to the laws of the country where they are domiciled. A colony, by contrast, presupposes a metropolitan country that directs its destiny. "To be a 'colony', a settlement requires a legal bond attaching it to the country whence the colonists come;" otherwise it is a group of emigrants and not a group of colonists.[36]

We are indeed correct in referring to the Old Assyrian settlements as permanent and not intermittent in the sense that the *kârû* and the *wabârâtum* exhibit the characteristics of full-fledged residence areas populated by Assyrians who accepted the idea of spending much of their lives away from Assyria, and who indeed married and maintained domiciles in their new homes. And our sources document clearly that the settlements were not simple transplantations of emigrants but "colonies", in that they were legally bound to Assyria.

In the traditional sense, "colony" involves political domination, or government, of the new country or its people — occupation and legislation, an element of fact and an element of law. The colonists "must preserve their dependence on, their submission to, the mother-country".[37] But this does not necessarily mean that the *natives* where the colonies are existing must also be bound to the mother-country of the colonists.[38] For the Assyrian traders, although fully integrated into the legal structures of their homeland, still experienced limits in their jurisdictional relationships with the indigenous populations. For while the prince and assembly of Assur supervised the affairs of the Assyrian settlements

[35] Cf. *ibid.*, 10-13.

[36] Cf. *ibid.*, 13f.

[37] Cf. *ibid.*, 14.

[38] Against Maunier, *ibid.*

through their intermediaries, the "Envoys of the City", not all relationships between Assyrian corporations or Assyrian individuals and individual Anatolian principalities were dominated by the implied threat of action by these Envoys.

Granting that "there must always be a legislative bond to reinforce the colony's actual attachment [to the mother-country]" we can also agree that domination has degrees and forms.[39] We have already rejected the idea of *de facto* political domination by the Assyrians, the attempt to assume command and to impose authority on a new country. But we may discuss domination in other ways. In the economic sense domination means that loans, contracts, exports of the country settled may be in the hands of the new settlers, hence a monopoly of the settlers or colonists.[40] More than anything else we may affirm an Assyrian *commercial monopoly* in Asia Minor. It is the monopoly of a rich, unified, well-developed, long-distance trading apparatus over a relatively undeveloped set of Anatolian city-state economies which have behind them only the individual traditions and experiences of single principalities. Our sources affirm the imposition of a *trading* "imperialism" and its carriers — the Old Assyrian traders — upon an area still operating as a system of separate and divided sovereignities, with no large-scale, unified economy. The Assyrians are tutors in economics, but do not thereby subvert the individual city-states and attempt to merge them into a land empire. It was sufficient that the Assyrian commercial operation blanket an area which had no previous experience in large-scale, large-area economic activity. The local economies seem almost absorbed in the process. We are confronted in our sources, then, with a situation in which single Anatolian principalities exist and exercise their political autonomy within the economic "empire" of a foreign group, which itself desires chiefly to exploit the situation for its own benefit. Emigration for commercial purposes need not be intensive. Nor is the domination thus exerted exclusively financial. It may also be cultural and intellectual.[41] And to be sure, the influx of money and trade into Anatolia was accompanied inevitably by writing and other features of Mesopotamian civilization. On the one hand, the Assyrians adopted Anatolian material techniques to create their residences and domestic utensils, while on the other, the Anatolian learned to write, and came in contact with a new cultural influence.

[39] Cf. *ibid.*
[40] Cf. *ibid.*, 14-15.
[41] Cf. *ibid.*

From the legal point of view "colonization" is dependence or allegiance in the sense that the "colonists" remain citizens of the country of their birth. They preserve rights in it and have duties toward it. This, of course, is represented not only by legal forms, but by outward symbols.[42] But for the situation reflected in the Cappadocian tablets, Assyrian colonization does not spell out dependence for the natives. Although there is *de facto* commercial domination, there was no *de jure* domination.[43] If not, then how are we to characterize the international political situation of the Old Assyrian period in Anatolia?

We propose that there was a system of shared sovereignty, or a parity-relationship between the Assyrians and the numerous Anatolian principalities; and we turn therefore to an exploration of this view.

How was it, in the absence of conquest, that the Old Assyrians managed to get residence quarters in the presently-known twenty-one cities of Anatolia? The emigration began, we feel, with merchants, who at first made relatively isolated trading expeditions to North Syria and Anatolia. First they may have established points of departure near to Assyria for journeys father to the west. The discovery of fragments of Cappadocian tablets at Yorgan Tepe (Nuzi) in Northern Mesopotamia seems to support this possibility for the script and orthography of these indicate they are older than the tablets from Level II at Kültepe. Also the presence of a *kârum* and several *wabârâtum* in North Syria and at the approaches to the great passes leading into the Anti-Taurus during the period of Level II at Kültepe speaks for an orderly progression and extension of influence from Assyria to the north-west. No doubt the pioneer traders reappeared in the new areas after long absences, but "they are already in a certain sense emigrees from their own country".[44] Their arrival in towns along the trade routes would be the occasion for establishing markets and fairs, which when set up in a new country are the beginnings of colonization.[45] For from these first contacts develop warehouses and residence quarters. One has only to cite the experience of Aegean peoples (especially the Greeks) and the Phoenicians, who founded such markets and warehouses, to credit the assumption.[46]

Having grown accustomed to the presence of Assyrian traders coming

42 Cf. *ibid.*, 16.
43 Cf. *ibid.*, 16-19.
44 Cf. *ibid.*, 10.
45 Cf. *ibid.*
46 Cf. *ibid.*, and R. B. Revere, "'No Man's Coast': Ports of Trade in the Eastern Mediterranian", (Chapter IV) in K. Polanyi, C. M. Arensberg and H. W. Pearson, *Trade and Market ...*, *op. cit.*, 38-63.

from beyond the Taurus barrier in their midst, the rulers of cities on the trade routes would have permitted, even encouraged their settling in special quarters which could be organized and furnished for the purposes of caravan trade. The process, as we have said, appears to have begun in cities close to Assyria, but the commercially strategic location of Kanis could not be overlooked. It was situated at the hub of a wheel; trade routes converged upon it from all directions, and especially was it the logical objective of those which cut through the mountain passes from North Syria. It then came to serve, we feel, as an administrative center for the other groups of Assyrians residing elsewhere.

The Assyrian traders were already familiar with the *kârum* structure in Mesopotamia. It served there, we recall, as a specialized quarter within the confines of a Mesopotamian city, devoted mainly to inter-city commerce. It had its own administration which was integrated into the larger city-administration dominated by the city-ruler and the assembly. Hence the natural form to adopt for purposes of organizing a foreign commercial establishment on a more or less permanent basis was ready-at-hand to the Assyrians abroad.

The *kârum*, as our sources depict it, followed the legislative principle of sovereignty of the whole. It is the *kârum ṣahir rabi*, or the whole *kârum*, which is invoked in serious legal cases within the Assyrian group, or in negotiation with the Anatolian princes. Although we encounter individual officials of the *kârum*, it is manifest that no single executive has the power to act for the *kârum*. And here the argument for an Assyrian prince at *Kaniš* is especially weak. For it is the *kârum qua kârum* which makes most of the important decisions.

It seems most natural to us that the basis for the establishment of a foreign group in a settled area be sought in the realm of negotiation and eventually, formal treaties. Provision must always be made for adjustments of conflict of interest between the new and the old groups. We have stressed, certainly, that our sources do not include any treaty as such, but always there appears behind the international relations we observe the implied presence of such treaties. The *kârum* of Anatolia was forced to take on a function which was alien to it in Mesopotamia. Its powers grew in scope from the relatively simple ones required at first to organize itself as a functioning commercial community to those requiring its attention to international arbitration with sovereign princes. Thus, we feel, the appearance of the Envoys of the City is to be explained: they supervised the affairs of their own nationals in the interst of the home government; and they provided guidance and sanction for any agreements struck between an Assyrian settlement and an Anatolian administration.

We feel it is possible to suggest from the information we have presented throughout an idea of some of the provisions of such treaties as may have pertained to Assyrian-Anatolian relations:

(1) *The Assyrians are guaranteed residence rights.* Perhaps no formal article to this effect would have appeared in the treaties, but would have been implicit. Land is turned over to the Assyrians on the periphery of the cities, but not within them. The Assyrians are allowed to purchase property, and do, indeed call upon indigenous craftsmen to perform services for them. Thus the Assyrian lived under the shadow of Anatolian civic life.

(2) *The Assyrians were allowed to govern themselves.* Since we have given sufficient evidence of this already, it requires no further elaboration.

(3) In instances of legal contacts between the Assyrian citizens and citizens of any particular Anatolian city, especially in the matter of redemption from debt, *the principle of ethnic solidarity in the interests of the subject is clear.* While most financial dealings between members of the different groups were privately undertaken, in the interests of fair play, a palace-administration can intervene to aid, but not absolve, a distressed indigenous debtor. For its part, the *karum* could sanction a financial arrangement by which its own members redeemed a colleague from bondage to an Anatolian, but did not itself initiate that action.

(4) *In religious matters, the principle of symbiosis prevails.* There is little doubt that oaths concluded between Assyrians and Anatolian rulers were protected by the gods of each contracting party.

(5) *In commercial dealings goods were sold "at the price", which suggests the idea of administered trade — a trade fostered by treaty,* although there was also a fringe market trading.

(6) *The local princes retained the right of first option to purchase Assyrian goods,* although the Assyrians appear to have had almost unlimited privileges beyond this. *The rulers also collected imposts from the caravans,* perhaps even the amounts which the Assyrians taxed their own traders.[47]

[47] Thus we question the importance of the inference taken by Prof. Lewy that because Assyrian traders are seen to pay charges such as the *nisḫatum* and the *išrâtum* to the *êkallum* as well as the *Bît Kârim*, these institutions must have been parts of the same "Assyrian" administrative apparatus in Anatolia (cf. "On Some Institutions ...", *op. cit.*, 38-39, w.n., 136-137). Can one automatically assume that the *nisḫatum* and the *išrâtum* which the *Bît Kârim* collected (among other charges) were the *same* taxes as paid to the *êkallum*?

If we deny the necessity of considering *kârum* and *êkallum* as member institutions

(7) *The Assyrians were allowed to make use of the palace warehouses,* while the palace administrations carries on both cash and credit dealings with the *Bît Kârim* establishments in their environments.[48]

(8) *The local princes provided protection for the caravans which passed through their territories, as well as guides for them. They also claimed the right of search and arrest over Assyrians who were suspected of dealing in restricted commodities.*[49]

---

of the alleged Assyrian imperial structure in Anatolia, we nevertheless affirm that they were quite interdependent. Evidence exists that they cooperated in deals involving metals, especially copper, and clothing. For the former, cf. *KTS*, 18, which appears to show an unnamed palace willing to pay for "good copper" (*erî'um maz/sî'um*), which is in supply at a *Bît Kârim*, with ordinary copper from its own stocks. This suggests that the Assyrians, because of their mobility and investment capital, were able to stock metals in various states of refinement, and to sell them to local potentates, no doubt at a substantial profit. Other instances in our texts which show how eagerly the various palaces desired to deal with the Assyrians for copper are *TC*, III, 25, and *KTHahn*, 14; for *aši'um*, cf. *BIN*, IV, 45, in which connection we recall that *aši'um* may have been a prime commodity, both for the Assyrians and the palaces (cf. the concern of the palaces to prevent secret traffic in this metal, Chapter Five, w.n. 17-18, above). An indication of *êkallum-kârum* dealings in which the *kârum* owed over two hundred *kutânu*-garments to a palace appears in *TC*, II, 16:16-18a.

[48] It even seems possible to assert that goods destined to be deposited in a *Bît Kârim* had *first* to pass inspection in a palace. There, after the usual purchases had been made and taxes collected, that part of a shipment destined for the *Bît Kârim* was taken together with goods purchased by the palace and conveniently stored in the palace warehouse. Other goods, not relegated either to palace or *Bît Kârim* were released (*zakâ'um*) for further disposition. Such a procedure seems to be indicated in *TC*, III, 158.

In another text, *KTHahn*, 13, we see that an Assyrian trader would prefer that his caravan avoid going up to a palace so as to avoid paying the *nisḫatum*, which would inevitably be levied upon his goods. His agents are instructed to "hide" the goods if possible: (6) *šu-ma pá-zu-ur-šu-nu ta-li-a* (7) *pá-zi-ra-šu-nu šu-ma pá-zu-ur-šu-nu* (8) *lá ta-li-a a-na êkallim*^{lim} (9) *šé-li-a-šu-nu-ma ê*[*kallum*^{lum}] (10) *ni-is-ḫa-tí-šu-nu li-i*[l_5-*qí*]-*ma* (11) *ṣubâtí*$^{hi\text{-}a}$ *šé-ri-da* ...

(On the practise of sheltering goods to avoid palace inspection, etc., cf. J. Lewy, "On Some Institutions ...", *op. cit.*, 24, n. 103). This text also shows that a trader had the right to refuse sale of his goods to the palace, for its sender specifically instructs his agents to accept only silver in exchange for his goods (cf. 11. 11b-17f.).

[49] A pertinent notice to the fact that guides were sometimes provided by the palaces for conveying caravans through their territories is provided by *TC*, III, 211:44b-45. It is reasonable to assume that the Assyrians depended upon the individual palaces for safe-conduct through their territories in time of danger. Frequently the so-called "travel-notebooks" of the Assyrian traders record payments to the watch-stations (*maṣṣârâtum*) who appear to have been staffed by indigenous guards (cf., e.g., the *rabi maṣṣârtim* official, Šulia, in *BIN*, VI, 160:5, and *BIN*, VI, 235:3, for another reference to a *r.m.*). If the Assyrian caravans occasionally find themselves in danger it is because the distances between towns on the trade routes were long, and not all the regions through which they passed were always politically stable. *KTHahn*, 1, for example, reports a trader's change in plans to go to *Waḫšušana*, for that region as well as

At the present time this is all that can realistically be proposed in the absence of any extant treaty-document or historical account wherewith to elucidate our period. We do not wish to imply that there was one model of a treaty which suited all negotiations, or that each prince was automatically included in such formal relationships. The presence of the Assyrian settlements in Anatolia for at least a century all told must have made negotiations between them and the Anatolian principalities quite traditional. Princes ascending the throne of their fathers would naturally have sought to enter into the same types of formal relations with the resident "aliens" as their predecessors had fostered and enjoyed; and it could also be conjectured that the occasional difficulties encountered by Assyrian caravaners in one or another region were in part owing to the fact that teaties had not been satisfactorily concluded with the princes of those areas.

We believe, in absence of evidence to the contrary, and with positive support of the arguments already presented throughout this study, that the Assyrian legal position in Anatolia reflects an organic development; Assyrian law grew in importance as the activities of the traders expanded, and as more and more the settlements became familiar features of the Anatolian milieu. Ultimately it may have found its greatest strength in its own traditional presence in Anatolia, in the condition, that is, of its being accepted as a familiar and orderly system side by side with the autocthonous legal systems of the area. Thus it would appear to be one permanent characteristic of a symbiotic relationship between members of the Semitic and the non-Semitic groups.

As our study draws to its end, we may sketch in some features of the Old Assyrian Period as a whole. The migration of the Assyrians to Upper Mesopotamia was probably accomplished after the entry of the Semitic Akkadians into the central region of the Tigris-Euphrates Valley. The Old Assyrian calendar suggests the agricultural origins of the immigrants, while certain features of dialect, legal protocol and methods of choosing officials distinguish them from the Semites of the South. Originally subsisting as farmers and herders, they adapted to an urban

---

Burušhattum were in "uproar" (*sà-aḫ-a-at-ni*: 1.4). Also cf. the steps taken to divide a caravan into three sections so as to insure that at least some part of it will get through to *Kaniš* (*TC*, 18). Normally, however, travel conditions during the Old Assyrian Period were peaceful, a sure indication of the willingness of the Anatolian princes to keep the trade routes open if they could. We stress the *desire* of the princes rather more than their ability at all times to accomplish this, for numerous indications in our sources suggest that relationships between the small indigenous rulers of Anatolia were less than stable, if not actually warlike.

style of life, which was at one and the same time heavily influenced by the older Sumerian material culture. In their new homeland the worshippers of Assur also came in contact with mining, and metallugical technology. Whether the Assyrians were themselves miners is uncertain; but there can be no doubt that they came upon substantial sources of the metal *annâkum*, as well as lesser sources of other valuable metals. Additionally, their cloth-producing industries provided an abundance of materials for trading purposes.

The emergence of Assyria as an economically important area was tempered by her long political vassalage to powers of the South, most notably Ur III. Her first opportunity to establish her independence came after the demise of that state, which was caused in part by the pressure of western Amorites upon her Euphrates boundary, and in part by internal weaknesses which fostered revolt among her vassals. Momentarily Assyria struck out at southern Mesopotamia under Ilušumma, but she was unable to establish either permanent occupation or lasting political influence there. She saw the whole territory contended for by rival city-states, and retired (or was forced to retire) in order to secure the northern areas for herself. Had she been already a strong military power capable of conquering a large and distant region such as Anatolia, she should surely have reduced her rivals in southern Mesopotamia.

However, the rise of Amorite states along the Euphrates and in Lower Mesopotamia during the twentieth and nineteenth centuries forced Old Assyrian activity into areas beyond the immediate reach of the southern powers. With access to metals, and with the opportunity of relatively unhampered movement along the routes which passed from northern Mesopotamia and into the passes of the Taurus and the Anti-Taurus, she developed new spheres of influence in Cappadocia. Having experienced the rise of the caravan trading company, which provided a usable apparatus for the pursuit of long-distance trading operations, Assyria could exploit the North and the West for economic gain. Her objectives were the export of surplus metals and clothing, and the garnering, in return, of valuable supplies of copper and silver from Anatolia. Her *kârum* and *wabârtum* settlements were distributed along the life-lines of North Syrian and Anatolian trade.

The greatest days of Cappadocian trade are exactly contemporaneous with the period of Old Assyria's greatest strength — the years covered by the reigns of Irišum I, Ikunum, Šarrum-kên I and Puzur-Aššur II. But the rise of Pitḫana and Anitta in central Anatolia, coupled with unrest on the Mesopotamian scene — an unrest which brought Assur, herself, under the dominance of Narâm-Sîn of Eshnunna for a brief period — served to interrupt the Cappadocian trading operation. In Anatolia *Kârum Kaniš*, with its host city, is destroyed, as no doubt were the other emporia. At home, the control of Assyria passes out of the hands of the Old Assyrian Dynasty, and is later to be claimed by the usurper Šamsi-Adad and his son Išmê-Dagan.

For a while the activities of Cappadocian trade are resumed; *Kârum Kaniš* is resettled. But its days, and the days of the homeland as an independent Assyrian state are numbered. For in Anatolia a new hegemony is being created by the Indo-European Hittites, while on the mountain borders of Mesopotamia the Hurrians are beginning to exert pressure on the lines of communication between the Assyrian settlements and Assur. And of greatest significance, the Old Babylonian Dynasty, one of the old Amorite dynasties, reaches its apogee in the reign of Hammurabi and his successors. All of these factors together bring increasing and unbearable pressures upon Assyria and its far-off communities. Assyria is swallowed up by Ḫammurabi, but neither he, nor the later kings of his dynasty, could succeed to the possession of the trading empire wrought by the Old Assyrians. For the Babylonians were themselves checked by the existence of independent states in western Mesopotamia, as well as by the Hittite and Hurrian powers on the north. The last phase in the drama occurs when Muršiliš I, the Old Hittite King, raids Babylon at the turn of the sixteenth century, an event which signals the full emergence of Anatolian power as a factor in the political life of Mesopotamia at mid-second millennium.

We believe it was the stimulus given to the Anatolian metal economy by the Old Assyrian traders which, ironically, prepared the way for the rise of the Old Hittite Kingdom, and for the blossoming of its successor, the Hittite Empire of the fifteenth century and later. All in all, to be sure, the century or century and a half of Assyrian commercial undertaking in Anatolia did not make of Assyria a great power. But it served as a catalyst for Anatolia, even as for the next phase of Assyrian power in Mesopotamia — the Middle Assyrian Kingdom — which was itself to contend with the Hittites, Hurrians and Babylonians during the second half of the second millennium. In sum, then, the Old Assyrian colonies of Anatolia represent a remarkable achievement in the history of ancient Near Eastern international relations: the establishment of a commercial system which bound together two regions in common enterprise without recourse, we fully affirm, to war and conquest.

APPENDIX A

THE OLD ASSYRIAN DOCUMENTS

I. THE FIND-SPOTS

In addition to Kültepe, Alişar Hüyük and Boğazköy, numerous Old Assyrian tablets have been found in other places, both in Anatolia and in Northern Mesopotamia. Individual tablets originating at *Anatolian* sites are: (a) One of twenty-five tablets in the Museum of Adana (No. 237b) is thought to come from Maymun Suyu, near Toprak Kale;[1] (b) The Cappadocian tablet of the Walter's Art Gallery, Baltimore (published by J. Lewy, *AHDO*, I [1937] 17f.), has been held by B. Landsberger to come from somewhere east of the Cilician Plain region;[2] (c) K. Balkan suggests that tablet No. 54 of those published by Gelb in *OIP*, 27 may have originated from one of the *Hüyüks* near Everek (Develi), south of Kayseri;[3] (d) Some encased tablets have been found near Malatya, according to Balkan;[4] (e) A tablet purchased at Uzunyayla in 1940 may have originated in the vicinity of that site.[5]

Cappadocian tablets found or purchased in *Northern Mesopotamia* are: (a) Several fragments of Cappadocian tablets originate from the site of Yorgan Tepe (Nuzi);[6] (b) A tablet of the Cappadocian type, and a building inscription, were reputedly found in Assur according to E. Forrer in *RLA*, 1, 235;[7] (c) I. J. Gelb has studied a tablet from the Diyala region

[1] Cf. K. Balkan, *TTKY*, VII, Seri — No. 28 (1955), 48, w.n. 21.

[2] Cf. *ibid.*, 48 and 51 w.n. 37-38.

[3] Cf. *ibid.*, 48.

[4] Cf. *ibid.*, 68, n. 21.

[5] Cf. *ibid.*, 48.

[6] These were published by Th. J. Meek in *HSS*, 10 (1935) as Nos. 223-227; cf. J. Lewy, "Notes on Pre-Hurrian Texts from Nuzi", *JAOS*, 58 (1938), 450-461. With Lewy, *loc. cit.* 459, Balkan believes that four of the five fragments published by Meek are older than the Cappadocian tablets of Kültepe Level II for reasons of orthography and archaism in language, *loc. cit.*, 48, w.n. 23-24.

[7] Cf. the notice by Gelb, *OIP*, 27 (1935) 8, and Balkan, *loc. cit.*, 48.

of Mesopotamia whose epigraphy appears to be typically Cappadocian;[8] (d) S. Smith refers to a number of tablets which Lord Percy reputedly obtained in the region of the Habur River, but these have not been published;[9] (e) The tablet published by J. V. Scheil, "Texte cappadocienne ninivite", was reputedly obtained in Mosul.[10]

II. CHECKLIST OF THE DOCUMENT SOURCES[11]

The numbers appearing after the title entry indicate the number of new texts presented in the volume. The following symbols are also used: *A* = Autograph copy; *B* = Transliteration; *C* = Translation. The bibliography is presented by date of publication and utilizes abbreviated titles according to the *Table of Abbreviations* given at the beginning of this study.

Th. G. Pinches, *PSBA*, 4 (1881-82), 11-18, 28-32 (2: *ABC*); A. H. Sayce, *PSBA*, 6 (1883-84), 17-25 (Tablet on p. 20f. republished, *ibid.*, 19, 289f.) (5: *BC*); V. S. Golenischev *Vingt-quatre tablettes cappadociennes de la collection W. Golenischeff* (1891) (No. 18= Šil. 5; No. 24= Šil. 6) (24:*ABC*); J. V. Scheil, RT 18 (1896) 74f. (1:*ABC*= Chantre No. 16); *idem*, in E. Chantre, *Mission en cappadoce* (1898) 93-109 (= Pls. 21-22) and Pl. 4 no. 7, Pl. 5 no. 8f. (No. 16= RT 18 [1896] 74) (19:*ABC*); A. H. Sayce, *PSBA*, 19 (1897) 286-91 (Tablet on pp. 289f. previously published, *ibid.*, 6 [1883-84] 20f.) (2:*BC*); *Collection De Clercq* 2 (1900) 174f. (1:*ABC*); A. H. Sayce, *Bab.* 2 (1908) 1-45 (Translations of 19 tablets of Golenishev, 2 of Chantre, of Sheil, RT 18 [1896] 74f., of Sayce, *PSBA*, 19 [1897], 287, all previously published. Three new tablets published here are: Gol. a= Šil. 4; Gol. b= Šil. 3; Gol. c) (3:*ABC*); Th. G. Pinches, *AAA*, 1 (1908), 49-80 (21:*ABC*); J. V. Scheil, *RT*, 31 (1909), 55f. (1:*ABC*); Fr. Thureau-Dangin, *Florilegium* (1909) 591-97 (1: =*LC*, No. 242); *idem*, *LC* (1910) Nos. 239-42 (No. 242= *Florilegium*, 591-97) (4:*A*); *idem*, *RA*, 8 (1911), 142-151 (Republished in TC as follows: pp. 142-45= No. 90; 145-48= No. 91; 148f.= No. 63; 149f.= No. 64) (5:*ABC*); A. H. Sayce, *Bab.*, 4 (= Edinburgh) (1911) 65-80 (3:*ABC*); *idem*, Bab. 6 (= *SUP*) (1912) 182-92 (see *BIN*, 6 [1944], 3) (10:*ABC*); G. Contenau, *TTC* (1919) (8 tablets previously published in *Bab.*, 2 [1908], one in *Bab.*, 4 [1911], and two in *PSBA*, 4 [1881-82] are

[8] Cf. I. J. Gelb, "A Tablet of Unusual Type from Tell Asmar", *JNES*, 1 (1942), 219-226.

[9] Cf. *CCT*, 5.

[10] Cf. J. V. Scheil, *RT*, 31 (1909), 55f.

[11] I am deeply indebted to Prof. Gelb of the Oriental Institute, Chicago, for supplying me with an initial working bibliography of document sources when I began my studies of the Old Assyrian settlements. The list given in the text has been elaborated from it.

here re-studied, along with new texts) (30:*AB*, partially *C*); *idem*, *TC* (1920) (Nos. 63, 64, 90 and 91 republished from *RA*, 8 [1911], 142-51) (147:*A*); L. W. King, *HT* (1920) (Pl. 50= No. 102, supposedly coming from Boğazköy. See *CCT* [1921] 5) (1:*A*); V. K. Shileiko, *IAIMK*, 1 (1921), 356-64 (No. 3= Gol. b; No. 4= Gol. a; No. 5= Gol. 18; No. 6= Gol. 24) (12:*ABC*); S. Smith, *CCT* (1921) (99:*A*); *idem*, *RA*, 21 (1924), 89f. (1:*BC*); *idem*, *CCT*, II (1924) (60:*A*); *idem*, *CCT*, III (1925) (74:*A*); J. Lewy, *KTS* (1926) (147:*A*); S. Smith, *CCT*, IV (1927) (108:*A*); A. T. Clay, *BIN*, IV (1927) (233:*A*); F. J. Stephens, *KTP* (1927), 101-136 (see A. H. Sayce, *Museum Journal*, 9 [1918], 148f.) (45:*A*, 9 fully or partially *BC*); Fr. Thureau-Dangin, *TC*, II (1928) (78:*A*); J. Lewy, *KTB*l (1929) (18:*ABC*); *idem*, *KTHahn* (1930) (40:*ABC*); *idem*, and G. Eisser, *EL*, I and II (1930 and 1935) (64 new text of 341:*BC*); J. Lewy, *TuM* (1932) (Approximately 108 tablets and fragments= about 84:*A*); G. R. Driver, *An Or*, 6 (1933) Pls. 1-8 (22:*A*); F. M. Th. Böhl, Leiden (1934), 36-43 (4:*BC*); T. J. Meek, *HSS*, 10 (1935), Nos. 223-27 (5:*A*); I. J. Gelb, *OIP*, 27 (1935) (62:*ABC*. Nos. 1-53 are tablets from Alişar Hüyük, Nos. 54-62 from Kültepe and elsewhere); J. Lewy, *TC*, III, 1 (1935) (81:*A*); *idem*, *TC*, III, 2 (1936) (114:*A*); A. Goetze, *Berytus*, 3 (1936), 76-82 (1:*ABC*); H. G. Güterbock, *MDOG*, 74 (1936) 64f. (1: *ABC*); J. Lewy, *TC*, III, 3 (1937) (81:*A*); *idem*, *AHDO*, 1 (1937) 106-108 (1:*ABC*); B. Hrozný, *AHDO*, 1 (1937), 87-90 (1:*BC*); *idem*, *SeD*, 2 (1939), 108-111 (1:*BC*); K. Bittel and R. Naumann, *MDOG*, 77 (1939) 23 (4:photographs); B. Landsberger, *TTAED*, 4 (1940), 7-31 (4:*BC*; No. 4= *KTP* [1927], No. 14); F. J. Stephens, *BIN*, VI (1944) (270:*A*); B. Landsberger and K. Balkan, *Belleten*, 14 (1950) (1:*ABC*); B. Hrozný, *ICK*, I (1952) (194:*A*); A. Goetze, *JCS*, 8 (1954), 145 (2:*A*); S. Smith and D. J. Wiseman, *CCT*, V (1956) (150:*A*); P. Garelli, *RA*, 51 (1957) (3:*ABC*); H. Otten, *KBo*, IX (1957) (40:*A* [includes all Boğazköy tablets found up to publication date in addition to four from the Berlin Vorderasiatischen Museum-]); K. Balkan, *TTKY*, VII, Seri — No. 31a (1957) (1:*ABC*, and several new Kültepe tablets and others previously untranslated are rendered in whole or in part, *BC*); L. Matouš, *JJP*, 11-12 (1957-58) (2:*ABC*); P. Garelli and D. A. Kennedy, *RHA*, 66 (1960) (1:*ABC*); *idem*, *JCS*, 14 (1960) (16:*ABC*); B. Kienast, *ATHE* (1960) (76:*ABC*);[12] *JCS*, 15 (1961), 127 (1:*A*); L. Matouš, *ICK*, II (1962), (348:*A*, mostly fragments); H. Lewy, *JCS*, 17 (1963), 103-104 (1:*BC*); P. Garelli, *RA*, 58 (1964), 53-68 (13:*ABC*); *idem*, *RA*, 58 (1964), 111-136

[12] Texts No. 1-53 were first offered as a Heidelberg Dissertation, 1957. All 76 are assigned to Level II of Kültepe-Kaniš by the author.

(11:*ABC*; one published text, *TC*, III, 1, 10:*BC*); *idem*, *RA*, 59 (1965), 19-48 (22:*ABC*); *WZKM*, 59/60 (1963/64), 117-118 (1:*ABC*); P. Garelli, *RA* 59 (1965), 149-176 (11:*ABC*); *idem*, *RA* 60 (1966), 93-152 (23 *ABC*); K. Hecker, *Die Keilschrifttexte der Universitätsbibliothek Giessen* (= *Berichte und Arbeiten aus der Universitätsbibliothek Giessen* 9 (Giessen, Universitätsbibliothek, 1966) (50 ABC $\neq$ 1 *BC*).

III. UNPUBLISHED TEXTS

H. H. von der Osten has estimated that Old Assyrian tablets are to be found in nearly every European and American museum containing Oriental antiquities.[13] Known collections of unpublished tablets include the one hundred-fifty at Leiden,[14] thirty-three at Geneva,[15] a small number at the University Museum, Philadelphia,[16] in addition to many tablets in the hands of private individuals.[17] With the appearance of *CCT*, V (1956), the British Museum has completed publication of its Old Assyrian holdings. Still to be awaited are publications of tablets in the *Vorderasiatischen Abteilung* of the Berlin Museum,[18] and those in possession of the Universities of Giessen and Tübingen,[19] as well as approximately eight hundred of the Kültepe tablets brought by Hrozný to Prague in 1925.[20]

IV. PUBLICATION OF TEXTS UNEARTHED AT KÜLTEPE, 1948

More then ten thousand new tablets have been discovered at Kültepe between 1948 and the present. These are in the possession of the *Türk Tarih Kurumu* (*Turkish Historical Society*), but only a mere handful of them have been referred to, and these mostly in reviews of excavations in progress.[21]

[13] Cf. *OIP*, 30, 3, 438, n. 88.
[14] Cf. *Leiden* (1934), 36-43.
[15] Cf. E. Sollberger, "The Cuneiform Collection in Geneva", *JCS*, 5 (1951), 19, where it is reported that G. Dossin intends to publish them.
[16] Prof. J. Lewy had recently before his death been studying the unpublished Kültepe documents of this museum; cf. *HUCA*, 27 (1956), 45, n. 170.
[17] Cf. *EL*, I and II, *passim*.
[18] Cf. Goetze, *Kleinasien* (1957), 68.
[19] Cf. *ibid*.
[20] The recent publication of 194 of Hrozný's texts appears as *ICK*, I (1952). For commentary on the appearance of this volume see Lewy, *HUCA*, 27, (1956), 1-2, w.n. 1-6. In 1962, Lubor Matouš brought out a second group, *ICK*, II.
[21] Almost every interim report of the Kültepe excavations brings word of new archives being discovered. Several texts are communicated in transliteration (in whole or part) by Balkan, *TTKY*, VII, Seri — No. 28, 43, 65f., 73. A recent publication of a letter

V. ORIGINS, DECIPHERMENT AND PUBLICATION HISTORY OF THE OLD ASSYRIAN TABLETS

The prototypes of Old Assyrian tablets were first studied and communicated to scholars by Th. G. Pinches in 1881.[22] He had discovered them not as a result of excavation, but while working in two different European institutions: the British Museum and the *Bibliothèque Nationale* of Paris. Up to then undeciphered and unclassified, his first specimens and (as it turned out later) many hundreds of similar tablets had been routinely collected by museum agents and other scholarly travelers, who were ignorant of their style and contents. The bazaars of Anatolia were the chief suppliers for Europe and America, but no one who searched for the places where the tablets lay buried succeeded in finding even one site for almost fifty years after Pinches' first communication.[23]

By 1894, after fruitful work by Golenishev,[24] Jensen[25] and especially Delitzsch,[26] the new tablets were clearly shown to have been written in an old dialect of Assyrian. But it was not until 1925 that one of those who kept exploring the central Anatolian Plateau for find-spots succeeded in identifying a main center of distribution. In that year the Czech Assyriologist, Hrozný, unearthed nearly a thousand tablets in the terrace mound lying adjacent to the larger mound of Kültepe.[27] Additional discoveries of Old Assyrian tablets were made at Alişar Hüyük between 1929 and 1932,[28] at Boğazköy in 1938 and 1953,[29] and at Yorgan Tepe (Nuzi) in 1931 *et. seq.*[30]

---

found in the palace on the Kültepe Main Mound is: K. Balkan, "The Letter of King Anum-Hirbi of Mama to King Warshama of Kaniš", *TTKY*, VII, Seri — No. 31a (1957).

22 Cf. *PSBA*, 4 (1881-82), 11-28; 28-32.

23 Cf. T. Özgüç, *TTKY*, V, Seri — No. 10 (1950), 109-110 (German translation) where the visits of Chantre in 1893-94, Winckler in 1906 and Grothe in the same year, are cited. Lewy, in *HUCA*, 27 (1956), 1, n. 2, notes also the visits of Belck and Hilprecht.

24 Cf. V. S. Golénishchev, *Vingt-quatre tablettes cappadociennes de la collection W. Golénischeff* (St. Petersbourg).

25 Cf. P. Jensen. "Die kappadokischen Keilschrifttafelchen", *ZA*, 9 (1894), 62-81.

26 Fr. Delitzsch, after studying twenty-one of the Golenishchev tablets, demonstrated conclusively in 1893 that the so-called Cappadocian tablets were written in Old Assyrian, although words of a non-Semitic idion had infiltrated into that dialect. Cf. "Beiträge zur Entzifferung und Erklarung der kappadokischen Keilschrifttafeln", *Königlich-Sachsische Gesellschaft der Wissenschaften, Philologisch-historischen Klasse. Abhandlungen, Bd. 14, No. 4* (Leipzig, 1894), 205-270 [230].

27 Cf. the brief description and bibliography of Hrozný's finds given in *Appendix B*, Ia and Ib, below.

28 Cf. *Appendix B*, II and IIa.

29 Cf. *Appendix B*, III and IIIa.

30 Cf. *Appendix B*, IV and IVa.

The great majority of texts has come from Kültepe; of the more than 10,000 at hand, less than one hundred come from all other sites. Less than one-third of the total have been published, mostly in autograph-copy, but only about six hundred have been translated.[31] As already noted, next to none of the texts unearthed since 1948 at Kültepe have been published.

VI. PHYSICAL AND EPIGRAPHICAL CHARACTERISTICS OF THE TABLETS

The average size of Cappadocian tablets is about 54 mm. × 48 mm. (roughly 2″ × 2″). In color they vary considerably from red and yellow to grey and black shades.[32] Characteristically pillow-shaped, they are slightly convex on both obverse and reverse surfaces. The tablets appear in two forms, either plain or enclosed. The enclosed, or so-called "case" tablet, has been placed in a clay envelope, upon which a duplicate or an abstract of its contents has been inscribed. This type of tablet preparation has been discussed by George Eisser in "*Beiträge zur Urkundenlehre der altassyrischen Rechtsurkunden vom Kültepe*", along with other notary practises, such as the rules governing the affixing of seals on contracts and legal decisions.[33]

The Cappadocian tablets are almost always ruled-off by horizontally incised lines, which slant somewhat upward to the right.[34] The heads of the upright wedges of the signs hang from these lines, and the signs, themselves, usually also slant forward to the right.[35] The shape of the wedges varies from a linear style, in which the wedges have no distinct heads and have been but slightly scratched into the clay surface, to the other extreme of deeply-engraved, largeheaded strokes which properly merit the designation "cuneiform". A third style compromises between the two. Sometimes the wedges are very elongated and flat, but sometimes they are narrow and higher than they are wide.[36] The writing of the internal elements of a sign also varies according to scribal idiosyn-

[31] Consult the bibliography of sources given in this Appendix, and the notations appended to each entry.

[32] Cf. *TTC*, (1919), 8f.

[33] *Festschrift Paul Koschaker 3* (Weimar, 1939), 94-126. See also G. R. Driver, *Semitic Writing* (London, 1948), 12.

[34] Cf. *BIN*, IV, 7; *CCT*, 5; Th. J. Meek observes, however, that Nos. 224-227 from Nuzu do not have the slant to the right, *HSS*, 10, xxv.

[35] Cf. *TCC*, 9.

[36] Cf. *TTC*, 8-9; *CCT*, 5.

cracy in that sometimes it is simple, but sometimes more complicated than normally would be expected.[37]

An unusual feature of Cappadocian writing is the single, vertical wedge occasionally used as a word-divider. It may have served as a device of punctuation, but if so, the principles of its use are unknown at present.[38] The Old Assyrian scribes followed normal Mesopotamian practise in not continuing a word from one line to the next. If space was lacking at the end of a line, they added any unaccommodated signs to the end of the line immediately below it.[39]

VII. THE OLD ASSYRIAN SYLLABARY

Cappadocian writing is predominantly syllabic. Logograms are sparingly used, mainly for designating trade goods, or to express notions such as "month" and the like. Very frequently these logograms are written with phonetic compliments.[40] Verbal ideas are not expressed logographically in the Cappadocian tablets.[41] Determinatives, also, are relatively rare.[42]

There are approximately one hundred-twenty signs in the Cappadocian syllabary, mostly of the consonant plus vowel (CV), or the vowel plus consonant (VC) types.[43] Voiced, voiceless and emphatic consonantal sounds are not distinguished from each other in the syllabary.[44]

The first compendium of Cappadocian signs was made in 1919 by G. Contenau in *TTC* (137f.). He compared these with signs from Ur, the Old Babylonian Dynasty and later Assyrian and Babylonian examples. In 1921, Sidney Smith appended a sign-list to his first volume of British Museum texts, *CCT* (Pls. A and B). In 1928, Fr. Thureau-Dangin offered "*Le syllabaire des tablettes cappadociennes*", in *TC*, II

[37] Cf. *TTC*, 9.

[38] Cf. *CCT*, 6; *CSQ*, 2, 12; *TTC*, 13-14; Driver, *Semitic Writing*, *op. cit.*, 42 w.n. 3; I. J. Gelb, "Notes on von Soden's Grammar of Akkadian", *BO*, 12 (1955), 97, sub 7b (review of *AnOr*, 33).

[39] Cf. *TTC*, 13.

[40] Cf. *OIP*, 27, 41, n. 7; *CCT*, 5-6; I. J. Gelb, *A Study of Writing* (Chicago, 1952), 114, 120 and 165.

[41] Cf. *TTC*, 13.

[42] Cf. *OIP* 27, 41, n. 7, and 63, n. to line 11.

[43] Cf. "Le syllabaire des tablettes cappadociennes", in *TC*, II, 4-6; also *An Or*, 27, *passim*.

[44] Cf. *OIP*, 27, 41, n. 7; Gelb, *A Study of Writing*, *op. cit.*, 69; R. Labat, *Manuel d'épigraphie akkadienne* (Paris, 1952), 20. S. A. Pallis, *The Antiquity of Iraq* (Copenhagen, 1956), points out that at Kültepe certain sounds were articulated differently than in the mother country, probably under the influence of Anatolian dialects of the neighborhood (p. 230 and 583).

(4-6). The most recent and comprehensive presentation of the sign-list appears in Rene Labat's, *Manual d'épigraphie akkadienne* (*passim*), together with a short sketch of Cappadocian syllabary characteristics.[45] A presentation of Cappadocian sign values (among others) appears in W. von Soden's *An Or*, 27 (1948), although no logographic values are given.

VIII. THE OLD ASSYRIAN DIALECT

The Old Assyrian dialect displays characteristics which, for the most part, are common to Assyrian of later periods. It would be extraneous, if not impossible, to treat of the subject here, even in small compass. As yet, no grammar of Old Assyrian has been written, although Professor Lewy had indicated that he would treat many of its problems in the near future.[46] At the present time the most comprehensive — though mainly comparative — treatment of the dialect may be found in von Soden, *An Or*, 33 (1952), *passim*. Beyond this, there exist only a very few articles on the subject.[47]

IX. TYPES OF OLD ASSYRIAN TEXTS

The Cappadocian tablets are mainly concerned with business ma tters For convenience they may roughly be divided into the following categories: (a) Business documents, proper; (b) Letters, the overwhelming majority of which discuss business conditions; (c) Legal documents; and (d) Letters which represent correspondence between political bodies and their representatives. In a category by itself is the so-called "Irišum-Inscription", found (in two copies) at Kültepe in 1948.

(a) The business documents, proper, include debt tablets, purchase orders and agreements, memoranda of inventory and deposit (or "entrusting") of goods, agreements about the transport of goods and the transfer of ownership of goods, contracts authorizing the financing of business enterprises, memoranda of settlement of accounts, liquidation of debt and the assumption of debt-obligations by guarantors. All these types of business records are treated in detail in G. Eisser and J. Lewy,

[45] *Loc. cit.*

[46] Proposed at the Fourth International Congress of Assyriologists at Paris in 1953, as reported in *Or ns*, 23 (1954), 173, before his death.

[47] Cf. this Appendix, Sections XI A and XI G.

EL, I and II (1930 and 1935), the standard and indispensable work on the subject.

(b) The letters about business activities and conditions represent correspondence between entrepreneurs and their employee-agents, who generally are under contractual relationships. While most publications of Cappadocian tablets usually include texts of all types, the volumes *CCT*, II-IV (1924-27) and *TC*, III, 1 (1935), are entirely devoted to letters. Of singular importance for entrepreneur-employee contracts is B. Landsberger's, "*Solidarhaftung von Schuldnern in den babylonisch-assyrischen Urkunden*".[48]

(c) The legal documents contain depositions in commercial disputes as well as records of decisions handed down by *kârum* and *wabârtum* courts. In this case there occasionally appear documents concerned with marriage, divorce, adoption and settlement of inheritances. Of special interest are several documents issued under the authority of local princes.[49]

(d) The letters reflecting the correspondence between political bodies of one kind or another and their representatives are relatively rare, there being no "official archives" among the Cappadocian tablets. Mostly these letters are concerned with administrative matters relative to Cappadocian trade, but several very important letters inform us directly of the relations between individual Anatolian princes and the Assyrians.[50]

(e) Finally, the so-called "Irišum-Inscription" is an account in variant texts, of the building activities undertaken at some time by Irišum I in the Temple of Assur at Assur. Its value as a historical source is questionable, since it seems to have been used at Kültepe as a school-exercise text, and hence may be anachronistic.[51]

X. OLD ASSYRIAN DOCUMENTS FROM ASSUR

The only other Old Assyrian documentary material contemporaneous with the Cappadocian tablets are the texts emanating from the reigns of several members of the Old Assyrian Dynasty. These are mainly building inscriptions, and have been published by Ebeling, Meissner and Weidner.[52]

48 *ZA*, N.F. 1 (v. 35), (1924), 22-36.
49 Cf. Chapter Five, above.
50 Cf. Chapter Four, above.
51 Cf. B. Landsberger and K. Balkan, "Die Inschrift des assyrischen Königs Irišum, gefunden in Kültepe, 1948", *Belleten*, 14, (1950), 219-268.
52 (= *IAK*).

XI. CHECKLIST OF SECONDARY SOURCES ESPECIALLY RELEVANT TO THE OLD ASSYRIAN PERIOD

The check-list is arranged by subject-matter, and the references are presented by date of publication within each division. Only the most important works of the last four decades are cited. A short form of citation is employed since all works are listed fully in the Bibliography at the end.

A. *Textual Commentary*

J. Lewy, *SATK* (1922); *idem*, "Bemerkung zu den altassyrischen Texten ...", *ZA*, N.F. 1 (v. 35) (1924) 148; F. J. Stephens, *CSQ*, 2 (1925) 11-58; J. Lewy, "Bemerkung zu den altassyrischen Texten ...", *ZA*, N.F. 3 (v. 37), (1926), 122-123; F. J. Stephens, "Notes on Cappadocian Tablets", *JAOS*, 46 (1926), 179-181; G. R. Driver, "Studies in Cappadocian Tablets", *RA*, 24 (1927), 153-179; *idem*, "Studies in Cappadocian Tablets", *Bab.*, 10 (1927), 69-137; *idem*, "Studies in Cappadocian Texts", *ZA*, N.F. 4 (v. 38) (1929), 217-232; B. Landsberger, "Zu Driver's Übersetzungen ...", *ZA*, N.F. 4 (v. 38) (1929), 275-280; *EL* (1930-1935); P. E. van der Meer, *Une correspondence commerciale* ... (1931); *idem*, "Fünf kappadokische Geschaftsbriefe", *Or Chr*, 3-Serie, 7 (1932), 126-137; M. David, "Beiträge zu den altassyrischen Briefen ...", *OLZ*, 36 (1933), 209-220; B. Landsberger and K. Balkan, "Die Inschrift des assyrischen Königs Irišum ...", *Belleten*, 14 (1950), 219-268 (Turkish and German); K. Balkan, *TTKY*, VII, Seri — No. 31a (1957); Reviews of *CCT*, V by L. Matouš, *BO*, 16 (1959), 176-183; K. Deller, *Or ns*, 27 (1958), 59-65, 184-198; P. Garelli, *RA*, 52 (1958), 42-44; *idem*, *JSS*, 3 (1958), 298-301; Reviews of *ATHE* by P. Garelli, *RA*, 55 (1961), 211-214; H. Hirsch, *WZKM*, 57 (1961), 43-58.

B. *History and Political Institutions*

G. Contenau, *TTC* (1919); E. F. Weidner, "*Der Zug Sargons* ...", *BKS*, 6 (1922), 57-99; J. Lewy, *SATK* (1922); *idem*, "Zur Geschichte Assyriens ...", *OLZ*, 26 (1923), 533-544; B. Landsberger, "Über die Volker ...", *ZA*, N.F. 1 (v. 35) (1924), 213-238; *idem*, *AHK* (1925), 1-36; J. Lewy, "Der *karrum* der altassyrisch-kappadokischen Stadte ...", *ZA*, N.F. 2 (v. 36) (1925), 19-28; *idem*, "'Kappadokische' Tontafeln und Frühgeschichte Assyriens ...", *OLZ*, 29 (1926), 750-761; 963-966; E. Ebeling, B. Meissner, E. F. Weidner, *IAK* (1926); S. Smith, *EHA* (1928); B. Hrozný, "L'invasion des Indo-Européens ...", *Ar Or*, 1 (1929), 273-299;

idem, "Narâm-Sîn et ses ennemis ...", *Ar Or*, 1 (1929), 65-76; M. David, *ZSS*, 52 (Review of *EL*) (1932), 496-503; B. Hrozný, Assyriens et Hittites ...", *Ar Or*, 4 (1932), 112-117; A. Goetze, *Kleinasien* (1st. Ed.) (1933); M. David, "Beiträge zu den altassyrischen Briefen ...", *OLZ*, 36 (1933), 209-220; H. G. Güterbock, "Die historische Tradition ...", *ZA* N.F. 8 (v. 42) (1934), 1-91, and *ZA*, N.F. 10 (v. 44) (1938), 45-149; J. Lewy, "La chronologie de Bitḫana et d'Anitta ...", *RHA*, 17 (1934), 1-24; I. J. Gelb, *OIP*, 27 (1935), 1-18; E. F. Weidner, "Ilušumas Zug nach Babylonien", *ZA*, N.F. 9 (v. 43) (1936), 114-123; B. Landsberger, *TTAED*, 4 (1940), 7-31; R. S. Hardy, "The Old Hittite Kingdom", *AJSL*, 58 (1941), 177-216; B. Landsberger, "Kommt *Ḫattum* 'Hettiterland' ...", *Ar Or*, 18, 1/2 (1950), 329-350; *idem*, "Hettiterland und Hettiter ...", *Ar Or*, 18 3/4 (1950), 321-329; J. Lewy, "*Ḫatta, Ḫattu, Ḫatti* ...", *Ar Or*, 18 3/4 (1950), 366-441; H. Otten, "Die hethitischen 'Königslisten' ...", *MDOG*, 83 (1951), 47-70; *idem*, "Zu den Anfängen der hethitischen Geschichte", *MDOG*, 83 (1951), 33-45; J. Klima and L. Matouš, "Les tablettes 'cappadociennes'", *RAI*, 2 (1951), 49-59; B. Landsberger, "Assyrische Königsliste ...", *JCS*, 8 (1954), 31-45, 47-73, 106-133; J. Lewy, "The *iššiʾakkum* of Kaniš ...", *PICO*, 23 (1954), 135-136; K. Balkan, *TTKY*, VII, Seri — No. 28 (1955); S. Lloyd, *Early Anatolia* (1956); J. Lewy, "On Some Institutions ...", *HUCA*, 27 (1956), 1-79; *idem*, "Apropos of a Recent Study ...", *Or ns*, 26 (1957), 12-36; D. O. Edzard, *Die "zweite Zwischenzeit" Babyloniens* (1957); A. Goetze, *Kleinasien* (2nd. Ed.) (1957); *idem*, "On the Chronology of the Second Millennium", *JCS*, 11 (1957), 53-61, 63-73; J. Mellaart, "Anatolian Chronology ...", *An St* 7 (1957), 55-88; K. Polanyi in *Trade and Market* ..., (1957), 12-26; K. Balkan, *TTKY*, VII, Seri — No. 31a (1957); H. G. Güterbock, "Kaneš and Neša ...", *Eretz Israel*, 5 (1958), 46-50; J. Lewy, "Some Aspects of Commercial Life ...", *JAOS*, 78 (1958), 89-101; G. Goossens, "Het Ontstaan van het Assyrisch Rijk", *MKAWB*, 22/3 (1960), 3-48; R. Borger, *Einleitung in die assyrischen Königsinschriften*, 1 (= HO) (1961); A. Goetze, "Hittite and Anatolian Studies", *BANE* (1961), 316-327; O. R. Gurney, *The Hittites* (3rd. Ed.) (1961); *idem*, *Anatolia*, 1750-1600 *B.C.*, *CAH*, rev. ed. of v. II, Ch. VI (1962); J. Mellaart, *Anatolia*, 4,000-2300 *B.C.*, *CAH*, rev. ed. of v. I, Ch. XVIII (1962); H. Lewy, "Neša", *JCS*, 17 (1963), 103-104; P. Garelli, *Les Assyriens en Cappadoce* (1963); J.-R. Kupper, *Northern Mesopotamia and Syria*, *CAH*, rev. ed. of v. II, Ch. 1 (1963); H. Lewy, "Notes on the Political Organization of Asia Minor ...", *Or ns*, 33 (1964), 181-198; M-J. Seux, "Remarques sur le titre royal assyrien *iššakki aššur*", RA 59 (1965), 101-109; H. Lewy, *Anatolia in the Old Assyrian Period*

(= *CAH*, rev. ed. of v. I, Ch. XXIV) (1965); *idem*, *Assyria, c.* 2600-1816 *B.C.* (= *CAH*, rev. ed. of. v. I, Ch. XXV) (1966).

C. *Economic Institutions and Business Practices*

B. Landsberger, "Solidarhaftung von Schuldnern ...", *ZA*, N.F. 1 (v. 35) (1924), 22-36; *idem*, *AHK* (1925), 1-36; G. Eisser and J. Lewy, *EL*, I and II (1930-35); P. van der Meer, *Une correspondence commerciale* ... (1931); S. Przeworsky, *Die Metallindustrie Anatoliens* (1939); I. J. Gelb, *OIP*, 27 (1935); B. Landsberger, *TTAED*, 4 (1940), 7-31; E. Bilgic, "Die juristisch-ökonomischen Keilschriftquellen ...", *Belleten*, 11 (1947), 571-602 (Turkish); R. J. Forbes, *Metallurgy in Antiquity* (1950); W. F. Leemans, *The Old Babylonian Merchant* (1950); S. E. Birgi, "Notes on the Influence of the Ergani Copper Mine ...", *JKAF*, 1 (1950-1951), 337-343; E. Bilgiç, "Änlichkeit und Unterscheid ...", *Belleten*, 15 (1951), 333-338 (Turkish); *idem*, "L'interet dans les textes economiques ...", *Belleten*, 15 (1951), 339-347; *idem*, "L'economie des metaux en Anatolie ...", *RAI*, 2 (1951), 99-100; J. Lewy, "Old Assyrian *ḫusârum* ...", *IEJ*, 5 (1955), 154-162; H. Lewy, "On Some Old Assyrian Cereal Names", *JAOS*, 76 (1956), 201-204; J. Lewy, "Some Aspects of Commercial Life ...", *JAOS*, 78 (1958), 89-101; W. F. Leemans, *Foreign Trade in the Old Babylonian Period* (1960); H. Limet, *Le travail du metal* ... (1960); P. Garelli, *Les Assyriens en Cappadoce* (1963); H. Lewy, "The Assload and Other Old Assyrian Measures of Capacity", Festschrift H. Th. Bossert (= *Anadolu Araştirmalari/JKAF* v. 2, Parts 1-2) (1965), 291-304; M. T. Larsen, *Old Assyrian Caravan Procedures* (Istanbul, 1968).

D. *Ethnology*

J. Lewy, "Lykier Syrer ...", *ZA*, N.F. 1 (v. 35) (1924), 144-148; B. Landsberger, "Über die Völker ...", *ZA*, N.F. 1 (v. 35) (1924), 213-238; J. Lewy, "Die Keilschriftquellen zur geschichte Anatoliens", *Nachrichten der Giessener Hochschulgesellschaft*, 6 (1927-1928), 35-43; *idem*, "Zur Amoriterfrage", *ZA*, N.F. 4 (v. 38) (1929), 243-272; M. S. Senyurek, "A Crainological Study of the Copper Age and Hittite Populations ...", *Belleten*, 5 (1941), 237-253; *idem*, "Human Skeletons from Kültepe", *Belleten*, 12 (1948) 323-343; T. Özgüç, *Die Bestattungsbrauche* ... (1948); E. Bilgiç, "Die Ortsnamen ...", *AfO* 15 (1945-1951), 1-37; B. Landsberger, "Kommt *Ḫattum* Hettiterland ...", *Ar Or*, 18, 1/2 (1950), 329-350; *idem*,

"Hettiterland und Hettiter ...", *Ar Or*, 18, 3/4 (1950), 321-329; J. Lewy, "*Ḫatta, Ḫattu, Ḫatti* ...", *Ar Or*, 18, 3/4 (1950), 366-441; M. S. Senyurek, "The Longevity of the Chalcolithic and Copper Age Inhabitants ...", *Belleten*, 15 (1951), 447-468; *idem*, "Fluctuation of the Crainial Index ...", *Belleten*, 15 (1951), 593-615; J. Klima and L. Matouš, "Les tablettes 'cappadociennes'", *RAI*, 2 (1951), 49-59; E. Bilgiç, "Recherches sur les tribus anatoliennes ...", *RAI*, 2 (1951), 102-103; I. J. Gelb, "A Contribution to the Proto-Indo-European Question", *JKAF*, 2 (1951), 23-36; A. Goetze, "The Cultures of Early Anatolia", *PAPS*, 97 (1953) 214-221; *idem*, "Some Groups of Anatolian Proper Names", *Language*, 30 (1954), 349-359; *idem*, "The Linguistic Continuity of Anatolia ...", *JCS*, 8 (1954), 74-81; B. Landsberger, "Assyrische Königsliste ...", *JCS*, 8 (1954), 31-45, 47-73, 106-120, 120-133: A. Goetze, "Suffixes in 'Kanishite' Proper Names", *RHA*, 66 (1960), 45-55; *idem*, "Cilicians", *JCS*, 16 (1962), 48-58; P. Garelli, *Les Assyriens en Cappadoce* (1963).

E. *Geography*

I. J. Gelb, "Studies in the Geography of Western Asia", *AJSL*, 55 (1938), 66-85; A. Goetze, *Kizzuwatna* ... (1940); J. Garstang, "Šamuḫa and Malatya", *JNES*, 1 (1942), 450-459; E. Bilgiç, "Die Ortsnamen in den kappadokischen Texten ...", *Belleten*, 10 (1946), 381-423 (Turkish); J. Lewy, "Naram-Sin's Campaign ...", *HEM* (1947), 11-18; E. Bilgiç, "Die Ortsnamen der 'kappadokischen' Urkunden ...", *AfO*, 15 (1945-51), 1-37; A. Salonen, *Die Landfahrzeuge* ... (1951); J. Lewy, "Studies in the Historic Geography ... II", *Or ns*, 21 (1952), 293-306, 393-425; A. Goetze, "An Old Babylonian Itinerary", *JCS*, 7 (1953), 51-72; S. Alp, "Die Lage von Šamuḫa", *Anatolia*, 1 (1956), 77-80; A. Salonen, *Hippologica Accadica* (1956); S. Smith, "Uršu and Haššum", *An St*, 6 (1956), 35-43; M. Falkner, "Studien zur Geographie ...", *AfO*, 18 (1957), 1-37; H. G. Güterbock, "Kaneš and Neša ...", *Eretz Israel*, 5 (1958), 46-50; B. Alkim, "Güney-Batı Antitoros ..." (Eng. Resume: "An Ancient Road-System in the Southwestern Antitaurus, *Belleten*, 23, 74-76), *Belleten*, 23 (1959), 59-73 (Turkish); J. Garstang and O. R. Gurney, *The Geography of the Hittite Empire* (1959); E. Laroche, "Études de toponymie anatolienne", *RHA*, 69 (1961), 57-98; J. Lewy, "Old Assyrian Evidence Concerning Kuššara ...", *HUCA*, 33 (1962), 45-57; H. Lewy, "Neša", *JCS*, 17 (1963), 103-104; P. Garelli, *Les Assyriens en Cappadoce* (1963); E. Weidner, "Assyrische Itinerare", *AfO*, 21 (1966), 42-46.

F. *Law and Legal Practices*

J. Lewy, "*TC*, 100, *LC*, 242 und das Eherecht ...", *ZA*, N.F. 2 (v. 36) (1925), 139-161; G. Eisser, "Bemerkung zu den altassyrischen Rechtsurkunden ...", *ZDMG*, 81 (1927), xlvi; *idem*, "Altassyrische Prozessgesetze ...", *ZSS*, 48 (1928), 579-582; J. Lewy, "Fragmente altassyrische Prozessgesetze ...", *MAOG*, 4 (1928), 122-128; G. Eisser and J. Lewy, *EL*. I and II (1930/1935); G. R. Driver and J. C. Miles, *The Assyrian Laws* (1935); A. Goetze, "Eine altassyrische Rechtsurkunde ...", *Berytus*, 3 (1936), 76-82; B. Hrozný, "Un nouveau texte juridique ...", *AHDO*, 1 (1937), 87-90; J. Lewy, "Old Assrian Documents ...", I and II, *AHDO*, 1 and 2 (1937/1938), 91f., 111-142; B. Hrozný, "Über eine unveröffentliche Urkunde ...", *SeD*, 2 (1939), 108-111; G. Eisser, "Beiträge zur Urkundenlehre ...", *Festschrift Paul Koschaker*, 3 (1939), 94-126; E. Bilgiç, "Die originallen Seiten ...", *DTCFD*, 9 (1951/1952), 239-250; G. R. Driver and J. C. Miles, *The Babylonian Laws* (1956); I. J. Gelb and E. Sollberger, "The First Legal Document ...", *JNES*, 16 (1957), 163-175; P. Garelli, *Les Assyriens en Cappadoce* (1963); H. Hirsch, "Eine Kleinigkeit zur Heiratsurkunde ICK 1,3", *Or. ns* 35 (1966), 279-280.

G. *Linguistics and Onomastica*

J. Lewy, *Das Verbum* ... (1921); *idem*, *SATK* (1922); F. J. Stephens, *PNC* (1928); A. Goetze, "Die kleinasiatische Personennamen ...", *ZA*, N.F. 6 (v. 40) (1931), 260-263; L. Oppenheim, "Les rapports entre les noms ...", *RHA*, 5 (1938), 7-30; M. Bar-Am, "The Subjunctive ...", *Or ns*, 7 (1938), 12-31; J. Lewy, "Studies in Akkadian Grammar ...", *Or ns*, 15 (1946), 361-415; E. Laroche, "Recherches sur les noms des dieux hittites", *RHA*, 46 (1946), 76-139 (also published as a monograph, 1947); E. Bilgiç, "Die Ortsnamen ...", *AfO*, 15 (1945-51), 1-37; J. Lewy, "Studies in Old Assyrian Grammar ...", *Or ns*, 19 (1950), 1-36; K. Balkan and B. Landsberger, "Die Inschrift des assyrischen Königs Irišum ...", *Belleten*, 14 (1950), 219-268; A. Goetze, "Hittite Courtiers and their Titles", *RHA*, 54 (1952), 1-14; E. Laroche, *Recueil d'Onomastique hittite* (1952); E. Bilgiç, "Die einheimischen Appellativa ...", *Ankara Universitesi Sumeroloji Enstitüsü Yayinlari*, No. 3 (1953-54) (Turkish and German); A. Goetze, "The Theophorous Elements ...", *Language*, 29 (1953), 263-277; *idem*, "The Linguistic Continuity of Anatolia ...", *JCS*, 8 (1954), 74-81; *idem*, "Some Groups of Ancient Anatolian Proper Names", *Language*, 30 (1954), 349-359; A. Kammenhuber, "Beobachtungen zur hettitisch-luvischen Sprachgruppe", *RHA*, 58 (1956), 1-21; H. Lewy, "On Some Old Assyrian Cereal Names", *JAOS*, 76 (1956), 201-204; J. Lewy, "Old Assyrian *izêzum* ...", *Or ns*, 28 (1959), 351-360; *idem*, "Grammatical and Lexicographical Studies", *Or ns*, 29 (1960), 20-45; A. Goetze, "Suffixes in 'Kaneshite' Proper Names", *RHA*, 66 (1960), 45-55; A. Kammenhuber, "Nominalkomposition ...", *ZVSGI-ES*, 77 (1961), 161-218; P. Garelli, *Les Assyriens en Cappadoce* (1963); H. G. Güterbock, "A Votive Sword with Old Assyrian Inscription", *Landsberger Festschrift* (= *Assyriological Studies No.* 16, Oriental Institute, Univ. of Chicago, 1965), 197-198; H. Lewy, "The Assload and Other Old Assyrian Measures of Capacity", Festschrift H. Th. Bossert (= Anadolu Araştirmalari/ *JKAF* v. 2, Parts 1-2, 1965), 291-304; H. Hirsch, "*Ṣubrum* und scheinbar Verwandtes", *AfO* 21 (1966), 52-55; *idem*, "Stoffe aus Šarzuwa", *AfO* 21 (1966), 58.

H. *Religion and Religious Practices*

The comprehensive work is now: H. Hirsch, *Untersuchungen zur altassyrischen Religion*, *AfO*, Beiheft 13/14 (1961); H. G. Güterbock, "A Votive Sword with Old Assyrian Inscription", *Landsberger Festschrift* (= *Assyriological Studies No.* 16, Oriental Institute, Univ. of Chicago, 1965), 197-198; L. Matouš, "Anatolische Feste nach 'Kappadokischen' Tafeln", *Landsberger Festschrift* (= *Assyrological Studies No.* 16, Oriental Institute, Univ. of Chicago, 1965), 175-181.

I. *Social and Cultural Institutions*

H. Ehelolf and B. Landsberger, "Der altassyrische Kalender", *ZDMG*, 74 (1920), 216-219; B. Landsberger, *AHK* (1925), 1-36; J. Lewy, "The Assyrian Calendar", *ACIO*, 20 (1940), 122-123; *idem*, and H. Lewy, "The Origin of the Week ...", *HUCA*, 17 (1942-43), 1-152c; B. Landsberger and K. Balkan, "Die Inschrift des assyrischen Königs Irišum ...", *Belleten*, 14 (1950), 219-268 (Turkish and German); J. Lewy, "On Some Institutions ...", *HUCA*, 27 (1956), 1-79; P. Garelli, *Les Assyriens en Cappadoce* (1963); K. Balkan, "The Old Assyrian Week", *Landsberger Festschrift* (= *Assyriological Studies* No. 16, Oriental Institute, Univ. of Chicago, 1965), 159-174.

APPENDIX B

CHRONOLOGICAL AND STRATIGRAPHICAL NOTES ON THE OLD ASSYRIAN SETTLEMENTS

I. EXCAVATIONS AT KÜLTEPE (KÂRUM KANIŠ)[1]

The site of Kültepe, situated about nineteen kilometers north-east of Kayseri (Gr: *Caesarea Mazaca*), and seat of *Kàrum Kaniš*, chief of the Old Assyrian settlements in Cappadocia, consists of two principal areas — a large mound which rises to a height of twenty-three meters above the surrounding plain, and a flat terrace platform standing about two and one-half meters above ground level. The terrace platform is roughly about 400 meters by 800 meters, and within its strata lie the remains of Assyrian inhabitation at the site.

Kültepe has been formally excavated twice, the first time by B. Hrozný in 1925, the second by the *Türk Tarih Kurumu* (*Turkish Historical Society*), which began a series of annual excavations in 1948. The following presentation includes a description of the results of both digs.

Ia: HROZNÝ'S EXCAVATION OF 1925

Hrozný began his soundings on the main mound and reached an average depth of from three to five meters, in two places eight meters. He uncovered a large edifice with thick stone walls, which he dated to the end of the Hittite Empire Period (ca. 1200 B.C.). The building appeared to have been burnt. Among the small finds within it were several fragments of reliefs and sculpture, a number of vases (including two very large examples from the Graeco-Roman Period), and various kinds of small craft objects.

In late September of the summer's dig which was to end in mid-

[1] The following summary of the Kültepe excavations is synthesized from the many interim reports which have been issued so far, as well as from the two formal volume-reports issued by the Türk Tarih Kurumu (for which cf. the checklist under Section If of this Appendix).

November, Hrozný began to excavate the terrace mound on information from his workmen that cuneiform tablets could be unearthed there. Within a week he had penetrated to about two and one-half meters below the surface, and had discovered great numbers of Cappadocian tablets. These he removed to Prague at the end of the season, and did not excavate at Kültepe again.

Ib: CHECKLIST OF REPORTS ON HROZNY'S EXCAVATION

B. Hrozný, "Rapport préliminaire sur les fouilles tchéchoslovaques du Kültépé (1925)", *Syria*, 8 (1927), 1-12; *idem*, "The First Czechoslovak Excavations in the Near East", *Central European Observer*, 4 (1926), 527-529; *idem*, "A 'Record Office' 4000 Years Old: New Materials for the History of Asia Minor's Earliest Civilisation", *Illustrated London News* (Oct. 2, 1926), 600f.

Ic: EXCAVATIONS OF THE TÜRK TARIH KURUMU, 1948 —

After a twenty-three year period, during which the site lay untouched, the *Türk Tarih Kurumu* selected Kültepe as the site most likely to produce important results for furthering knowledge of early Anatolian history, and resumed excavations. Under the direction of Tahsin and Nimet Özgüç two test areas, designated *A* and *B*, and lying about 120 meters from each other, were dug; area *A* was plotted close to Hrozný's earlier soundings for purposes of comparison. Excavations since 1948 have disclosed four inhabitation strata. Level IV, resting on virgin soil, is clearly pre-Assyrian. The Assyrian traders most likely arrived sometime during the period represented by Level III, but the most flourishing period of the *kârum* is seen in Level II. The period of Assyrian occupation continues through Level Ic (during which the *kârum* appears to have been abandoned), and Level Ib. Thereafter, Level Ia postdates the *kârum*, and is the last occupation stratum on the terrace-mound. A scheme of the stratification on the terrace-mound is presented in Figure 2.

Id: STRATIFICATION OF KÂRUM KANIŠ

A. *Level IV*

1. *Buildings:* Only incomplete building foundations were discovered in this level. These differ somewhat in plans and orientation from the building foundations of later levels considered as a whole. [Cf. *TTKY*, V, Seri No. 10, pp. 147-149; *TTKY*, V Seri — No. 12, pp. 139-140; *TTKY*, V Seri — No. 19, p. xx; *AJA*, 66 (1962), p. 73].
2. *Pottery:* Three types of pottery occur: (a). The so-called "Hittite"-monochrome ware, a fast wheel-turned, unpainted [mostly red-slipped and highly burnished] ware. This pottery appears for the first time in Central Anatolia in this level, though in a more restricted variety of shapes than later appears in Level II. The "Hittite"-monochrome accounts for 50% of the total bulk of Level IV pottery to date; (b). A handmade polychrome-painted ware, the so-called "Cappadocian" or Alishar III ware, which is technically less developed than its counterpart in Level II; (c). A handmade monochrome, coarse examples of Alishar III ware, less well-made than the handmade-polychrome. [Cf. *TTKY*, V Seri — No. 10, pp. 170-199; *TTKY*, V, Seri — No. 12, pp. 153-193; *AJA*, 66 (1962), p. 73; K. Emre, "The Pottery of the Assyrian Colony Period ...", *Anatolia* 7 (1963), pp. 87-99 [87; 99]].

	Kârum Ia	(Deserted)	
OLD ASSYRIAN PERIOD	*Kârum* Ib	(Destroyed by fire)	Old Assyrian Tablets
	Kârum Ic	(No occupation)	
	Kârum II	(Destroyed by fire)	Old Assyrian Tablets
	Kârum III		
	Kârum IV		

Virgin Soil

Fig. 2. Scheme of the Stratification on the Terrace-Mound at Kültepe.

The results of most recent excavation at Kültepe now allow Level IV to be considered *vis à vis* the stratigraphical situation on the Main Mound [see Figure 3]. It remains clear that *Kârum* Level IV is the earliest stratum inhabited on the terrace, but the origins of the city of *Kaniš* go much deeper, perhaps the equivalent of 1,000 years. The excavations of

1961 penetrated to the period of Early Bronze I [= *EB*, I], whose beginning, at a rough guess, is ca. 3,000 B.C. The following series of strata was uncovered [summarized from M. Mellink, *AJA*, 67 (1963), pp. 175-176]:

(1) *Early Bronze I*, an unburnt level with mudbrick houses on stone foundations, and tombs within the houses. Pottery is red or dark-burnished, handmade, with but few examples of a local painted style. The ceramic style is regional.

(2) *Early Bronze II*, which continues the *EB*, I period without a break. Several subsidiary building strata appeared, some of which disclosed burning. The pottery is characterized as typical "Copper Age" ware. An important discovery was the presence of imported Syrian wheel-made jars and corrugated cups, which suggests correlation with Syria and Cilician *EB*, II.

(3) *Early Bronze III*, whose architecture gradually becomes monumental. Three sub-divisions of the period were discerned, from the lower level to the higher: (a) *EB*, IIIc: an increase in so-called painted "Proto-Intermediate" type, no Alishar III ware as yet, but connections to Alishar are seen in a type of handmade depas-cup with red bands [Cf. *OIP*, 29, Pl. 1, b 139]. Syrian imports continue; (b) *EB*, IIIb: the discovery of a megaron room with white-plastered walls [Cf. *AJA*, 62 (1958), pp. 93f., and Seton Lloyd, *The Dawn of Civilization* (London, 1961), p. 187, fig. 4]. Some of the tombs of this level are built of stone, and rich gifts, including "Cappadocian"-type idols were found in them. Pottery now includes wheel-made plates of Troy II and Tarsus RB III type, as well as a little Alishar III ware, but much "Intermediate" ware and continued Syrian imports; (c) *EB*, IIIa: buildings are now large, having white-washed walls reinforced with internal buttresses and benches. Pottery is described as profuse [the "Intermediate" ware] and in much greater variety than earlier. Depas goblets occur, as do Syrian ring-burnished bottles. This level was burnt and destroyed. As yet no *EB*, IIIa material types have been found in the *kârum*-area.

Apparently the *Kârum* was founded [though not by the Assyrian traders] in the next period, Middle Bronze I [= *Kârum*, Level IV].

B. *Level III*

1. *Buildings:* This Level follows directly upon its predecessor without there being evidence of any catastrophe to interrupt the inhabitation

sequence. The foundations of buildings here in many places rest directly upon those of Level IV beneath. By all indications, the stratum was rather densely populated. Buildings have from two to four rooms and rest on foundations of skillfully-worked stone.

2. *Pottery:* The Hittite monochrome pottery dominates the styles in Level III, increasing in quantity and varieties of shape, while the hand-made "Cappadocian" or Alishar III ware begins to recede. The proportions are now estimated to be 70/75% of the former to 25/30% of the latter. A third ware, a wheel-made product with painted decoration in geometric designs, or with bird and tree patterns, or hook and S-shaped patterns, appears for the first time. Its shapes are similar to those of utensils in the "Hittite" monochrome. Generally speaking, the pottery of Level III corresponds to that of Level II above it in form and technipue. The difference between pottery in Levels IV and III is seen in the rise of greater quantities of wheel-made ware for the latter, and is estimated to be the result of a natural evolution. [Cf. *TTKY*, V, Seri — No. 10 and 12, cited above, and K. Emre, *op. cit.*, pp. 87 and 99].

C. *Relative Chronology of Levels IV and III*

Before going on to a discussion of the remaining levels on the *Kârum*-terrace and their correlations with the strata uncovered on the city-mound, it is desirable to set Levels III and IV in their general chronological and cultural milieu. We have seen that the foundations of *Kaniš* as a city go back to the *EB*, I period, to somewhere, therefore, within the chronological horizons of the period ca. 3,000-2,500 B.C. The first phase of *Kaniš*'s existence (*EB*, I) passes harmoniously and apparently peacefully into the second (*EB*, II, ca. 2,500-2,300 B.C.). It is during this period that the preliminary indications show evidence both of expanded contacts with Cilicia and Syria and of some local disruption in the life of the city [burning]. However, the Early Bronze City continued to grow, as is witnessed by the construction of larger buildings, and by continued contacts with outside cultures [Troy II in the West and Cilicia and Syria in the South]. The city's three phases (*EB*, IIIc, ca. ?2300-2200 B.C.; *EB*, IIIb, ca. ?2200-2100 B.C.; and *EB*, IIIa, ca. ?2100-2000 B.C.) come to an end through some sort of violence suggested by a burnt stratum.

Since no Old Assyrian tablets have to date been found in Levels IV and III, it is clear that these pre-date Assyrian occupation. Who the inhabitants of these early terrace-levels were cannot be known at the present time, nor can anything be safely deduced now about the circumstances under which they were founded [but see *Appendix C*, below, for the possibility that the earliest inhabitants were perhaps native Anatolian merchants].

In 1959, Tahsin Özgüç, the excavator of Kültepe, wrote of their chronology:

> The houses of Levels III-IV were built of short lived materials. The presence of Syrian imported pottery fragments in Level IV and the availability of dated parallels from the city-mound are sufficient evidence that the two levels cannot be thought to extend back into the third millennium B.C. It seems to us that assigning a length of more than 40-50-years each to levels III-IV is made improbable by our investigations on the city-mound [*TTKY*, V, Seri — No. 19-p. xx].

However, a serious scholarly dispute had developed over the possibility that the *Kârum* was founded during the reign of Ibbi-Sin (ca. 2040-2016 B.C.), and by Sumerians. It is important, therefore, to revue this dispute before going on to a summary of later levels at Kültepe.

In 1911, Fr. Thureau-Dangin published a seal impression from a Cappadocian tablet bearing the name of a certain Ur-lugal-banda, son of Ur-nigin-gar, a functionary of Ibbi-Sin, last king of the Third Dynasty of Ur.[2] In 1948, the Turkish excavators of *Kârum Kaniš* unearthed a tablet bearing a seal impression which similarly mentioned Ibbi-Sin. As Falkenstein was the first to note, the legend of the latter seal impression was almost identical with that published by Thureau-Dangin.[3] Since 1948, more examples of seal impressions in the style of Ur III, some mentioning Ibbi-Sin, have been discovered, so that now about a dozen are known.[4] All these impressions come from tablets found in Level II, and indicate either that an original seal in an authentic Ur III style had been used, or that the original seal had been somewhat altered by addition of new elements to its basic design.[5]

In 1928 Sidney Smith expressed the possibility that the seal published by Thureau-Dangin indicated, with other facts of Cappadocian tablet orthography, that Ur III was overlord of Assyria.[6] Most scholars

[2] "La date des tablettes cappadociennes", *RA*, 8 (1911), 142f.

[3] Cf. A. Falkenstein, Review of K. Bittel, *Grundzüge der Vor — und Frühgeschichte Kleinasiens* (Tübingen, 1945), in *Die Welt des Orients*, 1 (1949), 343, w.n. 5. For further comments cf. J. Lewy, "*Ḫatta, Ḫattu, Ḫatti* ...", *op. cit.*, 416-417, w.nn. 286-287.

[4] Cf. N. Özgüç in *TTKY*, V, Seri — No. 12 (1953), 230-231, and K. Balkan, *TTKY*, VII, Seri — No. 28 (1955), 63.

[5] N. Özgüç in *TTKY*, V. Seri — No. 12 (1953), 230-231.

[6] Cf. *Early History of Assyria* (New York, 1928), 155-157.

rejected the importance of this particular seal impression because the name of the seal's owner, Ur-lugal-banda, did not appear either as a contracting party, or as a witness, on the debt tablet over which the seal had been rolled. They concluded that the seal had been reused.[7] But following the appearance of the second seal impression mentioning the king Ibbi-Sin in 1948, Falkenstein was led to the conclusion that the merchant colony at *Kaniš* was founded by the Third Dynasty of Ur, and that Assur continued the undertaking after it had gained independence following the breakdown of Ur's power at the beginning of Ibbi-Sin's reign.[8] Other scholars who share this view include Bittel[9] and Otten.[10]

Dr. Nimet Özgüç, who made a special study of the seals recovered at Kültepe during 1948 and 1949 also believes that the hand of Ur III is to be seen at Kültepe. She remarks that during the period of Old Assyrian inhabitation there, the memory of Ur III was still very strong, although, for her, the presence of seals in the style of Ur III does not point directly to an absolutely definite connection between Ur and *Kârum Kaniš*.[11]

Despite the weight of opinion given above, it must be argued that the seal impressions in Sumerian styles on Cappadocian tablets do not indicate a direct connection between Ur III and Kültepe-*Kaniš*. First, it seems quite clear that the seal published by Thureau-Dangin was reused by a person who had gotten possession of it, a common enough practise in the ancient Near East. Nor is there any reason to believe that the other appearances of seals in Sumerian style were anything but reuses. The last ruler of Ur III, Ibbi-Sin, was hardly able to control the region round his own capital in southern Mesopotamia, let alone exert influence in Anatolia.[12] It has also been pointed out by Gelb, and Goetze, that no historical records exist to show that Ur III ever, in fact, did extend its power to Anatolia.[13] Beyond this, no names of Anatolian cities appear in the economic records of this dynasty.

With the discovery of the Early Bronze I-IIIa levels of the city-mound at Kültepe and the consequent clear indications of relations with Northern Syria, Cilicia and even Southern Mesopotamia [cf. Özgüç, "Early Anatolian Archaeology", *Anatolia*, 7 (1963), p. 2], we must alter the

[7] Cf., e.g., J. Lewy, "'Kappadokische' Tontafeln und Frühgeschichte Assyriens und Kleinasiens", *OLZ*, 29 (1926), 758, w.n. 2; G. Contenau, *La civilisation des Hittites et des Hurrites du Mitanni* (Paris, 1948), 40.

[8] A. Falkenstein, Review of K. Bittel, *Grundzüge ...*, *op. cit.*, 343, w.n. 5.

[9] Cf. K. Bittel, "Hethiter und Proto-Hattier", *Historia*, 1 (1950), 284.

[10] Cf. H. Otten, "Zu den Anfängen der hethischen Geschichte", *MDOG*, 83 (1951), 37.

[11] Cf. N. Özgüç in *TTKY*, V, Seri — No. 12 (1953), 231.

[12] Cf. Th. Jacobsen, "The Reign of Ibbi-Suen", *JCS*, 7 (1953), 36-47.

[13] Cf. Gelb, *OIP*, 27 (1935), 7, and Goetze, *Kleinasien* (1957), 66.

picture slightly in favor of admitting a certain familiarity of third millennium Mesopotamian dynasts with Central Anatolia. C. J. Gadd has shown a renewed interest in the credibility of Old Akkadian contacts with the area ["The Dynasty of Akkad and the Gutian Invasion", *CAH*, Rev. Ed. vol. I & II (1963 = Chap. XIX], and Machteld Mellink has recently published an analysis of a Baghdad Museum stele which tends to support "the credibility of pseudo-historical claims for the Akkadians to have taken their armies into Anatolia" ["An Akkadian Illustration of a Campaign into Cilicia?" *Anatolia*, 7 (1963), p. 114]. But it may not be supposed in the present state of our knowledge that either Akkad or Ur III, despite possible contacts with the edges or the center of the Anatolian Plateau, were responsible for founding the trading settlements which the Old Assyrians possessed in the nineteenth century, B.C. The reader is referred to *Appendix C* for further discussion of Mesopotamian-Anatolian contacts.

D. *Level II*

Level II is the richest of the four terrace platform levels in architectural remains and material objects. Its multi-roomed houses were lavishly planned, and its structures — easily identifiable as shops, storehouses and archive and administrative buildings — were so crowded together as almost to touch each other. All these structures were built according to Anatolian techniques and reflect Anatolian styles. Buildings having more than one storey, and possessing open courtyards, were discovered. The streets and houses in this level are oriented differently from those in Level III, which suggests that a change in the plan of the residence quarter took place.

It would be impossible to attempt a summary of the wealth of building remains uncovered at Kültepe for *Kârum* Level II. The reader should consult *TTKY*, V, Seri — No. 10, No. 12, and especially No. 19 (1959), which deals with the architectural materials found since 1950 in both Level II and I. Beyond this, the work-in-progress in Anatolian archaeology is summarized by M. Mellink in *AJA*, 59 (1955), 231-259; 60 (1956), 369-394; 62 (1958), 91-104; 63 (1959), 73-85; 64 (1960), 57-69; 65 (1961), 37-52; 66 (1962), 71-85; 67 (1963), 173-190; 68 (1964), 149-166; 69 (1965), 133-149.

(1) *Pottery:* the pottery of this Level is divided between examples of "Hittite" monochrome and polychrome. Very beautiful single pieces

were recovered, among them painted vessels in the form of snails, terracotta boxes, painted clay vessels in the shape of shoes (probably libation vessels), and painted animal rhyta in bull and lion shapes. In general three categories of pottery are discernable: (a) traditional native shapes that came into existence in Central and Western Anatolia in the third millennium B.C. continue to be used after undergoing a development in the technique of manufacture; (b) completely new shapes introduced by the Assyrian merchants or made possible by more refined use of the potter's wheel, including the adoption of a tradition of painted pottery prevalent in Northern Syria and Northern Mesopotamia (perhaps due to the influence of the Assyrian merchants); and (c) imitations of North Syrian and Northern Mesopotamian examples in shape, but manufactured in native techniques [a minor category by comparison with the first two]. According to Kutlu Emre [*op. cit.*, p. 99], "The relationship of the pottery of Level II with that of Level III is such that it can be considered the result of a natural evolution. The great variations seen in some types of ware can also be explained by the fact that Kültepe was a rich and very brilliant center."

(2) *Small Obects:j* Small objects abound in great variety. Funerary gifts were found in graves situated beneath the floors of houses, and include gold and silver diadems, headdresses, pins and similar articles. There is also a great variety of bronze weapons, leaden objects, objects of electrum and bone and precious stones.

(3) *Seals:* Most important was the discovery of some stamp and cylinder seals, though most of our examples of the seal-cutter's art come from seal impressions appearing on Cappacocian tablet envelope cases. The seal impressions may be categorized by style as follows: (a) seals in the style of Ur III, appearing either unaltered, or with modifications; (b) seals in the Old Babylonian style; (c) seals in the Old Assyrian style; (d) seals in a so-called "Syrianized" style; (e) seals in indigenous Anatolian styles.[14]

(4) *Tablets:* Thousands of tablets have come to light from Level II [for which see *Appendix A*]. It is now possible to list the archives both of Assyrian and native merchants discovered in the *kârum*. The list was originally given in *TTKY*, V, Seri — No. 19, pp. xxii-xxiii, with further reference to the exact locations on the terrace in which the individual archives were found. For the convenience of the reader we reproduce the list with references to the periodical literature in which the individual archives were first reported.

[14] Cf. N. Özgüç, *TTKY*, V, Seri — No. 12 (1953), 226-242.

Merchant	*Earlier Periodical Reference*
Šaktunua	*TTKY*, VII, — No. 28, p. 61; *Belleten* 76, p. 453.
Ṭâb-Aḫum	*TTKY*, VII, — No. 28, p. 46; *Belleten* 65, p. 111.
Uzup-Išqum	Prof. Julius Lewy
Galulu	*TTKY*, VII, — No. 28, p. 61; *Belleten* 82, p. 344.
Šarbunua	*Belleten* 82, p. 344.
Adad-Sululi	*TTKY*, V, — No. 10, p. 130; No. 12, p. 140
Alaḫum II	K. Balkan
B/Puzutâ	*TTKY*, VII, — No. 28, p. 46.
Alaḫum I	*Ibidem; Belleten* 65, p. 109.
Aššur-Emûqi	Belleten 71, p. 398 and 376.
Peruwa	*TTKY*, VII, — No. 28, p. 60; *Belleten*, 66, p. 299.
Uzua	*TTKY*, V, — No. 10, p. 133.
Lâqîpum	*Ibidem*, p. 128.
Šuppi-aḫšu	Dr. L. Matouš
Enna-Suin	*Belleten*, 82, p. 344; Prof. A. Goetze.
Ili-âlim	*Belleten*, p. 344.
Luzina	*TTKY*, VII, — No. 28, p. 46
Šarnika	*Belleten* 71, p. 399.
Enna-Aššur	Prof. J. Lewy

In 1961 two new archives were found, one belonging to a native merchant [Cf. *AJA*, 66 (1962), p. 73].

In 1962, some 2200 tablets were collected [*AJA*, 67 (1963), p. 175].

In 1963, about 200 new tablets were reported [*AJA*, 68 (1964), p. 151)].

(5) *Relative Chronology of Level II:* Considerable evidence exists both for estimating the duration of Level II and for establishing its chronology *vis à vis* the reigns of Old Assyrian kings.

On the basis of eponym-names (*lîmus*) collected from the tablets of Level II, it may be concluded that Level II lasted at least sixty-two years, but probably no more than eighty. This agrees well with the fact that no more than three generations of traders are attested at *Kaniš*.[15]

The materials from which the relative chronology of Level II may be determined are as follows:

(a) A seal impression on a Cappadocian tablet mentioning a son of the Old Assyrian King, Ikunum, who is almost certainly Sargon I, though K. Balkan reads the name as AN.LUGAL.(X), or "Ilum-šar-x".[16]

(b) A direct reference to Puzur-Aššur (II), called *mera' rubâ'im*, or

[15] Cf. Balkan, *TTKY*, VII, Seri — No. 28 (1955), 45-47, w. *Appendix*: "*Lîmus* from Cappadocian Tablets", 79-101.

[16] Cf. Balkan, *ibid.*, 51-54.

"son of the prince", in *OIP*, 27 58:24. The father is clearly Šarru-kên I.[17]

(c) The so-called "Irišum Inscription", found at Kültepe in 1948, and recording some building activities of Irišum in the Temple of Aššur in Assur.[18]

It seems reasonable to assert that the end of Level II inhabitation occurred no later than the end of Puzur-Aššur II's reign, but we may feel free to move up its last days into the reign of Sargon I.[19] As for the beginning of the Level, it seems reasonable to agree with Balkan that the first Assyrian inhabitants may have arrived in Anatolia during the last years of the reign of Irišum I.[20]

Using the chronology of Sidney Smith (Ḫammurabi = ca. 1792-1750 B.C.), we may assign the following absolute dates:[21]

17 But as noted in Chapter Two, n. 94, above, it is a matter of dispute whether the further reference to a *rubâ'um* ("prince"), in 1. 27 of the same text is to Šarru-kîn. Prof. Lewy thinks that the *rubâ'um* here indicated is his alleged Assyrian ruler of *Kaniš*, a conclusion we cannot accept. Cf. Lewy, "On Some Institutions ...", *op. cit.*, 31-35, w.n. 112-122.

18 K. Balkan and B. Landsberger, "Die Inschrift des assyrischen Königs Irišum ...", *op. cit.*

19 Balkan, *TTKY*, VII, Seri — No. 28 (1955), 58-63 (59). Cf. also T. Özgüç, *TTKY*, V, Seri — No. 12 (1953), 215-216, who adheres to the low chronology of Cornelius and Albright (Hammurabi = 1728-1686). Balkan follows the high chronology of Landsberger (Ḫammurabi = ca. 1900), *JCS*, 8 [1954], 120.

20 Balkan, *TTKY*, VII, Seri — No. 28 (1955), 59. For discussion of an earlier beginning of Assyrian inhabitation, cf. T. Özgüç, *TTKY*, V, Seri — No. 12 (1953), 216 (bottom), 217.

21 It is impossible to treat the absolute dating given above without a long discussion of the chronological problems which arise from the appearance of different information in the variants of the Assyrian King List (*KKL*). We generally accept Balkan's reconstruction of how the eighty years duration period of Level II — reconstructed from the *lîmu*-names available — may be fitted into the period of rule of the Old Assyrian Dynasty, subject to some reservations about his dates for the end of Level Ib. The reader is referred to *TTKY*, VII, Seri — No. 28 (1955), 58-59 for the argument.

We depart from Balkan as follows: (1). A total of 86 years (the number resulting from a subtraction of the length of reign attributed by the KKL to Irišum (*KKL*, no. 33) and Šamši-Adad I (*KKL*, n. 39) from the total number of years attributed by the scribes of Šalmanasser I to the reign kings, *KKL*, no. 33 to *KKL*, no. 39. These 86 years must be distributed for the reigns of Ikunum (*KKL*, no. 34), Šarru-kên I (*KKL*, n. 35), Puzur-Aššur II (*KKL*, no. 36), Narâm-Sîn (*KKL*, no. 37) and Irišum II (*KKL*, no. 38). Balkan assigns Ikunum 26 years, Šarru-kên I, 20 years, Puzur-Aššur II, 20 years, Narâm-Sîn "at least 15 years", and Irišum II, 5 years. Balkan's attribution of 15 years to Narâm-Sîn is admittedly a guess (*TTKY*, VII, Seri — No. 28, 58), and we prefer to accept the information of the Nassouhi king list variant, which notes that this king reigned only 4 years, on the theory that one should stick to the available evidence wherever possible. This means that we distribute 11 more years between Ikunum, Šarru-kên I and Puzur-Aššur II, hence: Irišum 40 years; Ikunum 29; Šarru-kên I 23; Puzur-Aššur II 25; Narâm-Sîn 4; Irišum II 5; Šamši-Adad I 33.

(2). Balkan assumes that the end of the Kültepe Level II period and the accession of

Assyrian King	*Kârum Kaniš*
Irišum I (1940-1901)	Beginning of Level II (ca. 1900?)
Ikunum [1900-1872]	Generation I of Assyrian Traders
Sargon I [1871-1849]	Generation II of Assyrian Traders
Puzur-Aššur II [1848-1824]	Generation III of Assyrian Traders [End of Level II during or at end of Puzur-Aššur II's reign]
Narâm-Sîn [1823-1820]	
Irišum II [1819-1814]	
Samši-Adad I (1813-1781)	[Beginning of Level Ib]
Išme-Dagan (1780-)	[End of Level Ib = ca. 1760/50 at latest?]

E. *Level I*

Level I, chronologically the latest, consists of three phases: (a) Level Ic, a period during which the *kârum*-area was temporarily uninhabited; (b) Level Ib, a bustling settlement inhabited by Assyrian merchants; (c) Level Ia, which seems to represent a transitional phase between the end of Assyrian occupation and the Hittite Empire Period.

(1) Level Ic: this is described as "*eine* 1.50 *m dicke, kompakte Erd- und Brand-Schicht*" by the excavator.[22] To judge by the rich objects found intact in the ruins of Level II, the Assyrians who inhabited the *kârum* during the subsequent period of Level Ib were unfamiliar with the circumstances of the catastrophe which engulfed that settlement; perhaps, as has been thought, the new settlers were not of the same generation as the merchants of Level II, for the foundations of buildings in Ib appear to have been laid atop the destruction stratum of Ic, and nowhere penetrate it.

Narâm-Sîn of Ešnunna to the throne of Assur as no. 37 of *KKL* (for which cf. A. Goetze, "An Old Babylonian Itinerary", *op. cit.*, 59), are possibly contemporaneous events. We need make no such assumption, however, although we agree with his assertion that "the end of this main period of the colonies should not be fixed at a date later than the end of the reign of Puzur-Aššur II" (*TTKY*, VII, Seri — No. 28, 59). For we may again point out that Puzur-Aššur is referred to in *OIP*, 27, 58:24 only as "the son of the Prince". Whether this son of Šarru-kên I came to the throne during the days before the destruction of Level II or not is not known at present. Consequently, nothing prevents us from adopting more flexible possibilities, namely that Level II either came to its end *during* the reign of Šarru-kên I, at its end, or some time during the reign of Puzur-Aššur II. To be sure, Balkan is aware of these.

For remarks on the chronology of the post-Level II period, cf. n. 23, below.

[22] Cf. T. Özgüç, *TTKY*, V, Seri — No. 12 (1953), 136; also *ibid.*, 112, 214f.

The dating of Level Ic is extremely difficult because the length of time represented by Ib, its immediate successor is at present unknown. Furthermore, there are no direct references from the published Old Assyrian tablets of Ib to any royal personage of Assur. Tahsin Özgüç reckons two generations and more for Level Ic, thereby generally agreeing with Prof. Julius Lewy's estimate of eighty years. However, we believe this estimate to be too long. It does not necessarily follow that because rich objects were found intact in the ruins of Level II that the builders of Ib houses were *two* generations younger. We point out that Level Ib most likely lasted until ca. 1750 B.C. This date represents the death of Ḫammurabi according to the chronology of Sidney Smith. By ca. 1760 B.C. Assur was captured by Ḫammurabi. In Anatolia, though there are no firm chronological data with which to establish the beginnings of the Old Hittite Kingdom, it would appear that ca. 1750 is a reasonable working hypothesis. Level Ib, then, has an approximate *terminus post quem* of ca. 1750 B.C. We have already suggested above that ca 1848-1824 is the time period within which Level II may have terminated. Closer approximation than this is not possible.

(2) Level Ib: the remains of Level Ib show that this phase of Assyrian inhabitation was as flourishing as Level II, but buildings are oriented in a different way from those in the previous stratum.

(a) *Buildings:* In *TTKY*, V, Seri — No. 19 (1959), Tahsin Özgüç generally summed up the archaeological character of *Kârum* Level Ib as follows:

In this phase all areas of the Kârum Kanesh were densely settled. There is no doubt that the city of level Ib covered a wider area than that of level II. The foundations of level Ib can be seen at various depths, gradually becoming lower from the center of the Kârum area towards the north and west. Many of the foundations are set on the levelled burnt debris of level II, some of them even intrude into the ruins of II. ... The buildings of Ib, in contrast to those of Ia, were erected closely together, i.e. the various units are made to stand side by side and back to back ...; complexes consisting of several buildings also occur. In this level there are also permanent community buildings. The outer doors of the houses open on to streets or squares. Individual buildings can easily be distinguished owing to the well-preserved condition of the hearths and ovens and especially because neighboring houses possess separate, although closely adjoining walls. [p. 71].

In all respects the city-plan of Level Ib shows a crowded pattern of building. Every parcel of ground is exploited in Ib. As a result

the city of level Ib has a denser style of building than any other one of the Kârum levels, especially more so than level II, whose area it exceeded. The effect of this situation also shows in the house plans. Occasionally somebody would want to use a small area which happened to be available at the time and the result was the addition of rooms which protruded oddly from the long facades. ... Originally the houses of each one of these levels [Ib and II] were built according to a definite plan. [*TTKY*, V, Seri — No. 19, p. 78].

Beyond this, recent reports show that the *kârum* as well as the citadel-mound were walled during the Ib period. The population appears to have increased over that of Level II, and the diameter of the Ib inhabited area is over one kilometer [*AJA*, 68 (1964), p. 152].

(b) *Pottery:* compared with Level II, the pottery of Ib shows great differences in many respects. New kinds of slip-techniques appear; painted pottery, in color and motif, is also quite different from Level II. Many forms came down from the Level II period without undergoing any changes, but a number of new forms appear for the first time in Ib. Most important, although commercial ties with Assyria appear to have grown weaker, they continued on. As a result

the import of goods from Northern Syria and Northern Mesopotamia went on. This is shown by the Habur jars, champagne cups and pilgrim flasks found in level Ib. ... These vases are different from the pottery imported during the first phase. Also ... vessels that were made in imitation of the North Syrian examples are different from those of level II. The foreign shapes as a whole did not last long and disappeared with the end of the Colony Period. Nevertheless, there is a possibility that this tradition was more lasting at the centres between Kaniş and Northern Syria and Northern Mesopotamia and also in the mountain areas to the South. [K. Emre, *op. cit.*, p. 95].

Indeed, the presence of the painted "Habur-ware" in Level Ib has chronological significance for this period, for Mallowan dates the first pieces of this ware to the reign of Šamši-Adad's younger son, Iasmaḫ-Adad, at Mari.[23]

(c) *Small Objects:* for these refer to *TTKY*, V, Seri — No. 19, pp. 102-110.

Level Ib was destroyed most likely by the Dynasty of *Kuššara*, which founded the Old Hittite Kingdom [Cf. *Appendix C*].

(d) *Tablets:* the tablets found in Level Ib cannot be tabulated precisely at the present time. The following list reproduces notices of finds in various periodicals and monographs since 1949:

1. In 1949, ten tablets were found in Ib, five of which were assigned

[23] Cf. M. E. L. Mallowan, "Excavations at Brak and Chagar Bazar", *Iraq*, 9 (1947), 82f.

to Level II according to their context. [*TTKY*, VII, Seri — No. 28, p. 65, n. 8].

2. In 1953, one tablet was found in Ib [*Ibidem*].

3. In 1954, nine tablets, of which five were attributed to archives of the Level II period. [*Ibidem*].

4. In the years 1957-59, twenty-eight tablets were found in Ib. [*TTKY*, V, Seri — No. 19, xix].

5. In 1962, about forty tablets, some in envelopes, came to light. One large tablet with a list of six native kings including the names of Inar, Waršama and Anitta was recovered from a building in the center of the *kârum*-area. [*AJA*, 67 (1963), p. 175].

6. In 1964, about ten new tablets referring principally to native merchants was discovered [*AJA*, 69 (1965), p. 135].

In 1955, K. Balkan outlined the chief characteristics which distinguished Level Ib tablets from those of Level II. In the former he noted:

1. Beginning of the omission of the rigid mimation rules of the Old Assyrian dialect.

2. The appearance of new ways of expression.

3. The appearance of new forms of contracts.

4. The absence of any trace of import-ware.

5. The non-occurrence of *lîmu*-names of this period in Level II.

The argument is presented in great detail in *TTKY*, VII, Seri — No. 28, pp. 42f. with the notes on pp. 65-67.

(e) *Relative Chronology of Level Ib:* the tablets and artifacts of *Kârum*-Level Ib and its matching level on the city-mound have produced some meaningful chronological data.

1. It is already clear that the level belongs to the period of the Anatolian conqueror, Anitta, and probably also to his father. The tablet reported to have been found in *Kârum* Ib which mentions the name of Anitta as well as those of Inar and Waršama [see above] offers further confirmation of the general contemporaneity of Anitta with these Kings of *Kaniš* during Ib. Previously the discovery of a dagger bearing Anitta's name as "prince" in the corresponding level on the city-mound served to establish the chronological horizon of the Ib period [see below].

2. From a study of the *lîmu*-names recovered from Ib tablets at *Kaniš*, and from tablets at Alishar Hüyük and Boğazköy-*Ḫattuša*, it is possible to date Level Ib to the period of Šamši-Adad I of Assyria (ca. 1813-1781 B.C.), and his successor, Išmê-Dagan. [Cf. H. Otten, *MDOG*, 89 (1957), p. 71].

3. It also seems clear that the tablets from Alishar Hüyük [Level 10T]

and Boğazköy-*Ḫattuša* [Level IV] are contemporary with each other and together with those from *Kârum Kaniš* Ib [Cf. Otten, *op. cit.*, pp. 68-79, and *TTKY*, VII, Seri — No. 28, pp. 45f.].

(3) Level Ia: this younger phase on the *kârum*-terrace can be distinguished from Level Ib because of considerable differences in level and through characteristics of construction. Unfortunately the level was subjected to the depredations of the local population, which removed stones from it for building and for other reasons. However, it appears that those buildings which survived the destruction of Ib were re-used, while in other instances new buildings were constructed on the debris of Ib building foundations [*TTKY*, V, Seri — No. 19, p. 67]. The excavator summarizes:

> The area of the Kârum ... became more limited in Ia than it had been in levels Ib or II; it began to look like a small town. Only the northern half of the ancient site was settled, whereas the southern half, mostly in this period, was abandoned as a ruined area. Moreover, the houses of the city had become rarer in level Ia, and rather wide open areas had developed among them. On the other hand, levels Ib and II obviously each contained a city of houses built closely together. [*Ibid.*, p. 69].

F. *The City-Mound of Kültepe*

Excavation in the main city-mound has revealed a series of inhabitation levels from the Roman Age back to Early Bronze I, though we do not as yet have as clear a picture as we do for the *kârum*-terrace. The following summarizes the stratification at the present time:

1. *Roman Level*
2. *Hellenistic Level* [During these late periods the site appears to have lost its importance and was no more than a small town].
3. *Phrygian Level* [in two phases, reportedly occupied from the 11th. through the 4th. centuries].
4. *Hittite Period* [younger phase, containing a building (temple or palace?) excavated by Hrozný].
5. *Hittite Period* [older phase? Presence of a "Hittite Megaron".].
6. *Palace in which the Dagger of Anitta was discovered.*
7. *Building in which tablets of the indigenous administration of Kaniš were found, including the Letter of Anum-Ḫirbi of Mama to Waršama, King of Kaniš* [This building is roughly contemporaneous with the Palace of No. 6, above].

8. *A large building* [roughly contemporaneous with *Kârum*-terrace Level II].

9. *Middle Bronze I stratum contemporaneous with Kârum-terrace Levels III and IV.*

10. *Early Bronze IIIa-c.*

11. *Early Bronze II.*

12. *Early Bronze I.*

A summary of the stratification on the Kültepe City-Mound and its correlation with that on the *Kârum*-terrace is presented in Figure 3.

TERRACE-MOUND	CITY-MOUND	RELATIVE CHRONOLOGY
**********	**********	**********
Kârum Ib	Middle	ca. ?1800-?1780 B.C.
Kârum Ic (no occupation)	Bronze III	?1750 B.C.
**********	**********	**********
Kârum II	Middle Bronze II	ca. 1900-?1824 B.C.
Kârum III	Middle	ca. 2000-1900 B.C.
Kârum IV	Bronze I	
	**********	**********
Virgin Soil	Early Bronze IIIa	ca. 2300-2000 B.C.
	Early Bronze IIIb	
	Early Bronze IIIc	
	Early Bronze II	ca. 2600-2300 B.C.
	Early Bronze I	ca. 3000-2600 B.C.
	Virgin Soil	

********** = *Evidence of Burning*

Fig. 3. Scheme of the correlations in stratigraphy between the Terrace-Mound and the City-Mound at Kültepe.

If. CHECKLIST OF REPORTS ON THE TÜRK TARIH KURUMU EXCAVATIONS, 1948 —

Three excavation reports have been issued in volume form to date. These are: T. Özgüç, *TTKY*, V, Seri — No. 10 (1950); T. and N. Özgüç, *TTKY*, V, Seri — No. 12 (1953); and T. Özgüç, *TTKY*, V, Seri — No. 19 (1959). The reader is referred to the interim reports of the excavations since 1948 which have appeared in such periodicals as *Orientalia* (Nova Series), *The American Journal of Archaeology*, *Anatolian Studies*, *Belleten*, *Archiv für Orientforschung* and *Anadolu*, *passim*.

II. ALIŞAR HÜYÜK

Alişar Hüyük lies within the Kizil Irmak (Halys) Basin, about half-way between Kültepe and the town of Çorum, to the north. It consists of a citadel mound and a terrace mound, which nestles against it. In this respect the topography of Kültepe and Alişar Hüyük are generally the same. The site was excavated between 1928 and 1932 under the direction of H. H. von der Osten.[24]

Fourteen inhabitation levels were uncovered on the terrace mound, the total representing a time span from the so-called "Copper Age" (third millennium, B.C.) to the period of Turkish domination (eleventh to eighteenth centuries, A.D.). Level 10 on the Terrace corresponds to the second millennium, roughly to the fall of the Hittite Empire, and includes in its earliest phases the period of Assyrian inhabitation. All of the Cappadocian tablets found at the site were unearthed in this Level. Three hoards were found on the floors of rooms, while individual pieces were recovered from refuse deposits in the Level.[25]

Oddly enough, there is no stratum on the citadel mound which is contemporaneous with Level 10 on the terrace, although all other periods from the early Chalcolithic to the late Turkish are represented. Von der Osten believes that originally there was such a stratum, but that the people who put an end to Hittite Imperial power completely levelled it in the process of building their own structures.

In the Old Assyrian settlement at Alişar, streets could be identified in the few large areas that were excavated. The extant building walls are of mud-brick, which rest on stone foundations. In some of the rooms the type of oval fireplace discovered at Kültepe was unearthed. All the pottery is wheelmade, as at Kültepe during the Assyrian period, though painted ware is rare. The Alişar pottery is slipped in a variety of colors, buff or yellowish-red to red shades. Bronze and copper were the metals most commonly found, though iron appears sporadically. Seals and figurines, and objects in bone and ivory are numerous.

[24] Cf. excavation reports appended to this section.

[25] Cf. *OIP*, 29, 2 (1930-32), 108, and the "Table of Correlations", which provides a guide to the different systems of strata designation used during the entire course of the campaigns, p. 459, fig. 513.

IIa. CHECKLIST OF REPORTS ON THE EXCAVATIONS AT ALIŞAR HÜYÜK

H. H. von der Osten, *OIP*, 5 (1929); *idem*, and E. F. Schmidt, *OIP*, 6 and 7 (1930/32); E. F. Schmidt, *OIP*, 19 and 20 (1933); H. H. von der Osten, *OIP*, 28-30 (1937). *The Cappadocian Tablets from Alişar:* For the find circumstances see H. H. von der Osten, *OIP*, 29 (1937) 108-110; *idem*, *OIP*, 30 (1937) 434; The fifty-three tablets from Alişar are presented in I. J. Gelb, *OIP*, 27 (1935) 19-54, and Pls. 1-31.

III. BOĞAZKÖY

Boğazköy, site of the ancient Hittite capital, *Hattušaš*, is located within the Kizil Irmak (Halys) Basin of Central Anatolia, some one hundred-fifty kilometers east of Ankara, and thirty kilometers northwest of Yozgat. It is a huge, sprawling ruin encompassed by a great city wall, whose perimeter is several miles at the least. The land area within the walls is characterized by several flat terraces and rock escarpments, on which traces of buildings have been found. In the northern part of the city area lies a great, many-roomed ruin of a Hittite Empire period temple (Temple I). Southeast of this is an elevated terrace called *Büyükkale*, which was the residence area of the Hittite rulers. Farther to the south and south-west lie other rock terraces upon which temples and other buildings of the Empire period were situated.

On *Büyükkale* sporadic excavations since 1906 have disclosed five inhabitation levels. These are: I and II a/b, which correspond to the post-Phrygian and Phrygian periods; III, which represents the Hittite Empire Period; IV a-d, which is generally designated "Old Hittite"; and V, which probably corresponds to the beginning of the second millennium, or earlier. Levels IVd and perhaps, in part, Level V, encompass the Old Assyrian Period.[26]

Cappadocian tablets have been found in different places at the site, and at different times. According to K. Bittel and R. Naumann, the most recent excavators of Boğazköy, a fragment of a Cappadocian tablet was found close to the Level V dig on the rocky ground nearby, but it is not certain that the tablet belongs to this stratum.[27] Only bare traces of

[26] Cf. E. Weidner, "Boğazköi", (Ausgrabungen und Forschungsreisen), *AfO*, 17, 1 (1954-55), 204-205.

[27] Cf. K. Bittel and R. Naumann, *Boğazköy-Hattuša I. Architektur, Topographie, Landeskunde und Seidlungsgeschichte*, *WVDOG*, 63 (1952), 39.

settlement, consisting of fragmentary and unconnected remains of walls, were found in V. On the basis of sherds of a very primitive, handmade pottery (similar to that of Alişar I), Level V was dated to the end of the third millennium. The Level also showed extensive signs of destruction by fire.[28]

On *Büyükkale* in 1953, excavation revealed that Level IVd was most probably the level corresponding to the period of the Old Assyrian merchants. Pottery sherds similar to those discovered at Kültepe were found.[29] In addition, three Cappadocian tablets also appeared, a circumstance which makes it likely that the fragment reported by Bittel and Naumann as coming from Level V may in fact belong to IVd.

At another point in the city, in the northern Lower City (the residence quarter north of Temple I), four Cappadocian tablets were discovered together in 1938.[30] In this area only two distinct building levels could be identified. The Upper Level, so-called, was dated roughly to the Hittite Empire Period on the basis of Empire texts and seal finds. Its predecessor, the Lower Level, contained Cappadocian texts; it rested upon virgin soil, and generally covers the period from about 2,000 to 1,600 B.C. According to the excavators, probably the whole terrace area north of Temple I existed from the period when Old Assyrian traders flourished in Anatolia. The artifacts (and especially the pottery) of the Lower Level differ in no way from those usually designated "Old Hittite".[31]

Besides the small funds of tablets mentioned above, several individual tablets were found within or near the limits of Boğazköy. In 1936 H. Güterbock published the text of a tablet discovered in a valley west-south-west of Yerkapu (in the Upper City) about two kilometers away from the 1938 findspot.[32] The remains in the valley included "Hittite" pottery sherds and stone material coming from simple house walls. The latest pottery finds here (1952) have been dated to the Hittite Empire Period.[33] For text copies of 40 Old Assyrian texts from Boğazköy-*Hattuša* see now Otten, *KBo*, IX (1957), Nos. 1-40, with *idem*, *MDOG*, 89 (1957), 68-79.

[28] Cf. *ibid.*
[29] Cf. E. Weidner, *AfO*, 17, 1 (1954-55), *op. cit.*, 204-205.
[30] Cf. K. Bittel and R. Naumann, "Kappadokische Tontafeln", *MDOG*, 77 (1939), 22f. and Pl. 24.
[31] Cf. K. Bittel and R. Naumann, *Boğazköy-Hattuša I.*, *op. cit.*, 99-102.
[32] Cf. "Texte", *MDOG*, 74 (1936), 64-66.
[33] Cf. K. Bittel and R. Naumann, *Boğazköy-Hattuša I.*, *op. cit.*, 124, and the supplementary map, "Beilage 1", the notation, "Seidlung".

KÜLTEPE *Terrace*	KÜLTEPE *City-Mound*	ALISHAR HÜYÜK *Terrace*	ALISHAR HÜYÜK *City-Mound*	BOĞAZKÖY *City*	BOĞAZKÖY *Büyükkale*
*********	*********	*********	*********	*********	*********
Karum Ib (Tablets)	Middle Bronze III	Level 10T (Tablets)		Level 4 (Tablets)	Level IVd
Karum Ic no occupation					
*********	*********				
Karum II (Tablets)	Middle Bronze II				
Karum III	Middle	Level 11T	Level 5M		
Karum IV	Bronze I				
	***********				
	Early Bronze IIIa				
	Early Bronze IIIb		Level 6M		
		Level 12T			
	Early Bronze IIIc		Level 7M		
		Level 13T	Level 8M		
	Early Bronze II	Level 14T	Level 11M		
	Early Bronze I	Virgin Soil	Level 12M		
			Level 14M		
			?Level 19M		

********* = *Evidence of Burning*.

Fig. 4. Scheme of the correlations in stratigraphy between Kültepe, Alishar Hüyük, and Boğazköy.

IIIa. CHECKLIST OF REPORTS ON THE BOGAZKÖY EXCAVATIONS AND TABLETS

O. Puchstein, *Boğazköi. Die Bauwerke. WVDOG*, 19 (1912); K. Bittel, *Boğazköy. Die Kleinfunde der Grabungen*, 1906-1912. *WVDOG*, 60 (1937); *idem*, and R. Naumann, *Boğazköy-Hattuša I. Architektur, Topographie, Landeskunde und Siedlungsgeschichte. WVDOG*, 63 (1952); K. Bittel and H. G. Güterbock, *Boğazköy, Neue Untersuchungen in der hethitischen Hauptstadt. APAW*, 1935, Phil.-Hist. Klasse 1; K. Bittel and R. Naumann, *Boğazköy II, Neue Untersuchungen hethitischer Architektur. APAW*, 1938, Phil.-Hist. Klasse 1; K. Krause, *Boğazköy, Tempel V. Istanbuler Forschungen*, 11 (1940); K. Bittel, R. Naumann and H. Otto, *Yazilikaya, Architektur, Felsbilder Inschriften und Kleinfunde. WVDOG*, 61 (1941); K. Bittel, R. Nauman, *Boğazköy III. Funde aus den* Grabungen 1952-55. *DOG*, 2 Abh. (1957).

Interim reports of the Boğazköy excavations have appeared in *MDOG*, 1931-40; 1952 —, and *AJA*, *passim*.

The Cappadocian Tablets from Boğazköy.

Chantre (1898), No. 7 (Pl. IV), and Nos. 8 and 9 (Pl. V); Eight tablets were reputedly discovered by H. Winckler according to E. Forrer, *ZDMG*, 76 (1922), 186f., but E. Weidner in *BKS*, 6 (1922), 99, n. 2 and J. Lewy, *ZA*, N.F. 2 (v 36) (1925), 27, n. 3 refer to one tablet only. (See *Kleinasien* [1957] 68 with n. 1); L. W. King published one tablet supposedly coming from Boğazköy in *HT* (1920), No. 102; K. Bittel, *MDOG*, 70 (1932), 28, Pl. 13; H. G. Güterbock, *MDOG*, 74 (1936), 64f.; Four tablets found in 1938 are published by K. Bittel and R. Naumann, *MDOG*, 77 (1939), 22f. and Pl. 24; (See K. Balkan *TTKY*, VII, Seri — No. 28 [1955] 49f. for a transliteration and translation of one of them, Bo. 249/e); for tablets discovered at Boğazköy from 1955 on, see H. Otten, *MDOG*, 87 (1955), 24 and M. Mellink, *AJA*, 62 (1958), 95, where some fifty Old Assyrian tablets are reported as coming from the most recent phase of Level 4, north of Temple 1. Further, see H. Otten, *KBo*, IX (1957), for copies of forty Old Assyrian texts from Boğazköy, and *idem.*, *MDOG*, 89 (1957), 68-79.

IV. YORGAN TEPE (NUZI)

Yorgan Tepe is situated in Northern Mesopotamia, some thirteen kilometers southwest of Kirkuk. It is a low mound, measuring roughly 200 meters square, and rising on the average of five meters above the surrounding plain. It was excavated during the period 1925-31 under the direction of E. Chiera, R. Pfeiffer, and R. Starr, respectively.[34]

Twelve inhabitation strata have been disclosed at the site. Levels XII-XA, the lowest, are designated "Prehistoric"; Level X, "Late Prehistoric"; Levels IX-III, "*Ga. Sur*", which denotes the name of the settlement during Akkadian occupation; Levels III-IIA, "Intermediate"; Levels IV-I, "*Nuzi*", the name of the settlement during the period of Hurrian occupation; and "Partho-Sassanid", which is intrusive in *Nuzi*, Stratum I and above.[35]

It is not by any means certain that there was an Old Assyrian *settlement* at Yorgan Tepe. Only five Cappadocian texts, and these in fragmentary form, have been found at the site. All come from Level IIA. Their position is 1.27 meters below the first Nuzi (or Hurrian). Level, and immediately above the levels which yielded 222 Akkadian texts. Thus they appear to fall into the transitional period during which the domination of the site passed from the Akkadians to the Hurrians. In a general way they appear to date from an earlier period than the other Cappadocian tablets, but little more can be inferred from them.[36]

IVa. CHECKLIST OF REPORTS ON THE YORGAN TEPE EXCAVATIONS AND TABLETS

R. F. S. Starr, *Nuzi* (Cambridge, Mass., 1937-39): On the Cappadocian tablets from Nuzi see: T. J. Meek, *HSS*, 10 (1935), Nos. 223-227; *idem*, "The Akkadian and Cappadocian Texts from Nuzi", *BASOR*, 48 (1932), 25; J. Lewy, "Notes on Pre-Hurrian Texts from Nuzi", *JAOS*, 58 (1938), 450-461.

BIBLIOGRAPHICAL ADDENDUM TO APPENDIX B

I. *Kültepe*:

Tahsin Özgüç, "The Art and Architecture of Ancient Kanish", *Anatolia* 8 (1964), 27-48.

Idem, "Recent Archaeological Research in Turkey: Excavations at Kültepe-Kaniş", *An St* 15 (1965), 24-25.

[34] Cf. R. F. S. Starr, *Nuzi I* (Cambridge, Mass., 1939), xxxiii-xxxvi.

[35] Cf. *ibid.*, *Appendix A*, 507-522, for a convenient chronological summary.

[36] Cf. J. Lewy, "Notes on Pre-Hurrian Texts from Nuzi", *JAOS*, 58 (1938), 450-461.

Approximate Dates	KÜLTEPE-*KANIŠ* City	KÜLTEPE-*KANIŠ* *Kârum*	Kings	ALISHAR HÜYÜK City	ALISHAR HÜYÜK Terrace	BOĞAZKÖY-*ḪATTUŠA* Kings City	BOĞAZKÖY-*ḪATTUŠA* Büyükkale	Kings	Assyrian Kings	Mesopotamian Kings
1750	**********	**********	**********	**********	**********	**********	**********	**********		
	MB III	Ib Ic	Anitta Pitḫana Waršama Inar		10T	Anitta Pitḫana? Ḫarbatiwa [4] *rubâtum*	IVd	Anitta Pijušti	Išmê-Dagan 1780- Šamši-Adad I 1813-1781 Erišum II 1819-1814 Narâm-Sîn 1823-1820 Puzur-Aššur II 1848-1824 Sargon I 1871-1849 Ikûnum 1900-1872	Ḫammurabi 1792-1750 Sîn-muballiṭ 1812-1793 Apil-Sîn 1830-1813 Sabium 1844-1831 Sumulael 1880-1845 Sumuabum 1894-1881
1824	************	************								
	MB II	II	Labarša Warpa+ *rubâtum*							
1900 1950 2000	MB I	III IV		5M	11T					
	******									
2300	EB IIIa-c			6M 7M	12T					UR III 2124-2016
2600	EB II		Zipani?	8M 11M	13T 14T			Pamba?		Narâm-Sîn 2380-2325 Sargon/Akkad 2467-2413
3000	EB I			12M 14M						
				19M						

********** = Burned Level

Fig. 5. Proposed Relative Chronology of the Old Assyrian Period.

Alkim, U. Bahadir, "Recent Archaeological Research in Turkey: Exploration and Excavations in the District of Islâhiye", *An St* 15 (1965), 29.

Mebrure Tosun, "Styles in Kültepe Seal Engraving as Expressions of Various Cultural Influences", *Festschrift Landsberger* (= *Assyriological Studies No.* 16, Oriental Institute, Univ. of Chicago, 1965), 183-188.

Machteld Mellink, "Archaeology in Asia Minor", *AJA* 70 (1966), 139-159, with addenda, *AJA* 70 (1966), 279-282.

W. Orthmann, "Kültepe", *AfO* 21 (1966), 170.

Nimet Özgüç, "Kültepe Mühür Baskilarinda Anadolu Grubu (= The Anatolian Group of Cylinder Seal Impressions from Kültepe", *Or N.S.* 35 (1966), 339-340.

II. *Boğhazköy*:

Franz Fischer, "Boğhazköy und die Chronologie der altassyrischen Handelsniederlassungen in Kappadokien", *Istanbuler Mitteilungen* (1965), 1-16.

APPENDIX C

THE OLD ASSYRIAN COLONIES IN THE SETTING OF ANATOLIAN CULTURAL HISTORY

The Old Assyrian colonies of the second millennium B.C. occupy a distinctive position in the sequence of Anatolian cultural development. They represent, as we have seen, the first evidences of a political and economic system which is significantly documented and can therefore be studied from detailed textual sources as well as from the ample archaeological record. They further represent a pivotal point between prehistoric and historic cultural forms in Anatolia, all the more important because they originate within the cultural sphere of Mesopotamia.

The principal recent discovery of novel character from the excavations at Kültepe demonstrates that during the last phase of the Early Bronze Age (ca. 2000 B.C.) a previously unencountered and highly important culture existed in Central Anatolia. Kültepe in this period had wide-reaching contacts, with Northern Syria, with Cilicia, and even with Southern Mesopotamia. As Tahsin Özgüç succinctly puts it:

> The Assyrians came to an area they knew and were familiar with. For the development of Central Anatolian art, the influence of these connections became of much importance. Kültepe has shed light on the question of the origin of Central Anatolian painted pottery, on the date of the alabaster idols, on the existence of temples of megaron type and above all on the monumental architecture of the Early Bronze Age.[1]

The realization of Kültepe's importance as an import and trade center during the pre-Assyrian period leads now to a renewed interest in the historical and literary evidence for Mesopotamian connections with Anatolia during the latter part of the third millennium. It is proposed in this Appendix to set out the major outlines of this evidence as we have it at the present time, and to enclose it within the Anatolian cultural sequence from the Early Bronze Age through the formative period of the Old Hittite Empire.

[1] "Early Anatolian Archaeology in the Light of Recent Research", *Anatolia*, 7 (1963), 2.

Anatolia by no means experienced a unified cultural development. Rather, it is the archaeologist's fashion to define as many as seven cultural regions beginning with the Early Bronze I [= EB I] Period: (1) the Northwest; (2) the Southwest; (3) the Eskişehir-Ankara region; (4) the Konya Plain; (5) the Cilician Plain; (6) Central Anatolia; and (7) the Pontic Region.[2] Nor can one fit the numerous cultures of early Anatolia into one comprehensive chronological scheme. However much these difficulties prevent the historian from arriving at a synthesis which will gain scholarly consensus at the present time, it is still possible to present an interpretation generally acceptable enough to serve as useful background for the period of Old Assyrian trading activity.

With the possible exception of the Plain of Cilicia, where newcomers seem to intrude, the EB age seems everywhere to have developed from the Late Chalcolithic.[3] Tahsin Özgüç cites Büyük Güllücek and to some extent Alaca Hüyük as affording good samples of this Late Chalcolithic culture in central Anatolia.[4] Houses of two to four rooms, thin-walled, sharply profiled pottery of predominantly black and gray color, stamp seals, idols, large copper weapons, earrings, finger rings, pins and other jewelry made of copper and lead are typical of this region in this period.[5] The communities surveyed are not merely villages but seem to have advanced beyond the normal description of village culture. The beginnings of a metallurgy which may be called "flourishing" in EB I may be attributed to the Late Chalcolithic period.[6]

Both Özgüç and James Mellaart point to a generally unbroken development from the Late Chalcolithic to the Early Bronze.[7] Towns and villages do not suffer conflagrations, and the architecture, stamp seals and idols continue without interruption.[8] Metallurgy appears to have taken important strides forward.[9] It is the second phase of EB culture in Anatolia that displays an impressive advance over earlier cultural phases. Two significant features which now appear are a great progress in metal-working and an increase in trade.[10] EB II is definitely a city culture as evidenced by the fortress at Alişar Hüyük, that at Troy II, the

[2] Cf. James Mellaart, "Anatolia, c. 4000-2300 B.C.", *CAH*, rev. ed., Vol. I, Ch. 18 (1962), Map 1, p. 13.
[3] *Ibid.*, p. 9.
[4] Özgüç, *op. cit.*, p. 9.
[5] *Ibid.*
[6] Mellaart, *op. cit.*, p. 9.
[7] *Ibid.*, and Özgüç, *op. cit.*, p. 9.
[8] Özgüç, *ibid.*
[9] *Ibid.*, and Mellaart, *op. cit.*, p. 9.
[10] Özgüç, *op. cit.*, p. 10.

town of Poliochni V, the series of shrines or temples in Beycesultan XIV-XVI, the small fort of Ahlatlibel and the town wall and houses of Tarsus EB 2.[11] At Kültepe a temple of the megaron-type is contemporary with EB IIIb.[12] At Alaca Hüyük, Horoztepe and Mahmatlar rich royal tombs testify to the wealth of the ruling city-aristocracies, as do those from the ruins of Troy IIg and Poliochni V, the tombs of Dorak, the finds from the Yortan cemetery, Ovabyindir and the graves of Ahlatlibel.[13]

Özgüc points to a basic subsistence substratum of agriculture and husbandry for the Early Bronze Age, as indeed existed earlier in the Late Chalcolithic, but the evidence of trade and variety of metal-working in the EB shows that "in Central and Northeast Anatolia metallurgy had by now become as important as agriculture".[14] It is clear that gold, silver, copper, bronze, electrum and even iron were expertly used, and that casting and hammering were both employed.

It is not surprising that this efflorescence of metallurgical activity occurred during EB II and later, although we do not know precisely how it was stimulated. In north-western and central Anatolia there are rich deposits of gold, silver, copper and iron. From the Konya Plain, commanding two great silver mines of Bulgar and Bereketli-Maden, a trade route passed through Cilicia and on to Syria and Mesopotamia, which lacked precious metals. In the south-west, too, gold, copper, silver and iron were distributed to the Aegean via the Meander Valley, while further to the north and west a Trojan maritime culture was instrumental in importing tin and producing good tin bronzes.[15] Mellaart concludes about EB I and II that "the great prosperity of Anatolia ... was based mainly on the systematic exploitation of its metal wealth and on its ability to trade it to its neighbors, not only Syria and Mesopotamia, but Egypt, Greece, the Balkans and the Pontic Steppe as well".[16]

While there is no reason to deny the existence of a meaningful system of local kingdoms in Central Anatolia and its contiguous lands during the Chalcolithic, such a system is most forcefully attested for the heart of the Early Bronze Age. We are in the presence of full urban communities which boast royal seats. Such royal fortresses as discovered at Troy and Ahlatlibel (in the vicinity of Ankara), and the evidence of large city-sites such as Poliochni, Beycesultan, Alaca Hüyük, Alişar Hüyük, Kültepe and

[11] Mellaart, *op. cit.*, p. 26.
[12] M. Mellink in *AJA*, 67 (1963), p. 175, and Özgüç, *op. cit.*, p. 10.
[13] Özgüç, *op. cit.*, p. 10, and Mellaart, *op. cit.*, p. 26.
[14] Özgüç, *op. cit.*, pp. 10-11.
[15] Mellaart, *op. cit.*, p. 10.
[16] *Ibid.*

Tarsus show conclusively that a number of important kingdoms, both large and small, existed.[17] Özgüç thinks that "the metal industry and especially the metal trade were probably under direct control of the local kings", and that this system makes more comprehensible the significance of trade in the later period when Old Assyrian colonies were established in the area.[18]

We need recall now that Kültepe was itself an important city of the pre-Assyrian period and a center for imports from Syria and Cilicia, among others. It must already have been a fairly large and independent kingdom to judge only by the megaron temple discovered for its EB IIIb phase, a temple which "approaches that of the largest Megaron of Troy II".[19] Yet we can say little at present about its comparative status. Several neighboring sites, Alaca Hüyük and Horoztepe especially, have royal tombs displaying a remarkable wealth — richer indeed than the hoard of Troy II — while burials covering at least two or three generations of local Anatolian rulers have come to light.[20] Indeed, the evidence of conflagrations in southern and northern cities of the Anatolian Plateau suggests much internecine warfare during the Early Bronze Age.

Two circumstances of singular importance must now be brought into the discussion of the Early Bronze Age in Anatolia, — the first, that in its middle phase (EB II), the period roughly equivalent in archaeological correlation to the period of the Royal Tombs at Alaca Hüyük and to Troy II, the Old Akkadian Dynasty was the dominant dynasty in Mesopotamia (ca. 2467-2287 B.C.);[21] the second, that a series of violent burnings was visited upon the Middle and Late EB sites of Anatolia, a phenomenon which marks the transition to the Middle Bronze Age [= MB] and to the first appearance of inhabitation on the *kârum*-terrace mound at Kültepe. An inquiry about the Old Akkadian Dynasty is important because of the texts which associate it in one way or another with adventures in Northwestern Syria, Cilicia and Asia Minor; that concerned with the destruction of EB civilization because of the possibility that the Indo-European peoples who later will coalesce into the political entity we know as the Hittite Kingdom are implicated. The two questions are not closely related, but their implications for Anatolian history and the backgrounds of Old Assyrian colonization are evident.

17 *Ibid.*, p. 26.
18 Özgüç, *op. cit.*, p. 11.
19 *Ibid.*, p. 13.
20 *Ibid.*, p. 14.
21 For the difficulties involved in dating the cultures of Central Anatolia, see Mellaart, *op. cit.*, pp. 8-9, 43-44.

ANATOLIA AND THE OLD AKKADIAN DYNASTY

We may think of the reign of Lugalzaggesi, sole ruler of the Third Dynasty of Uruk (ca. ?2492-2468 B.C.), as preparing the way for the area-wide, even international control of the Dynasty of Akkad, for it is this king who campaigns far to the west of Lower Mesopotamia, conquering for the first time the region from the Lower Sea to the Upper Sea (the Mediterranean). The defeat of Lugalzaggesi by Sargon of Akkad (ca. 2467-2413 B.C.) insured that the latter, too, would follow in the same path. Completing his conquest of the Sumerian heartland through victories over Ur, Lagash and Umma, Sargon appears also to have fought as many as thirty-four battles, which resulted in his controlling the Persian Gulf and making of Akkad a terminus for the trade from lands along its shore as well as from those who made use of its waterway to reach Mesopotamian ports.[22]

Southern Mesopotamia secure, Sargon's troops were led up the Euphrates toward conquest in Syria. At Tuttul (modern Hit) Dagan is said to have given Sargon "the Upper Land, Mari, Iarmuti, Ibla, up to the cedar forest and the silver mountains". This is authenticated by information from the Chronicle and omens that Sargon "set up his images in the West".[23] In sum, probably by the eleventh year of his reign, Sargon had conquered up to the Amanus Mountains of Lebanon (= the Cedar Forest), and the Taurus Range (= the Silver Mountains). The inclusion of Iarmuti suggests that Sargon had obtained a coastal port on the Mediterranean, and of Ibla, that he had reached the area of the great Euphrates bend north of Carchemish.

Granted, then, that Sargon reached the limits of North Syria. Did he go beyond? Later tradition suggests that he penetrated even into Anatolia. The "King of Battle" story places Sargon's influence deep in the Plain of Konya, especially in connection with the city of *Burušḫanda* (Old Assyrian: *Burušḫattum*; Hittite: *Paršuḫanda*), but the information comes to us from a text found in Egypt with the Amarna Letters (first half of the 14th. century, B.C.). Despite details which suggest a genuine historical foundation, the entire composition is cast in the mode of the fabulous, in which legend and poetic imagination predominate. It represents, as is generally thought, a composition which has combined some valid historical memory of Semitic presence in Asia Minor (perhaps

[22] C. J. Gadd, "The Dynasty of Agade and the Gutian Invasion", *CAH*, rev. ed., Vol. I, Ch. 19 (1963), p. 8.

[23] *Ibid.*, p. 11.

the recollection of the Old Assyrian colonies of the period long after the reign of the Akkadians) with a vivid appreciation of Sargon as a legendary hero.

Recently C. J. Gadd has gathered together further indications which may add some support to the tradition of a north-westerly campaign by the founder of the Old Akkadian Dynasty. None of these is on a tablet of contemporary date, and the chief one, an account alleging that Sargon campaigned to the "land of Uta-rapaštum" is nonetheless still decked out in the trappings of legend. However one tablet speaks of the loss of *Burušhanda* in the time of Narâm-Sîn, fourth king of the Akkadian Dynasty, "as though", says Gadd, "it had been the most distant bound of the Akkadian possessions".[24] Another tablet of late Assyrian times, with unfortunately no greater authority than those discussed above, gives a compilation of geographical names, all allegedly those of places that comprised Sargon's empire. Two places called "Anaku" ("Tin [or 'Lead'] Country") and "Kaptara" (most likely the Biblical "Kaphtor", or "Crete"), are listed as "lands beyond the Upper Sea" (the Mediterranean). To a small degree the veracity of these places as parts of Sargon's holdings to the north and west is enhanced by the mention of Sargon in the omens as having crossed the sea in the West.[25] The correlative of "Tin/Lead Country" is unclear; perhaps the metal-bearing regions of Bulgar Maden of Ak Dağ or of Ala Dağ in the Taurus should here come into consideration.

Of Sargon's conquests in the North the omens mention Subartu, of which later Assyria was a significant part. Inscriptions found at Nineveh, at Assur and at Nuzu (known as *Gasur* in the Old Akkadian period) make it certain that the Akkadians controlled the Assyrian homeland in the twenty-fifth century. Further conquests brought the hill country to the east and north-east of Mesopotamia into Sargon's empire, as finally did campaigns to Elam and its vicinity bring in "almost the entire mountainous region in south-western Persia".[26]

We should not imagine that what is generally called the "empire" of Sargon was really a strong, tightly-administered political organization. The late Chronicle and omens speak of a revolt of all the lands against Sargon, probably in his old age, but a total catastrophe was averted. Nonetheless Rimuš (ca. 2412-2398 B.C.) and Maništusu (ca. 2397-2381 B.C.), Sargon's sons and successors, had to fight hard to retain the

[24] *Ibid.*, p. 15.
[25] *Ibid.*, pp. 15-16.
[26] *Ibid.*, p. 19.

dynastic possessions. They succeeded in passing on to Narâm-Sîn (ca. 2380-2325 B.C.) a considerable heritage.

Narâm-Sîn had to earn his claim to being "king of the four regions" by hard fighting, though it is impossible to establish a chronology for his reign, nor can truth be fully separated from legend when the events of his reign are considered. Two texts speak of large-scale revolts, one of twenty, another of seventeen kings, whose realms extended from Anatolia to the Persian Gulf. The authentic inscriptions of his own reign attribute victory to Narâm-Sîn in nine battles.[27] A combination of information reliable for the period of his rule, and that borne by tradition and incorporated into the larger accounts of the empire-wide revolt, make it, in the words of Gadd, "hardly too much, therefore, to believe that Narâm-Sîn exercised some authority, however incomplete, over districts in the south-east of Asia Minor, where his grandfather before him had accomplished the same phenomenal march which Narâm-Sîn or his flatterers heralded as a pioneer effort."[28]

Given the uncertainty of our knowledge about the presence, under whatever circumstances, of the Akkadians in Anatolia, we may still note with some special interest that the text which reports the revolt of seventeen kings against Narâm-Sîn mentions among others of the rebels a certain Pamba, king of *Ḫatti*, a Zipani, King of *Kaniš*, a Huwaruwas, King of *Amurri* (in Syria), and a Ti[š]binki, King of *Kursaura*. All these places are styled as kingdoms, and if the literary tradition behind this text is correct, it affords support to what archaeology attests about the existence of rich and powerful city-state lands during the peak of Early Bronze Age cultural development in Anatolia.

The inference of materials recovered from the city-mound of Kültepe for this period that a significant *trade* relationship between Central Anatolia and Syrian and Cilician sites existed offers reasonable presumption that Anatolian and Syro-Mesopotamian cities were well known to each other through some sort of political involvement as well. This involvement may have been validated by treaties or other forms of regulation. Judging by the ease with which early conquering kings from Lower Mesopotamia could usually move to the approaches of the Lebanon and the Taurus, it does not strain credulity to assert that Sargon and Narâm-Sîn could easily have been granted homage in the form of tribute or gifts by Anatolian city-rulers, who either felt actually threatened, or thought it wise to follow a cautious policy in regard to these

[27] *Ibid.*, p. 27.
[28] *Ibid.*, p. 29.

potentially dangerous outsiders. It need not be false at all, even if the authenticity of the Narâm-Sîn text just discussed be doubted, to infer that the numerous city-states of Anatolia during the middle and later Early Bronze Age could form alliances for a common purpose and again dissolve them. Thus, even if we cannot prove that Pamba, King of *Ḫatti*, and Zipani, King of *Kaniš*, were actual rulers, we can believe that the city-state kingdoms of *Ḫatti* and of *Kaniš*, among others, already functioned within an Anatolian system of small, independent kingdoms.

Between the fall of the Old Akkadian Dynasty, and the reestablishment of centralized political power in Mesopotamia by the Third Dynasty of Ur (ca. 2124-2016 B.C.) following the anarchic period of Gutian control of Mesopotamia (ca. 2256-2132 B.C.), the cities of the old Sumero-Akkadian region seem to have lost important contact with the regions of the Taurus and the western Anti-Taurus. It is Gudea of Lagash who resumes this contact, and it is the Third Dynasty of Ur which recreates internal Mesopotamian unity and area-wide trade from the Persian Gulf to the Mediterranean.

THE END OF THE BRONZE AGE IN ANATOLIA

In Anatolia the waning of the Early Bronze Age is witness to widespread destruction. Mellaart's studies to date allow him to assert that at the end of EB II "a catastrophe of such magnitude as to remain unparalleled until the very end of the Bronze Age"[29] struck Western and Southern Anatolia. The picture drawn is one of severe reduction in the total number of sites immediately following EB II in these areas, as well as a significant diminution of the EB III inhabited area compared to its EB II predecessor in sites where both cultures occur. Many towns and villages were deserted; inhabited areas seem to have become grazing grounds of nomads. Mellaart provisionally interprets the evidence to suggest that those responsible for this wave of destruction were the Luwians, an Indo-European-speaking people who originally came from Europe and destroyed the Troy I culture at the end of EB I. Subsequently, having become "Anatolianized", they descended upon Western and Southern Anatolia under the impact of newcomers from the north-west at the end of EB II.[30] The technical questions, of course, will be solved only after patient and continuous excavation and interpretive

[29] *Op. cit.*, p. 46.
[30] *Ibid.*, pp. 48-49.

study, but for our purposes we may see the end of the EB II phase (or to be less precise, the end of the Early Bronze Age itself), as a period during which the old Anatolian city-state system is subjected to the impact of new populations and social forms. Let us consider the effect of this impact upon the region of Central Anatolia.

Tahsin Özgüç points out that "In the Kayseri Plain there are signs of violent burning in various levels belonging to the late and middle phases of the Early Bronze Age".[31] Kültepe [EB IIIa] and Alaca Hüyük [Stratum 5] are two such important cities which were affected. About this catastrophe and these sites Professor Goetze writes:

> Alaca Hüyük ended in a catastrophe, and this catastrophe has left its mark wherever excavations have been conducted. It is this break, ushering in the Middle Bronze Age, with which the Hittite period begins. Much as it took over from the preceding period — in fact, it is so much that the ethnic change would hardly be recognizable to the archaeologist — nevertheless, the texts which fortunately begin to become available at this point — first in Kültepe and then in Boğazköy — teach us that the Hittites, or at least close relatives of the Hittites, were present in Anatolia at the beginning of the Middle Bronze Age.[32]

Although the weight of scholarly opinion supports this interpretation Özgüç denies that the Hittites were responsible for bringing the rich EB culture to an end. A treatment of his reasoning will allow a convenient transition to a discussion of the appearance of Old Assyrian traders in Anatolia.[33]

Özgüç believes that the Hittites were a minority when they came to Anatolia and remained so for a period of time afterward. On the other hand, the princes of North and Central Anatolia "lived in rich and fortified cities" and "were experienced in the use of all kind of weapons".[34] Therefore these princes "cannot have fallen victims to Hittite invaders who were of a lower level of civilization and small in numbers".[35] Further, "The Hittites were too insignificant to be responsible for the simultaneous and ubiquitous destruction and burning of these cities".[36]

Such statements appear to show little if any familiarity with the realities of ancient Near Eastern history. One need only point to Amorite successes over substantial Sumerian-controlled cities or Israelite successes over strong Canaanite cities of Palestine to dismiss the hypothesis that

[31] *Op. cit.*, p. 3.
[32] A. Goetze, "Hittite and Anatolian Studies", *BANE* (1961), p. 319.
[33] *Op. cit.*, p. 3.
[34] *Ibid.*
[35] *Ibid.*
[36] *Ibid.*

per se a technologically inferior, even numerically inferior, group cannot conquer important cities and make inroads into an entrenched urban system.

What appears likely to the present writer is that the entrance of Indo-European elements into Anatolia produced a period of unsettling conditions for a few centuries (?ca. 2300-2000 B.C.). During this period as a whole the general outlines of conflict between the newcomers and the indigenous Anatolian (Hattian) principalities may at first have resembled that between semi-nomadic groups and urban centers, which easily could have disrupted urban life everywhere, or in specific regions from time to time. Not all the evidence of violence associated with the end of the Early Bronze Age need be attributed to the Indo-Europeans. Many of the destroyed sites may have suffered at the hands of their own traditional city-rivals, who could exploit the generally upsetting conditions to their own advantage. It may even be thought that some may have acted in consort with the more mobile groups of foreigners, who, it must be remembered, might not be so considered a few generations after their appearance in an area. It is not too far-fetched to see in the situation an analogy to the Amarna Age of Palestine. Özgüç rightly speaks of the predominant continuity of Anatolian culture between the Early and Middle Bronze Ages as exhibited by material remains, and stresses that changes are due to a local development under the influence of the South.[37] Certainly he is also right in marking as their greatest achievement that the Hittites "adopted the local culture and ... assimilated it, making it function as their own culture and art".[38]

Still it should be asked whether use of the term "Hittite" for the period before the founding of the Old Hittite Kingdom (ca. 1750 B.C.) is meaningful. We think not. The political state which we characterize by the term was in effect a coalescence of a number of Indo-European dialect groups (i.e., Luwian, Palaite, Neshite, etc.) and also included important non-Indo-European groups (the indigenous Anatolian [Hattic] population) as well as important Hurrian elements. We deal before ca. 1750 B.C. with a symbiotic situation. The Old Assyrian tablets of the nineteenth century still show us a basically Hattian system of political centers within which, indeed, at least some Indo-European centers (whether villages, tribal areas, amphictyonic leagues, new-founded or appropriated cities) also existed. We shall return to this topic in some detail below.

[37] *Ibid.*, p. 4.
[38] *Ibid.*

During the later period of Indo-European entrance into and settling down within Anatolia, the Third Dynasty of Ur had re-established political and economic hegemony in Mesopotamia and the heartlands of Syria. It would be short-sighted to say that because no evidence makes a good case for Sumerian *incursion* into Anatolia that a *resumption of trade contacts* between Mesopotamia and Anatolia did not ensue.[39] The point need not be argued in detail. It has been dealt with sufficiently within the body of this work.[40] Suffice it to say that the commercial energies and achievements of this Dynasty made it the most prosperous in Mesopotamian history to its time.

The fortunes of Assyria from the Old Akkadian period through the end of the Ur III period were mixed. It had been a part of the Akkadian sphere of control under Sargon and Narâm-Sîn, but had suffered under the depredations of the Gutians to judge by the condition of the ruins at Assur.[41] Afterward it returned to the control of the southern Dynasty of Ur. The incursions of Amorites, the defection of a number of city-state governors and Elamite aggression brought an end to the rule of this Dynasty, and Assyria became independent, a contender with Isin, Ešnunna and Der for hegemony in Mesopotamia.[42] Well into his reign Išbi-Irra of Isin (ca. 2017-1985 B.C.) succeeded in driving the Elamite garrison out of Ur, consolidating a small city-state system in the south, and taking over Ur's lucrative trade with Tilmun. Edzard cites the economic texts of Isin to show that Išbi-Irra took over the Ur III state system, strengthened it, therefore probably organized Isin like Ur III.[43] Ešnunna, independent since the third year of Ibbi-Sin, engaged in somewhat continual conflict with Der for superiority and political influence, finally losing to her in the reign of Bilalama. For her part, Der's own independence and control ended during the reign of Iddin-Dagan of Isin (ca. 1974-1954 B.C.). The reign of Iddin-Dagan's son, Išmê-Dagan (ca. 1953-1935 B.C.) is important for our synthesis because an oracle of his time relates that Ninurta brought Sumer and Akkad back into order.[44] If this is an oblique reference to previous disorder

[39] Cf. *OIP*, 27 (1935), p. 7, also fn. 81 for references to Ur III trade with Mari, Ibla and Uršu, the latter two, located on the West Syrian edges of Anatolia, being traditionally the economic gateways to the Taurus and the Anti-Taurus for early Mesopotamian kings.

[40] Cf. *Appendix B*, discussion of the Ibbi-Sin seal impressions.

[41] Gadd, *op. cit.*, p. 43.

[42] Dietz O. Edzard, *Die "Zweite Zwischenzeit" Babyloniens* (Wiesbaden, Otto Harrassowitz, 1957), pp. 44f.

[43] *Ibid.*, p. 65.

[44] *Ibid.*, p. 77.

caused by an enemy attack,[45] then there is reason to suspect the campaign reported by Old Assyrian sources in which Ilušuma of Assur (ca. ?1960-1940 B.C.) attacked the south and proclaimed the "freedom" [*andurarum*] of Der, Nippur, Ur and some other southern Mesopotamian cities.[46]

There can only be conjecture about the causes of Ilušuma's attack on southern Mesopotamia. Perhaps it was merely opportunistic. We think it may more likely have represented an attempt by the founder of the Old Assyrian Dynasty to capture control of the trade routes to Elam and of the Tilmun trade, which represented an important economic life-line to a people of the North. The Assyrian incursion was ephemeral, and apparently there were no repercussions from the southern cities which threatened the stability of dynastic rule at Assur. What is useful emerges as a chronological datum: Ilušuma's successor, Irišum, came to the throne of Assur about 1940 B.C. Toward the end of Irišum's reign [= ca. 1901 B.C.] it can be proposed with some certainty, Old Assyrian colonial trading activity as represented by the founding of *Kârum Kaniš* Level II begins.[47] Therefore the raid of Ilušuma into the south, and which cannot be earlier than ca. 1953 B.C., the first year of Išmê-Dagan of Isin, belongs to the same climate of motivation and action which culminates in the Assyrian trade movement to the west only a few decades later in the reign of Irišum. Granted these are only suggestions, but what is more reasonable than to suppose that Assyria's freedom of action, guaranteed to her by her autonomy, was the opportunity, denial to her of southern sources of trade, the motivation, for her endeavor to exploit the commercial routes leading into the heart of Anatolia? In the south Isin gave way to Larsa as the chief power, and the latter took over the Tilmun trade,[48] while subsequent Amorite penetrations kept lower Mesopotamia disorganized and must certainly have presented a kind of barrier to Assyrian aspirations in these regions.

It is now clear that the *kârum* area of Kültepe was in existence and had passed through two archaeologically defined periods before the first Assyrians arrived there.[49] At some (probably short) time after the burning of the city, which signals an end to the Early Bronze Age period, the *kârum* area was founded. Who the inhabitants of Levels IV and III were cannot be discerned at present for these levels have left no documents. Yet there is a continuity of life on the *kârum*-terrace uninterrupted by

[45] *Ibid.*
[46] Cf. *IAK*, pp. 6-9 [w. p. 8, n. 6].
[47] Cf. *Appendix B.*
[48] Edzard, *op. cit.*, p. 100.
[49] Cf. *Appendix B.*

any violence, though a change in material culture is evident in Level III over that which is characteristic of Level IV. It seems reasonable to assume that indigenous persons — small traders, craftsmen, and the like — inhabited the area and were involved in their doubtlessly small and local activities. Some support is given this assumption by the evidence of native Kanishean businessmen living in the *kârum* and working with the Assyrian traders of Levels II and Ib.[50] It is unlikely that the native Anatolians were brought into the Assyrian trading orbits only as a result of Assyrian choice or decision. Most probably the local businessmen provided a convenient liaison between the Semitic and the native population, and this could certainly have come about if a group of such entrepreneurs was already in existence doing business in each and every city-state of Anatolia. This is by no means to imply that prior to the arrival of Assyrian traders there was already a *kârum-organization* such as is known from Level II and thereafter. Indeed, nothing prevents the assumption that local merchants were somehow organized, though we know nothing of this save the later, ubiquitous, role of the Anatolian palace-organizations.

THE POLITICAL CLIMATE OF ANATOLIA AT THE DAWN OF ASSYRIAN COLONIZATION

The political map of Anatolia was fairly well stabilized when Assyrians appeared in Anatolia and were allowed to set up their commercial facilities (*kârû* and *wabâratum*) at the various cities. Of course we do not know by what stages the Assyrian network of settlements grew, but probably *Kaniš* was the first, and hence the nuclear, settlement because it became the controller of the others. Yet, admittedly, it could have happened that the earliest founded *kârû* were closest to Assyria, and that the successes of these prompted further gradual expansion to the west. However it was, the Level II tablets reveal different types of territorial organizations among the Anatolians. Several were called "lands" (*mâtû*). Others were smaller, single city-states, which we know could be autonomous, could head their own systems of vassal dependencies, and could be partners in alliances without necessarily having the status of a *mâtum*. Furthermore, not every head of a *mâtum* bore the same rank.[51]

The important inference to be taken from these facts is that Anatolia,

[50] Cf. *TTKY*, V, Seri — No. 19, xxii-xxiii [xxiii], and *AJA*, 68 (1964), p. 151.
[51] Cf. Ch. Three, above.

itself, must already have developed the system of *parity* and *vassalage* treaty arrangements which we know so well from the Hittite state treaties of the New Empire.[52] We may concisely review the evidence from the Old Assyrian tablets for both types of relationships between the indigenous states during the periods of Kültepe *kârum* Levels II and Ib.

For the entire period of Assyrian occupation we have a total of thirty-two Anatolian principalities named in the Old Assyrian texts. From the Old Hittite Inscription of Anitta, we may add two not named as kingdoms in the Assyrian texts — *Ḫatti*, and *Harkiuna* — and acknowledge three others whose names have not survived.[53] Beyond this, the names of the kingdoms of *Kuššara*, *Neša*, *Ulama*, *Zalpa*, *Šalatiwar* and *Burušḫattum* — all known previously — recur in the Anitta Inscription. Eschewing absolute chronological preciseness for the moment, we may generally attempt to sketch out the Anatolian political environment presented by our sources. For Level II:

1. There exist the large territorial states of *Kaniš*, *Waḫšušana*, and *Burušḫattum*. The ruler of the latter country is styled "Great prince" (*rubâ'um rabî'um*).

2. In one town of Eastern Anatolia, *Ḫaḫḫum*, the ruler is called "king" (*šarrum*), but he does not thereby seem to be entitled to be thought of as a powerful ruler.[54]

Lacking specific information about the sizes of the *mâtû* mentioned in [1.] above, we may still conclude that *Kaniš* was a substantial territorial kingdom of the Kayseri Plain, *Waḫšušana* of the southern central Plateau, and *Burušḫattum*, perhaps a larger kingdom centered in or near the Plain of Konya. It is highly probable that *Burušḫattum* was a weightier political influence or force in Anatolian political affairs than either of the others.[55]

How many of the other kingdoms of the Level II period were fully independent, how many were vassals of *Kaniš*, *Waḫšušana* or *Burušḫattum*

[52] Cf. J. Pirenne, "La politique d'expansion hittite envisagée à travers les traités de vassalité et de protectorat", *ArOr*, 1/2 (1950), pp. 373-382.

[53] Cf. the translation of the Anitta Inscription in H. Otten, "Zu den Anfängen der hethitischen Geschichte", *MDOG*, 83 (1951), pp. 40-42, with ref. to 11. 17-19.

[54] Cf. Ch. Three, above.

[55] To be sure, inferences taken from titles alone are bound to be suspect without corroborating information about the political *actions* or *functions* of the state or ruler involved. The title of the "great prince" at *Burušḫattum* may have become merely traditional by Level II times. However, H. Otten, *op. cit.*, p. 43, stressing the continued importance of *Burušḫattum* in tradition, cites its appearance as the objective of Sargon of Akkad's campaign, and its re-appearance at the end of the Anitta Inscription, as justifying the opinion of its preeminent status in early Anatolian history.

we do not know. An Old Assyrian text [*ATHE*, 66] attests a treaty-relationship between *Kaniš* and *Waḫšušana*.[56] In fact, it was a *sine qua non* of Assyrian trade that *the local rulers themselves* be on good terms with each other, the peaceful relations being affirmed by formal oaths. Between *Kaniš* and *Waḫšušana* we can certainly postulate a *parity-type* of treaty from ATHE 66, and can assume that such a relationship also existed between *Kaniš* and *Burušḫattum*, and between *Burušḫattum* and *Waḫšušana*, although *Waḫšušana* may have been a large-state vassal of the former (see below). We stress these relationships as being in addition to the treaty-agreements between the *Assyrians* and the local princes.[57]

The Anum-Ḫirbi Letter (above, Chapter 3), the evidence of as yet unpublished texts from Kültepe, and the Anitta Inscription,[58] give us considerably more information about the Anatolian city-states for the period of Kültepe *kârum* Ib, the late period of Assyrian trade. The Anum-Ḫirbi letter shows us two treaty partners, *Kaniš* and *Mama*, each of which controls a system of vassals. The Kanishean and the Mamean rulers each are styled as "prince" (*rubâ'um*), which shows that a "great prince" such as was the ruler of Burušḫattum during Level II, required probably a *large* system of vassals to merit the title. The kingdom of *Kaniš* seems to have continued its status as a *mâtum* into the period of Ib. *Mama* appears as a newcomer to the political scene but only because we lack information to compare her Ib status with what it may have been earlier. We recall that *Mama* was the seat of an Assyrian *wabârtum* during the period of Level II.

The Anitta Inscription throws a great deal of light on the political conditions of the last phase of Assyrian activity in Anatolia. From it we learn not only of the rivalry between *Kuššara* and *Neša*, but of the entrance of *Neša* into the political orbit of *Kuššara*, and its rise, under Anitta (and probably earlier under Pitḫana), to a center of contention for power in inner Anatolia. We learn further of a large coalition headed by the ruler of *Ḫatti* raised to check the expansion of *Neša*. The members of this coalition cannot be named altogether precisely. The city of *Ḫarkiuna* is one; and *Zalpa*, a *mâtum* in this period, was indeed in the forefront.[59] This coalition also appears to have had as its political base the territory of north-central Anatolia, the region of the Halys River Basin north of the Kayseri Plain. Finally, two more enemies of *Neša* are named:

[56] Cf. 11. 9-12, with commentary. For further commentary on these lines cf. P. Garelli *AfO*, 20 (1963), 169, and H. Hirsch, *WZKM*, 57 (1961), p. 57.

[57] Cf. Chs. Four through Six, above.

[58] Cf. Otten, *op. cit.*, pp. 40-42.

[59] *Ibid.*, 11. 23; 31-44.

Šalatiwara [= Old Assyrian *Šalatu(w)ar*] and *Burušḫanda* [Old Assyrian *Burušḫattum*].[60] The area in which these two cities are located denotes the political sphere of south-central Anatolia. The culmination of Anitta of *Neša*'s triumphs is the handing over to him by the ruler of *Burušḫattum* of gifts which symbolize the transfer of title to Anatolian political hegemony.

The events mentioned above seem to have taken place a short time *after* the years in which the rulers of *Kaniš* and *Mama* controlled their own systems of vassals independent of outside authority. The conquests of Anitta produce the first wide-spread control of Anatolia by a single city — *Neša.* This hegemony will pass to the Hittites and a new political age in Anatolia will begin. It is the *terminus post quem* of the Old Assyrian Period. We need now look back again to the period of Level II to ask whether the cities of *Ḫatti* and *Zalpa*, coalition allies against *Neša* in the period of Ib, were also then important kingdoms.

While the textual evidence for the appearance of *Ḫatti* in Level II tablets is controversially interpreted, the recovery of a growing, but as yet a small, number of Old Assyrian texts from Boğazköy-*Ḫattuša* dating to the period of *Kaniš* Ib allows the strong assumption that *Ḫatti* [Old Assyrian *Hattuš*(?)] was the site of an Assyrian *kârum* during the period of Level II as well.[61] Granted, this is an argument from silence for the Level II period, but the emergence of *Ḫatti* as a powerful kingdom so relatively close to *Kaniš*, *Zalpa* and other major Assyrian trade centers cannot but lead to the assumption of its earlier importance.[62] For its part, *Zalpa* is well attested as both the seat of a *kârum* and of an apparently powerful kingdom during the period of Level II. If we now list the names of those cities discussed above which were either capitals of *mâtû*, or were otherwise strong centers of political power, and match them against the list of places where the Assyrians located their major trading settlements, the *kârû*, we note the following correlations:

Major Political Center	Kârum
Burušḫattum	*Kârum Burušḫattum*
Ḫattuš	*Kârum Hattuš*
Kaniš	*Kârum Kaniš*
Waḫšušana	*Kârum Waḫšušana*
Zalpa	*Kârum Zalpa*

60 *Ibid.*, 11. 52-54, 64-72.

61 Cf. *TTKY*, VII, Seri — No. 31a, p. 58.

62 So, if we grant some validity to the tradition which included *Ḫatti* as an enemy of Narâm-Sîn in Akkadian times.

If we exclude two kingdoms boasting *kârû* in Syria [*Uršu* and *Niḫria*],[63] and two in Eastern Anatolia [*Ḫurama* and *Ḫaḫḫum*],[64] as being outside the political sphere of Central Anatolia, then we are left with two within the north-central sector of the Anatolian Plateau which appear to play no role as yet attested in the political activities undertaken solely between the indigenous rulers themselves. A prince of *Tamnia* of Level Ib times is in trade negotiations with representatives from *Kârum Durhumit* (in a neighboring kingdom), which perhaps suggests that Durhumit was the seat of political power for its region. If *Tamnia* was within *Durḫumit*'s orbit as a vassal, then the Assyrians of *Kârum Durḫumit* would naturally seem to be the proper *Assyrian* representatives for the Prince of *Tamnia* to deal with, as they were stationed in their overlord's city.[65] The haughty attitude of the Tamnian ruler toward the Assyrians as attested by the text kt f/k 183 (see above, Chapter IV) perhaps refers to an earlier time when *Tamnia* was autonomous and important enough to have been negotiated with by envoys from *Kârum Kaniš* instead of the Assyrians posted at *Durḫumit*. In any event, if this explanation of *Tamnia*'s position suffice, we see that only *Durḫumit* remains unmentioned as a functionary in the power politics of the Assyrian Period. This may be explained if we consider that *Ḫatti*, *Zalpa* and *Durḫumit* are all to be located in the basin of the Halys River, and that *Durḫumit* may well have been subordinate to the other two.[66]

The emergence of *Mama* as the center of a system of vassals in the Ib Period suggests only that no larger power in her south-eastern region stood in the way of her expansion to the borders of the land of *Kaniš*. She had previously been a small kingdom, the site of an Assyrian *wabârtum*. It is of great interest that the name of *Waḫšušana* is missing from the account of Anitta's victories in the South. It may have been reduced or absorbed by the power of *Burušḫattum*.[67] Since the Anitta Inscription ends with an account of the defeat of *Šalatiwara* and the submission of the Prince of *Burušḫattum*, we may assume that *Waḫšušana* had lost its influence to *Šalatiwara* by the period of Ib. If this is so, then it is under-

[63] Cf. Ch. 1.

[64] *Ibid.*

[65] Cf. discussion of kt f/k 183 in Ch. 4, above.

[66] In *KTP*, 14 [above, Ch. 4] exactly the same situation is seen. The ruler of *Wašḫania* approaches the envoys of *Kârum Waḫšušana*, the Assyrian representatives stationed in the city of the chief political center of the region, in order to enter trade negotiations.

[67] Indeed Prof. Landsberger has argued that *Waḫšušana* was one of two lands [with *Burušḫattum*] that made up the domain of the "Great Prince" of *Burušḫattum*: *ArOr*. 18, 1/2 (1950), p. 338.

standable how *Mama* might have become the major power of the south-east, the territory bordering upon that of *Waḫšušana*.

The strong position of *Kuššara* under Pitḫana is a novelty for the Ib period. Perhaps a *wabârtum* was there located.[68] In any event its king was strong enough to capture *Neša* and use that city as a base for his and Anitta's campaigns of expansion. Before we treat of this and its connections to the founding of the Old Hittite kingdom, we may summarize our proposals of the previous paragraphs:

1. When the Assyrians came to Anatolia they found a political situation in which, while many cities had rulers who could be styled *rubâ'um*, or "Prince", only about five or six were dominant, being either full-fledged *mâtû* or controllers of significant systems of vassals. One *mâtum*, *Burušḫattum*, wielded a powerful influence in south-western Anatolia, but apparently did not (or could not) make inroads into the central and north-central areas of the Plateau.

2. An Assyrian *kârum* was founded in each of the major royal seats. We may conjecture that *Kaniš* was chosen as the center of the Assyrian *kârum*-system because it was the closest and most conveniently reached political center in Central Anatolia, it being directly approached from the passes of the Anti-Taurus. In other words, *the distribution pattern of kârû in Central Anatolia coincides with the distribution of the major indigenous kingdoms.* These kingdoms divide the region as follows: *Burušḫattum* controlled the south-west; *Waḫšušana*, the south-central area; *Kaniš*, the Kayseri Plain; *Ḫatti* and *Zalpa* (in some relationship), the Halys River Basin. We propose also that the *wabârtum*-settlements were located in the lesser political centers, some inside Anatolia, some in North Syria.

THE END OF THE HATTIAN POLITICAL SYSTEM AND THE RISE OF *NEŠA*

A crisis in the political system as we have discussed it appears to have been ushered in with the destruction of the second level on the city-mound and on the *kârum*-terrace at Kültepe. Is there any possibility of determining the perpetrators of this destruction? Our synthesis is based upon the information of the Anitta Inscription, our inferences about the political make-up of Anatolia during the period of Level II, and an

[68] Cf. Ch. 5, n. 95, above.

examination of the question whether *Kaniš* is to be identified with *Neša* as has been proposed recently by Güterbock.[69]

1. The violent destruction visited upon *Kaniš*, and which brought an end to Level II was not the result of an ephemeral raid. The excavators note not only that the condition of the *kârum*-remains suggests a swift and surprise attack, but also that *Kaniš* afterward appears to have been deserted for at least a generation.[70] Therefore, as *Kaniš* was the center of a major kingdom, we see the enemy as the center of another major kingdom or collection of allies. The attack could not have been the work of a minor opponent.

2. The recovery of *Kaniš*, as witnessed by Level Ib on the *kârum*-terrace and the corresponding level on the city-mound containing the palace of Inar and Waršama, shows a return of the city to independent status, to its older position as leader of its own political system of vassals.

One possible interpretation of the events mentioned above, and which we shall attempt to develop, is that the interruption of *Kaniš*'s peaceful and prosperous condition, and of her dynastic line, was an early move in the series of events which eventually led to the ascendancy of Pitḫana and Anitta. An attack upon a kingdom like *Kaniš* presupposes not only a major opponent, but an opportunity for that opponent to act, — in other words, a moment when *Kaniš* might have experienced a weakening of her position for one or another reason. Do we know of any such moments citied in the documentary sources? One, of course, is the time when a certain Labarša "seized the kingdom",[71] but this event appears to have taken place *before* the destruction of Level II. A second is reported by the Anitta Inscription, and becomes meaningful only if we can equate *Kaniš* and *Neša*: at some time before Anitta's reign, a certain Uḫna, King of *Zalpuwa* (*Zalpa*), is reported to have carried off the statue of the city-god of *Neša*.[72] Let us propose the hypothesis *Kaniš* = *Neša* to test whether the archaeological and documentary evidence from Kültepe can then be integrated with the statements of the Anitta Inscription. A summary of this important historical document is now required.

1. Both Pitḫana and his son, Anitta, are rulers of the Kingdom of

[69] The *Kaniš* = *Neša* thesis was first suggested by E. Forrer as an hypothesis [*Glotta*, 26 (1938), 190, n. 1], revived as such by H. G. Güterbock in *Eretz Israel*, 5 (1958), 46-50, taken up by K. Balkan [*TTKY*, VII, Seri — No. 31a, 58f.], and O. R. Gurney, *op. cit.*, 7. Sedat Alp has recently contributed further arguments in its favor ["Kaniš=Aniša=Niša", *Belleten*, 107 (1963), 377-386].

[70] Cf. *Appendix B*.

[71] =*ICK*, 178.

[72] Cf. Otten, *op. cit.*, p. 41, 11. 39f.

Kuššara. But in the days of Pitḫana the ruler of the city *Neša* did something [text broken] which incurred the hostility of *Kuššara*. After a strong attack by night Pitḫana captured *Neša*, took its king prisoner, but treated the population as though they were his own flesh and blood; he did them no harm.[73]

2. Pitḫana's successor, Anitta, fights a number of enemies who had allied against him, and conquers, depopulates and curses several of their cities. Only the city of *Ḫarkiuna* can clearly be recognized in the text.[74] The city of *Zalpuwa* (*Zalpa*) appears in a broken context.[75] But when we consider that Pijušti, King of *Ḫatti* is named as leading a coalition of allies against Anitta "*for a second time*"[76] and that *Zalpuwa* (*Zalpa*) appears to be part of this coalition,[77] it is reasonable to conclude that Anitta encountered a major enemy alliance led by *Ḫatti* and *Zalpa*, and involving most likely the chief vassals of these kingdoms within the Inner Halys Basin, and scored a victory. Yet this victory was indecisive in that Anitta did not yet destroy the cities of *Ḫattuš* or *Zalpuwa/Zalpa*.

3. The second encounter with the alliance of the north-central Plateau ended with Anitta as undisputed master of Central Anatolia. The *Zalpuwa*-lands were defeated, as were the *Ḫatti*-lands with its capital city, though we do not read of the fate of *Zalpuwa*, itself. Its king (Ḫuzziya), however, is brought to *Neša* as prisoner.[78] We should at this point evaluate the information of the Inscription about prior relations between *Zalpuwa/Zalpa* and *Neša*.

At some earlier time, reports Anitta, a king of *Zalpuwa* named Uḫna had carried off the statue of Šiušummi, *Neša*'s deity, to his own city.[79] Although it is not specifically mentioned, *Neša* must have suffered a major defeat and destruction for this to have happened. Such an event must have transpired before Pitḫana of *Kuššara* took possession of *Neša*, for this city is secure and on the ascendant during the reigns of Pitḫana

[73] *Ibid.*, 11. 7-9. While we do not know what caused the hostility between *Kuššara* and *Neša*, we do see that *only the king* of *Neša* is considered to be the real enemy. That this is noteworthy is seen when we consider that in his own campaigns Anitta does destroy and depopulate a number of enemy cities. Apparently, then, some bond of relationship between the populations of *Kuššara* and *Neša* ran deeply enough for Pitḫana to show the Nešians favor. This allows one to suppose that the people of the two cities belonged to the same "ethnic" or "linguistic" stock, and that the removal of the hostile king of *Neša* did not affect the resumption of harmonious relationships.

[74] Otten, *op. cit.*, p. 40, l. 23.

[75] *Ibid.*, ll. 31-32.

[76] *Ibid.*, l. 36.

[77] *Ibid.*, ll. 38-44.

[78] *Ibid.*, ll. 43-44.

[79] *Ibid.*, ll. 39-40.

and Anitta. How long before Pithana's capture of *Neša* the attack by *Zalpuwa/Zalpa* took place we cannot, of course, know. But we note that *Neša* must then have had a reduced influence, must even have been a vassal of *Zalpuwa* after her defeat. Her king must have served *Zalpuwa*, either as a puppet ruler chosen from the Neshite line itself, or placed on the throne from outside. In some way the rulers of *Neša* under *Zalpuwa* may have seemed to be illegitimate rulers over the Neshite population, especially since the Neshite deity, himself, was in detention. If the population of *Kuššara* and of *Neša* belonged to the same ancestral stock, the magnanimous treatment of *Neša*'s inhabitants by Pithana could well be explained. The victory against *Neša*'s king would have been seen as a restoration rather than an indiscriminate victory.

The religious implications of *Zalpuwa/Zalpa*'s victory over *Neša* and *Kuššara*'s subsequent capture of *Neša* are very significant. Both Pitḫana and Anitta are worshippers of "the Weather-god of Heaven" [Ḫalma-šiutta].[80] Anitta built a temple to this Ḫalmašiutta, and also to the Neshite god, Šiušummi, in *Neša*, after his conquests.[81] Thus Anitta restored the local deity which had been carried away by *Zalpuwa/Zalpa*, and introduces the god of his dynasty to *Neša* as a superior deity, who is nonetheless on the most harmonious terms with Šiušummi. This is clearly proven in the way that Anitta describes his taking of *Hattuš*(*a*). It is the Nesian god, Šiušummi, who "delivered it over" to Anitta's god, Ḫalmašiutta. Hence the city-god of *Neša*, in an act of revenge, presents the capital of the enemy coalition [which had included *Zalpuwa/Zalpa*, his own humiliator] to the god of Anitta, who restored him.[82] This is an excellent example of religious syncretism and synthesis as a result of political activity. It makes it highly probable that as a consequence of Anitta's victories, the "Weather-god of Heaven" was raised to a position of supremacy in pre-Hittite Anatolia without the displacement of local deities.

We suggest that several pieces of evidence from Kültepe may correlate with the information summarized above:

1. The massive destruction layer which represents the end of Level II on the *kârum*-terrace and on the city-mound could be explained as the effects of the invasion of Uḫna, king of *Zalpuwa/Zalpa*, if the equation *Kaniš* = *Neša* stands up.[83]

[80] *Ibid.*, l. 2, and ll. 20, 51, 56-57.
[81] *Ibid.*, ll. 56-57.
[82] *Ibid.*, ll. 46-47.
[83] Also proposed by K. Balkan, *TTKY*, VII, Seri — No. 31a, p. 59.

2. If so, then the kings Inar and Waršama of *Kaniš* represent the rulers of the period in *Kaniš/Neša* (Ib) when the city had a diminished political influence. This is supported by the evidence of the Anum-Ḫirbi letter, the haughty communication in which the ruler of *Mama*, a town earlier unimportant enough to warrant only the presence of an Assyrian *wabârtum*, now is seen to treat the Kanishean ruler as an equal, and to upbraid him for failing to keep his vassals in line as well as for resorting to trickery in the matter of a treaty-oath. Note also that:

3. Pitḫana took over *Kaniš/Neša* by a night attack (= by surprise?) but did not apparently visit any great destruction on the city, a fact which seems to agree with the condition of the Level Ib at Kültepe.[84]

4. The Anitta Inscription reports that Anitta fortified *Neša*[85]. The archaeological report of the 1963 excavations reveals apparently that both the Kültepe citadel-mound and the *kârum*-terrace were walled for the first time during the period of Ib.[86] Also the increase in population inferred by the excavators from the size of the *Kârum* Ib area is compatible with the importance of *Neša* under Pitḫana and Anitta.

5. Some important confirmation that Anitta is contemporary with Inar and Waršama is suggested by the finding of a large tablet in the *Kârum* Ib level in 1962 containing a list of six native kings including the names of Inar, Waršama and Anitta.[87]

When we recall that *Kârum* Ib appears to have lasted for about a generation after its founding before it and the corresponding level on the citadel-mound were again destroyed, we see that the events discussed in the preceding paragraphs may be fitted into the time available as inferred from the archaeological results. If *Kaniš/Neša* was destroyed by *Zalpuwa/Zalpa* [end of Level II], existed as a small defenceless city [Level Ic, period of no tablets], revived as a small kingdom under Inar and Waršama, but a kingdom that was obliged to wage wars and enter into a parity-pact with *Mama* [Level Ib with the evidence of the Anum-Ḫirbi Letter], then Pitḫana's capture of the city and Anitta's campaigns from it follow reasonably within view. So also does Anitta's loss of power to another dynasty as witnessed by the destruction of Kültepe Level Ib and the subsequent inauguration of Level Ia, the beginning of the Hittite Period.

The chronological reconstruction derived from the data of the Old

[84] Otten, *op. cit.*, p. 40, ll. 5-9. See also above note 73.

[85] *Ibid.*, l. 55.

[86] *AJA*, 68 (1964), p. 152.

[87] *AJA*, 67 (1963), p. 175.

Assyrian texts and relevant materials does not seriously dispute this interpretation. Kültepe Level II comes to an end approximately between ca. 1848 and 1824 B.C.[88] Allowing about one or two generations for the period of Ic on the *kârum*-terrace, when there was no occupation after the destruction of Level II, and perhaps 30 yr. for Level Ib, we may postulate a date of between ca. 1775 and 1755 B.C. for the destruction of Pitḫana's and Anitta's city, *Kaniš/Neša*. This would place the period of *Kârum* Ib wholly within the reign of Šamši-Adad I of Assyria (ca. 1813-1781, B.C.), and partly within that of his successor, Išme-Dagan, and would account for the re-occupation of the *kârum* at Kültepe, which one assumes depended upon a return of stability to the Assyrian royal line initiated by Šamši-Adad. Of course, we cannot insist on exact initial and terminal dates for Level Ib, which may have to be altered slightly upward or downward as new evidence becomes available.

Returning now to the question of the Hittites, who put an end to Anitta's reign at *Kaniš/Neša*, — is there any connection between the former and the *Kuššaran* Dynasty of Pitḫana and Anitta? Hittite tradition acknowledges that the original seat of the early kings of *Ḫattuša* was *Kuššar(a)*.[89] Yet it was Anitta of *Kuššara* who, having made *Neša* his capital, fought with the king of *Ḫattuša* of his own time, destroyed the city, and cursed it forever.[90] How can the move of later kings of *Kuššara* to *Ḫattuša* then be reconciled with the earlier hostility of the two cities? H. G. Güterbock proposed a change of dynasty at *Kuššara*, an hypothesis which O. R. Gurney also accepts as the most likely one.[91] Gurney further attributes the move by Ḫattušiliš I to *Ḫattuša* to strategic considerations.[92] These appear to be most reasonable explanations. The present writer would put forth another possibility, namely that the Dynasty of *Kuššara* might have been a parallel line to that of Pitḫana and Anitta. When these kings shifted their center of power to *Kaniš/Neša*, it is likely that the government of *Kuššara* continued on in local hands. A falling out between Anitta and a new power-system building up with *Kuššara* as its center is not beyond possibility. This would account for the destruction of *Kaniš/Neša*, the survival of *Kuššara*, and the preservation of the account of Pitḫana's and Anitta's deeds in the earlier period.

The move to *Ḫattuša* would seem to have been a peaceful one according

[88] Cf. *Appendix B.*

[89] Cf. O. R. Gurney, "Anatolia, c. 1750-1600 B.C.", *CAH*, rev. ed. Vol. II, Ch. 6 (1962), p. 13.

[90] Otten, *op. cit.*, p. 41, ll. 44-48.

[91] Gurney, *op. cit.*, p. 9 w.n. 5.

[92] *Ibid.*, pp. 13-14.

to present knowledge, and here perhaps we can conjecture that the first culmination of that "religious federalism" which characterizes the consolidation of the Hittite kingdom took place — a union of the dominant "Weather-god of Heaven", who became the "Weather-god of *Ḫatti*", and the "Sun-Goddess of Arinna", perhaps even on the model of events by which the *Kuššaran* deity under Anitta became the benevolent suzerain of the Neshite god, Šiušummi. The question is too complicated, the evidence too obscure, to make this an assertion. But the hypothesis is warranted: the Hittite federal system is based upon a careful *inclusion* of all manner of local gods into a divine system which Pirenne has suggested reflects the methods of Hittite treaty-operations in the international sphere.[93] The joining of the chief Weather-god of Anatolia of *Kuššaran* tradition and the "Sun-Goddess of Arinna", whose lands seem primarily to have included north-central Anatolia, must represent the confluence of *Kuššaran* and *Ḫattušan* power in a peaceful manner. Are we permitted to see the joining of the two at Yazilikaya as the highest representation in religious art among the Hittites of the memory of this early unity? Whether these specific notations stand or not, we must certainly see in the initiative of Pitḫana and Anitta an impetus which brings an end to an older state-system of Anatolia and leads to the beginning of a new political activity which culminates in the formation of the Old Hittite Kingdom.

[93] Pirenne *op. cit.*, pp. 373-374.

BIBLIOGRAPHY

A. BOOKS

Andrae, Walter, *Die archaischen Ischtar-Tempel in Assur*, *WVDOG*, 39 (Leipzig, Hinrichs, 1932).

Arensberg, Conrad M. (See Polanyi, Karl).

Balkan, Kemal, "Kaniš Kârum'unun Kronoloji Problemleri Hakkinda Müşahedeler" [Observations on the Chronological Problems of the Kârum Kaniš], *TTKY*, VII, Seri — No. 28 (Ankara, Türk Tarih Kurumu Basimevi, 1955).

——, "The Letter of Anum-Ḫirbi, King of Mama, to Warshama, King of Kaniš", *TTKY*, VII, Seri — No. 31a (Ankara, Türk Tarih Kurumu Basimevi, 1957).

Bezold, Carl, *Babylonisch-assyrisches Glossar* (Heidelberg, Carl Winter's Universitätsbuchhandlung, 1926).

Bilgiç, Emin, "Die einheimischen Appellativa der kappadokischen Texte und ihre Bedeutung für die anatolischen Sprachen", *DTCFY*, 96 (Ankara, Türk Tarih Kurumu Basimevi, 1954).

Bittel, Kurt, "Boğazköy. Die Kleinfunde der Grabungen, 1906-1912", *WVDOG*, 60 (Leipzig, Hinrichs, 1937).

——, *Grundzüge der Vor- und Frühgeschichte Kleinasiens*, 2nd. ed. (Tübingen, Ernst Wasmuth, 1950).

——, and Hans G. Güterbock, "Boğazköy. Neue Untersuchungen in der hethitischen Hauptstadt", *APAW*, *Phil.-hist. Klasse*, 1 (Berlin, Walter de Gruyter & Co., 1935).

——, and R. Naumann, "Boğazköy II. Neue Untersuchungen hethitischer Architektur", *APAW Phil.-hist. Klasse* 1 (Berlin, Walter de Gruyter & Co., 1938).

——, and R. Naumann, Boğazköy III. Funde aus den Grabungen, 1952-1955, *ADOG*, 2 (Berlin, Gebr. Mann, 1957).

——, and R. Naumann, "Boğazköy-Hattuša I. Architektur, Topographie Landeskunde und Seidlungsgeschichte", *WVDOG*, 63 (Stutt-

gart, Kohlhammer, 1952).
——, R. Naumann and H. Otto, "Yazilikaya. Architektur, Felsbilder, Inschriften und Kleinefunde", *WVDOG*, 61 (Leipzig, Hinrichs, 1940).
Borger, Riekele, *Einleitung in die assyrischen Königsinschriften*, 1 (= *Handbuch der Orientalistik*, Leiden, E. J. Brill, 1961).
Cavaignac, Eugene, *Les Hittites* (Paris, Libr[e] A. Maisonneuve, 1950).
Chantre, Ernest, *Mission en Cappadoce* (Paris, E. Leroux, 1898).
Clay, Albert T., *Letters and Transactions from Cappadocia* (= *BIN*, IV, New Haven, Conn. Yale University Press, 1927).
Contenau, Georges, *La civilisation des hittites et des hurrites du Mitanni*, 2nd ed. (Paris, Payot, 1948).
——, "Tablettes cappadociennes I", *TCL*, IV (Paris, Paul Geuthner, 1920).
——, *Trente tablettes cappadociennes* (Paris, Paul Geuthner, 1919).
Deimel, Anton, *Sumerisches Lexikon*, 7 vol. (Rome, Pontificium Institutum Biblicum, 1930).
Delaporte, Louis, *Les Hittites* (Paris, La Renaissance du livre, 1936).
——, *Les peuples de l'Orient méditerranean*, I (= *Le Proche-Orient asiatique*, 3rd ed., Paris, Les presses universitaires de France, 1948).
Delitzsch, Friedrich, *Assyrisches Handwörterbuch* (Leipzig, Hinrichs, 1896).
Driver, G. R., *Semitic Writing* (London, Oxford University Press, 1948).
——, and John C. Miles, *The Assyrian Laws* (Oxford, The Clarendon Press, 1935). *Idem*, *The Babylonian Laws* (1956).
Ebeling, Erich, and Bruno Meissner, *Reallexikon der Assyriologie*, I and II (Berlin and Leipzig, W. de Gruyter & Co. 1932-1938).
——, Bruno Meissner and Ernst Weidner, "*Die Inschriften der altassyrischen Könige*", *AOB*, 1 (Leipzig, Quelle und Meyer, 1926).
Edzard, Dietz O., *Die "zweite Zwischenzeit" Babyloniens* (Wiesbaden, Otto Harrassowitz, 1957).
Eisser, Georg and Julius Lewy, "Die altassyrischen Rechtsurkunden vom Kültepe", I and II, *MVaG*, 33 and 35, 3. Heft (Leipzig, Hinrichs, 1930 and 1935).
Fisher, William B., *The Middle East*, 2nd. ed. (London, Methuen, 1952).
Forbes, Robert J., *Metallurgy in Antiquity* (Leiden, Brill, 1950).
Forrer, Emil., *Die Boğazköi-Texte in Umschrift*, 2 vols. (= *WVDOG*, 41 and 42, Leipzig, Hinrichs, 1922-1926).
Frankfort, Henri, *The Birth of Civilization in the Near East* (New York, Doubleday & Co., Inc., 1956).

Friedrich, Johannes, *Hethitisches Wörterbuch* (Heidelberg, Carl Winter Universitätsverlag, 1952).

Garelli, Paul, *Les Assyriens en Cappadoce* (= *Bibliothèque Archéologique et Historique de l'Institut Français d'Archéologie d'Istanbul*, Vol. XIX, (Paris, Librarie Adrien-Maisonneuve [Dépositaire], 1963).

Garstang, John, and Oliver R. Gurney, "The Geography of the Hittite Empire", *Occasional Publications of the British Institute of Archaeology at Ankara*, 5 (London, 1959).

and L. A. Mayer, *Index of Hittite Names*, Section A, Geographical, Part I (British School of Archaeology in Jerusalem, Supplementary Papers I) (London, 1923).

Gelb, Ignace J., "Inscriptions from Alishar and Vicinity", *OIP*, 27 (Chicago, University of Chicago Press, 1935).

——, *Old Akkadian Inscriptions in the Chicago Natural History Museum* (*Fieldiana, Anthropology*, V, 44, No. 2) (Chicago, Chicago Natural History Museum, 1955).

——, *A Study of Writing* (Chicago, University of Chicago Press, 1952).

Goetze, Albrecht, *Kizzuwatna and the Problem of Hittite Geography* (New Haven, Conn. Yale University Press, 1940).

——, *Kleinasien* (= *Kulturgeschichte des alten Orients*), in I. von Muller, *Handbuch der Altertumswissenschaft*, III, I, iii (Munchen, C. H. Beck, 1933).

——, *Kleinasien*, 2nd. ed. (= *Kulturgeschichte des alten Orients*), in I. von Muller, *Handbuch der Altertumswissenschaft*, III, I, iii (Munchen, C. H. Beck, 1957).

——, *Verstreute Boğazköi-Texte* (Marburg, Im Selbstverlag, 1930).

Golenishchev, V. S., *Vingt-quatre tablettes cappadociennes de la collection W. Golenischeff* (St. Petersbourg [no publ. cited], 1891).

Goossens, G., *Het Ontstaan van het Assyrisch Rijk*, *Mededelingen van de Koninklijke Academie voor Wetenschappen, Letteren en Schone Kunsten van België. Klasse der Letteren*, 22/3 (Brussel, Paleis der Academiën, 1960).

Güterbock, Hans G. (See Bittel, Kurt.)

Hazard, H. W. (See Strauz-Hupé, R.)

Hirsch, Hans., *Untersuchungen zur altassyrische Religion*, *Archiv für Orientforschung*, Beiheft 13/14, Graz, 1961).

Hrozný, Bedrich, *Inscriptions cunéiformes du Kultépé*, I (= *Monografie Archivu Orientálního*, XIV, Praha, Orientalni Ustav, 1952).

Kaplan, Abraham (See Lasswell, Harold D.).

Kienast, Burkhart, *Die altassyrischen Texte des Orientalischen Seminars der Universität Heidelberg und der Sammlung Erlenmeyer* (*Basel*) (= *Untersuchungen zur Assyriologie und Vorderasiatischen Archäologie*, 1, Berlin, de Gruyter, 1960).

King, Leonard W., *Hittite Texts in the Cuneiform Character from Tablets in the British Museum* (London, British Museum, 1920).

Koschaker, Paul, *Babylonisch-assyrisches Bürgschaftsrecht* (Leipzig and Berlin, B. G. Teubner, 1911).

Kraus, K., "*Boğ azköy, Tempel V*", *Istanbuler Forschungen*, 11 (Berlin [no publ. cited], 1940).

Kupper, J.-R., *Les nomades en Mésopotamie au temps des rois de Mari* (= *Bibliothèque de la Faculté de Philosophie et Lettres de l'Université de Liège*, 142, Paris, 1957).

Labat, Réné, *Manuel d'épigraphie akkadienne* (Paris, Imprimerie Nationale de France, 1952).

Lasswell, Harold D. and Abraham Kaplan, *Power and Society* (New Haven, Conn., Yale University Press, 1950).

Leemans, Wilhelmus F., *Foreign Trade in the Old Babylonian Period* (Leiden, Brill, 1960).

——, *The Old Babylonian Merchant: His Business and His Social Position* (Leiden, Brill, 1950).

Lewy, Julius (See also Eisser, Georg).

——, *Das Verbum in den altassyrischen Gesetzen* (Berlin, Im Selbstverlag, 1921).

——, *Die altassyrischen Texte vom Kültepe bei Kaisariye* (Konstantinopel, Antiken-Museen zu Stambul, 1927).

——, *Die Keilschrifttexte aus Kleinasien* (*Texte und Materialien der Frau Professor Hilprecht Collection of Babylonian Antiquities im Eigentum der Universität Jena*, I) (Leipzig, Hinrichs, 1932).

——, *Die Kültepetexte der Sammlung Rudolf Blanckertz, Berlin* (Berlin, Heintze & Blanckertz, 1929).

——, *Die Kültepetexte aus der Sammlung Frida Hahn, Berlin* (Leipzig, Hinrichs, 1930).

——, *Studien zu den alt-assyrischen Texten aus Kappadokien* (Berlin, Im Selbstverlage, 1922).

——, "Tablettes cappadociennes, III", *TCL*, XIX-XXI (Paris, Paul Geuthner, 1935-1937).

Limet, H., *Le travail du métal au pays de Sumer au temps de la IIIe dynastie d'Ur* (= *Bibliothèque de la Faculté de Philosophie et Lettres de l'Université de Liège, Fasc.* 155, Paris, 1960).

Lloyd, Seton., *Early Anatolia* (Baltimore, Md., Penguin Books Ltd.,

1956).

Matouš, Lubor, *Inscriptions cunéiformes du Kültepe*, Vol. II (Prague, Éditions de l'Académie Tchécoslovaque de Sciences, 1962).

Mayer, L. A. (See Garstang, John).

Meek, Theophile J., *Old Akkadian, Sumerian, and Cappadocian Texts from Nuzi* (= *Excavations at Nuzi*, III, Cambridge, Mass., Harvard University Press, 1935).

Meer, P. van der, *Une correspondance commerciale assyrienne de Cappadoce* (Roma, Imprimerie Pie X, 1931).

Meissner, Bruno (See Ebeling, Erich).

Meyer, Eduard, *Geschichte des Altertums*, I² (= *Die altesten geschichtlichen Völker und Kulturen bis zum XVI Jahrh.*), 2nd. ed, Stuttgart & Berlin, J. G. Cotta, 1913).

——, *Reich und Kultur der Chetiter* (Berlin, Karl Curtius, 1914).

Miles, John C., (See Driver, G. R.).

Naumann, R. (See Bittel, Kurt).

Oppenheim, A. Leo, and others, eds., *The Assyrian Dictionary of the Oriental Institute of the University of Chicago* (Chicago, The Oriental Institute, 1956).

Osten, Hans H. von der, "Explorations in Central Anatolia, Season of 1926", *OIP*, 5 (Chicago, University of Chicago Press, 1929).

——, "The Alishar Hüyük, Seasons of 1930-1932", Part I, *OIP*, 28 (Chicago, University of Chicago Press, 1937).

——, "The Alishar Hüyük, Seasons of 1930-1932", Part II, *OIP*, 29 (Chicago, University of Chicago Press, 1937).

——, "The Alishar Hüyük, Seasons of 1930-1932", Part III, *OIP*, 30 (Chicago, University of Chicago Press, 1937).

——, and Erich F. Schmidt, "The Alishar Hüyük, Season of 1927", Part I, *OIP*, 6 (Chicago, University of Chicago Press, 1930-1932).

——, and Erich F. Schmidt, "The Alishar Hüyük, Season of 1927", Part II, *OIP*, 7 (Chicago, University of Chicago Press, 1930-1932).

Otten, Heinrich, "Keilschrifttexte aus Boghazköi" (= *Wissenschaftliche Veröffentlichung der Deutschen Orient-Gesellschaft*, 70 Berlin, Gebr. Mann, 1957).

Otto, H. (See Bittel, Kurt).

Özgüç, Tahsin, *Die Bestattungsbrauche im vorgeschichtlichen Anatolien* (Ankara, Ankara Universität, 1948).

——, *Kültepe-Kaniş. New Researches at the Center of the Assyrian Trade Colonies* (= *Türk Tarih Kurumu Yayinlarindan*, 5, No. 19 Ankara, Türk Tarih Kurumu Basimevi, 1959).

——, *Kültepe Kazisi Raporu*, 1948 (= *Türk Tarih Kurumu Yayinlarindan*, 5, No. 10, Ankara, Türk Tarih Kurumu Basimevi, 1950).

——, and Nimet Özgüç, *Kültepe Kazisi Raporu*, 1949 (= *Türk Tarih Kurumu Yayiolarindan*, 5, No. 12, Ankara, Türk Tarih Kurumu Basimevi, 1953).

Pallis, Svend A., *The Antiquity of Iraq* (Copenhagen, E. Munksgaard, Ltd., 1956).

Pearson, Harry W. (See Polanyi, Karl).

Polanyi, Karl, Conrad M. Arensberg, and Harry W. Pearson, *Trade and Market in the Early Empires* (Glencoe, Ill., The Free Press, 1957).

Przeworsky, S., *Die Metallindustrie Anatoliens* (Leiden, 1939).

Puchstein, O., "Boghazköi, Die Bauwerke", *WVDOG*, 19 (Leipzig, Hinrichs, 1912).

Ramsay, William M., *The Historical Geography of Asia Minor* (= Royal Geographical Society. Supplementary Papers, IV, London, John Murray, 1890).

Salonen, Armas, "Hippologica Accadica", *AASF*, Ser. B, Tom. 100 (Helsinki, Suomalainen Tiedeakatemia, 1956).

——, *Die Landfahrzeuge des alten Mesopotamien nach sumerisch akkadischen Quellen* (= *Annales Academiae Scientiarum Fennicae*, Ser. B, Vol. 72/73, Helsinki, 1951).

Schmidt, Erich F. (See also Osten, Hans H. von der).

——, *The Alishar Hüyük, Seasons of* 1928 *and* 1929. Part I. *OIP* 19 (Chicago, University of Chicago Press, 1932-1933).

——, *The Alishar Hüyük, Seasons of* 1928 *and* 1929. Part II. *OIP* 20 (Chicago, University of Chicago Press, 1932-1933).

Smith, Sidney, *Cuneiform Texts from Cappadocian Tablets in the British Museum* (Parts I-IV. London, British Museum 1921-1927).

——, *Early History of Assyria* (New York, E. P. Dutton and Co., 1928).

——, and D. J. Wiseman, *Cuneiform Texts from Cappadocian Tablets in the British Museum*. Part V (London, British Museum, 1956).

Soden, Wolfram von, *Akkadisches Handwörterbuch* (Wiesbaden, Otto Harrassowitz, Appearing in fascicles from 1959).

——, "Das Akkadische Syllabar", *Analecta Orientalia*, 27 (Rome, Pontificum Institutum Biblicum, 1948).

——, "Grundriss der akkadischen Grammatik", *Analecta Orientalia*, 33 (Rome, Pontificum Institutum Biblicum, 1952).

Stamp, L. Dudley, *Asia*, 8th Ed. (London, Methuen, 1950).

Starr, Richard F. S., *Nuzi* I (Cambridge, Mass., Harvard University Press, 1939).

Stephens, Ferris J., "Old Assyrian Letters and Business Documents", *BIN*, VI (New Haven, Conn., Yale University Press, 1944).

——, *Personal Names of Cappadocia* (New Haven, Conn., Yale University Press, 1928).

Strauz-Hupé, R. and H. W. Hazard eds., *The Idea of Colonialism* (New York, Praeger, 1958).

Thomson, R. Campbell, *A Dictionary of Assyrian Chemistry and Geology* (Oxford, The Clarendon Press, 1936).

Thureau-Dangin, Fr., "Lettres et contrats de l'époque de la première dynastie babylonienne", *TCL*, I (Paris, Paul Geuthner, 1910).

——, "Textes cappadociennes, II", *TCL*, XIV (Paris, Paul Geuthner, 1928).

Walther, A., "Das altbabylonische Gerichtswesen", *LSS*, 6 (Leipzig, Hinrichs, 1917).

Weber, Otto, *Boğazköi-Studien*, 10 Parts (Leipzig, Hinrichs, 1917-1924).

Weidner, Ernst (See Ebeling, Erich).

B. PERIODICALS

Albright, William F., "The Epic of the King of Battle. Sargon of Akkad in Cappadocia", *JSOR*, 7 (1923), 1-20.

Alkim, B., "Güney-Bati Antitoros Bölgesinde eski bir yol Sebekesi" (= English Resume: "An Ancient Road-System in the South-Western Antitaurus"), *Belleten*, 23 (1959), 59-73 (Turkish), 74-76 (English).

Alp, Sedat., "Die Lage von Šamuha", *Anatolia*, 1 (1956), 77-80.

——, "Kaniş = Anişa = Nişa: Erken Hitit Çağinin Bir Başkenti" (= German Translation: "Kaniš = Aniša = Niša: Eine Hauptstadt der frühethitischen Periode"), *Belleten*, 27 (1963), 367-376 (Turkish), 377-386 (German).

Anderson, J. G. C., "The Road System of Eastern Asia Minor with the Evidence of Byzantine Campaigns". *JHS*, 17 (1897), 22-44.

Balkan, Kemal, and Benno, Landsberger, "Die Inschrift des assyrischen Königs Irişum gefunden in Kültepe 1948", *Belleten*, 14 (1950), 219-268.

Bar-Am, Moshe, "The Subjunctive in Cappadocian Texts", *Or ns*, 7 (1938), 12-31.

Bilgiç, Emin, "Änlichkeit und Unterscheid zwischen altbabylonischen und kappadokischen Urkunden in bezug auf allgemeine Wirtschaft-

grundsatze und Schuldrecht", *Belleten*, 15 (1951), 333-338 (Turkish).
——, "Asurca Vesikalara Göre Etilerden Önce", *Sumeroloji Arastirmalari, Sumeroloji Enstitüsü Nesriyati*, No. 1 (1940-1941), 913-950.
——, "L'économie des metaux en Anatolie avant les Hittites d'après les documents en lague assyrienne", *RAI*, 2 (1951), 99-100.
——, "L'interet dans les textes économiques cuneiformes", *Belleten*, 15 (1951), 339-347.
——, "Die juristisch-ökonomischen Keilschriftquellen, ihr Charackter und ihr Inhalt", *Belleten*, 11 (1947), 571-602 (Turkish).
——, "Die originellen Seiten im Eherecht der vorhethitischen Bevölkerung Anatoliens", *DTCFD*, 9 (1951-1952), 239-250.
——, "Die Ortsnamen der 'kappadokischen' Urkunden im Rahmen der alten Sprachen Anatoliens", *AfO*, 15 (1945-1951), 1-37.
——, "Die Ortsnamen in den kappadokischen Texten und ihre Lokalisierungsversuche", *Belleten*, 10 (1946), 381-423 (Turkish).
——, "Recherches sur les tribus anatoliennes d'après les tablettes cappadociennes", *RAI*, 2 (1951), 102-103.
Birgi, S. E., "Notes on the Influence of the Ergani Copper Mine on the Development of the Metal Industry in the Ancient Near East", *JKAF*, 1 (1950-1951), 337-343.
Bittel, Kurt, "Hethiter und Proto-Hattier", *Historia*, 1 (1950), 267-286.
——, "Die James Simon Grabung in Boghazköy September, 1931", *MDOG* 70 (1932), 1-23.
——, and R., Naumann, "Kappadokische Tontafeln", in *MDOG*, 77 (1939), 23.
Böhl, F. M. Th., "Mededelingen uit de Leidsche Verzameling van Spijkerschrift-inscripties, II. Oorkonden uit de Periode van 2000-1200 v. Chr.", *Mededeelingen der Koninklijke Akademie van Wetenschappen, Afdeeling Letterkunde*, Deel 78, Serie B, No. 2 (1934), 36-43.
Boissier, A., "Étude de deux tablettes cappadociennes de la mission Chantre", *AIBL* (1895), 348-352.
Çambel, Halet, "Archaologischer Bericht aus Anatolien", *Or ns*, 20 (1951), 236-251.
Cowan, Thomas J., "The Principle Structure of Community Reviewed", in Carl J. Friedrich, ed., *Community* (= *Nomos*, II) (New York, The Liberal Arts Press, 1959), 180-187.
David, Martin, "Beitrage zu den altassyrischen Briefen aus Kappadokien", *OLZ*, 36 (1933), 209-220.
——, "Review of *EL*, I and II", *ZSS*, 52 (1932), 496-503.
Delitzsch, Fr. "Beiträge zur Entzifferung und Erklärung der kappado-

kischen Keilschrifttafeln", in *Königlich-Sachsische Gesellschaft der Wissenschaften. Philologisch-historischen Klasse. Abhandlungen.* Bd. XIV, No. 4 (Leipzig, S. Hirzel, 1894, 207-270).

Deller, K., "Zu einer neuen Veröffentlichung altassyrischer Texte" (Review of *CCT*, V), *Or ns*, 27 (1958), 59-65.

Dhorme, P., "Les nouvelles tablettes d'el-Amarna. IV. La tablette de Sargon l'Ancien", *RB* (1924), 19-32.

Dossin, G., "Un cas d'ordalie par le dieu fleuve d'après une lettre de Mari", *SeD*, 2 (1939), 112-118.

Driver, G. R., "Cappadocian Texts at Oxford", *An Or*, VI (1933), 69-70, with Pl. I-VIII.

——, "Studies in Cappadocian Tablets", *Bab.* 10 (1927), 69-137.

——, "Studies in Cappadocian Tablets", *RA*, 24 (1927), 153-179.

——, "Studies in Cappadocian Texts", *ZA*, N.F. 4 (v 38) (1929), 217-232.

Ehelolf, H. (See Landsberger, B.).

Eisser, Georg, "Altassyrische Prozessgesetze unter den kappadokischen Urkunden?", *ZSS*, 48 (1928), 579-582.

——, "Beiträge zur Urkundenlehre der altassyrischen Rechtsurkunden vom Kültepe", *Festschrift Paul Koschaker*, 3 (1939), 94-126.

——, "Bemerkung zu den altassyrischen Rechtsurkunden aus Kappadokien", *ZDMG*, 81 (1927), xlvi.

Emre, Kutlu, "The Pottery of the Assyrian Colony Period According to the Building Levels of the Kaniş Karum", *Anatolia*, 7 (1963), 87-99.

Evans, Geoffrey, "Ancient Mesopotamian Assemblies", *JAOS*, 78 (1958), 1-11.

——, "Ancient Mesopotamian Assemblies — an addendum", *JAOS*, 78 (1958), 114-115.

Falkenstein, A., "Review of K. Bittel, *Grundzüge der Vor- und Frühgeschichte Kleinasiens* (Tübingen, E. Wasmuth, 1945) in *Die Welt des Oriens*, 1 (1949), 342-344.

Falkner, M., "Studien zur Geographie des alten Mesopotamiens", *AfO*, 18 (1957), 1-37.

Forrer, Emil, "Die kappadokisch-assyrischen kolonien und ihr Ursprung" (= Paragraph 11 *et. seq.* in the article "Assyrien" Paragraphs 1-48) *RLA*, I (1928), 232a-234a, ff.

——, "Die Inschriften und Sprachen des Hatti-Reiches", *ZDMG*, 75 (1922), 174-269.

Garelli, Paul, "La religion de l'Assyrie ancienne d'après un ouvrage recent", *RA*, 56 (1962), 191-210.

——, "Tablettes cappadociennes de collections diverses", *RA*, 58 (1964),

53-68, 111-136; *RA* 59 (1965), 19-48; to continue.
——, "Trois tablettes cappadociennes du Musée du Rouen", *RA*, 51 (1957), 1-10.
——, and D. A. Kennedy, "Un nouveau prince anatolien?" *RHA*, 66 (1960), 37-44 (See also under Kennedy, D.A.)
Garstang, John, "Hittite Military Roads in Asia Minor", *AJA*, 47 (1943), 35-62, with Pl. 17.
——, "Šamuḫa and Malatya", *JNES*, 1 (1942), 450-459.
Gelb, Ignace J., "A Contribution to the Proto-Indo-European Question", *JKAF*, 2 (1951), 23-36.
——, "Notes on von Soden's Grammar of Akkadian", *BO*, 12 (1955), 93-111.
——, "Studies in the Topography of Western Asia", *AJSL*, 55 (1938), 66-85.
——, "A Tablet of Unusual Type from Tell Asmar", *JNES*, 1 (1942), 219-226.
——, and E. Sollberger, "The First Legal Document from the Later Old Assyrian Period", *JNES*, 16 (1957), 163-175.
Goetze, Albrecht, "Die Annalen des Muršiliš", *MVaG*, 38 (1933).
——, "Bemerkungen zu den hethitischen Text AO 9608 des Louvre", *RHA*, 1 (1931), 18-30.
——, "Cilicians", *JCS*, 16 (1962), 48-58.
——, "The Cultures of Early Anatolia", *PAPS*, 97 (1953), 214-221.
——, "Eine altassyrische Rechtsurkunde auf einer Tontafel in Beyrouth", *Berytus*, 3 (1936), 76-82.
——, "Hattušiliš; der Bericht über sein Thron-besteigung nebst den Paralleltexten", *MVaG*, 29, 3 (1925).
——, "Hittite and Anatolian Studies", *BANE*, (1961), 316-327.
——, "Die kleinasiatischen Personennamen auf -uman, -umna in den kappadokischen Tafeln", *ZA*, N.F. 6 (v. 40) (1931), 260-263.
——, "The Linguistic Continuity of Anatolia as Shown by its Proper Names", *JCS*, 8 (1954), 74-81.
——, "An Old Babylonian Itinerary", *JCS*, 7 (1953), 51-72.
——, "On the Chronology of the Second Millennium", *JCS*, 11 (1957), 53-61; 63-73.
——, "Some Groups of Ancient Anatolian Proper Names", *Language*, 30 (1954), 349-359.
——, "Suffixes in 'Kaneshite' Proper Names", *RHA*, 66 (1960), 45-55.
——, "The Theophorous Elements of Anatolian Proper Names from Cappadocia", *Language*, 29 (1953), 263-277.

——, "Texts and Fragments", *JCS*, 8 (1954), 144-145.
Gurney, Oliver R., "Anatolia, c. 1750-1600 B.C." *Cambridge Ancient History*, Rev. Ed. of Volumes I and II (1962), 1-32.
Güterbock, Hans G., "Die historische Tradition und ihre literarische Gestaltung bei Babyloniern und Hethitern bis 1200", *ZA*, N.F. 8 (v. 42) (1934), 1-91; *ZA*, N.F. 10 (v. 44) (1938), 45-149.
——, "The Hurrian Elements in the Hittite Empire", *Journal of World History*, 2 (1954), 383-394.
——, "Kaneš and Neša: Two Forms of One Anatolian Place Name?" *Eretz Israel* 5 (1958), 46-50.
——, "Texte", *MDOG*, 74 (1936), 64ff.
——, "Türkische Beiträge zum Studium des Alten Orients", *AfO*, 15 (1945-1951), 128-135.
Hallo, William W., "Zariqum", *JNES*, 15 (1956), 220-225.
Hardy, Robert S., "The Old Hittite Kingdom", *AJSL*, 58 (1941), 177-216.
Hogarth, David G., and J. A. R. Munro, "Modern and Ancient Roads in Eastern Asia Minor", *Royal Geographic Society*, Supplementary Papers, III, Part 5 (London, John Murray, 1893), 643-739.
Hrozný, Bedrich, "Assyriens et Hittites en Asie Mineure vers 2000 av. J.-C.", *Ar Or*, 4 (1932), 112-117.
——, "The First Czechoslovak Excavations in the Near East", *Central European Observer*, 4 (1926), 527-529.
——, "L'invasion des Indo-Européens en Asie Mineure vers 2000 av. J.-C", *Ar Or*, 1 (1929), 273-299.
——, "Narâm-Sîn et ses ennemis, d'après un texte hittite", *Ar Or*, 1 (1929), 65-76.
——, "Un nouveau texte juridique du Kültepe", *AHDO*, I (1937), 87-90.
——, "Rapport préliminaire sur les fouilles Tchechoslovaques du Kültépé (1925)", *Syria*, 8 (1927), 1-12.
——, "A 'Record Office' 4000 Years Old: New Materials for the History of Asia Minor's Earliest Civilisation", *ILN* (Oct. 2, 1926), 600f.
——, "Über eine unveröffentlichte Urkunde vom Kültepe (ca. 2000 v. Chr.)", *SeD*, 2 (1939), 108-111.
Jacobsen, Thorkild, "Early Political Development in Mesopotamia", *ZA*, N.F. 18 (v 52) (1957), 91-140.
——, "Primitive Democracy in Ancient Mesopotamia", *JNES*, 2 (1943), 159-172.
——, "The Reign of Ibbi-Suen", *JCS*, 7 (1953), 36-47.
Jensen, P., "Die kappadokischen Keilschrifttafelchen", *ZA*, 9 (1894), 62-81.

Kammenhuber, A., "Nominalkomposition in den altanatolischen Sprachen des 2. Jahrtausends", *ZVSGI-ES*, 77 (1961), 161-218.

Kennedy, D. A. and P. Garelli, "Seize tablettes cappadociennes de l'Ashmolean Museum d'Oxford", *JCS*, 14 (1960), 1-23 (See also Garelli, Paul).

Klima J., and Matouš, L., "Les tablettes 'cappadociennes'", *RAI*, 2 (1951), 49-59.

Kohn, H., "Reflections on Colonialism", in R. Strauz-Hupé, *Idea of Colonialism* (New York, Praeger, 1958), 3-4.

Landsberger, Benno, "Assyrische Handelskolonien in Kleinasien aus dem dritten Jahrtausend", *Der Alte Orient*, 24 (1925), 1-36.

——, "Assyrische Königsliste und 'Dunkles Zeitalter'", *JCS*, 8 (1954), 31-45; 47-73; 106-120; 120-133.

——, "Hettiterland und Hettiter in den Kültepe Tafeln (Berichtigung zu dem Artikel *Ar Or*, 18, 1-2, 329-350)", *Ar Or*, 18, 3-4 (1950), 321-329.

——, "Kommt *Hattum* 'Hettiterland' und *Hatti'um* 'Hettiter' in den Kültepe-Tafeln vor?", *Ar Or*, 18, 1-2 (1950), 329-350.

——, "Review of J. Lewy, SATK (Berlin, Selbstverlag, 1922)", *OLZ*, 28 (1925), 229-233.

——, "Solidarhaftung von Schuldnern in den babylonisch-assyrischen Urkunden", *ZA*, N.F. 1 (v 35) (1924), 22-36.

——, "Über die Völker Vorderasiens im dritten Jahrtausend", *ZA*, N.F. 1 (v 35) (1924), 213-238.

——, "Vier Urkunden vom Kültepe", *TTAED*, 4 (1940), 7-31.

——, "Zu Driver's Übersetzungen 'kappadokische' Briefe", *ZA*, N.F. 4 (v 38) (1929), 275-280.

——, and Kemal Balkan, "Die Inschrift des assyrischen Königs Irišum, gefunden in Kültepe, 1948", *Belleten*, 14 (1950), 219-268.

——, and Ehelolf H., "Der altassyrische Kalender", *ZDMG*, 74 (1920), 216-219.

Laroche, E., "Recherches sur les noms des dieux hittites", *RHA*, 46 (1946), 76-139 (As a volume, Paris, 1947).

——, "Études de toponymie anatolienne", *RHA*, 69 (1961), 57-98.

Lewy, Hildegard (See also Lewy, Julius).

——, "Marginal Notes on a Recent Volume of Babylonian Mathematical Texts", *JAOS*, 67 (1947), 305-320.

——, "Neša", *JCS*, 17 (1963), 103-104.

——, "On Some Old Assyrian Cereal Names", *JAOS*, 76 (1956), 201-204.

Lewy, Julius, "Apropos of a Recent Study in Old Assyrian Chronology", *Or ns*, 26 (1957), 12-36.

——, "The Assyrian Calendar", *ACIO*, 20 (1940), 122-123.

——, "Bemerkungen zu den altassyrischen Texten aus Kappadokien", *ZA*, N.F. 1 (v 35) (1924), 148-151.

——, "Bemerkungen zu den altassyrischen Texten aus Kappadokien", *ZA* N.F. 3 (v 37) (1927), 132-133.

——, "La chronologie de Bitḫana et d'Anitta de Kuššara", *RHA*, 3 (1934-1936), 1-8.

——, "Fragmente altassyrische Prozessgestze aus Kaniš", *MAOG*, 4 (1928), 122-128.

——, "Grammatical and Lexicographical Studies", *Or ns*, 29 (1960), 20-45.

——, "*Ḫatta*, *Ḫattu*, *Ḫatti*, *Ḫattuša* and 'Old Assyrian *Ḫattum*'", *Ar Or*, 18, 3-4 (1950), 366-441.

——, "The *išši'akkum* of Kaniš and the Old Assyrian Empire", *PICO*, 23 (1954), 135-136.

——, "Kappadokische Tontafeln", *ERV*, 6 (1925), 212-219.

——, "'Kappadokische' Tontafeln und Frühgeschichte Assyriens und Kleinasiens", *OLZ*, 29 (1926), 750-761, 963-966.

——, "Der *karrum* der alt-assyrischen-kappadokischen Stadte und das alt-assyrischen Grossreich", *ZA*, N.F. 2 (v 36) (1925), 19-28.

——, "Die Keilschriftquellen zur Geschichte Anatoliens", *Nachrichten der Giessener Hochschulgesellschaft*, 6 (1927-1928), 35-43.

——, "Lykier Syrer und Choriter Syrer". *ZA*. N.F. 1 (v 35) (1924), 144-148.

——, "Nâram-Sin's Campaign to Anatolia in the Light of the Geographical Data of the Kültepe Texts", *Halil Edhem Hatira Kitabi*, I (= *HEM*), *TTKY*, VII Seri — No. 5 (1947), 11-18.

——, "Notes on Pre-Hurrian Texts from Nuzi", *JAOS*, 58 (1938), 450-461.

——, "Old Assyrian Documents from Asia Minor (about 2000 B.C.). — I and II", *AHDO* I and II (1937-1938), 91f.; 111-142.

——, "Old Assyrian Evidence concerning Kuššara and its Location", *HUCA*, 33 (1962), 45-57.

——, "Old Assyrian *husârum* and Sanchunyaton's Story about Chusor", IEJ 5 (1955), 154-162.

——, "Old Assyrian *puru'um* and *pûrum*", *RHA*, 5 (1939), 117-124.

——, "The Old Assyrian Surface Measure *Šubtum*", *Analecta Biblica*, 12 (1959), 216-226.

——, "On Some Institutions of the Old Assyrian Empire", *HUCA*, 27 (1956), 1-79.

——, "Some Aspects of Commercial Life in Assyria and Asia Minor in the Nineteenth Pre-Christian Century", *JAOS*, 78 (1958), 89-101.

——, "Studies in Akkadian Grammar and Onomatology", *Or ns* 15 (1946), 361-415.

——, "Studies in the Historic Geography of the Ancient Near East. — II", (= "Old Assyrian Caravan Roads in the Valleys of the Habur and the Euphrates and in Northern Syria"), *Or ns*, 21 (1952), 293-306; 393-425.

——, "Studies in Old Assyrian Grammar and Lexicography", *Or ns*, 19 (1950), 1-36.

——, "*TC.*, 100, *LC* 242 und das Eherecht des alt-assyrischen Rechtsbuches *KAV*, Nr. 1", *ZA*, N.F. 2 (v 36) (1925), 139-161.

——, "Les textes paléo-assyriens et l'Ancien Testament", *RHR*, 110 (1934), 29-65.

——, "Zur Amoriterfrage", *ZA* N.F. 4 (v 38) (1929), 243-262.

——, "Zur Geschichte Assyriens und Kleinasiens im 3. und 2. Jahrtausend v. Chr.", *OLZ*, 26 (1923), 533-544.

——, and Lewy, Hildegard, "The Origin of the Week and the Oldest West Asiatic Calendar", *HUCA*, 17 (1942-1943), 1-152c.

Mallowan, M. E. L., "Excavations at Brak and Chagar Bazar", *Iraq*, 9 (1947), 1-259.

Matouš, Lubor, "Zwei 'kappadokische' Tontafeln im Nationalmuseum zu Krakow", *JJP*, 11-12 (1957-58), 111-118 (See also Klima, J.).

Meek, Theophile J., "The Akkadian and Cappadocian Texts from Nuzi", *BASOR*, 48 (1932), 2-5.

Meer, P. van der, "Fünf kappadokische Geschaftsbriefe", *Or Chr*, 3, Serie, 7 (1932), 126-137.

Mellaart, James, "Anatolia, c. 4000-2300 B.C.", *Cambridge Ancient History*, Rev. ed. of Vol. I and II (1962), 1-53.

——, "Anatolian Chronology in the Early and Middle Bronze Age", *An St*, 7 (1957), 55-88.

——, "The End of the Early Bronze Age in Anatolia and the Aegean", *AJA*, 62 (1958), 9-33.

Mellink, Machteld, "Anatolian Chronology", in Robert W. Ehrich, *Chronologies in Old World Archaeology* (Chicago, University of Chicago Press, 1965), 101-131.

——, "Archaeology in Asia Minor", *AJA*, 60 (1956), 369-384; *AJA*, 62 (1958), 91-104; *AJA*, 64 (1960), 57-69; *AJA*, 66 (1962), 71-85; *AJA*, 67 (1963), 173-190; *AJA*, 68 (1964), 149-166; *AJA*, 69 (1965), 133-149.

Mendelsohn, I., "Gilds in Babylonia and Assyria", *JAOS*, 60 (1940),

68-72.

Munro, J. A. R. (See Hogarth, D. G.).

Oppenheim, A. Leo, "A Bird's-Eye View of Mesopotamian Economic History", in Karl Polanyi and others, ed., *Trade and Market in the Early Empires* (Glencoe, Ill., The Free Press, 1957), 27-37.

Oppenheim, L., "Les rapports entre les noms de personnes des textes cappadociens et des textes de Nuzi", *RHA*, 5 (1938), 7-30.

Osten, Hans H. von der, "Anatolische Wege", *Eranos* (*Acta Philologica Suecana A. Vilelmo*), 49 (1951), 65-84.

Otten, Heinrich, "Die altassyrischen Texte aus Boğazköy", *MDOG*, 89 (1957), 68-79.

——, "Die Ausgrabungen in Boğazköy im Jahre 1954. Die Inschriftlichen Funde", *MDOG*, 88 (1955), 33-36.

——, "Inschriftliche Funde der Ausgrabungen Boğazköy 1953", *MDOG*, 87 (1954), 13-25.

——, "Keilschrifttexte", *MDOG*, 91 (1957), 73-84.

——, "Zu den Anfängen der hethitischen Geschichte", *MDOG*, 83 (1951), 33-45.

Özgüç, Tahsin, "Archaeological Journeys in the Plain of Elbistan and the Excavation of Karahöyük", *Belleten*, 12 (1948), 232-237.

——, "Early Anatolian Archaeology in Light of Recent Research", *Anatolia*, 7 (1963), 1-21.

——, "The Dagger of Anitta", *Belleten*, 20 (1956), 33-36.

——, "Summary of Archaeological Work in Turkey (Kültepe)", *An St*, *passim*.

Özgüç, Nimet, "Selas from Kültepe", *Anatolia*, 4 (1959), 43-53.

——, "Die Siegel der Schicht I B im *Kârum-Kaniş* von Kültepe", *Belleten*, 22 (1958), 13-19.

Parsons, Talcott, "The Principal Structures of Community: A Sociological View", in Carl Friedrich ed., *Community* (= *Nomos* II) (New York, The Liberal Arts Press, 1959), 152-179.

Pinches, Th. G., "The Cappadocian Tablets Belonging to the Liverpool Institute of Archaeology", *AAA*, 1 (1908), 49-80.

——, "Communication", *PSBA*, 4 (1882), 11-18; 28-32.

Pirenne, J., "La politique d'expansion hittite envisagée à travers les traités de vassalité et de protectorat", *Ar Or*, 18, 1-2 (1950), 373-382.

Sayce, A. H., "Assyriological Notes", *PSBA*, 19 (1897), 286-291.

——, "The Cappadocian Cuneiform Tablets", *Bab.*, 2 (1908), 1-45.

——, "Cappadocian Cuneiform Tablets from Kara Eyuk", *Bab.*, 4 (1911), 65-80.

——, "The Cappadocian Cuneiform Tablets of the University of Pennsylvania", *Bab.*, 6 (1912), 182-192.
——, "The Cuneiform Tablets of Kappadokia", *PSBA*, 6 (1884), 17-25.
——, "The Cuneiform Tablets of Kappadokia", *Records of the Past*, new series, 6 (London, 1892), 115-131.
Scheil, J. V., "Tablette cappadocienne du Musée de Constantinople", *RT*, 18 (1896), 74f.
——, "Texte cappadocienne ninivite", *RT*, 31 (1909), 55f.
——, "Textes cunéiformes", in E. Chantre, *Mission en Cappadoce* (Paris, Leroux, 1898), 93-109.
Senyurek, Muzaffer, "A Crainological Study of the Copper Age and Hittite Populations of Anatolia", *Belleten*, 5 (1941), 237-253.
——, "Fluctuation of the Crainial Index in Anatolia, from the Fourth Millennium B.C. to 1200 B.C.", *Belleten* 15 (1951), 593-615.
——, "Human Skeletons from Kültepe", *Belleten*, 12 (1948), 323-343.
——, "The Longevity of the Chalcolithic and Copper Age Inhabitants of Anatolia", *Belleten*, 15 (1951), 447-458.
Shileiko, V. K., "Documenty iz Gi͡ul-Tepe", *Izvesti͡ia Rossiiskoĭ Akademii Istorii Material'noi Kul'tury*, I (1921), 356-364.
Smith, Sidney, "Miscellanea", *RA*, 21 (1924), 89f.
——, "Uršu and Haššum", *An St*, 6 (1956), 35-43.
Sollberger, E., "The Cuneiform Collection in Geneva", *JCS*, 5 (1951), 18-20.
Stephens, Ferris J., "The Cappadocian Tablets in the University of Pennsylvania Museum", *JSOR*, 11 (1927), 101-136.
——, "Notes on Cappadocian Tablets", *JAOS*, 46 (1926), 179-181.
——, "Studies of the Cuneiform Tablets from Cappadocia", *CSQ*, 2 (1925), 11-58.
Thureau-Dangin, Fr., "Un acte de repudiation sur une tablette cappadocienne", *Florilegium* (1909), 591-597.
——, "La date des tablettes cappadociennes", *RA*, 8 (1911), 142-151.
——, "Notes assyriologiques", *RA*, 24 (1927), 81-84.
Weidner, E., "Boğazköi", *AfO*, 17, 1 (1954-1955), 204-205.
——, "Der Zug Sargons von Akkad nach Kleinasien; die alteste geschichtlichen Beziehungen zwischen Babylonien und Hatti", *BKS*, 6 (1922), 57-99.
——, "Ilušumas Zug nach Babylonien", *ZA*, N.F. 9 (v 43) (1936), 114-123.

C. MAPS

Duran, Faik Sabri, "Türkiye (1:2,000,000)", Istanbul, Kanaat Yayinlari, 1948.

"Karte der türkischen Republik", in *Petermann's Geographischer Mitteilungen*, 81 (1935), Tafel 22.

INDEX

1. SUBJECTS

Alishar Hüyük, stratification of, and tablets, 216, 219.
Anitta, conquests of, 155-156. (*See also* Pitḫana, conquests of.)
Anitta Inscription, 155, 237-239, 241, **242-244.**
Anatolia, cultural development of in Early Bronze Age I Period, 225-226.
——, end of the Early Bronze Age, 231 f.
——, meaningful system of local kingdoms during Chalcolithic and Early Bronze Age, 226f.
——, not annexed to Assyria by force, 170.
——, Old Akkadian Dynasty and, 228-231.
——, political climate at the dawn of Old Assyrian Colonization, 236f., 241.
——, territorial organizations, 236.
Anatolian administrations, power of search and arrest over Assyrians, 150.
Anatolian city-state armies, 157.
Anatolian cultural development, roll of Old Assyrian Colonies in, 224.
Anatolian palaces, police functions of, 152-153.
Anatolian political centers, correlated with Assyrian *kârû*, 239-240.
Anatolian political environment, sketched from Old Assyrian sources, 237-238.
Anatolian population in early Second Millennium, 27.
Anatolian princes, interference in the affairs of Assyrian businessmen, 142.
Anatolian principalities, 73, 75f.
——, location of Old Assyrian settlements in, 74f.
——, named in Old Assyrian texts, 237.
Anatolian rulers, 73f.
——, chronology of, 74.
Anum-Ḫirbi letter, and implications, 97-101, 238.
Assur, jurisdiction of over Assyrian settlements, 167-169.
Assyria, Old Akkadian and Ur III periods, 234-235.
Assyria, under Sumerian rule, 45-46.
Assyrian colony, environment of, 26.
——, *kârum*-type, 26.
——, *wabârtum*-type, 26.
Assyrian colonies, distribution of, 27.
——, locations of, 34-44.
Assyrian customs, 28.
Assyrian gods in Anatolia, 169.
Assyrian government at Assur, administrative structure of, 61-64.
——, relationships to *kârû* and *wabârâtum*, 60.
Assyrian *kârû* and *wabârâtum*, in Cappadocian trade, 162.
——, not colonies in the imperial sense, 171.
Assyrian law in Anatolia, 161 f.
Assyrian merchants, arrival in Anatolia, 24.
——, exports from Anatolia, 25.
——, imports from Assur, 24-25.
Assyrian political institutions, structure of, 161.
Assyrian power, distribution of, 164.
——, forms and scope, 163-164.
Assyrian quarters in Anatolian cities, 28.
Assyrian ruler at *Kaniš*, critique of theory of, 103f.

——, hypothesis of, 101-105.
Assyrian settlements, types of, 25.
——, and the Assyrian "community", 165-166.
——, as *colonies*, 171f.
Assyrian subject in Anatolia, definition of, 162.
"Assyrian System", 73.
Assyrian-Anatolian, legal interrogation, 142-147.
——, parity-relationships, 177-181.
——, relations based on oaths, treaties and law, 116-129, 139f.
Assyrians, arrival of in Anatolia, 235-236.
——, ethnic origin of, 27.
——, non-coercive force in Anatolia, 169.
——, symbiotic relationships with Anatolians, 28-29.

Boğazköy (*Ḫattuša*), stratification of, and tablets, 217-219.

Cappadocian trade, based on commercial treaties, 51-52.
——, effect upon Anatolia, 58.
——, goods in, 56-58.
——, organization and division of labor, 52-56.
——, origins, 51.
——, studied as an aggregate of groups, 162-163.
——, supervisory powers of Assyrian government over, 58-59.
——, transport, 58.
Colonization, conditions attending, and characteristics of, 173-177.
——, relationship to conquest, 172f.
Colony, idea of and preconditions for, 92-94.

Detention of Assyrian goods, 132-138, 148-150, 152.
Diplomatic encounters, Old Assyrian letters giving information about, 114f.

Geography of Assyrian colonies, 31-34.
Great Prince of *Burušḫattum*, relationship to Assyrians, 139f.

Hattian (Early Anatolian) political system, end of, 241f.
Hittites, entry of into Anatolia, 232f.
——, relationship of to Kuššaran Dynasty of Pitḫana and Anitta, 246-247.

Imprisonment of Assyrian businessmen, 147-148.
Indigenous administration of *Kaniš*, attempted reconstruction of, 109-113.

Kaniš, city mound, description of, 29-31, 214-216.
Kaniš, city of, history, 24.
——, hub of a system of radiating routes, 36f.
——, identification with *Neša* hypothesized, 242-245.
Kaniš, kingdom of, 88f.
——, controversial scholarly opinion about, 89f.
Kârum, etymology and meaning of, 25-26.
——, proposed definitions of, 90-91.
Kârum-house (*Bît Kârim*), center of administrative and commercial life of *kârum*-settlements, 59-60.
Kârum Burušḫattum, 34, 36, 37, 140, 141, 147, 156, 239, 241.
Kârum Durḫumit, 34, 38, 118, 119, 120, 121, 139, 240.
Kârum Ḫaḫḫum, 34, 39, 126, 240.
Kârum Ḫattuš, 34, 37, 119, 156, 239, 241.
Kârum Ḫurama, 35, 43, 142, 143, 145, 146, 240.
Kârum Kaniš, 35, 69, 108, *et passim*.
——, administrative structure, 65-69.
——, financial center and legal sovereign of Assyrian settlements in Anatolia, 65f.
——, founding of, 235.
——, history of, 23.
——, location of, 23.
——, stratification of, 23-24, 199-214.
Kârum Niḫria, 35, 43-44, 240.
kârum-settlements, Old Assyrian textual references to, 34-35.
Kârum Tamnia (= *Tawinia*), 35, 38, 118, 119, 120.
Kârum Tawinia. See *Kârum Tamnia*.
Kârum Uršu, 30, 35, 39, 240.
Kârum Waḫšušana, 35, 36, 37, 115, 116, 119, 120, 123, 149, 153, 239, 241.
Kârum Zalpa, 35, 38, 156, 239, 241.
Kültepe, chronology of *Kârum* Levels, Ib and Ia, 213-214.

——, chronology of *Kârum* Levels II, 209-210.
——, chronology of *Kârum* Levels III and IV, 203-206.
——, excavations at, 199.
——, excavations of the Türk Tarih Kurumu, 1948, 200.
——, external contacts of in Early Bronze Age, 224.
——, Hrozny's excavation of in 1925, 199-200.
——, stratification of the city-mound, 214-215.
——, stratification of the *kârum*-terrace, Level I, 210.
——, stratification of the *kârum*-terrace, Level II, 206-210.
——, stratification of the *Kârum*-terrace, Level III, 202f.
——, stratification of the *Kârum*-terrace, Level IV, 201-202.

Mesopotamian city institutions, 46f.

Neša, rise of, 241f.

Old Assyrian Dialect, 191.
Old Assyrian documents, checklist of sources, 185-187.
——, find spots of, 184-185.
——, from *Assur*, 192.
——, origins, decipherment and publication history of, 188-189.
——, physical and epigraphical characteristics of, 189-190.
——, publication of texts unearthed at Kültepe, 1948, 187.
——, types of, 191-192.
——, unpublished texts, 187.
Old Assyrian Dynasty, 45-46.
Old Assyrian Empire, theory of an, 94-96f.
Old Assyrian Period, general characteristics, 181-183.
——, secondary sources for, 193-198.
Old Assyrian Syllabary, 190-191.
Old Hittite Kingdom, formation of, 247.

Pitḫana, conquests of, 155-156. (*See also* Anitta, conquests of).
Private trading entrepreneurship through trading companies, 50-51.
Professional trader, 48-49.
Revolt at *Ḫaḫḫum*, 127.
Routes between Old Assyrian colonies, 35-44.
Royal personages at *Kaniš*, evidence for, 106-107.

Sovereignty in Anatolia, 161.

Treaty arrangements, parity and vassalage, 237
Ur III Dynasty, 234.

Wabârtum of *Badna*, 35, 43, 152, 153.
Wabârtum of *Ḫanâknak*, 35, 43.
Wabârtum of *Karaḫna*, 35.
Wabârtum of *Mama*, 35, 39, 100, 149, 240.
Wabârtum of *Šalatu(w)ar*, 35, 37, 156.
Wabârtum of *Šamuḫa*, 35, 43, 151, 152.
Wabârtum of *Tuhpia*, 35, 38.
Wabârtum of *Ulama* (var: *Walama*), 35, 37.
Wabartum of *Wašḫania*, 35, 36, 115, 119.
Wabârtum of *Zalpa*, 35, 38, 148.
Wabârtum-settlements, Old Assyrian textual references to, 35.

Yorgan Tepe (*Nuzi*), stratification, 220-221.

2. GEOGRAPHICAL NAMES (ANCIENT)

Akkad, 45, 96.
Amkuwa (var: Akkuwa, Ankuwa), 76, 153, 154.
Amurri, 230.
"Anaku", 229.
Assur (=Qal'at Sherqat), 25, 43, 44, 45, 52, 54, 56, 57, 59, 61, 62, 63, 64, 67, 68, 73, 94, 95, 96, 100, 101, 102, 103, 107, 115, 117, 118, 140, 141, 147, 148, 149, 162, 164, 165, 167, 168, 170, 182, 229, 234, 235.
Awal, 45.

Badna, 43, 77, 152, 153.
Baradum (Parattum), 105.
Burušḫanda (Parsuḫanda), 228, 229, 239. *See also* Burušḫattum.
Burušḫattum, 37, 74, 77, 95, 107, 108,

116, 139, 140, 141, 147, 150, 151, 156, 165, 237, 238, 239, 240, 241.

Dadania, 77.
Der, 45, 234.
Durḫumit (var: Dur/Turmitta), 38, 77f, 118, 119, 120, 121, 139, 240.
Durmitta, *see* Durḫumit.

Eshnunna, 45, 101, 183, 234.

Gasur, see Nuzi.

Ḫaḫḫum, 39, 42, 78, 123, 125, 126, 127, 128, 129, 135, 237, 240.
"Halys Assyria", 94, 102, 105, 147.
Ḫanaknak, 43, 78.
Ḫarkiuna, 78, 237, 238, 243.
Ḫatti, 156, 230, 231, 237, 238, 239, 240, 241, 243, 247.
Hattuš, 95, 119. *See also* Hattušaš.
Ḫattuš(a), 78, 244, 246.
Ḫattušaš, 37, 38. *See also* Hattuš.
Ḫudurut, 78.
Ḫurama, 43, 79, 107, 142, 143, 145, 146, 240.

Iarmuti, 228.
Ibla, 228.
Isin, 45, 234, 235.

Kaniš, 23, 24, 38, 79f., *et passim*.
Kaptara, 229.
Karaḫna, 80.
Kismar, 45.
Kursaura, 230.
Kuššara, 73, 80f., 151, 156, 237, 238, 241, 243, 244, 246, 247.

Lagash, 228, 231.
Larsa, 45, 235.
Luḫuzad/tia, 81, 107, 142, 143, 144, 145, 146.

Mallita, 37.
Mama, 39, 42, 81, 97, 100, 149, 151, 238, 239, 240, 241, 245.
Mari, 42, 45, 228.

Naduḫtum, 81, 129, 130, 131, 154.
Nenašša, 37, 82.
Neša, 73, 82, 156, 237, 238, 239, 241, 242, 243, 244, 245, 246.
Niḫria, 43, 44n, 82, 240.
Nineveh, 45, 229.
Nippur, 45.
Nuzi, 28n., 177, 229.

Paḫatima, 82f.
Parattum, *See* Baradum.
Parsuḫanda, *See* Burušḫanda.
Pa/puruttum, 83.

Qatara, 83.

Sibuḫa, 84, 100.
Simala, 84.
Sirmiya, 155.
Sis/zum, 107n.
Šalaḫšua, 83, 107, 154.
Šalatiwar(a), 156, 237, 239, 240. *See also* Šalatu(w)ar.
Šalatu(w)ar, 37, 69, 83f.
Šamuḫa, 43, 84, 151, 152.
Šiḫwa, 84.
Širmuin, 84.
Širun, 84.

Taišama, 85, 100.
Tamnia (var: Tawinia, Tawnia), 38, 85f., 118, 119, 120, 121, 122, 139, 157, 240.
Tarakum, 85.
Tegarama, 86, 105.
Tilimria, 86.
Timilkia, 39, 86.
Troy, 225, 226, 227.
Tuḫpia, 38, 86, 106, 151.
Turmitta. *See* Durḫumit.
Tuttul, 228.

Ulama (var: Walama), 37, 86f, 149, 150, 151, 237.
Umma, 228.
Ur, 45, 95, 96, 101, 228, 231, 234.
Uršu, 39, 40, 42, 87, 100, 240.
Ušša, 87.

Waḫšušana, 36, 37, 87f, 106, 108, 115' 116, 119, 120, 123, 148, 149, 150, 153' 165, 237, 238, 239, 240, 241.
Wašḫania, 36, 87, 106, 115, 116, 117, 118, 119, 120, 153.

Zalpa (var: Zalpuwa), 35, 38, 88, 132, 135, 136, 137, 148, 152, 156.
Zalpaḫ, 35n, 38.
Zalpuwa (*See also Zalpa*), 237, 238, 239, 240, 241, 242, 243, 244, 245.

3. GEOGRAPHICAL NAMES (MODERN)

Ahir Bel Pass, 41.
Ahlatlibel, 226.
Aksaray, 37.
Alaca Hüyük, 225, 226, 227, 232.
Alishar Hüyük, 28, 29, 30, 37, 38, 76, 114, 154, 174, 225.
Ambararasi, 42.

Besni, 43.
Beycesultan, 226.
Boğazköy, 28, 37, 38, 119.
Büyük Güllücek, 225.

Cihanbeyli, 36.

Derende, 42,
Diyarbekir, 42, 44.
Dorak, 226.

Elbistan, 41, 42.
Ergani Pass, 42, 44.

Firnis, 42.

Gök Bel, 41.
Göz Bel Pass, 41.
Göksun, 41.
Göksun-Maraş Passage, 42.
Gürün, 42,
Gürün-Darende-Harput Road, 43.

Hacinoğlu, 42.
Harput, 39, 42, 43, 125.
Horoztepe, 226, 227.

İncesu, 36.

Kadinhani, 36.
Kayseri, 36, 38.
Keban Pass, 41.
Konya, 36.
Konya Plain, 27, 37, 39.
Kültepe, 28, 30, 35f, *et passim*.
Kuru Çay Pass, 42.

Mahmatlar, 226.
Malatya, 39, 42, 43.
Maraş, 41, 42, 43.
Mardin, 43.

Niğde, 36.

Obruk, 36.
Ovabyindir, 226.

Polat, 43.
Poliochni, 226.

Samsat, 43.
Samsum, 35.
Sivas, 38.
Siverek, 43.

Tarsus, 35.

Yeşilhisar, 37.
Yortan cemetery, 226.

4. ROYAL AND OFFICIAL NAMES

Aludhuharša, *rabi E-zi*, 111.
Anitta, 73, 74, 76, 77, 79, 80, 81, 82, 154, 155, 156, 157, 158, 182, 213, 214, 237, 238, 239, 240, 242, 243, 244, 245, 246, 247.
Anum-Ḫirbi, 81, 97f, 100, 214, 238, 245.

Bilalama, 234.

Dakiki, 101f.

Erišum. *See* Irišum.

Ḫabuala, *Pu/Burullum rabûm*, 77.
Ḫabuala, *rêi'um ša rubâtim*, 107.
Ḫalk/giašu, *rabi ḫuršâtim*, 80.
Ḫalk/giašu, *rabi simmiltim*, 80, 104, 108, 109, 110, 112.
Ḫammurabi, 183, 209, 211.
Ḫarbatiwa, 76, 153.
Ḫattušiliš I, 246.
Ḫuwaruwas, 230.
Ḫuzziya, 88, 243.

Iasmaḫ-Adad, 212.

Ibbi-Sîn, 204, 205, 234.
Iddin-Dagan of *Isin*, 234.
Ikunum, 182, 208, 210.
Ilušum(m)a, 45, 46, 95, 96, 102, 103, 182, 235.
Inar, King of *Kaniš*, 79, 100, 213, 242, 245.
Irišum I of Assyria, 23, 62, 182, 192, 209, 210, 235.
Irišum II of Assyria, 210.
Išbi-Irra, 234.
Išme-Dagan of Assyria, 96, 171, 183, 210, 213, 246.
Išme-Dagan of *Isin*, 234, 235.

Kulakula, *rabi alpâtim*, 111.
Kuraa, *rabi nappâḫî*, 109, 112.

Labarša, 79, 108, 242.
Lugalzaggesi, 228.

Maništusu, 229.
Muršiliš I, 183.

Narâm-Sîn of *Akkad*, 24, 45, 95, 229, 230, 231, 234.
Narâm-Sîn of *Eshnunna*, 210.

Pamba, 230, 231.
Peruwa, *rabi simmiltim*, 76, 80, 81, 154.
Pijušti(š), 78, 243.
Pitḫana, 79, 80, 82, 155, 156, 157, 158, 182, 238, 241, 242, 243, 244, 245, 246, 247.
Puzur-Aššur I of Assyria, 45, 101, 102, 103.
Puzur-Aššur II of Assyria, 95, 103, 105, 182, 209, 210.

Rimuš, 229.

Sargon of *Akkad*, 45, 95, 228, 229, 230, 234.
Sargon I of Assyria, 94f, 182, 208, 209, 210.
Ṣilulu, 101 f.
Šamši-Adad I of Assyria, 96, 165, 183, 210, 212, 213, 246.
Šubunaḫšu, *rabi alaḫḫinim ša rabi sikkitim*, 112f.
Šulgi, 95.
Šulia, *rabi paššure*, 111.

Tarḫuala, *ahu rabi simmiltim*, 109, 112.
Tiglath-Pileser I of Assyria, 117.
Tišbinki, 230.
Tukulti-Ninurta I of Assyria, 117.
Turupani, 80.

Uhna(š), King of *Zalpuwa*, 88, 242, 243, 244.
Ur-Nammu, 95.

Warp/ba, 79, 104, 107, 109, 110, 112, 113.
Waršama, 79, 97, 100, 213, 214, 242, 245.
Wašḫuba, *rabi mahîrim*, 109, 112.

Zipani, 24, 230, 231.

5. FOREIGN WORDS AND PHRASES

abu, 54n. 48, 121.
âlam eppaš, 122f.
âlam mahârum, 63n. 104.
âlum, 59, 62w.n.98, 64, 164, 165, 167, 168, 169.
amûtum, 51n.35, 57, 59.
andurârum šakânum, 45n.3.
annâk qâtim, 57n.62.
annâkum, 25, 56w.nn. 58 and 61, 57, 59, 182.
annâkum kunûkum, 57.
apâlum, 124n.43.
arkammaš, 133n.70.
ark/gammani, 133n.70.
aršâtum, 58.
aši'um, 142, 145, 148, 149, 150, 179n.47.
âwîli, 154.
âwîli rabi'ûtim, 66.
âwilum ša nikkassî, 69.

bêl âlim, 73.
bêl ḫa-[*ti?*]*-tim*, 82.
bêli atta, 130.
biriqani, 58.
bîruttum, 69.
Bît Âlim^{ki}, 59, 62.
Bît Kârim, 30, 59, 124n.44d, 179n.47.
Bît Lîmim, 59n.83.

chiton, 57.

daianû, 69.

DAM.KAR, 48, 49, 50. *See also tamkârum*.
dîn âlim, 63n.103.
dîn âlim^{ki} *u rubâ'im*, 164, 165.
dîn kârim, 67.
dîn wabârtim, 67n.121.
dišpum, 58.

êkallum, 76, 77, 78, 79, 81, 82, 83, 84, 86, 87, 88, 179n.47.
elâ'um, 126n.51.
ellatum, 50n.32.
e/irbum, 60n.89, 118n.19, 134n.75, 151, 155.
eriqqâtum, 58.
erî'um maz/sî'um, 179n.47 (180).
eširtum, 68, 82, 84, 126.

gamrum, 60n.89, 62n.101.
g/kaššum, 69, 77, 82, 83, 84, 85, 87, 88, 151.

ḫabiri, 154.
ḫamištum, 67.
ḫamuštum, 53, 68.
ḫuluqqâ'ê, 136, 137.
ḫusârum, 57, 59.

ikribu, 51n.35, 133n.70.
ikribu ša ilim, 136.
išratum, 60n.89, 105w.n.72, 179n.47.
iššî'âkkum, 61w.n.95, 94, 101, 102, 103, 104, 164, 165.

kabâsum, 133n.67.
KAR, 25.
kârum, *See* Subject Index.
kârum ṣahir rabi, 178.
kutânu, 57, 145.

lapâtum, 60n.88, 124n.44d.
laputtâ'um, 64.
lîmu, 59, 68, 74, 208, 213.
luqûtum, 54n.51, 56n.58.

magârum, 124n.44e.
mâlikim ša rubâ'im, 86.
mâmîtam tammu'um, 117.
mâmîtum, 129.
masâhum, 122.
maškû, 58.
maṣṣârâtum, 180n.48.
mâtum, 73, 116w.n.14, 150, 236, 237, 238, 239, 241.
mazâ'um, 122.
metum-hamšat, 60n.89.
mišittum ša ellatim, 60n.88.

nadâ'um 60n.88.
nadânum, 60n.88.
namedum, 65n.115, 66.
napâlum, 60n.88, 124n.43.
naruqqum, 53.
naṭalum, 125n.46.
nêmelum, 53.
nibûm, 69, 77.
nikkassî šasâ'um, 60n.88.
NIMGIR.URU, 101.
nipiltum, 55n.54.
nisḫatum, 59n.84, 60n.89, 107, 179n.47.
nîš âlim^{ki} *u rubâ'im*, 63, 164.
nuâ'um, 73n.1, 145.

paṭrum, 63.
puḫrum, 62.
Pu/burullum, 77, 83, 152, 153, 154n.86.
Pu/burullum rabûm, 77, 154.

qaṣṣârum, 56n.57.
qâtum, 59n.84.

rabi alaḫḫinim ša rabi sikkitim, 113.
rabi alpâtim, 111.
rabi E-zi, 111.
rabi ḫuršâtim, 80.
rabi kakke, 156n.104.
rabi mahîrim, 109, 110n.92, 112.
rabi maṣṣârtim, 180n.48.
rabi nappâḫî, 109.
rabi paššure, 111.
rabi sikkitim (var: *sikkatim*), 78, 86, 87, 88, 149, 150, 151.
rabi simmiltim, 76, 80, 108, 109, 110, 111, 112, 113n.115, 147, 148, 156.
rabi siparrim, 156n.104 (157).
rabi ṣabim, 112n.109, 157.
rabi šarîqî, 112n.109.
râbiṣum, 64w.n.108, 82, 84, 86, 144, 145, 149, 151, 167.
rêi'um ša rubâtim, 107.
rubâtum, 76, 79, 81, 86, 87, 107, 112, 113.
rubâ'um, 61w.n.94, 62, 64, 73, 74, 76, 78, 79, 80, 81, 82, 84, 85, 86, 87, 88, 94, 103, 105, 106, 109, 110, 111, 112, 113, 156.
rubâ'um rabî'um, 74, 76, 77, 80, 82, 140, 156, 237, 240n.67.
rubâ'û, 127, 128.

sarridum, 56n.57.
sika šarri, 83. *See also ṣittum šarri.*
s/šinaḫila, 81, 130n.60.
ṣibtum, 53.
ṣittum šarri, 60n.89.
ṣuhârum, 56n.57.
ša kîma iati, 53n. 47 (54).
šaddu'âtum, 59n.84, 60.89.
šalištum, 67.
šalšâtum, 53.
šamalla'um, 52w.n.39, 53, 55.
šamnum, 58.
šaqâlum, 60n.88.
šaqil-ṭatim, 69.
šar kiššatim, 165.
šarrum, 61, 74, 78, 80, 82, 83, 84, 85, 88, 128.
šîbûtum, 62w.n.100.
šipru(m), 119, 135, 136, 137.
šipru GAL (or *E.GAL*), 131n.65.
šiprû ša âlim^{ki}, 63, 65, 69, 117, 123, 167, 168.
šiprû ša Kârim Kaniš, 65.
šiprû (of *wabârtim*), 65n.112.
šitrum, 58.
šugari'aum, 63.

tamkârum, 50, 51, 52n.39, 54, 55.
tašši'âtum, 60n.89.
têrtum, 131n.63.
tibnum, 58.
tunica, 57.
ṭa'tum (var: *ṭa'tum ša ḫarrânim*), 60n.89.
ṭuppum, 63.
ṭuppum ša âlim^{ki}, 63n.103.
ṭuppum ša âlim^{ki} *u rubâ'im*, 63n.103.
ṭuppum ša rubâ'im, 63n.103.
ṭupšarrum, 69.

ummeânum, 52, 53, 55, 105n.74 (106).

wabârtum. See Subject Index.
waklum, 64, 69.
waššurum, 131n.62.
waṣitum, 60n.89.

zakâ'um, 180n.48.
ZI.GA šarri/u, 83. *See also ṣittum šarri.*

6. OLD ASSYRIAN DOCUMENTS PRESENTED AND DISCUSSED IN THE TEXT

CCT II 48, 142.
CCT IV 19c, 146n.40.
CCT IV 30a, 123-129.
EL 252, 142w.n.21, *et seq.*
G/t 35, 97-99.
Kt f/k 183, 118-123.
KTHahn 3, 153n.77.
KTP 6, 155n.88.
KTP 14, 114-118.
TC III 75, 129-132.
TC III 85, 132-138.
TC III 271, 148n.51 (149).
TTC 27, 139n.1 (140f.).
VAT 6209, 151n.68.